Five for
Hollywood

Five for Hollywood

John Parker

A LYLE STUART BOOK
Published by Carol Publishing Group

First Carol Publishing Group Edition 1991

Copyright © 1989 by John Parker

A Lyle Stuart Book
Published by Carol Publishing Group
Lyle Stuart is a registered trademark of
Carol Communications, Inc.

Editorial Offices	Sales & Distribution Offices
600 Madison Avenue	120 Enterprise Avenue
New York, NY 10022	Secaucus, NJ 07094

In Canada: Musson Book Company
A division of General Publishing Co. Limited
Don Mills, Ontario

Published by arrangement with Macmillan London Limited

Queries regarding rights and permissions
should be addressed to: Carol Publishing Group,
600 Madison Avenue, New York, NY 10022

Manufactured in the United States of America
10 9 8 7 6 5 4 3 2 1

Library of Congress Cataloging-in-Publication Data

Parker, John, 1938 Aug. 5-
    Five for Hollywood / John Parker.
        p.   cm.
    "A Lyle Stuart book."
    Includes bibliographical references and index.
    ISBN 0-8184-0539-2
        1. Motion picture actors and actresses--United States--Biography.
    2. Taylor, Elizabeth, 1932-   . 3. Clift, Montgomery. 4. Hudson,
    Rock, 1925-1985. 5. Wood, Natalie. 6. Dean, James, 1931-1955.
    I. Title.
PN2285.P35   1991
791.43'028'092273--dc20
    [B]   91-9271
                                                  CIP

To Val

Contents

viii

Acknowledgments

As will be evident from the text, many people have assisted me in the preparation of this book, which is based on more than one hundred interviews and extensive bibliographic and archive research. I would like to express my deepest gratitude to those who gave up their time to talk to me, or who helped in other ways.

In particular, I thank those who were kind enough to show me hospitality in their own homes while they provided me with invaluable reminiscences, especially Miss Maureen Stapleton, who invited me to her apartment in a charming town hidden away in the heart of Massachusetts, which I reached after a four-hour bus ride from New York. Maureen, who has intimate knowledge of the characters in this book through both friendship and work, had an incredible recall of events over her forty-year career. In Hollywood, among the many I visited was Julie Harris – who starred with James Dean in *East of Eden* – in a borrowed home (she usually resides on the east coast), where she provided Earl Grey tea and fresh berries while we talked. In New York I breakfasted with the Broadway character actor William LeMassena, at his home in Greenwich Village, who spent several hours leading me painstakingly through the life of his friend Montgomery Clift. In London I joined Charlton Heston for tea at the Athenaeum and, with hardly an interruption for my questions, he gave me a long and fascinating commentary on Hollywood in the fifties, which is referred to at various points in this book. Susannah York broke rehearsals to provide a detailed account of filming *Freud* with Clift. These are just a few examples of the assistance I received and enjoyed.

I also owe a special debt to Professor Ronald L. Davis of the Southern Methodist University in Texas (and to his assistant Tom Culpepper) for granting me access to the SMU Oral History Collection on the Performing Arts, of which he is Director (see below), and for the following interviews: Walter Abel, Don Ameche, Pandro S. Berman, George Chakiris, George Cukor, Edward Dmytryk, Doris Day, Ann Doran, Stanley Donen, John Houseman, Rock Hudson, Ross Hunter, Gene Kelly, Virginia Mayo,

Richard Ney, Gregory Peck, Jane Powell, Tony Randall, Barbara Rush, Emily Torchia, Hal B. Wallis, Robert Wise, William Wyler. Among the quoted material in the book are recollections from Rock Hudson, which are based on reported interviews, the author's own interview in 1981, but largely on a lengthy conversation with Professor Davis, recorded on 24 August 1983. The SMU collection was started in 1972 and is part of the University's DeGolyer Institute for American Studies. Its aim is to gather primary source material for future writers and cultural historians on all branches of the performing arts and it now contains hundreds of recorded interviews. The collection is particularly strong, however, in the area of motion pictures and includes taped interviews with celebrated performers as well as behind-the-scenes personnel, many of whom are now dead. The use of this material is restricted to terms agreed between the University and the interviewee. I was given full access to the transcripts of many interviews and am grateful to the SMU and the interviewees for permission to use extracts from them.

My thanks also go to the staff of the American Film Institute Library, Los Angeles; the Library of the Motion Picture Academy of Arts and Sciences, Los Angeles; the Performing Arts Library at the Lincoln Center, New York; the British Museum Library; the British Museum Newspaper Library, Colindale, London; and Edda Tasiemka of the Hans Tasiemka Archive, London, who once again provided me with a daunting collection of research material. I am also grateful to Michael Pettitt of the Los Angeles Superior Court for his assistance with transcripts in the case of Marc Christian versus the Estate of Rock Hudson, and Mark Miller.

John Parker
Northamptonshire, 1989

Introduction

The Golden Age of Hollywood was all but over and the dream factories that had peddled and perpetuated their mythology of glamour, wealth and success – the very essence of the Great American Dream – saw themselves descending into a long nightmare: a slow and painful disintegration of all that had gone before.

In their heyday, great stars like Garbo, Chaplin, Davis, Gable, Niven, Flynn and Bogart attracted audiences of two hundred million a week and could expect fifteen thousand fan letters during the course of seven days. Behind them, creating and manipulating the illusion, were the movie moguls, the autocratic dictators of the great studios who boasted that they could make anyone a star; and into their production-line system they pushed the eager aspirants, who were in truth as fragile and as volatile as the celluloid on which their image was delivered to the world.

Mass adoration of these idols of the silver screen had reached hysterical proportions by the mid-forties and, as the moguls surveyed the crowds who turned out in their thousands to catch a glimpse of their favourite star in person, they believed their own publicity hype – that the great, golden days could never end. Their confidence turned them into arrogant bullies; but those men who could once honestly claim that they knew exactly what the film-going public wanted were losing their grip, ignoring the changes that were almost upon them.

Their stars were returning from the war with grey-tinged temples, some with their past auras shattered. Nepotism and politics fused with the wealth and glamour. Senator Joseph McCarthy's anti-communist witch-hunts stopped Hollywood dead in its tracks. Television and a new law ending the studios' monopoly control of cinema chains delivered the fatal wounds, and the moguls buried their heads in the sand and allowed it to happen.

Into this turmoil came the bright new stars, fresh-faced and innocent. Before them lay pressures and money unheard of even in the mink-lined existence of the past, as the moguls and their successors – lawyers, bankers, agents and conglomerates – fought to retain their place in the burgeoning business of entertaining the new affluent society.

I have chosen five young people whose lives and careers seem to me to epitomise that era in the glamour capital of the world: Elizabeth Taylor, Natalie Wood, Montgomery Clift, Rock Hudson, and James Dean. They were actors of vastly differing qualities and backgrounds, but in the fifties, when they broke through the star barrier, they were all considered sensational. More than that, their lives, personal and professional, became so incredibly intertwined that no Hollywood scriptwriter could have imagined the plot, the surprising twists and turns, the coincidences and the real-life, larger than life, dramas that emerged.

The Hollywood dream enveloped them all – five young people who, year after year, clung to their own belief that beyond the hill they were climbing lay the ultimate part, the role in a play or film that would make them. And eventually, in their different ways, each of them found it; but with it came not just supremacy in their profession but also the awful pressures that every star must face: the criticism, the hypocrisy, the backstabbing, the searching inquisitions into their private lives, and, after the adulation, the rejection.

These five came through together, almost hand in hand, sharing their fears and doubts, their hopes and aspirations. Their personal lives were marked by their professional involvement with each other, which in some cases developed into sexual desire before giving way to deep, platonic friendships which would survive as long as they lived. They saw each other through good and bad, and fate often brought them together at times of traumatic developments in their lives. Their stories, set in the scheming, deluding world of Hollywood, are for me an irresistible study – a searing, often tragic, account perhaps unequalled in the annals of Hollywood.

They came together in the fifties, when something of the old Hollywood lingered on. Elizabeth Taylor, the unadulterated product of the studio system, was the most glamorous and sought-after actress in the world. When she played *The Girl Who Had Everything*, that was exactly what she seemed to be. In ten years' time she had become the first million-dollar star, while the extravagance, dramas and scandals of her private life made her 'the most famous woman in the world'.

Her lifelong and devoted friend Montgomery Clift was the darling of Broadway in the forties, a theatre actor of repute before he was lured, reluctantly, to Hollywood. Clift was the creator of modern hero-worship, idolised by millions of young men and women, and in his wake followed Marlon Brando, James Dean and the rest. But he was a man possessed, who slipped tragically and inexplicably into a pit of hedonistic excess and insecurity, destroyed by his inner torment.

Rock Hudson was also a leader. Created and honed by his agent and studio into fifties beefcake, his clean-cut, all-American image made him the world's top-rated male star until demand for this kind of cinematographic hero dwindled during the sixties and evaporated altogether in the seventies.

Like Elizabeth Taylor, Natalie Wood virtually grew up on a studio lot and knew no other life in her early years. She too made the difficult transition from perfect child star to successful young actress and, after *Rebel Without a Cause*, she and James Dean became known as the first American teenagers, the idols of their generation. In his short career, Dean personified the onset of youth rebellion, which would be taken up on the campuses in the sixties with new heroes like the Beatles and Dylan.

Dean once said, 'To me, the only success, the only greatness is immortality.' He achieved that ambition when he drove off in his Porsche to an early death, leaving the character he had carefully invented captured for ever on a few pieces of celluloid. At least he did not live long enough to display his weaknesses; nor did he have time to destroy his own image. The spectacular tragedy of his death was matched in different ways, but equally sensationally, by the early departures of Clift, Wood and Hudson. Now, of the five characters whose lives I have set out to chronicle, only Taylor remains – tarnished, perhaps, but still the total star.

What survives is a wide cross-section of their work, good and bad, for continual reshowing on television and at specialist festivals. More important, their films are the remnants of an art form which can never be repeated. But comparison between then and now is not my aim in this book; nor is it my intention to adjudicate on the merits of actors and actresses of that era. The picture I paint for you is, I hope, one which accurately displays their highs and lows – the build-up to a delirium of great success, the self-doubt and the exploitation, the sexual curiosity and passions, the attempts to escape through alcohol and drugs – until we see our five young lives literally and dramatically torn apart. The system that created them was, in part, to blame.

Chapter One

Heading for the Hills

Elizabeth got there first. She arrived in Hollywood early in 1940, her wide oval eyes with their natural dark outline and her fresh-faced innocence reminiscent of Judy Garland a few years earlier. Now Judy was having her breasts strapped down to stay fourteen by day, and dating band-leader Artie Shaw by night, and already aware that Benzedrine was available on request from the studio pharmacy.

Born in England on 27 February 1932, Elizabeth Taylor had spent an idyllic middle-class childhood. Her parents, Francis and Sara Taylor, were American. Francis managed a London art gallery owned by his wealthy uncle, Howard Young, and they led a comfortable pre-war life with a home in Hampstead, London, and a country retreat in the heart of Kent, where Elizabeth was surrounded by goats, chickens, rabbits and a pony. But as the war clouds gathered in March 1939, Francis sent his wife, their ten-year-old son Howard and seven-year-old Elizabeth to Sara's parents' home in Pasadena. He followed in September, when war in Europe became a reality, and, with the packages of paintings brought from London, set up shop in Hollywood.

Elizabeth and Howard were enrolled at a school near the Taylors' new home in Pacific Palisades, where they found themselves surrounded by the children of famous Hollywood families. Sara was anxious for her daughter to continue the singing and dancing lessons she had enjoyed in England; at the age of three she had been one of a group of children from her ballet school who performed before the Duchess of York and her daughters, the Princesses Elizabeth and Margaret Rose. Elizabeth had a loud, clear voice and her English accent made her stand out in Hollywood, so that soon Sara's friends were beginning to comment on the little girl's natural abilities.

At first Sara had no thoughts of allowing Elizabeth to join the throngs of children in Hollywood whose mothers were drilling them in song and dance and dragging them towards studio gates; but as a former Broadway actress herself, perhaps her enthusiasm for the profession which she had given up when she married Francis was reawakened. They were certainly in the right place at the right time.

Child stars were still among Hollywood's leading box-office attractions. In the wake of Shirley Temple, Jane Withers, Jane Powell and Judy Garland they remained enormously popular with the public, and the success of Deanna Durbin's films was such that, virtually alone, they saved Universal from bankruptcy. The studios rewarded their greatest assets lavishly and child stars ranked among the biggest earners. In the summer of 1940, for example, when Judy Garland went on a promotional tour with *The Wizard of Oz*, Metro–Goldwyn–Mayer gave her a $10,000 bonus and a new seven-year contract at $2000 a week. None of this was lost on Sara.

When the wife of MGM producer John W. Considine, Jr, suggested that Elizabeth should audition for her husband, the Taylors agreed. Soon the child was being ushered into the producer's office in the giant Metro studio, where she sang her exercise scales to Mr Considine. Louis B. Mayer, the autocratic boss of MGM, saw her for a fleeting moment as he was passing through and said, 'Sign her, sign her.' They offered Sara a $100-a-week, seven-year contract for Elizabeth; Universal, however, where Sara was friendly with the wife of an executive, made it $200, and in the spring of 1941, at the age of nine, Elizabeth Taylor officially became a Hollywood actress.

Within a few weeks she stood alone on a vast stage at Universal in front of a casting committee who were looking for a bright, breezy little child for a new musical. Elizabeth did not get the part, and in fact she was offered only one tiny role by that studio, in a bit of nonsense called *Man or Mouse*, starring Alfalfa Switzer, which took her all of three days to complete. Nothing else came along. She collected her $200 a week for the full year and then they let her go. When that first film was retitled *There's One Born Every Minute* and released in 1942, Elizabeth was billed as an exciting young newcomer, but by then she had already left Universal.

Now anxious for her daughter to continue her career in films, Sara secured an audience with Hedda Hopper, one of the two awful but influential gossip giants of Hollywood, to ask her advice. Hedda listened to Elizabeth's rendition of 'The Blue Danube' and said frankly that the child's future should not be tied to her singing. Recalling that moment in her autobiography, *The Whole Truth and Nothing But*, Hedda wrote:

I liked, and pitied, her from the start when her mother, bursting with ambition, brought her to my house one day to have her sing for me. Sara had never gotten over Broadway and she wanted to have a glamorous life again through her child. It struck me as a terrifying thing to ask a child to sing for a stranger. But in her quivering voice, this shy creature with enormous violet eyes piped her way through the song. It was one of the most painful ordeals I have ever witnessed.

Painful or not, Sara persisted, and that summer Francis heard by chance that MGM were looking for a girl with an English accent for a new film called *Lassie Come Home*, starring Roddy McDowall, whose fame had recently been secured by his appearance in *How Green Was My Valley*. The very next day, Elizabeth found herself back in the MGM studios, where the low-budget unit was preparing to go into production with the screenplay of Eric Knight's novel about a collie dog which is parted from its master (Roddy) and finds its way home through seemingly insurmountable obstacles. In an age of gloomy news from the war fronts of Europe, *Lassie* brought a charming, tear-laden relief, and cinema audiences and critics were at one in their acclaim. Elizabeth's acting was applauded, and the Taylors' lives would never be the same again.

That performance won for Elizabeth the part that was to launch her into stardom. *National Velvet* was already being discussed while she was working on *Lassie*, but first MGM had earmarked their new child protégé for two more films – *Jane Eyre*, for which she was loaned out to 20th Century–Fox, and MGM's own prestigious *The White Cliffs of Dover*, in which she was once again teamed up with Roddy McDowall. They became two of the most highly promoted films of 1944, but neither provided Elizabeth with any great challenge.

National Velvet was the opportunity she was waiting for. The unlikely tale of a girl named Velvet who nurses a sick horse called The Pi back to health, dresses up as a boy and wins the Grand National, it offered a fully-fledged starring role, which Elizabeth was determined to secure. She knew she *was* Velvet, and she spent every waking moment at the local stables, improving her riding and learning to steeplechase. She and her mother cried with joy when producer Pandro S. Berman announced that she had got the part and was to star with Mickey Rooney, Donald Crisp and Angela Lansbury. Now she had arrived in the big league.

Filming was completed in October 1944, and what Berman produced was a classic children's fairy story which had adult audiences equally enthralled. There was no hiding Elizabeth's delight, nor that of MGM and Louis B. Mayer, to whom she had become a very important young person. Her life changed overnight. She was removed from her normal school, Hawthorne High (where the other children were spending more time studying her than attending to their teacher), and put into the studio education system, which was operated under the watchful eye of the Los

Angeles Education Board. When she was working on a picture she had
to be given at least three hours' tuition before three in the afternoon
each day; at all other times she was required to follow a normal
curriculum arranged for the studio's moppets. But in truth, lessons were
of secondary importance; from now on she was totally immersed in her
training in the art of acting to the camera. And, as Judy Garland, Mickey
Rooney and Roddy McDowall could testify, the life of a young star entailed
many pressures. 'Whichever way you slice it,' said McDowall, 'you are
loading the child with a terrific amount of responsibility.'

* * * * *

For Natalie Wood that responsibility came even earlier in life. Towards
the end of 1943, as Elizabeth was about to start work on *National
Velvet*, little Natasha Gurdin stood with her mother, Marie, in Santa
Rosa, a smallish community outside San Francisco, as part of a crowd
waiting hopefully to be spotted by a film crew who had come to town.
Director Irving Pichel was shooting location scenes for *Happy Land* for
20th Century–Fox, with Don Ameche and Frances Dee, and was hiring
locals as extras. Marie Gurdin was determined that she and Natasha
would be at the front of the queue.

Marie was a tall, darkly attractive woman, a Russian of French
extraction, with an air of mystery about her. Like Elizabeth's mother,
she had a theatrical background. She had been a ballerina in Russia, but
in 1935 she fled Stalinist oppression and went to China, where she met
and married her first husband, who brought her to California. The
marriage lasted only months after that, and in 1937 she was married
again to another exiled Russian, Nicholai Zaharenko, whose name was
somehow Americanised to Gurdin. Their daughter Natasha was born
on 20 July 1938.

Nicholai spoke hardly any English and, as a lowly carpenter, his work
was spasmodic. Poverty drove Marie to seek any opportunity and news
of Pichel's arrival in town sent her dashing to the point where extras
were being recruited. In the crush, Irving Pichel suddenly found a
five-year-old child with huge black eyes being thrust into his arms. It
was Natasha Gurdin, a lively little girl with a flair for mimicry, whose
mother's friends had already compared her to Shirley Temple. On cue
to her mother's instructions, she began an instant audition.

All she had to do for the movie was drop an ice-cream and cry. She
demonstrated perfectly, and that was that. Natasha had gained her first
screen part – and more: Pichel promised that when another good part
came along, he would send for her. Marie took him at his word, though

few of her friends in the neighbourhood believed she would ever hear from him again.

When Pichel looked at Natasha on screen, he was captivated by her presence. Eighteen months later, when he was casting *Tomorrow Is Forever* and looking for a child to play alongside Orson Welles and Claudette Colbert, he returned to Santa Rosa to find her. On the strength of the promise of a screen test for her daughter, Marie packed the family up and moved to Los Angeles, rather to the bemusement of Nicholai.

Natalie remembered those first steps into the movie industry for the rest of her life.

I could hardly read, so my part had to be told to me and then I would memorise it. Also I had to speak with a German accent and learn some lines of German. Orson Welles was wonderful to me. He was always helpful. He was quite temperamental also, but never to me.

Welles himself summed her up after that first movie: 'She was a born professional, so good that she was terrifying.'

Tomorrow Is Forever, in which she appeared under the new name Pichel had invented for her, brought Natalie instant acclaim. She received widespread praise in the notices. The child 'eats your heart out', commented Louella Parsons, that other great Hollywood gossip, and *Box-office*, the film-industry trade paper, voted her the most talented young actress of 1946. Even before the film was released, several other producers were clamouring to sign her. At the age of eight she was experiencing the accolade bestowed on stars, and when she attended promotional activities laid on by the studio publicists, fans were grabbing at her hair to steal her bows.

Pichel had become Natalie's mentor. He idolised the young girl, whom he saw as a daughter, and a couple of years later he actually tried to adopt her. When he mentioned the prospect to Marie one day on the set, she thought he was joking and said, 'Sure, you can have her whenever you please.' Natalie recalled: 'A few nights later, he turned up at our apartment with a couple of lawyers and brought the adoption papers with him. My father was so angry, he ordered him out. But it all blew over, and Irving continued to promote my career.'

Pichel rushed her into another film, *The Bride Wore Boots*, then 20th Century–Fox signed her for *The Ghost and Mrs. Muir*, with Rex Harrison and Gene Tierney, and before the shooting had finished she was cast as Maureen O'Hara's daughter in *Miracle on 34th Street*. It was a film that in some ways illustrated the life that Natalie had been thrust into: a childhood lost, the mysteries of early youth never to be experienced.

Reflecting on those days, years later, Elizabeth Taylor said of the world she and Natalie knew: 'What happened to both of us is that we lost our childhood. We were never allowed to be just ordinary kids. Never. We both grew up in front of the camera, and going into the commissary and seeing cowboys and Indians having lunch together.' Natalie herself recalled:

> The strange thing is that, as a child in the movies, I didn't think of myself as being any different to other children. If I got up each morning and went to work, as I did, then you assume that all children of your age did exactly the same thing. It was only when I met people outside the studios, away from that very enclosed environment, that it began to dawn on me that life was different for other people.

Marie Gurdin lived for her daughter's new-found fame, and for its fortune. She was beginning to believe the studio's publicity material, that Natalie Wood was a child wonder. Everything the family did now revolved around her, and her half-sister Olga (from Marie's first marriage), whose own ambitions had lain towards the theatre, now became so fed up with her mother's single-minded approach to Natalie's career that she left the Gurdin household to return to her own father. Marie admitted that she had only one thought: 'I raised Natalie to be a movie star and I completely subordinated my life, that of my husband and my two other daughters to help Natalie get ahead.'

By the end of 1946, it seemed that her ambitions were realised: Natalie had certainly arrived.

*   *   *   *   *

The mid-1940s, however, brought fresh problems for the studio heads as they watched their pre-war idols returning from the hostilities, tired, unsure of themselves, their temples tinged with grey. Hollywood was running short of young male leads.

Louis B. Mayer sent his talent scouts off to New York and Broadway to 'discover' some new actors, and, not for the first time, he turned his attentions to a young man named Montgomery Clift, who in the previous twelve months had become the darling of the stage. But Clift, who had earlier turned down Mayer's offer of a starring role in *Mrs. Miniver*, continued to reject film offers.

Mayer had sent him airline tickets which had been returned, pleaded with him on the telephone, and sent subordinates to try to talk him round. Monty was in love with his art: acting – and that meant acting with a capital A – on the stage. He was in love with his friends, and with

New York, and he was strangely tied to his mother, with whom he still lived, although often he could not abide her.

To those who challenged his reasoning in rejecting Mayer's offers, Monty would say with resolution: 'Look, I'm not odd. I'm just trying to be an actor; not a movie star, an actor. I can't play something I'm not interested in, and if *I'm* not interested in it, how can I possibly expect the audience to get interested?' He stuck rigidly to that rule and, like his contemporary Marlon Brando, turned down dozens of scripts. Neither was he impressed by the lure of money; it had simply never been necessary. When his agents pleaded with him to consider doing a film that would earn him $100,000 instead of accepting $100 a week on Broadway, he chose the latter.

Like Elizabeth Taylor, Monty Clift had had a comfortable upbringing. He was born on 17 October 1920 into a wealthy stockbroking family. William and Ethel Clift, with their three children – twins Roberta and Montgomery, and their elder brother William, Jr – had established a home in Omaha, Nebraska (the city which also produced Brando), though almost immediately after the twins were born Ethel began taking the children on lengthy trips. Sometimes it would be to another part of America, more often it was abroad; and when Bill Clift moved to New York as an investment banker, he took a bachelor home while renting a place in Bermuda for his wife and children. After the season on the sunshine island, Ethel would take the youngsters off to Europe, to Switzerland, France or Germany, and they would be separated from their father for weeks, if not months, on end. It was a strange family life, which Monty was always reluctant to discuss.

For almost eight years Ethel and the children spent much of their time in Europe, and Monty became fluent in three European languages. Their lifestyle was one which even upper-class American children seldom saw. They mixed with only the best European families; the children became proficient in the 'expensive' sports – fencing, riding, tennis, skiing and so on. They had private tutors for their lessons and Ethel, whose domination was total, created a schoolroom atmosphere within the home, so that her children got the feeling of formal education.

The travelling stopped after the Wall Street Crash, when Bill Clift could no longer afford to give his family the lifestyle Ethel had arranged for them. They eventually set up home in Sarasota, Florida, and it was here, in a local theatrical group, that Monty took his first acting role, at the age of thirteen. Ethel at first tried to discourage him: her family were professional people; but gradually, through his own persistence, she warmed to the idea and began pushing him towards a career in the theatre.

The following year, 1934, they moved to Sharon, Massachusetts. In the neighbouring town of Stockbridge a play called *Fly Away Home* was being staged prior to a possible move to Broadway. It deals with a divorced couple whose children are intent on reuniting them, and Monty's chance came when a boy originally cast for one of the roles dropped out. Monty quickly despatched himself to the theatre for an audition and secured the part, much to Ethel's delight.

Bill Clift was less taken with the prospect; perhaps the danger signs around his son, a polite, over-sensitive, highly intelligent boy, were beginning to occur to him. He was given specific cause for concern when two English actors in the cast, known homosexuals in their late twenties, began to take an unhealthy interest in the Clift boy; yet inexplicably Bill and Ethel did nothing to stop the association. Some of Monty's friends later pinpointed this as the start of his drift into homosexuality, and perhaps the feelings that would eventually control his emotions were actively aroused at this time. Whatever its beginnings, homosexuality became Monty's way of life, and with it, in those early years, came the constant fear of discovery in an age when sex between consenting males was scandalous and criminal.

Monty's commitment to his work was intense, and word of his potential talent spread quickly. A succession of sensitive and stylish roles made him one of Broadway's most sought-after young actors. After two seasons in *Fly Away Home*, then two shortlived flops, Clift secured the lead in *Dame Nature* and, at seventeen, returned to Broadway in a starring role that won him good reviews. With his base now seemingly assured on Broadway, the Clift family moved permanently to an apartment in Manhattan, although when Monty's work took him on out-of-town tours, Mrs Clift was invariably at his side.

The role that set him alight came when Alfred Lunt and his wife Lynn Fontanne were casting for *There Shall Be No Night*, a new play by Robert Sherwood with a strong anti-war message; it was Monty's first in a series of dramatic roles voicing youth's protest against conflict. The play opened in April 1940, with Lunt, as always, directing and co-starring with his wife, and settled in for a good run.

In the Lunt company Monty met and became firm friends with William LeMassena, who went on to become one of Broadway's most popular character actors. Billy recalled for me his early days with Monty:

These were among the happiest days of my life. Monty's parents were kind and generous, and took a close interest in everything we were doing. Because I was Monty's best friend at the time, they gave me a room at their apartment in Manhattan; it was a superb place furnished lovingly with good American colonial furniture, and the pictures on the walls were all originals; it was all the type of stuff you'd only find in museums today. It was a perfectly charming household and they saw we never wanted for anything. Sunny [Mrs Clift] would see that when we went to the theater, we had the best seats; I mean if I'd gone on my own I'd be in the 55 cents rows.

Lunt gave them eighteen months' work before closing the play when America joined the war in December 1941. Clift always recognised this period as the most useful and formative in his career. He observed:

I watched Lunt and Lynn go on, night after night, and I watched them rehearse close at hand. For a young actor, the experience was just unforgettable. What I was learning here was a skill, a profession, an art form to which I could apply my own interpretation. Few actors get that kind of experience so early on in their career.

For years Monty had suffered from amoebic dysentery and colitis and as a result he was ruled unfit for military service. After the play's closure, he and Billy were not long without work. Billy said:

Monty had become a name on Broadway already and producers and directors were all looking out for him. And there is no doubt, this boy was an extraordinary person; he was when I first met him and he remained so, basically, until his death. In those early days on Broadway . . . he didn't drink or smoke and it is no exaggeration to say that he had the innate, organic morality of a saint at that time. Very early on, I learned that any kind of transgression that violated his friendship would hurt him tremendously and leave him helpless with emotion; cruelty, any kind, whether to animals or children, just injured him. He couldn't cope with it. It wasn't his upbringing, it was just the genius of him.

Monty believed firmly in a defined moral code and he could not cope with deceptive or ruthless people. In the life that lay ahead of him, it was a faith that was to be shattered many times, with devastating effect.

In April 1942 he and Billy were cast in a new play, *Mexican Mural*, directed and staged by Bobby Lewis, and it was in this production that Monty first met a number of people who were to become major influences in his life: Kevin McCarthy and his wife Augusta, Mira Rostova and Libby Holman. The show was not a huge success and closed after a few months. Then director Elia Kazan cast Clift for a new Thornton Wilder play, *The Skin of Our Teeth*. Kazan had a known aversion to homo-sexuals, stemming from his close association with the Group Theatre, that band of intellectual and passionate rebels who formed around Lee Strasberg and Clifford Odets in the 1930s and who, among other things, denounced homosexuality as an evil in society and a threat to the theatre (even though there were a number of severe cases within their own midst).

Kazan liked Clift, however, and took him to his home. Monty would curl up in a foetal position at the feet of Kazan's wife, Molly, who, like Lynn Fontanne, became one of his many surrogate-mother figures. As Kazan encouraged Monty in his career, he suggested that the young actor's polite, sensitive image had not gone unnoticed and that continuing to live at home, under his mother's influence, would merely encourage rumours about his sexual preferences. So he moved out of the family apartment into his own place, a small suite at the top of some dimly lit stairs over a laundromat on East 55th near Lexington, albeit only a couple of hundred yards from his parents. His relationship with his parents remained stable for the moment, though now that he was living alone it began to deteriorate as other friendships blossomed.

Professionally, Monty's star had risen to such a degree that the Hollywood scouts were getting restless for him. He rejected them all: movies were not for him. A temporary setback occurred when an attack of colitis forced him to leave the Kazan play and confined him to hospital for several weeks; he spent months undergoing treatment. This was perhaps another significant point in his life: through these bouts of illness his interest in medical matters and drugs began to grow; prescription medication became almost a fascination, and he wanted to discover the effects of the various kinds of pills and painkillers he was required to take.

He came back to Broadway at the end of 1943, appearing successively in Thornton Wilder's *Our Town* and Lillian Hellman's *The Searching Wind*, in which he played a young man returning from war. Then in May 1945 he achieved top billing for his performance in the new Elsa Shelley play, *Foxhole in the Parlor*. Once again it was a wartime plot, in which Clift played the weary, disillusioned hero torn by the futility of conflict. Though audiences and reviewers alike were tiring of war plays, Monty rose above the drab script and received rave reviews; suddenly he had elevated his status in the eyes of the critics and the theatre-going public, and there were now crowds waiting to see him at the stage door. Scripts and offers from Hollywood came thick and fast, and soon Monty found himself face to face with Louis B. Mayer, who had summoned him once again to Los Angeles with a round-trip air ticket and the promise of something big.

This time Monty agreed to fly to Hollywood for talks. As he entered the inner sanctum, Mayer pushed across the desk a seven-year contract and issued the immortal line: 'Sign up with Metro and we'll make you a big star.' He could never believe that anyone could refuse such an offer.

Clift was, in fact, by now ready to come to Hollywood. Billy Le-Massena reckoned that the parts he had been playing recently on Broadway helped in that decision: 'We sat talking in a coffee shop about the offers he was getting, and he told me he was fed up with doing the sensitive stuff; he wanted a complete change, like a western or something.' Monty was totally unprepared for a seven-year tie-up, however. He explained to Mayer, hesitantly but politely, that he would like to do pictures for MGM but only on the basis of one at a time and that he wanted script approval, which was virtually unheard of in Hollywood in those days. He did his best to make Mayer see that a man so engrossed in acting for the theatre could not contemplate sacrificing his conscience and skill simply for the guarantee of seven years of big money.

Louis B. didn't see. He began his reply by saying that he fully appreciated Clift's feelings, but then he contradicted himself and blew up: 'Who the fuck do you think you are? Do you think we're going to pump money into you, building you up into a big, big star and then let you go back to New York? Well, if you think that, you got another think coming. Get outta here!' Monty walked out of the office leaving behind him a scene that many others knew only too well. Having shouted himself into an emotional rage, Mayer was in tears.

At the same time, Howard Hawks at United Artists was looking for a strong talent to cast alongside John Wayne and Walter Brennan in what was to become one of the most famous westerns of all time – *Red River*. He had been impressed by Clift's recent performances on Broadway and sent him the script.

Monty was intrigued; the idea of a western was challenging. He could see, as Hawks could, that this was something completely different to the stage acting that had consumed his life so far; it would give him the chance to develop new, unexplored dimensions in his abilities. Furthermore, he would be up against Duke Wayne and, as Hawks perceived, the meetings of two such extreme talents would make an unexpected and electrifying piece of casting. Monty accepted.

So, in 1946, Montgomery Clift had arrived in Hollywood. It was the first of many excursions, and it would soon lead to the beginning of his long love-affair with Elizabeth Taylor.

* * * * *

In the very week that Monty Clift came to Hollywood to start filming, a young man who began life as Roy Scherer, Jr, was now known as Roy

Fitzgerald after his mother's divorce and remarriage, and who was soon to become Rock Hudson, reached California. He had not the slightest experience of acting, nor had he any inkling of how he could break into the profession. All he did know for sure was that he wanted to be a movie star.

He was born on 17 November 1925 in Winnetka, Illinois. Roy Scherer senior left his family in poverty when his son was five and Roy junior was brought up by his mother, Katherine, a big, cheerful woman who had been a telephone operator. Her influence over her son was very strong and it was she who inspired his boyhood dream of becoming a movie star. She would listen admiringly as he recited dialogue from movie magazines, and by the time he was ten he was delivering groceries and cleaning chickens for the local butcher to earn enough money to see two movies a week at the Winnetka picture house.

Katherine had married Wallace Fitzgerald when Rock was eight. The boy's relationship with his stepfather was not a happy one; in an interview in 1957 he recalled:

As soon as he came on the scene, he took all my toys away. He used to beat me, saying he wanted to make a man of me and once when I asked him if I could have drama lessons, he walloped me across the head and that was that.

Katherine also had mixed feelings about her argumentative husband; before Rock was fifteen she had divorced him, remarried him and divorced him again. Out on her own, with her son at her side, she took a job as a live-in housekeeper for a wealthy family, and she and Rock shared a bed in the servant wing before they moved to a tiny room over a drug store. 'She was my mother, my father, and my big sister,' Rock said, 'and I was like a brother to her.'

Rock took a job as a truck-driver until he was called up for war service. He spent two and a half uneventful years in the Navy as an aircraft mechanic, then, when the war was over, went back to Winnetka. His ambition to be a movie star had never waned, however, and after six months as a piano remover he determined to make himself 'available for discovery'. He moved with his mother to Los Angeles, where his own father, Roy Scherer, was living. He gave his son a job selling vacuum cleaners, but it lasted only a few weeks: Rock failed to sell a single machine, and the reunion between father and son, after so many years apart, was not a success.

After all his avid reading of movie-fan magazines, it seemed perfectly feasible to Rock that he would be 'noticed', and he began hanging around outside studio gates for hours at a time, waiting for some producer to be attracted by his all-American-boy image and whisk him away to stardom. 'Believe it or not,' he said years later, 'I was so naive, I really did think that those stories about people being discovered were true. It may sound foolish but that's what I did, and nothing happened.'

Over the years Hudson gave various versions of how he was eventually 'discovered' and, as usual, the studio publicity people merged fact with invention. The story that seems most credible is his own early account of how he met Henry Willson, the famed Hollywood agent who once handled Joan Fontaine and Lana Turner.

Unnoticed but undaunted, Rock had some pictures of himself taken for $65 and mailed them to studios and agents. The response was nil. Then he heard that the David O. Selznick studio was casting and left one of his photographs with a reception clerk. The following day he was summoned to the studio, where he met Willson, then acting as talent scout for Selznick. And there it began.

Willson, recalling their first meeting, said: 'I saw in him a face that could flip a lot of women. Sure, he was gawky, he could hardly speak because of his shyness, he had a terrible, nasal midwestern drawl, a twisted eyetooth and a stoop. But I knew I could change all that.' He was so confident that he took Hudson under his wing and soon a Hollywood veteran was describing the Willson protégé as a 'wholesome boy, who doesn't perspire, has no pimples, smells of milk and has the appeal of cleanliness and respectability; this boy is pure'.

What Rock did not know was that he had become associated with one of Hollywood's most evil exploiters of young men and women – a homosexual who would sell his own soul, and those of his clients, in the furtherance of his quest for sex and money. Roy Fitzgerald was ready and willing to do Willson's bidding to realise his dream of movie stardom. But at what price?

* * * * * *

There could be no better example of an all-American boy from a small town than James Dean – a homespun youth whose own limited experience of life mirrored that of the generation that made him its idol. Not a lot happened to Dean in the first eighteen years of his life: his adolescence was as uneventful as that of millions of young men around the world.

He was born on 8 February 1931 to Winton and Mildred Dean in Marion, Indiana, where his father worked as a dental technician. Later Winton's work took them to Santa Monica, California, and Mildred, who had been reluctant to leave her family, sent pictures of Jimmy, her only child, back home almost weekly. With no friends, she showered her son with affection and time. She made him toys, including a cardboard theatre, and wrote plays which they performed together with rag puppets. He had few friends either; as a newcomer he was regarded as an outsider.

Jimmy was nearing his ninth birthday when Mildred died of breast cancer, and Winton, deeply in debt through hospital bills, sent his son back to Indiana to live with his aunt and uncle, Ortense and Marcus Winslow, on their 300-acre farm at Fairmount. Winton stayed in California and seldom saw the boy.

There Jimmy remained, in the hub of a protective and caring family, and future writers on the life and times of James Dean would have to use all their imaginative powers to discover anything truly 'different' in his background. It is true that his Hollywood contemporaries said later that he made continual references to his mother's death, over which he seemed to blame himself: 'I must have been bad for her to leave me' was an oft-quoted saying attributed to him. But to Ortense and Marcus, and to his teachers at Fairmount High, he was a fairly normal, slightly moody boy, who was a good worker, a good athlete and got into no serious trouble. A passion for speed first emerged at fifteen, when he persuaded his uncle to buy him a motorbike.

At this stage of his life, Jimmy spoke with forceful clarity, his voice carrying to the back of any hall – a complete contrast to the slurred mumble that became his trademark. Ortense encouraged his obvious talent for drama and arranged for him to give a reading to the Fairmount Women's Temperance Movement. The pastor of the local Wesleyan Church, Dr James DeWeerd, also became an important influence on the boy. DeWeerd, a Silver Star hero of the Second World War and a friend of Winston Churchill, taught Dean to appreciate art, classical music and philosophy. In their long, searching discussions at DeWeerd's home, the pastor urged him to think of life beyond Fairmount, whose small-mindedness he often criticised in his Sunday sermons.

On 9 April 1949 Jimmy made headlines in the *Fairmount News*: 'James Dean was awarded first place honors in the National Forensic League contest with a reading of "The Madman" by Charles Dickens. By winning first place, he is eligible to enter the national speaking tournament of the NFL.'

From that moment, Dean set his heart on becoming an actor. The die was cast.

Chapter Two

The Shadow of Inquisition

The end of the war opened up new horizons for the film industry; but it did not pick up the challenge. The immediate post-war era proved to be disastrous for Hollywood. Even the biggest names were forced into old-fashioned, lightweight films which took little account of what the movie-going public, fresh from the turmoil of the past five years, wanted. The loyalty of a vast audience of fans was tested to the limit.

A major contributing factor was the sinister shadow cast by Senator Joseph McCarthy as he began his purge on Communism in all walks of American life. As the investigations and public hearings began to name and crucify writers, directors and actors, the studios were thrown into a state of blind panic through fear of producing anything that could be seen as un-American. The effect was an air of mistrust, deceit, double-dealing, and the complete undermining of the industry. The disarray and distortions that resulted from the televised hearings of the House of Representatives Committee on Un-American Activities (HUAC) was catastrophic. As the examination of the political undertones in the movie industry spread into an unprecedented witch hunt, the blacklist of suspected Communists became 'the Great List'.

The beginning of the purge towards the end of 1946 and the start of the hearings themselves in April 1947 stifled the output of any picture that was the slightest bit controversial. Message pictures were quickly ruled out. 'If you want to send a message, use Western Union,' said Jack Warner. Even films like the William Wyler classic *The Best Years of Our Lives* were scrutinised. At the hearings, initially held behind closed doors, Richard Nixon asked Warner if he was making any anti-communist movies comparable to his anti-Nazi material during the war. Warner managed to produce only one example, *Up Until Now*, but that was not enough for Nixon. He insisted that Hollywood had a positive duty to attack the Communists through the movies. In the years before the HUAC hearings, pictures with social and psychological themes amounted to almost thirty per cent of Hollywood's output; in 1948 the figure had dropped to twenty per cent, and in 1949 to eighteen per cent – but among these were deliberate anti-communist propaganda films like *The Red Menace, The Red Danube, Guilty of Treason, I Married a Communist, I Was a Communist for the FBI, The Iron Curtain.*

Howard Hughes, one of the HUAC's greatest supporters, began his own purge of suspected Communists when he bought RKO in 1948. He hired teams of investigators to spy on virtually every employee of the studio. Phones were tapped, private eyes snooped on top executives. On lists of names, those that came back circled in red were dismissed, their names wiped off the credits of films made by RKO as far back as 1931.

Hughes called his head of production, Dore Schary, to a meeting in a tiny office in Romain Street (he never set foot inside the RKO studios) and asked him if he was a Communist. 'No,' replied Schary, 'but I am an extreme Liberal.' Goodbye, Mr Schary.

Hughes switched the output of the studio from sociological themes to a peculiar mix of sex and right-wing extremism aimed at spreading the anti-communist message, like *I Married a Communist* (subsequently retitled *Woman on Pier 13*), which included the line, written by Hughes himself, 'I'm no Commie. If people like you don't wake up ... the Communists will take over.'

* * * * *

Such was the turmoil of Hollywood as it headed towards the end of the decade. Perhaps it was a further sign of stagnation that the list of the top ten women stars had hardly altered since 1940. Judy Garland, now twenty-three, once divorced and just married to Vincente Minnelli, her director in *Meet Me in St. Louis*, was still one of Louis B. Mayer's main box-office attractions and he had recognised that fact by raising her salary to $3000 a week, with a bonus of $15,000 for her performance in *The Clock*. Also in that list were Ingrid Bergman, after *Casablanca*; Greer Garson, who had won an Oscar for *Mrs. Miniver* in 1942 and had collected five other nominations since; Bette Grable and Bette Davis.

Elizabeth Taylor would soon be outpacing them all. After *National Velvet*, young womanhood set in and, in usual Hollywood fashion, had been advanced a little. She shook off the child-star image in *Life With Father*, released in 1947, in which she got third billing alongside William Powell and Irene Dunne; the following year, in *A Date with Judy*, she got a screen kiss from the much older Robert Stack, which was very much commented upon in the fan magaziness; then she had Peter Lawford as her fiancé in *Julia Misbehaves* and married him in her next film, *Little Women*.

Now she *was* a star, an achievement marked in typical Hollywood style by the presentation on her sixteenth birthday of a pastel-blue Cadillac with a gold key from her parents and her very own, completely complete wardrobe from MGM. What made Elizabeth different from many other young stars was that she was in the process of making a smooth transition from childhood to young womanhood. Judy Garland had accomplished it; Natalie would soon follow; but many other child stars fell by the wayside and were never seen again. Those prophetic enough to realise it could see that in Elizabeth Taylor and Natalie Wood Hollywood had created two young talents who would see in the next era of movie-making, and throughout their teens they were in constant demand. Elizabeth recalled: 'Natalie and I jumped straight from child-hood into womanhood, both of us. Natalie never stopped working and I never stopped working. She never went through that awkward age, nor did I. We were doing our growing up in front of the camera.'

Unlike Judy Garland, whose private life got out of control in her teens because her mother, Ethel, allowed the studios to try to force her real character into the publicity image they had created for her, and to overtax her energies with one film after another, both Elizabeth and Natalie remained under the strict supervision of their parents and the studio chaperons now required by law.

Elizabeth had received a lot of controlled media attention and encour-aging reviews, in spite of some of the fairly average movies she appeared in as MGM, like other major studios, struggled to find its way. Now, however, the newspapers and magazines were beginning to turn to her private life for stories – and in that they were aided by the ever-vigilant studio publicity department. When Elizabeth went publicly on a date with the all-American football and basketball hero Glenn Davis, it was no accidental encounter. The studio had arranged it, and in the end it backfired, as so many publicity stunts did. The gallant Lieutenant Davis, on leave from the Army before going to Korea, was as famous on the sports pages as Miss Taylor was in the entertainment sections. They had seven more very public dates that summer, before Glenn was finally shipped out for his tour of duty, all of them eagerly covered by the newspapers.

Elizabeth played the part to perfection; perhaps, momentarily, she thought that she was in love for the first time, but even the studio did not want it to be for real. Davis did not know that; he was twenty-four and serious enough to think she was his girl. He sent her his gold football chain to wear around her neck and wrote to her daily. He went to war clearly under the misapprehension that he might just possibly be getting engaged to one of the world's most beautiful and famous young women.

Of course, all this most opportune publicity had nothing at all to do with the fact that MGM had just cast Elizabeth in a new film, *Conspirator*, to star with Robert Taylor – as his wife, no less. She was sent to London in November 1948 for the location work and she went as a star, with all the trappings – and with Miss Melinda Anderson of the Los Angeles Schools Department, who was there to make sure that Elizabeth did at least three hours of lessons a day. From a lesson in English or mathematics, she would hurry back to the filming, perhaps to a love-scene in the arms of her co-star.

On screen, she looked a young adult. Her proportions had filled to a rounded bloom – a striking rose with a startlingly natural beauty that required almost no make-up. That was what attracted Michael Wilding, then one of Britain's most popular actors and twenty years older than Elizabeth. They met during her filming and, as he watched her in the studio canteen, he said to Stewart Granger: 'Rather than ask a waitress for the salt, that Taylor chit gets it herself, wiggling her hips; then she wiggles her way back again past my table.' They had a number of meetings; clearly she made a profound impression on him and on the day she left England he was at the airport to kiss her goodbye.

Unknown to Elizabeth, another, more senior, suitor was watching all the newsreels of her in the privacy of his legendary seclusion and when she returned to America in February 1949 he attempted to attract her to his side. Howard Hughes, whose tentacles had embraced some of Hollywood's most famous female stars, had deviously plotted to get to Elizabeth through her parents. He said he wanted to buy some paintings from her father, began inviting them to dinner and suggested that they might like to bring Elizabeth along. But his attempts came to naught. She showed not the slightest interest in even seeing him, let alone in joining her parents at his dining table, and so he cancelled the order for the paintings. Hughes would not let it rest there, however. He had an insatiable appetite for young women, and he did not like rejections.

Glenn Davis was back from Korea and eager to take up where he had left off. Elizabeth went to the airport to meet him, surrounded by the usual barrage of cameras, once again put on red alert by MGM publicity. She shed a tear on his arrival, wiped the lipstick from his cheeks, and repeated the gesture for a cameraman who had missed the shot.

Davis was at her side when she attended the Academy Awards that spring, but he did not fit in with the glamour and razzmatazz; he knew that as soon as he arrived under the arc-lights. Not many days passed before they parted, with a brief and formal statement from the MGM press office announcing that they had reached the conclusion that their lives were too different and too busy to assure their happiness. The headlines were huge over such earth-shattering news, for everyone in the world had been expecting them to marry.

Within a week, Elizabeth had received a proposal of marriage from another of America's most eligible young men, William Pawley, Jr, son of a multi-millionaire whom she had met not long before at her uncle's house. When he saw in the papers that she had broken with Glenn Davis, Bill Pawley wrote to her from his home in Florida, proclaiming his undying love. His proposal followed rapidly, and Elizabeth realised that she was in love, seriously this time and for ever. Encouraged by her response, Bill caught the next plane to Los Angeles with a 3½-carat solitaire diamond ring in his pocket. With the approval of her parents and Louis B. Mayer, she accepted his ring and said yes, she would love to marry him because he was the only man in the world for her.

Three weeks later Elizabeth and her mother flew down to the Pawley homestead for the official announcement. News of her intentions travelled ahead of her and, to Bill Pawley's dismay, they were mobbed and jostled by the hordes as she landed at Miami. From then on they were followed and spied on from every angle. Bill had already decided upon his next move: he asked Elizabeth to renounce her screen career when she became his wife. She replied, perhaps then in all honesty, 'After my next picture.'

Bill worshipped her. When she returned to Hollywood to start pre-production work on her next, aptly titled film, *Father of the Bride*, with Spencer Tracy, he phoned her daily and flew to Los Angeles whenever he could. It all seemed idyllic. The gossip writers were already discussing Elizabeth's forthcoming rehearsal for her own wedding as she threw a bridal shower for Jane Powell, who married Geary Steffen in September.

In that same week, two days before the Powell wedding, MGM called Sara and Elizabeth into the studio. The news was terrific. She was being loaned to Paramount for a highly starred role in *A Place in the Sun*. It was to be her first major romantic role and she was to play alongside Montgomery Clift; best of all, George Stevens was directing. Elizabeth cried with joy. She couldn't believe it. Montgomery Clift. George Stevens. It was all too much.

Her position in Hollywood changed instantly. Stevens was one of the best and most acclaimed directors, and the fact that he had selected Elizabeth was praise in itself. Bill Pawley, however, did not share Elizabeth's rapture. 'I thought you were going to give it all up?' he enquired in the first tones of displeasure he had shown her.

'But, Bill,' she pleaded, 'I must do this one film. I do love you, I do, I do . . .'

He put the phone down and flew to Los Angeles for a confrontation.

Within twenty-four hours the engagement was off and Bill was flying back to Miami with tears in his eyes. Twenty-four hours after that, Elizabeth's misery over the broken engagement was lifted when her father threw a party on the night of Jane Powell's wedding. She was gloomy at first, but soon she got into the party mood and was photographed apparently having a good time. One young man never took his eyes off her that night and finally he managed to get an introduction.

'Miss Taylor,' said a Paramount executive, 'I would like you to meet Nicky Hilton.' And they danced the night away.

* * * * *

Elizabeth was yet to meet Montgomery Clift. Since *Red River* he had come to the brink of international fame, but he was not at all keen on what he had found in Hollywood. For one thing, the film – about the first cattle drive from Texas to Abilene, Missouri – had not been a happy initiation into the world of movie-making. Although Monty had thrown himself into the part, quickly learning to ride and handle steers, neither John Wayne nor Howard Hawks took to him as a man, although Hawks praised his acting. As personalities, they were poles apart, and only the cheery Walter Brennan could inject some light relief. Monty took it all tremendously seriously and would go off into deep thought, memorising his lines and trying different approaches to a scene. At the end of it, he sensed that he would not like the finished article. He would have to wait eighteen months before he could see it, for Howard Hawks became locked in a legal battle with the film's backer, Howard Hughes, who wanted to tamper with the edited version and disliked the ending. Although it was completed in 1947, it was not released until the end of 1948, and in fact Monty's second film, *The Search*, was out before it.

In Hollywood, however, Monty was already being hailed as a future star. It was he who started the migration of young New York actors to the film capital. Behind him came Marlon Brando, Paul Newman, James Dean, Steve McQueen, Anthony Perkins, George Peppard and others; but it would always take something special to prise Monty himself from New York.

Apart from his overriding desire to be a Broadway person, all his roots were there: his mentors, his friends, his lovers, his advisers, his coaches, his mother and his mother-substitutes. He was bound by a complex pattern of relationships.

Male lovers came and went in relative secrecy; he was almost paranoid about attracting attention to his homosexuality, which, in the forties, was still very much taboo. Phyllis Thaxter, an actress whom he met while she was starring in a Broadway production of *Claudia*, had become a cover in that respect. They were so close that many people expected them to marry, but Phyllis always knew it would never happen. Billy LeMassena said that Monty could charm and captivate any woman, and he was never short of female company; but while he loved women for their society, he preferred men in bed.

Billy and Monty were often together, and his other closest friends were actor Kevin McCarthy and his wife Augusta. He was also the admired companion of writers like Thornton Wilder, Truman Capote and Tennessee Williams, and dined with famous actresses like Marlene Dietrich. But something in Monty was changing. When he returned from his first excursions to Hollywood, Billy noticed the difference: 'I found he was drinking and smoking; not heavily, but the momentum was gathering; you could see that. Now that may seem innocent, but believe me the way Monty had been before I left for war service, it came as a shock.' Billy also noticed that Clift's interest in prescription drugs had increased and he had built up a library of medical books, which he read avidly.

At the same time, Monty had grown increasingly hostile towards his parents for no apparent reason. They still lived close by and Mrs Clift visited regularly; but even her ardour was being tested by the strange 'friends' appearing at the apartment, and the language that Monty deliberately used in her presence was a shock to her.

Two other women in his life held sway in their different ways; both had come to him, like the McCarthys, through their appearance in *Mexican Mural* in 1942. The first was the Russian Mira Rostova, whose family had fled to New York from Berlin at the start of the war. She was five years Monty's senior, and they became devoted to each other, though in a professional sense only. Her influence was to manifest itself throughout his career, to which she seemed happy to apply her energies.

Libby Holman was a different matter. Once described by Noël Coward as a 'fag hag', she was almost twice Monty's age and had been a star of Broadway musicals in the late 1920s. She achieved national notoriety in 1932 when she was charged with murdering her husband, Zachary Smith Reynolds of the affluent tobacco family. Reynolds was just twenty when she married him eight months earlier, and was heir to a very large pile of cash and masonry. She maintained that Zach, angry about her continued appearance on stage and about his own failings in the matrimonial bed, stood in front of her and shot himself through the head. The Reynolds family, who feared that some of their $30 million tobacco fortune might slip into Libby's bank account, promptly encouraged the district attorney to charge Libby with murder, claiming that it was she, not he, who had pulled the trigger.

At her trial, the defence produced some disturbing evidence about Zachary's sexual background; his homosexual urges had overwhelmed any normal relationship with Libby and he had shown strong suicidal tendencies. At this point, the prosecution decided to drop the case and Libby collected $750,000 from his estate. Four months later, she gave birth to a son, Christopher Smith Reynolds.

Libby remained a social leper for most of the thirties, but with her new-found wealth she put up some of the backing for *Mexican Mural* in the vain hope of a comeback. The scandals, however, were not yet at an end. Libby had since married an actor, Ralph Holmes, another homosexual who declined into a depressed state and soon took his own life with a couple of handfuls of sleeping pills.

From the mid-forties onwards, Libby and Monty were the closest of friends and, as she searched for new pleasures in her well-endowed but empty life, she was among those who encouraged Monty towards the good times. As his personal conflicts over his Hollywood career and his homosexuality intensified, Libby became a willing participant with him in long bouts of drinking, experimenting with drugs and strange sexual excursions into strip-joints and whorehouses which went against his apparent leanings but satisfied her perverted whim. What they got up to in private has always remained a matter of colourful speculation. As Billy LeMassena once said, the idea of the handsome young idol of Broadway going to bed with an unattractive, older woman was repulsive. Monty himself told of wild scenes at Libby's magnificent home, filled with the aromas of erotic eastern perfumes and joss-sticks, topped up with marijuana and pep pills.

Clift's lifestyle was aided by the $60,000 straight fee he got from *Red River*. His agent, Leland Hayward, kept reminding him that there was plenty more where that came from, and contracts would arrive with blank spaces for Monty to fill in the figures and return them to Hollywood. After his long career on Broadway, and his final acceptance of a move into films, producers and directors were falling over themselves to sign him. It was not just a sign of Monty's own incredible achievement of star status even before his first film had been released; it was a further indication of how badly the studios needed new talent. But he never wavered from his original view: he would go to Hollywood only on his own terms.

Other, more important, developments in New York were drawing Clift into a new approach to acting, and setting a style that would launch the angry young American men and women of the fifties. They began with Elia Kazan's determination after the war to try to re-establish the ideals of the disbanded Group Theatre. He wanted 'to do something about the American actor' over and above the enormous contribution he had made to the theatre as a director. Between 1942 and 1947 he had staged more than a dozen plays on Broadway, including *The Skin of Our Teeth*, in which Montgomery Clift had shown new depth, *Deep Are the Roots*, *All My Sons* and *A Streetcar Named Desire*, in which Marlon Brando made his breakthrough.

In 1947, with Bobby Lewis and Cheryl Crawford, he founded the Actors Studio, a controversial centre where actors could learn and experiment with their craft. They initially gathered twenty-six actors who would represent the first intake of students. Clift and Brando were among them, although they were never true products of the school since they had both established their own styles before they began attending Kazan's classes. Lee Strasberg, who introduced the Stanislavski 'Method' technique of acting at the studio when he arrived in 1948, actually warned his future generation of actors against the slouching, mumbling style adopted by Brando and subsequently by James Dean. The Method technique, in simple terms, is a series of exercises in which an actor learns to draw from his own emotional experiences, from inside his own mind and body, to create the character he is portraying. The exercises involve long, deep periods of concentration, sometimes ending with an explosion of physical acts, which can be violent and sexual or calm and deliberate. Many actors dismissed it as worthless hocus-pocus, and said it merely threw up tricks and stunts which got in the way of true acting. Charlton Heston described it to me as being 'like masturbation; a lot of fun but it gets you nowhere.'

Clift, in many ways, had already worked out his own 'method', which was obvious in the intensity with which he approached his work, but there is no doubt that attendance during the early days of the Actors Studio gave him added depth. He brought these new dimensions to his style with a sensitive and expert treatment of his role for Fred Zinnemann in *The Search*, released in 1948, the story of an American GI in the aftermath of the war who adopts a dirty-faced, homeless boy in the ruins of Germany. One magazine critic wrote that Clift's performance would bring tears from a turnip. Zinnemann said: 'He had an aura I had seldom experienced in other actors. His presence on the screen was electrifying and he got much more out of the part than was written down.'

Some of Clift's magnetic appeal had to do with the coaching he got from Mira Rostova. At nights they would rehearse his lines; during the following day's shooting she was always on set, somewhere behind the cameras, and at the end of a take Clift would look towards her for a nod of approval or a grimace signalling that he should do it again. Zinnemann tolerated her presence on the set for weeks, then finally walked over to Monty and said quietly: 'Who's directing this movie, anyway?' Mira retreated, never to be seen on Zinnemann's lot again. But in private she continued to rehearse Monty with an intensity that astounded his colleagues.

Clift's performance in *The Search* made him an instant star and sent the youth of America into raptures. He got rave notices and a Best Actor nomination in 1948 Academy Awards, alongside Dan Dailey, Lew Ayres, Clifton Webb and Laurence Olivier, who eventually won it for *Hamlet*.

All the popular magazines began to feature him. *Life* put him on the front cover; *Look* dubbed him the most promising young actor on Hollywood's horizon. All over the nation, Montgomery Clift Appreciation Clubs were springing up. His face, his sensitivity, his style were all very personal – nothing like the stereotyped male stars of the silver screen, like Gable, Cooper, Stewart or Fonda. Monty Clift was different; a loner with an almost indefinable sexual appeal which a dozen writers in the big-selling magazines tried to analyse but failed.

Fans began wandering up and down the street where he lived, and when they located his apartment they could hardly believe that their hero lived here, in such ordinariness. At first he loved the adulation; then, as it became relentless and incessant, he began to hate it:

I suppose it was exhilarating to begin with but then it gets sickening . . . you become public property. In Hollywood I am not an actor, I am a hot property. Fanmail came in torrents, and then they find you in a restaurant or wherever, and they grab you and push their faces forward and say, 'You . . . you are . . . you are Montgomery Clift, aren't you?' Sometimes they will come to my door, and ring and ring until I answer and they just don't care if you are naked, or wrapped in a chinchilla rug.

Whatever it was that caught the mood of the nation's youth also brought Hollywood running again. Paramount offered him a three-picture contract worth $350,000 and this time he accepted.

The first film, *The Heiress*, put him alongside Olivia de Havilland and Ralph Richardson, with William Wyler directing, in a lavish production based on Henry James's novel *Washington Square*. The elegant Miss de Havilland looked upon Monty with horror when he arrived on the set wearing what had become his very personal uniform of scruffy T-shirt, a pair of tired jeans and a jacket ripped and holey. Later, at a swish party, he was seen stuffing items from a plate of buffet food into his mouth by hand until morsels of food were hanging from his lips – a habit to which his New York friends had recently become accustomed. As the evening progressed, he was to be found crawling on his hands and knees as walking became increasingly difficult through the haze of wine.

Billy LeMassena noticed that Monty's drinking was getting gradually worse: he had never seen him like this before in his life and put it down to the evil Monty had discovered in Hollywood. Often he would turn on his parents and call them all sorts of names, or have a tantrum on the floor. Billy went on:

He would say, 'Mother you are a cunt.' The Clifts were broken-hearted. They couldn't understand it, none of us could, or what had suddenly caused it. Looking back, I think he had found a total denial of the life of order he once knew. I think it is a cop out to blame his mother's influence in his upbringing. No, it was a whole reversal of behaviour. His had been a life of coded behaviour, impeccable manners, politeness, clean living, and when he got to Hollywood he found the people high up couldn't be trusted. He could no longer take people at their face value, and that's what set him off. Obviously, we talked about these things; I said it was like he was climbing up a ladder on the side of a building and having the compulsion to fall back into space. He was turned by Hollywood, no question of that. There was an evil that confronted him and he couldn't handle it.

After *The Heiress* and a semi-documentary called *The Big Lift* filmed in Germany for 20th Century–Fox, Clift dashed back to California to begin work on his second film for Paramount, *A Place in the Sun*, and discovered that the studio had fixed him up with a date. He was to take Elizabeth Taylor, his new co-star, to the première of *The Heiress* at Grauman's Chinese Theater on Hollywood Boulevard. Although one of the better and more conscientious studios, Paramount was going through a bad time financially after a couple of major failures; anything that could bolster their flagging fortunes – like, for instance, the publicity value of an offscreen romance between the stars of their newest movie – would be all to the good.

Elizabeth couldn't wait to meet him. She had heard stories about him. She had seen his two pictures. She was totally fascinated. Quite soon the feeling would be mutual.

When he first discovered what was in store, Monty said defiantly to his Paramount paymasters, 'You've got to be joking.' He had no intention of escorting that child anywhere. She was seventeen. He was twenty-nine and he was taking Mira if he went at all. Paramount, who were paying him a large fee and had a contractual hold over him, insisted: get in the limousine, pick up Elizabeth Taylor, smile at the cameras, stay sober and show at least a bit of interest. Typically, once the realisation that he *must* escort Miss Taylor dawned on him, Clift gave it his best, arriving spic and span, on time, sober and clutching Elizabeth's hand so tightly that they looked like long-lost brother and sister.

A couple of hundred yards from the theatre, Mira and the publicity man who was her escort got out of the car to walk the rest of the way, leaving Monty and America's all-American girl to arrive in classic Hollywood style, amid the popping of flashbulbs, the movie newsreels and the lights, the microphones thrust under their noses.

Elizabeth was surprised to discover he was more nervous than she, a veteran of so many premières compared to his few. Monty took to 'the child' straight away. He kept calling her 'Bessie Mae' and when she asked why he had given her a nickname he replied, 'The whole world calls you Elizabeth Taylor, but only I will call you Bessie Mae.' At the end of the evening he escorted her back to her front door, kissed her gently on the forehead and she swirled away inside the house, completely captivated. All she could see now was the thrill of working with Monty.

* * * * *

Clift had moved into a circle of Hollywood and New York film intelligentsia; he was a must for anybody's list for an intellectual gathering. A lot of New York actors and writers used to gather at Gene Kelly's house in Beverly Hills; celebrities like John Garfield, Norman Mailer, Frank Sinatra, Judy Garland and Leonard Bernstein might drop in. Charlie Chaplin and his new wife Oona also gave salon-type get-togethers. Monty and Chaplin became the best of friends and remained so, until the HUAC and the FBI eventually hounded Charlie into exile. The HUAC had become the talking point of every social event and Monty, though no political animal, had many friends who liked to indulge in such discussion. A lot of them were being called to give evidence to the HUAC hearings and to declare their dislike of Communism. Gene Kelly too was eventually forced to give an oath that he had never been a Communist.

The air of mistrust also affected George Stevens. He had already been badgered by Paramount over the importance of *A Place in the Sun* and in the months of preparation he had been forced to make an about-turn on his original thinking of a message movie in tune with Theodore Dreiser's book, *An American Tragedy* (renamed for the film). With the spectre of the HUAC growing daily, the blacklist which virtually prevented an actor, writer or director from working once they had been 'named' had become a menacing reality. In common with anything else which might be considered the slightest bit un-American, Stevens's original script had been scrutinised and the studio rejected it as too strong. He had to rewrite it and had now been working on it for two years. Although he admitted despondently that he had lost much of the original impact because of the enforced frothy overlay, he still believed that he could project Dreiser's book for what it was: a statement on the double standards of America's middle-classes towards money and status.

Eventually the script was approved. Stevens knew that Clift was exactly right for the part of George Eastman, a young man from a modest background who hitch-hikes across the country to enter the social strata of his uncle's wealthy family. Ignored and shunned by his new-found relatives, he forms a tacky relationship with a factory girl, Alice Tripp (superbly played by Shelley Winters, who was coached for the test by Norman Mailer and who for the rest of her life played the girl most men would like to murder). She, of course, becomes pregnant by Eastman.

Meanwhile, confronted by his relatives' wealth, he has become consumed by ambition and is encouraged towards a quest for position and power when he falls in love with Angela, the rich little bitch played by Elizabeth Taylor. Eastman takes the whining Alice Tripp out on a lake in a rowing boat and dumps her over the side, thus leaving himself free to enjoy both the riches his family is now bestowing upon him and Angela's love.

The film is one of Stevens's masterpieces. Its many unexpected twists and turns culminate in Eastman's arrest and execution for murder, and there is a magnificent death-cell scene for Elizabeth.

Monty Clift helped turn Elizabeth Taylor into more of an actress than she had ever been. He coaxed and coached her gently and intelligently, just as Mira Rostova watched his own every move and action. When the movie was released, even the most hostile of the critics – who as a body had never been particularly fond of Elizabeth – came out with gushing praise. One wrote, '. . . all the uncomfortable, preening mannerisms that have brought a touch of nausea to her recent screen portrayals, are valid. The conceit, artificiality that mar her playing in most ingenue roles are not only acceptable but essential to her rendition of Miss Rich Bitch'.

Ironically, behind the scenes there had been more than a touch of realism to contribute to such a powerful performance from the teenage star. As the making of the movie progressed, she had become deeply fond of Monty Clift, to the point that she knew she was in love with him. She had, during those weeks, even written girlish love-letters (which for some reason Monty eventually gave to one of his male lovers). She was yet to become painfully appraised of the fact that he was homosexual.

Paramount saw a main chance and was ready and willing to throw its two stars to the wolves. The day before the filming of the heart-breaking final scene in the death cell, headlines in the evening papers announced to the world in big type: 'CLIFT AND TAYLOR TO WED'. The Taylors' house was mobbed immediately by reporters and cameramen. Elizabeth broke down and wept. 'Monty will think I've done this,' she cried to her mother. 'I can never face him tomorrow.'

Tears welled up in her eyes next day as she met Monty on the set to shoot the final scene. Her lines called for a sobbing farewell to George Eastman; in her heart Elizabeth felt she might also be saying goodbye to Montgomery Clift. The emotion was supercharged and at the end of it George Stevens shouted: 'Print it!' The lights faded and they walked off the set, Elizabeth still crying.

'Are you all right?' asked Stevens.

'Yes, I'm OK,' replied Elizabeth.

Paramount publicists, doubtless with Stevens's approval, had deliberately leaked the romance story to double effect: gaining free attention for the film, and goading the two actors into an emotional finish. As Elizabeth would discover in future encounters with the director, Stevens was never beyond such tactics.

The filming had ended. Elizabeth's eyes searched for Monty. With hardly a goodbye, he signalled Mira Rostova to his side and they prepared to leave. The film had drained him.

'What are you doing for a rest?' he asked Elizabeth. 'I'm getting out of here tonight. I'm flying down to South Carolina to meet up with Libby Holman.' That only hurt Elizabeth more.

In fact, the newspaper stories of his alleged impending marriage to Elizabeth had nothing to do with Monty's hasty departure from Hollywood. What drove him were his own sexual hang-ups, and his fascination with Libby Holman. He simply had to return to unwind in the bosom of his friendships and his mother-substitutes.

Later, when the truth of Monty's homosexuality had become clear to her, Elizabeth understood all this. Looking back at the early days of their friendship, she admitted that at first Monty played the ardent male with her, then just as it seemed that he had overcome his inhibitions about making love, he would turn up with some obvious young man he had picked up. Elizabeth didn't know what she was supposed to do; finally she just had to say, 'Look, Monty, I'm always here, whenever you need me,' and leave it at that.

Elizabeth settled for that friendship and looked for nothing more. But in the years to come, she gave and gave; he would be one of her most demanding, yet excitingly attractive friends.

At that moment, however, as Monty turned on his heels, the situation was not quite as clear or clean-cut as it became in retrospect. Elizabeth ran off the set, tears streaming down her face from the mixed emotions of confused reality and the electric-chair death of her screen-lover, George Eastman. No one, said Stevens, could have played that scene better.

*　*　*　*　*

The day was not over for Elizabeth yet. She went out later to be cheered up: a meal at Lucey's restaurant with friends soon had her giggling again and one man in particular helped her forget. Not by chance, Nicky Hilton was in the party. And with that night, with Monty gone and, she thought, a love lost, she found her first husband.

Chapter Three

Mirages

The star system, which finally disappeared in the late fifties, was at the start of the decade still very much part of the way Hollywood was run. Studios were still pampering the stars to retain their services at the lowest possible cost. Many established actors, however, and certainly some of the newer arrivals, such as Montgomery Clift, Charlton Heston and Marlon Brando, were trying to keep their freedom so that they would not be pushed into some of the mediocrity that had dogged the veterans. The writing was already on the wall and the end of the system was in sight.

Charlton Heston saw it happening when he arrived in Hollywood in 1950. He was only the second actor to get a non-exclusive contract which meant that he could work for anyone. Heston told me:

Hal B. Wallis, who hired me for my first picture, was a very shrewd man. He recognised the studio system would no longer be there in five years' time. When I arrived, the major studios all still had thirty or forty actors under contract; the younger, less experienced ones would all get work, every so often they would be called for a small role or a bit-part. They all got their acting lessons, their dance lessons, their speech therapy and the young directors under contract got their training with director tests and they all got a lot of times in to bat. But that was beginning to come apart.

Heston remains convinced that the end of the system was bad for Hollywood: 'You can't learn your craft, you can't get audience exposure, you can't practise and, more importantly, you can't fail, if you don't get a chance to appear.'

Clark Gable, on the other hand, became bitter and outspoken about the life, and about those around him. He expressed these feelings in an interview soon after his return from war service:

They're absolute bastards. They encourage us to be larger than life, give actors anything they want, take any crap provided they interest the public, but the moment they slip – oh, brother! Look at the young talent on the Metro lot, Garland, Taylor, Gardner, Rooney . . . they'll probably ruin them all.

* * * * *

Before long the old-style mechanics of Hollywood would also be criticised and shunned by James Dean, who, by 1949, was edging closer to his goal. He had persuaded his father to allow him to come to live with him in Santa Monica. There was no local drama course he could follow in Fairmount and he had set his heart on registering with the University of California at Los Angeles (UCLA) in the autumn to begin his acting studies in earnest. Winton Dean and his new wife, Ethel, were a strange premonition of Jimmy's film-parents in *Rebel Without a Cause*: two middle-aged people out of touch with youth. They rejected both the idea of Jimmy's becoming an actor and his enrolment at UCLA for a drama course, insisting instead that he should go to Santa Monica City College to try for a physical education major.

After nine years apart, reunion between father and son was not easy, although both tried to make it work. Dean accepted his father's wish to go to the City College even though it would make him look foolish back in Fairmount. There, in true American local-newspaper fashion, the farewell party for one of the town's young men had been reported, along with the news that Jimmy would be entering UCLA for drama studies that fall. Fairmount was kept informed; the *Fairmount News* dutifully recorded that his grandparents, Mr and Mrs Charles Dean, had received a letter from their grandson telling them that he had joined the Playhouse Theater Guild in Santa Monica.

He also enrolled in the drama courses at the City College. His tutors later remembered him as a polite, enthusiastic, untroubled student, anxious and eager to learn everything he could about the art. But rebellion was welling up: life with father was restrictive. Within a year of arriving in Santa Monica, Dean had left his father's house and was heading for Beverly Hills and UCLA – into Hollywood through the back door.

* * * * *

Meanwhile, round at the front door, Rock Hudson had been knocking for over a year; success and opportunity did not come rushing towards him. Since his meeting with Henry Willson, his yearned-for movie career had hardly moved off the ground. Willson himself had gone back into the agency business after his spell as chief talent scout with the now disbanded David O. Selznick studio and he became noted for some of the young actors he rechristened and guided to stardom. They included Merle Johnson, whom he tagged Troy Donahue; Francis Durgin, who became Rory Calhoun; and Art Gelien, renamed Tab Hunter. Willson operated as a seemingly respectable Hollywood agent. He had a hotline to Louella Parsons and Hedda Hopper, and in one interview for *Parade* magazine he went as far as to suggest that he saw himself as something of a do-gooder for the young hopefuls arriving in Hollywood:

> I get five thousand letters a year and sixteen thousand phone calls from aspiring actors or actresses. I'm what you might call a Salvation Army worker at heart. Kids in this business know it and they come to me. I earn seventy-five thousand a year, but don't have a buck to show for it. Why? because I'm spending it all on these youngsters.

Although his claims were exaggerated for the purpose of attracting more business, Willson certainly had a reputation as a starmaker. But around him there was an aura of predatory evil, and many attractive young men were drawn in to satisfy his own homosexual yearnings. More than that, they became caught in a web of vice in which they were almost forced to indulge on the promise of an important acting role in exchange for sexual duties. Willson's secretary, Phyllis Gates, said:

> He had total confidence in himself and his ability to manipulate clients and customers. His principal method was sex . . . behind the façade of the witty bon vivant was a hard-boiled Machiavelli who would do anything. He was a virtuoso at arranging sexual affairs, young studs for a producer's wife . . . boys for a producer or director if they preferred it. . . . it was pimping, and blackmail. God help the poor client who refused to play Henry's game. He would begin a campaign of vilification that could ruin an actor's reputation.

Almost from his arrival in Los Angeles Rock Hudson could be found in what would now be termed gay bars, although publicly he was deeply protective of his heterosexual image. He was seduced by Willson at an early stage in their relationship, undoubtedly initially led into the affair by the promise of stardom, for Willson was not the attractive he-male of the kind that would normally win the attentions of his young protégé. He was overweight, with a round, pudgy face, receding hair and the handshake of a wet fish. But both he and Rock had insatiable sexual appetites.

For more than a year after their first meeting Willson hawked Rock around the studios and not one showed the slightest interest. He took him to parties, positioned him in prominent places, showed him off to fan-mag writers and generally tried to get his newcomer's face where it mattered. He was spending more on Rock than he had done on any of his other clients and eventually persuaded Raoul Walsh, a Warner Brothers director, to put him under personal contract. Walsh gave him a bit-part in *Fighter Squadron*; it was a furniture role, standing around somewhere at the back of a couple of shots, and it did not even merit a credit when the film was released. Rock had to say one line: 'Pretty soon, you are going to have to get a bigger blackboard,' and he fluffed it thirty-eight times.

After that, he didn't make another picture for almost a year, but Walsh and Willson continued to invest their own money in their husky hopeful. They paid for acting classes and for diction experts to iron out his midwestern drawl; tap-dancing lessons got rid of some of his lurching clumsiness. None of it completely cured his appalling shyness. There were four or five more screen tests and in one for 20th Century–Fox he was so bad that the studio kept the film to show in studio classes – as an example of how *not* to act.

After that, Walsh only ever used Rock for personal jobs – like chauffeuring or painting his house – while continuing for the next year to finance his tuition and rehearse him for screen tests. Finally, a successful test at Universal International in 1949 induced the studio – then desperately short of developing male talent – to offer Rock a contract. William Goetz, head of International until it merged with Universal, had taken over as head of the new joint studio and, like his father-in-law Louis B. Mayer, had set out to recruit a stable of young talent that would provide Universal with a galaxy for tomorrow. The policy of training new talent worked, just as it had for Mayer: among those Goetz recruited at that time were Jeff Chandler, Tony Curtis, Piper Laurie and Barbara Rush. Willson and Walsh sold him Rock for $9000, equivalent to the amount they calculated they had spent on him, and Hudson got his first movie salary of $125 a week.

Rock spent long, hard days going through intensive courses laid on by the studio. As the months went by, he evolved into a curious mixture of all-American-boy beefcake, yet with a quality of innocence and naivety, and without any clearly defined persona.

Henry Willson remained convinced that Hudson would become a star and retained an unhealthy, possessive hold over him. When Willson had free time, he would call Rock for dinner or lunch; they were to be seen regularly in Hollywood restaurants. Off the set and away from the studio crowd, Rock preferred to spend his time with two new friends, Mark

Miller and George Nader, who were to become his closest confidants in
later years. Miller, a year older than Rock, was a singer; Nader was an
actor five years his senior. The two had been together since they met in
a chorus line in 1947 and they shared a house in Studio City. George
described how 'Whenever he was lonely, Rock would call up and say,
"Hi, it's me. Can I come around?" and we'd drink, or play cards or go
to the beach.' Occasionally Mark and George arranged for another to
join them to make a foursome for dinner and so that, privately, Rock
could indulge his sexual leanings. Mark, George and Rock made a
fine-looking bachelor threesome, all healthy, fit and imposing young men
with lithe, tanned bodies, though George says that neither he nor Mark
was involved with Rock sexually.

Hudson had no difficulty in finding male partners, but whenever he
had a lover staying with him he would never let him answer the telephone;
he never allowed himself to be photographed with another man and his
romantic encounters were arranged with clandestine precision to prevent
any chance of gossip. The rampant writings of the gossip columnists and
scandal sheets were always a threat and already it was, in the real sense,
a double life.

* * * * *

The gossips, at that moment, were paying more attention to Elizabeth
Taylor after a hint of a forthcoming betrothal to Nicky Hilton. At
Christmas 1949, Conrad Hilton himself invited the Taylor family to stay
with him at a hotel he had bought at Lake Arrowhead. Nicky had
arranged it all to get Elizabeth to his side and Sara was suitably impressed.
At the Christmas party, Elizabeth rifled the gifts and discovered Nicky's
present to her in the mound around the tree: a tiny package containing
the most expensive set of diamond earrings, with dangling pearls. On
Christmas Day, Nicky took Elizabeth's father into the library and popped
the question: 'Sir, I would like your permission to ask Elizabeth to marry
me.' Francis Taylor agreed, with the proviso that she should finish her
schooling before Hilton spoke to her.

Elizabeth was still only seventeen and, although she was now earning
close on $2000 a week, she was still required by law to graduate.
Her diploma was a foregone conclusion, because of Miss Anderson's
persistence over schooling during the past few years; but she had to
receive the diploma through the correct channels and that meant an
official graduation ceremony at a proper school.

MGM, of course, fixed it as they fixed everything. They arranged a
presentation at Los Angeles University High School at the end of January

1950, and that was too good an opportunity for the publicists to miss. They moved in in force to make Miss Taylor's graduation a day to remember. The wardrobe people dressed her in cap and gown, brought a huge silver-grey limousine to drive her to the school and then, to the bewilderment of the 191 other graduation students, who were unaware of the anticipated arrival of such a celebrity, she was led to the single vacant seat in the front row. In their midst she was like royalty, nodding politely to the girls on either side as she took her place and waited for her name to be called. The photographers, alerted by MGM, were already moving into position to secure a prime shot of The Graduate. Walking towards the dais, hips wiggling slightly, she could hardly be described as the typical schoolgirl. She received her diploma from a headmaster she had never met before and then she was gone, whisked away in the limousine towards a sophisticated evening in the arms of her beloved Nicky.

Before that night was out, she had agreed to be his bride. She had been waiting all evening for him to ask; her father had warned her. When he finally did ask, 'Elizabeth, will you marry me?', she acted surprised and giggly.

'Oh, Nicky – but what about my career?' she replied, remembering Bill Pawley.

'I love you, and I love your career,' said Nicky. 'It will make no difference at all.'

Husband number one was betrothed. Louella Parsons beat the formal family engagement announcement by revealing the secret the following day. She phoned Elizabeth to say, 'Sorry, darling. I hope you're not too upset. But a little bird told me and I just had to run the story.' The little bird turned out to have been Conrad Hilton. Publicity is publicity, whether you run a film studio or a chain of hotels. And the 4½-carat diamond engagement ring Nicky had given his fiancée sparkled before the cameras of the world.

At MGM the studio heads could scarcely believe their good fortune. Among the Elizabeth Taylor films still to go on general release was *Father of the Bride*, which the studio adroitly arranged to première four weeks after the Taylor–Hilton wedding. It all seemed just too good to be true.

Soon presents were flowing in from all over the world. MGM gave armfuls of expensive outfits – suits, evening gowns, coats, every type of clothing to fit anyone and everyone connected with the wedding. Conrad Hilton sent round a hundred shares of Hilton Hotel stock, plus tickets for an all-expenses-paid European honeymoon. Sara Taylor gave her daughter a white mink stole, and Francis gave them a superb oil painting.

In April Elizabeth flew to New York for some presentations and telephoned Monty Clift from the back room of a drugstore. 'Will you come and visit me when I am married?' she asked him.

'Somehow, Bessie Mae, I don't think dear Nicky is my kind of guy.'

She flung the phone down and didn't speak to him again before the wedding. But Monty's doubts mirrored her own. She wanted so much to be a bride; it was the only route to complete womanhood. She was a virgin, a teenage mind in an adult body. As she wrote later:

> I had always had a strict and proper upbringing and that was absolutely necessary, living the existence I did. The irony is that the morality I learned at home required marriage, I couldn't just have an affair . . . I guess I never gave myself the time to find out whether it was love or infatuation. I always chose to think I was in love . . . but I didn't have my own yardstick.

Elizabeth did have severe doubts over whether she should go ahead with the marriage and some of her friends even suggested that she should plead with Monty to marry her so that she could get out of marrying Hilton. But by then it was too late. Even a disagreement over whether or not she should sign a piece of paper agreeing that any children of the marriage would be brought up in the Roman Catholic faith did not present a serious enough obstacle. She demurred for a few days, then eventually signed.

In *Father of the Bride*, Spencer Tracy tells Elizabeth, 'You look wonderful, kitten . . . just like a princess in a fairy tale,' and that's how it was on her day – only bigger, much bigger, and better, much, much better. As the fleet of MGM limousines ferried the wedding party and star guests to the Church of the Good Shepherd on the afternoon of 5 May 1950, the crowds were pressing around the barriers; three or four thousand people straining for a look at the bride, along with all the stars MGM could muster and dozens of others besides. Fred Astaire and Ginger Rogers were among the first to arrive; June Allyson, Dick Powell, Greer Garson, Esther Williams and Janet Leigh, to name only a few, followed briskly, waving to the screeching fans, some stopping to sign a hasty autograph, never missing an opportunity.

Then came the bride, a stern-faced but glowing picture of virginal whiteness, in a satin gown, high-necked and unrevealing, decorated with seed pearls and lilies of the valley. She half turned on the steps and, with her father, posed briefly to satisfy the shouts of a posse of photographers. Then she was walking down the aisle towards her groom before a mass of faces she failed to see.

In a mere twenty minutes it was over. Elizabeth Taylor had become

Mrs Conrad Nicholas Hilton, Jr, and that day's newspapers quoted her as saying: 'He is my darling. I shall love no other until my dying day.'

The crowds were still waiting to cheer them as the happy couple emerged smiling, joyous and coy. Before them lay the task of a thousand handshakes; there were so many at the reception that it took four and a half hours for them to greet the guests.

Then the honeymoon. It lasted five months, and when it was over so was the marriage.

They went to Pebble Beach for their wedding night, arriving exhausted. Next day they travelled up to Chicago, where they picked up a Cadillac and drove to New York to board the *Queen Mary*, heading for Europe; the Caddy came too, to provide them with suitable sightseeing transport. The bridal suite on board was not available: the Duke and Duchess of Windsor had first call on that, free of charge, whenever they were crossing the Atlantic and the Hiltons' honeymoon voyage coincided with their return to Paris after an elaborate excursion through America and Mexico. The Windsors were enchanted by the young Hiltons; Wallis revelled in the company of anyone rich and famous.

Then it was London, Paris, Rome, Venice – an exhausting whirlwind of parties and invitations awaited them. In London, MGM had already arranged for *Father of the Bride* to open during the frantic newspaper coverage of the honeymoon, so that Elizabeth and Nicky could arrive to give the movie an unbelievable send-off with publicity worth a million dollars. In Paris, Elsa Maxwell threw a lavish party for them, attended by the Windsors and other assorted dispossessed European royalty, as well as various leading showbiz figures. In Rome, the press pack followed Elizabeth's every move to the set of *Quo Vadis?*, in which she had agreed to appear in a cameo spot as one of the hundreds of Christian slaves fleeing from the lions in the Colosseum. She received no billing, but her presence brought the picture massive exposure. Then it was back to Paris for another round of socialising, culminating in a glamorous ball at which Elizabeth wore $150,000 of diamonds loaned to her for the evening by a Paris jeweller.

It was at that ball that the strain began to show. Elizabeth, with her fairly sheltered upbringing, had never experienced such continual partying, nor was she used to the constant company of men and women much older than herself. She began to tire of the need for unfailing politeness in the face of boredom; she was fed up with having to dance with flirting older men and talk to dowdy older women whose lives revolved around name-dropping. To cap it all, that night she and Nicky had a very public argument when he said he was going gambling. She was photographed in tears and the whole scene was recorded, with all due exaggeration, to be served up in the following day's newspapers around the world.

The rows got worse. Nicky ignored Elizabeth's pleas not to leave her alone and she wanted to return to California. Nicky would not have it. The rows and battles continued for another two weeks, until finally he agreed to go back to New York, where they would separate. There was no other course; embarrassing though it was, Elizabeth was determined.

Back in America, she contacted MGM and asked them to send someone to accompany her on the flight back to California to help ward off the army of photographers who were chasing her and the gossip columnists who wanted the low-down on the state of her marriage. She left Nicky in New York and at the stopover in Chicago was surprised to find him, not the studio minder, waiting for her. They ran into each other's arms, agreeing that they had been childish about the whole business. Of course they could make a go of it. She would learn to cook and become a housewife. He would curtail his drinking and stop going out on gambling jaunts.

Nicky flew back to Los Angeles with her and they found an apartment – a rented property because Nicky, always cautious with the family budget, did not feel that the purchase of a house was a commitment he yet wished to make. They tried to become as conventional in marriage as their professional lives would allow. Both went back to work immediately, he to Hilton and she to MGM, where work was piling up. There were retakes to do for her latest film, *Father's Little Dividend*, and discussions for her next.

Elizabeth's friends discovered she had changed a great deal while she was away. Her weight had dropped by almost ten pounds; she was smoking heavily; and, for the first time in her life, she was taking sleeping pills to get some rest before an early start at the studio or to quell the anguish of her marital situation. Always, in the past, she had gone to bed early before work the following day. Nicky's appetite for parties which went on well into the night did not do her any good at all and soon he was disappearing on his own, dismissing her idea of an evening's entertainment as 'kid's stuff'.

More rows, more separations; and soon it was affecting her health. She stopped eating properly and became prone to fainting. The studio insisted that her doctor called almost daily and, to make sure that she was never alone in her depressed state, Peggy Rutledge, who had been secretary to Bob Hope's wife, was hired as her secretary and companion.

In the autumn, Elizabeth went to New York, seeking the comforting, soothing words and friendship of Monty Clift.

* * * * *

In fact, Monty was in worse shape than Elizabeth, but her arrival did him a good turn. He had recently returned from London, where he had attended the royal première of *The Heiress*, and he was full of the experience. He had been presented to the Queen, dined with Laurence Olivier, had supper with Noël Coward and everyone called him 'Monty Darling'. In England, just as in America, he had become an established name, soon to be enhanced further with the release of *A Place in the Sun*.

Monty had moved on from London to Italy for further promotional work but, without telling his studio people, he suddenly got on a plane back to New York. Libby Holman had telephoned. Her son Christopher, just seventeen, had been killed in a climbing accident on Mount Whitney. Clift dashed back to be with her and kept vigil night and day for weeks. Libby's sorrow and mourning for her dead son turned into an alcoholic haze, punctuated by bouts of excessive drug-taking in which Monty was invariably her partner. Once, during this spell, he was found prostrate near Bloomingdales, half-naked. By chance it was a friend who discovered him and brought him back to his own apartment.

His drinking had become a severe problem and he had begun, secretly, to see Dr William V. Silverberg, one of New York's seemingly most respectable – and most expensive – psychiatrists at a time before therapy had become the fashionable resort of the rich and famous. Barely a week went by without Clift consulting him, at considerable cost, but eventually theirs became something much more than a doctor–patient relationship and Silverberg's methods and motives were challenged by Monty's closest friends. Billy LeMassena said:

> I think we were all shocked at the speed with which Monty's addictions had caught hold. But this man Silverberg was no good influence at all; as it developed, it was clear to everyone that he was actually encouraging Monty into excesses, rather than preventing them.

At the start of their consultations it was all fairly straightforward. Monty clearly needed help and, because he was in a state of mind where he did not want to give up drinking, Silverberg brought in Dr Ruth Fox, a specialist in alcohol abuse, who immediately hospitalised him. Four days' cold turkey in Regent Hospital did some good; but it did not last.

Elizabeth's arrival in the middle of this crisis helped him, temporarily, into a more rational state. He listened to her troubles about her marriage, he was her shoulder to cry on. Though in desperate need of straightening out himself, Monty could always hide his own problems for the sake of a friend in need. He was generous to a fault in that respect and, sober, he was the best friend anyone could have. He and Elizabeth dined out

at his favourite Italian restaurant, and he took her home to see his
parents. He was the soul of compassion. Sometimes they were joined by
Roddy McDowall, who had arrived in New York looking for work. Like
Elizabeth, he had become Monty's devoted friend.

*   *   *   *   *

Elizabeth returned to California in a happier frame of mind, but her
marriage to Nicky Hilton got no better. Towards the end of 1950 she
telephoned Monty to tell him that they were definitely getting a divorce.
By early December the news had leaked out into the newspapers.

MGM's press people were bombarded with phone calls and issued a
pert statement which put the blame firmly at Nicky's door: 'They have
fought about his gambling and playing around and ignoring her as a
wife'. It ended in Los Angeles in late January, when, in the drama of a
crowded courtroom, Elizabeth, nervous and ill from strain, tears streaming from her eyes, told how Nicky 'has left me alone so many nights'.
The judge gave her the freedom she sought, and the marriage to the man
she would love to her dying day was over after just seven months and
twenty-four days.

Elizabeth returned to the witness stand for a few moments at the
insistence of the photographers, refused the judge's offer of alimony, and
then she was gone. Rather than returning to her parents' home she
moved into a five-roomed apartment with her secretary. For the first
time in her life, she was an independent spirit.

Howard Hughes, meanwhile, viewed the publicity over Elizabeth's
divorce with glee. Secretly, he arranged for friends to offer her the use
of a house in Palm Springs for a brief holiday to help her regain strength
and composure. While she was there, he arrived one day, unannounced,
carrying a handful of loose jewels. They were hers. All she had to do
was marry him. Elizabeth laughed and tossed the glittering stones in his
face. But Hughes still hadn't got the message.

Chapter Four

Ambitions

Hollywood at the start of 1951 was an uneasy place. This was the beginning of the age of aspiration and acquisition: the motor car, hi-fi, television, jet travel, greater personal freedom, a more sexually aware outlook encouraged and promoted by the Kinsey Report.

That year saw general television programming introduced and, though few of those running the film industry regarded television as a major threat, it gave audiences an instant view of the world, live drama and shows, where once they had had to queue at the local cinema. Hollywood, meanwhile, seemed lost, producing a huge mixed bag of low-budget comedies, big-budget musicals and religious epics, interspersed with tales of wartime heroics. Of course, some superb pictures came out of these categories, particularly in the musical field – classics such as *Annie Get Your Gun*, *Showboat*, *Seven Brides for Seven Brothers* and *Singin' in the Rain*. But in spite of them, cinema audiences were evaporating by the week.

Television was not the only cause; just as important was a Supreme Court ruling ordering that studios rid themselves of monopoly interest in cinema chains. The effect was catastrophic. The studios no longer had a guarantee that their second-string B-movies, and even some of their low-quality A-movies, would be shown; nor did they attempt to fill the void by making B-movies for television. Charlton Heston recalled:

The Supreme Court ruling was the thing that really ended the studio system. In hindsight, it was terribly unfair but eventually it led to the opening up of the film industry. One of several results from that was that it was beneficial to only fifteen or so actors like me, and five writers, and eight directors. Television provided an opportunity for a whole generation of actors, writers and directors to come through. The studios wouldn't allow any of their contract players or directors to have anything to do with television, so that wiped out a whole colony of people who were willing and able to do it. The theatre people wouldn't do it either; they thought it was all rather tacky, and the new medium was left to a bunch of twenty-four-year-olds whose basic qualification was that they were unemployed. . . .

Here we were, racketing around inventing a medium because the networks didn't know how to do it either. I remember the people at CBS came to me and a young director I was working with and said, 'Can you do *Macbeth* in ninety minutes?' Sure, we said. 'Can you do it with ten days' rehearsal?' Yes, we said. And from then on, in the space of eighteen months for Studio One, I did *Julius Caesar*, *The Taming of the Shrew*, *Jane Eyre*, and lots more. An actor doesn't draw breath who isn't going to be good in one of those parts. All this happened because of the studio system; it couldn't happen today because they wouldn't do it that way, nor would they do that kind of material.

Stars of the future, like Jack Lemmon, Walter Matthau, and James Dean, all got started in the early days of television, doing live drama shows. The old Hollywood was dying on its feet and for the great showmen like Louis B. Mayer, the end was in sight.

One of the last acts of the man who had created Elizabeth Taylor and so many others had been to fire the leader of his poppet-pack, Judy Garland. By 1950 she had become a shattered wreck and her arrival for work and the fulfilment of her studio commitments were spasmodic and tardy. Her marriage to Vincente Minnelli had collapsed (they were divorced in 1951), and her drug-taking and drinking caused so much alarm at MGM that they sent an official warning that cancellation of her contract was being considered. Judy refused to take a cure, angrily insisting that there was nothing wrong, but almost immediately she locked herself in her bathroom and tried to commit suicide by cutting her wrist with broken glass.

Garland, who had made MGM millions and was still on $5000 a week and receiving two thousand fan-letters a day, was finally sacked after fifteen years with the studio. Elizabeth Taylor, who had become one of her most sympathetic friends during their years together at the same company, wept with her. Judy was penniless and left Metro owing them $9000, about half of a loan they had made her a year earlier. She walked off the lot, never to return, screaming, 'Those bastards, those fucking bastards.'

Next, in 1951, the unimaginable happened. Louis B. Mayer, who for so long, for good or evil, had been a supreme force in the industry, himself became a victim of the ruthlessness he had fostered and practised. He too departed. MGM profits had hit rock bottom and Dore Schary, who moved to MGM when he was sacked by Howard Hughes and who was twenty years younger than the sixty-six-year-old studio boss, took over. Nick Schenck, president of MGM in New York, gave Schary a big stock option. Upset, Mayer began rallying forces from among the executives who had been living in his shadow for years and ordered them not to co-operate with Schary. As the months wore on, Mayer volunteered to take a cut in his $1 million-a-year salary. Then, when he thought he had mustered enough strength, he wrote to Schenck: 'Either I or Schary must have control at MGM.'

Schenck replied: 'Goodbye Louis.'

Some mourned his departure; others rejoiced. Elizabeth Taylor had mixed feelings. She had seen him at his best and his worst.

* * * * *

As the old gave way to the new, James Dean and Rock Hudson were among the surge of newer names. They were thrown together for the first time in 1951 when both won parts in a Universal low-budget picture called *Has Anybody Seen My Gal?* Dean had one line. He and a gang of other kids march into the town's drug store, where Charles Coburn stands behind the counter being shown how to run the fountain by soda-jerk Rock Hudson. Jimmy says, 'Hey, Gramps, I'll have a choc malt, heavy on the choc, plenty of milk, four spoons of malt, two scoops of vanilla, one mixed with the rest and one floating,' and Coburn replies, 'Would you like to come in Wednesday for a fitting? Thank you.'

Hudson and Dean did not work together again until *Giant* four years later. Worlds apart in their views of Hollywood and acting, they were going down completely different roads. Rock's credits were already creeping up, recognition and confidence growing each month. The turning-point from bit-player to supporting actor came when Universal picked him for the role of Speed O'Keefe in the Jeff Chandler movie *Iron Man* at the start of 1951. He was still green but Henry Willson assured him, 'This is it, my boy . . . you've made it to the ladder. Now all you have to do is climb.'

Next, he appeared in *Bend of the River* in a supporting role to James Stewart. When the film was premièred in Portland, Oregon, the stars flew up for the first night. Outside the theatre stood a small band of fans shouting, 'We want Rock!' Henry Willson had hired a rent-a-crowd, who were in better voice than James Stewart's followers. Rock remembered:

I just couldn't believe it. There were these people shouting my name. I was on a real high. I just got real drunk that night and came down to earth the next day. I went out walking just to be recognised; I even stood beside my picture in a store window but no one noticed. It was a leveller, a real lesson to me that night.

Recognised or not, the climb was on and the fan mags began to take notice. Four more pictures were lined up by the Universal B-movie unit, including *Scarlet Angel* with Yvonne de Carlo, *The Lawless Breed*, *The Golden Blade* and *Taza, Son of Cochise*. It was unimportant material, but Rock knew that he could never take on heavy, meaningful scripts and, at the moment, the thought of it scared him.

*   *   *   *   *

James Dean's aspirations had so far failed to yield such promising results. He had achieved his ambition by enrolling for a theatre arts major at UCLA in the autumn of 1950 after walking out on the physical education course that his father had wanted him to complete. Even UCLA could retain his attentions for only a few months, however, and then he was off again, looking for serious work as an actor. He appeared in only one play at UCLA, cast as Malcolm in the university's major production of *Macbeth*. He was not a great success. Someone called him 'the world's worst Malcolm' and Dean despondently agreed. However, Isabelle Draesmar, the Hollywood agent, saw him and thought he showed sufficient talent to take him on to her books. That gave him the incentive to go on trying.

His first paid job came when an advertising agency turned up looking for all-American boys to appear in a one-minute television commercial for Coca-Cola. Jimmy was there, pushing to the front. As happened so often in his short life, there was an odd coincidence in that the commercial was shot in Griffin Park, Los Angeles, where the planetarium scene for *Rebel Without a Cause* was filmed three years later. Among the boys in the commercial was Nick Adams, a young man who had just hitch-hiked from New York to find work as an actor and who was to become close to both Jimmy and Natalie Wood, appearing with them in *Rebel*.

In that commercial the face of James Dean stood out from the crowd and soon he was called up again by the same director to appear with Roddy McDowall and Gene Lockhart in a semi-religious play specially filmed to go out on Easter Sunday. Jimmy, playing John the Apostle, had three lines, but it was sufficient for the girls at the Immaculate Heart High School to form a James Dean Appreciation Society and throw a party in his honour.

He was learning his craft as best he could, watching his heroes

Montgomery Clift and Marlon Brando. He read Hemingway and in moments of fantasy talked of becoming a bullfighter. (Clift had gone one better and had Hemingway to dinner in New York; he said afterwards that he found him boring.) Dean picked up a part here and a part there, but more often he was to be found working as an usher at CBS or parking cars.

After his solitary film role in *Has Anybody Seen My Gal?* he was ready to move on and in other directions. He had long discussions with the actor James Whitmore, who agreed to give him lessons in Method acting, which had made its way from New York to California as the students of Strasberg and Kazan came west. Towards the end of the summer of 1951, Whitmore told Jimmy that he should now go to New York himself; try it, challenge himself with the opportunities of real acting, live on stage and live on television. In a later interview Jimmy said, 'There's always someone in your life who opens up your eyes. For me, that's Whitmore. He made me see myself and gave me the key.'

He mustered some finance from the Reverend James DeWeerd back in Fairmount, with whom he had kept up a regular correspondence; further backing was enlisted from his surrogate-parents Marcus and Ortense, and soon he was heading east to Manhattan to the domain of his idols, Clift and Brando.

* * * * *

Elizabeth Taylor, in the meantime, was trying to get her life back together after the trauma of her divorce and MGM was anxious to get her straight back into another movie to capitalise on the success of her performance in *A Place in the Sun*. Their choice of script was hardly the vehicle to achieve that aim. It was a lightweight comedy, *Love Is Better Than Ever*, in which she was to play opposite Larry Parks, whose sole claim to fame so far was his portrayal of Al Jolson in *The Jolson Story*.

The director was a relative unknown, Stanley Donen, a first-rate choreographer who had been brought to Hollywood by Gene Kelly after they had worked together on Broadway in *Pal Joey*. Elizabeth had never heard of Donen and, after flicking through the script, she wasn't too happy about the movie either. MGM insisted, however, and finally she met Donen. Something clicked between them straight away; they began dating and soon the newspapers were getting plenty of mileage out of Elizabeth's new affair. There was criticism from the gossips because Mr Donen still had a Mrs Donen at home, and then the couple made front-page news when Donen became the unwitting bystander in a bitter estrangement between Elizabeth and her mother.

Although she had only just celebrated her nineteenth birthday, Elizabeth wanted to retain her independence and, against her mother's wishes, was still sharing her apartment on Wilshire with Peggy Rutledge. The row that had been brewing with Sara suddenly flared up when she arrived on her parents' doorstep with Donen. It ended with the door being banged shut in Elizabeth's face, mother and daughter both weeping. Donen helped Elizabeth away, leaning on his arm, and sped her off to her apartment, where she collapsed in a dead faint. She was rushed to hospital amid rumours of an overdose; reporters and cameramen surrounded the place in an instant and her four days in seclusion were accompanied on the outside by unstinting press coverage.

Worse was to come when she went back to work to start filming with Larry Parks. The HUAC hearings had been resumed and were reaching fever pitch. Names were being named by prominent Hollywood people to get themselves off the hook in the new round of investigations chaired by Congressman John Wood of Georgia and the threat of blacklisting became a reality to those who failed to co-operate, answering the Committee's questions with the words: 'I must respectfully decline to answer the question on the grounds that the information is privileged under the Fifth Amendment of the United States Constitution', the right which protected witnesses against giving evidence that might be self-incriminating. However, the Fifth Amendment had failed to protect the famous Hollywood Ten: writers Dalton Trumbo, Alvah Bessie, Albert Maltz, Lester Cole, John Howard Lawson, Ring Lardner, Jr, Sam Ornitz, producer Adrian Scott and directors Herbert Biberman and Edward Dmytryk. All had been cited for contempt after they refused to answer the Committee's questions in the first round of hearings in 1947 and, after lengthy and costly legal battles, they were imprisoned for up to twelve months. Various studio executives subsequently gave the Committee a pledge that they would purge all Communists from their midst. When Dmytryk was released, he found himself back before the Committee in 1951 and this time agreed to give names and answer questions, though he said afterwards that he named only those of whom he knew the Committee was already aware. Despite his new testimony, Hollywood, for the moment, had become a closed shop to him and he went off to find work in Britain.

Elia Kazan was also forced to give evidence and, much to the disappointment of some of his closest friends, named Communists he had known in the Theatre Group of the late thirties and beyond.

In March 1951 Larry Parks found himself before the Committee and was asked the usual question: 'Are you, or have you ever been, a member of the Communist Party? Will you co-operate and help us ascertain those who are or have been members of the Communist Party?' Parks hesitated. Yes, he had been a member of the Communist Party but was no longer. Then he pleaded: 'Please do not force me into a choice of going in contempt of this Committee and going to jail, or forcing me to crawl through the mud and be an informer.' He did not want to name other people. 'This is not the American way . . . to force a man to do this is not American justice.'

The HUAC did not agree; nor had they with the dozens who had made similar pleas. Parks surveyed his position and finally gave in, naming twelve people whom he knew to have been members of the Communist Party. It was still not enough to get him off the hook. His own admissions were sufficient to end his career. The film he was making with Elizabeth Taylor was put on the shelf by MGM, and Parks made only three more pictures before he died in 1975.

Still lurking in the background was Howard Hughes. Elizabeth's divorce had filled him with delight, renewing his hopes of luring her towards him, and now he began spreading a totally unfounded rumour that she was surrounded by Communists. He telephoned newspaper columnists and the studio with his 'news', his plan being to extract her from the mêlée of publicity that the rumours would cause and to take her into his care. He once even sent her mother a note offering her $1 million if she would persuade Elizabeth to marry him. Sara replied that her daughter was not for sale. His telephone calls were rejected at the Taylor apartment. Elizabeth hated him.

The débâcle over Donen and now Parks and Hughes was just too much. Elizabeth collapsed again. She was ordered to bed and doctors diagnosed an ulcer and colitis. All she could eat was baby food. The work she had done on *Love Is Better Than Ever* seemed wasted and MGM were as mortified as she was. They still had no film to bring Elizabeth back to the screens in early 1952, and they disliked what they thought was going on with Donen. She had already attracted enough wayward publicity and, coming on top of the Judy Garland fiasco, Dore Schary was worried.

In April 1951 MGM released the picture she had made with Spencer Tracy and Joan Bennett, *Father's Little Dividend*, shot before *A Place in the Sun*. Elizabeth turned up at the Hollywood première with Stanley Donen at her side. Five days later, Donen's wife Jeanne filed for divorce and Metro were not amused. Hasty discussions followed behind Elizabeth's back.

However innocent the couple's friendship, the studio wanted him out of her life and Pandro Berman, who had produced her in *National Velvet*, came up with the answer. She was cast in *Ivanhoe*, which Berman was producing with some great names from both sides of the Atlantic: Robert Taylor, Joan Fontaine, George Sanders, Finlay Currie, Felix Aylmer, Emlyn Williams and Megs Jenkins. Since most of the location work was to be shot in England, Elizabeth would be taken out of the Hollywood arena, away from Donen and away from the gossip columnists. That motive was apparent to all, for *Ivanhoe* could hardly be described as a major follow-up to *A Place in the Sun*. Her lines could almost be written on a cigarette packet, and she knew it. There were tantrums, but MGM insisted and Elizabeth needed the money. She could not face a suspension, without salary, and in the end agreed. Soon she was on her way.

There was a stopover in New York while she transferred from aircraft to the Atlantic liner *Liberté* on 18 June and out of the waiting crowds came a friendly face: Monty Clift arrived to surprise her.

'Hiya, Bessie Mae,' he called out, and it needed all her self-control to stop herself grasping him in her arms in front of the cameras. It was a brief reunion.

'What's going on with you and Stanley Donen?' Monty asked.

'Friends,' Elizabeth reassured him. 'Just friends, like you and me.'

Then she was gone again with her little entourage of Peggy Rutledge and Metro publicist Malvina Pumphrey, with her husband Kenny, who were keeping a close eye on their charge, as instructed by the studio. They were still unsure whether she would actually get on the boat.

Elizabeth's arrival in England was greeted by a mass of press coverage. Michael Wilding scanned the papers, picked up the telephone and dialled Elizabeth's hotel.

'Welcome!' he cried. 'Are you lonely?' Elizabeth shrieked with delight and agreed instantly to an invitation to dinner that night. Within a week, and after several more dinners, caviare and champagne, she was blooming. She was eating properly, her baby food was discarded and the assortment of pills prescribed back in Beverly Hills was tossed away.

Wilding was slim, six feet tall, with blue eyes, a warm wit and the most charming manner. Elizabeth was on hand to celebrate his thirty-ninth birthday on 23 July. She was exactly half his age. Years later she recalled the attraction he held for her at that particular time in her life: 'To me he represented tranquillity, security, maturity . . . all the things I needed in myself. But of course I would discover you can't get them by touching someone else.'

For the next eight weeks, during the shooting of *Ivanhoe*, they were often together – lunching, dining, trips to the country, boating on the Thames. Elizabeth was smitten again. She knew eyebrows would be raised; and he certainly knew it. Not long before his reunion with Elizabeth he had been escorting Marlene Dietrich and there had been some speculation about his intentions. 'I'm too old for you, darling,' he protested when Elizabeth asked him bluntly why he hadn't proposed to her. But she was not to be put off; before she left London that summer, he was a willing participant in a secret engagement which could not become official until Wilding had dealt with one problem – divorce from his existing wife, Kay. On her last day in London, Elizabeth also patched things up with her parents by sending them a telegram to demonstrate that she was deliriously happy and 'can't wait to see you'. The telegram was signed Elizabeth – and Michael Wilding.

Although she had loved being in England again, she was glad to leave and to put *Ivanhoe* behind her. She would never regard it as a significant part of her career, later describing it as a medieval western, a 'piece of cachou'. Hollywood thought differently: the movie eventually received an Oscar nomination for Best Film of 1952, along with *High Noon*, *The Quiet Man* and *The Greatest Show on Earth*, which won the award.

After a brief holiday in the south of France, Elizabeth returned to New York and embarked upon what she described as her first spree, courtesy of Monty Clift and Roddy McDowall. Her press people had gone back to Hollywood and she checked in at the Plaza Hotel, initially for four days. She was given a huge, sumptuous suite and the management said, 'No charge, Miss Taylor, this is complimentary.'

Sara and Francis Taylor flew in for a tearful reunion with their estranged daughter and celebrated their twenty-fifth wedding anniversary with her before moving on, leaving the young star to go on the town with Monty and Roddy. Drinks in Gregory's, dinner at the Pavilion and other classy restaurants, and they paid no attention to the occasional press photographer who happened upon them. Then came the day when the hotel management presented Elizabeth with a bill for $2500. The 'complimentary' stay had been for the four days for which she had originally checked in; the balance was for food, drink and the room rate for the remaining days. Her face froze when she saw the amount and she promptly announced that she would move to another hotel.

Monty found her a single room at a smaller place, the St Regis, and while he and Roddy were helping her pack, things went haywire. Large amounts of Martini were drunk; a huge bouquet of five dozen chrysanthemums, which had been delivered to Elizabeth earlier that day, was used for mock sword-fighting – and five dozen chrysanthemums drop a lot of petals; someone ran round the suite turning all the pictures upside down. Later Elizabeth sent messages of apology to the staff who were left to clean up the mess, and had chocolates and presents delivered.

Naturally, the news travelled. When Michael Wilding read about it in London, he telephoned and said he would be joining her in New York the following weekend. By coincidence, Nicky Hilton also called. He wanted to fly to New York to meet her again to discuss final details connected with their divorce. He arrived in town before Wilding and so within the space of a few days she was photographed on the spree with Monty, dining with her ex-husband and meeting her intended. The newspapers could not have wished for more.

It was no coincidence that MGM called Elizabeth back to Hollywood. Michael Wilding went with her and introduced her to some of his closest friends, including Stewart Granger. (It was Wilding's lifelong friendship with Granger that inspired Hedda Hopper in her book *The Whole Truth and Nothing But* to make allegations about Wilding's sexual ambiguity. Wilding sued for £3 million and won a huge out-of-court settlement and an apology.)

One thing was certain. After her meeting with Nicky, Elizabeth was more convinced than ever that she was deeply in love with Michael, and she displayed a huge sapphire ring on her engagement finger. Her parents were similarly charmed, but friends were less enthusiastic about her marrying a man twice her age. Louella Parsons and Hedda Hopper gave her some pointed advice, too, as rumours spread that she would soon remarry.

Howard Hughes still hovered on the fringes of Elizabeth's life. He had 'bought' Jean Simmons from J. Arthur Rank in London, which suited Jean because of her plans to marry Stewart Granger. Granger remembers a day when Hughes came over to his house, doubtless having heard that Elizabeth Taylor was there:

> Michael and Elizabeth were staying with us, living in sin just before their marriage. Hughes came over, and we all sat around talking. Now he liked women who were well endowed, and I noticed he was constantly looking down the front of Jean and Elizabeth's dresses, and there was plenty to see there, because both were as he liked them. I said jokingly, 'Howard, which one would you like? Take your pick.' He thought I was serious. Here we were playing with a man we thought was a nice guy; we were teasing a cobra.

* * * * *

It was during the winter of 1951–2, at the Actors Studio in New York, that Montgomery Clift saw James Dean for the first time. Someone had told him 'This kid is an echo of you, Monty.' Clift did not want to know. He found it unnerving to watch anyone whose work bore the remotest resemblance to his own. It was not difficult, however, to spot the influence of both Monty and Marlon Brando in Dean's developing style and he did not appear to want to hide it. In letters to friends, he was signing himself 'James Brando Clift Dean'. He also got hold of Clift's telephone number and called several times, but when Clift answered the phone Dean was too nervous to talk and hung up. He did the same to Brando. Monty heard about it and got angry: 'Who is that fucking creep, anyway?' Such idolatry of one's peers is not unusual in Hollywood: George C. Scott, when already a name himself, used to do the same to his idol, James Cagney, and, when he heard Cagney's voice, would disintegrate into tears.

Dean was also forming his own style, much more violent and staccato than Monty's. Billy LeMassena recalled an incident at the Studio:

> I saw Jimmy do a scene from *Caligula* that was hair-raisingly wonderful. I remember he had on a pair of GI shoes; Libby Holman was involved, playing his mother, and he hauled off as if he was going to kick her in the face. She was lying on the floor but it was all so daring and real that I was really taken in by him. He came so close to kicking her that everyone thought she'd be seriously injured.

Dean's appearances at the Studio were irregular, partly due to the need to earn a living. Any dollar would do: washing dishes, waiting on tables, Jimmy did it all. When he was out of work he walked the streets of New York, watching people and learning. What the initial teachings of Method acting had instilled in him was the power of observing others, picking up mannerisms, stoops, voices, images that he could store in his mind for use later. He mimicked people he met on the street, or studied the movements of down-and-outs in wino alleys. New York became his spiritual home because it had everything he wanted, except, at present, the finance to live.

The cruelty of life in the city, impoverished and often alone, was in fact fostering a complete change in his character, his outlook and even his appearance. The podgy, rounded face, fresh and healthy from his farm days, had given way to tauter, thinner lines; his jaw and cheekbones were more prominent and classical; his torso was slimmed by an empty stomach, revealing the protruding muscles of youth.

His friend from UCLA days, Bill Bast, arrived from Hollywood, seeking fame in the city as a writer. He had sufficient cash to rescue Dean from what he described as very unpleasant conditions. As they made their way through the heart of Manhattan, searching for work and subsistence, the city streets became what they become to all who live there for any length of time: a village in which everyone knows everyone, and what they are up to.

Trudging around Broadway and the blocks off in the theatre district, they would meet familiar faces, like Roddy McDowall's; in casting line-ups Jimmy would be vying for parts with Paul Newman and Steve McQueen. At the Neighborhood Playhouse, a great training ground run by the legendary Sandford Meisner, McQueen – in between selling ballpoint pens – was emerging slowly into the spotlight. He and Dean ran parallel, penniless and often at a low ebb.

New York at that time was the melting pot of future great talents. Television was having a great influence: directors like Fred Coe and Robert Wise were creating a totally new medium for the acting profession; new writers, like Mel Brooks and Woody Allen, were providing television with a fresh approach, different to all that had gone before. In other spheres, writers such as Arthur Miller, Gore Vidal and Tennessee Williams were pushing their stories to sexually adventurous heights. At the Actors Studio, Marilyn Monroe was being coached, along with other new faces – Rod Steiger, George C. Scott, Paul Newman, Carroll Baker, Zero Mostel, Grace Kelly – in preparation for future challenges on the west coast.

*   *   *   *   *

In the spring of 1952 some of the New York actors who had already made it arrived in Hollywood for the Academy Awards. Montgomery Clift was nominated Best Actor for *A Place in the Sun*, Marlon Brando for *A Streetcar Named Desire*; Karl Malden was nominated Best Supporting Actor in *Streetcar*, Kevin McCarthy for his role as Biff in Arthur Miller's *Death of a Salesman*. In the event Humphrey Bogart won Best Actor for *The African Queen*, while George Stevens won the Oscar for Best Director with *A Place in the Sun*.

Elizabeth Taylor did not attend the ceremony, however. A month earlier, she had boarded a plane for London to marry Michael Wilding.

As soon as London heard the news, Wilding was besieged by newsmen. Although a star in Britain, he had never received such press attention and he was astounded by it. The story was as sensational in England as it was in America. Here was one of the world's most glamorous and famous young movie stars marrying a man already well past the halfway mark to his threescore years and ten. The morning before Elizabeth's arrival, he puffed quietly at his pipe, displaying the nonchalance and *savoir-faire* of the typical Englishman that he was: 'People forget she has been through a very trying time . . . she wants to be married to someone who will love and protect her and that someone, by some Heaven-sent luck, turns out to be me. I will not let her down.'

It was a simple ceremony, lasting ten minutes, at Caxton Hall, London's most famous registry office, on 21 February, six days before Elizabeth's twentieth birthday. The British actress Anna Neagle, who was to star in Wilding's next picture, and her husband Herbert Wilcox, the producer, were the two witnesses: outside there were three thousand others. Elizabeth waved and chatted gleefully. At a press conference she said that in Michael she had found lasting happiness, of that she was sure. When questioned about her career she told reporters, 'I shall never put my career first. All I want is to be Mike's wife and start a family.'

At MGM the press cuttings were being perused and that remark about her career did not go unnoticed. Metro gave the happy couple just three months of married bliss – a delightful honeymoon in the French Alps, followed by Elizabeth's second try at being a good housewife in Wilding's Mayfair apartment; then the recall came.

It was more of a challenge, a threat even, than a polite request for her to return to work. During her absence, the studio had rolled out an old hit from 1932 entitled *A Free Soul*, starring Lionel Barrymore (who won an Oscar for his performance), Norma Shearer and Leslie Howard. It was the story of a society girl who meets a gangster, dumps her regular beau and goes off into the night with the undesirable interloper, whereupon Leslie Howard (the society boy) shoots the youthful Clark Gable (the gangster), thus propelling the latter into stardom. Now it was to be reworked to star Elizabeth Taylor as the society girl, with the new and apt title of *The Girl Who Had Everything*. In the new version, William Powell was to take the role played by Barrymore, Gig Young was the society boy, and the handsome Fernando Lamas was the gangster.

MGM, fearing that Miss Taylor might rebel, threw in a three-year contract for Michael Wilding for good measure. Elizabeth could not shun such an offer lightly, because by now she had a secret of her own: she was pregnant – a fact which she bestowed upon her masters only after a month of negotiating new contracts. Metro took the news in good part and hid the true feelings of some of the executives by lavishing congratulations upon the newly-weds. Behind closed doors they discussed the nuisance value of their star's happy event.

There were other matters to sort out. Neither Elizabeth nor Wilding was awash with cash and when they returned to Beverly Hills to house-hunt the only property that seemed right for them would cost $150,000 after renovations and furnishing. Elizabeth wanted that house. The question was: how? They could raise a good portion of the asking price between them, but then there was the refurbishment and furniture. Elizabeth went to the studio and, having just signed their lives away to MGM for some considerable time hence, the Wildings now became totally committed to Metro, who coughed up with a loan to help them buy the house of their dreams. The condition was that even though she would be heavily pregnant by the time the film was ready for release, Elizabeth must go on a promotional tour.

Furthermore, when Elizabeth finished making *The Girl Who Had Everything*, which was rushed into production before she became too obviously pregnant on screen, MGM placed her on suspension without salary for getting pregnant without their permission. The idea was that by the time she had had her baby in January 1953, she would be anxious to return to work to start earning again.

They had reckoned without her new spirit and confidence, gained from her first real happiness as a married woman and from motherhood. When MGM gave her an awful script for *All the Brothers Were Valiant*, to which they had already assigned her with Robert Taylor and Stewart Granger, she read the words – and refused. (Ann Blyth, who took the role planned for Elizabeth, probably wished she had done the same.)

MGM did not take it lightly. They promptly renewed Elizabeth's suspension from the lot, this time at a vastly reduced salary – hardly enough to keep her Cadillac and his Jaguar in fuel.

Chapter Five

Star Status

Hollywood, the ultimate soap opera, had started the fifties by confusing itself with reality. Billy Wilder raked the embers of a dying era in 1950 with his direction of *Sunset Boulevard*, in which William Holden plays Joe Gillis, a young newspaperman who comes to California in search of success. The film opens to reveal him lying face down in a swimming pool as a voice-over says, 'Poor devil, he always wanted a pool.'

Back-tracking, the film shows Joe's arrival in California and his eventual discovery and seduction by the fading star Norma Desmond, played by Gloria Swanson. They meet as Joe hides in the grounds of her house to dodge debt collectors; she is burying her pet chimpanzee. Recognising her, Joe says, 'Hey, I know you. You used to be big,' to which Miss Swanson gives the retort, mischievously written by Wilder himself, 'I am big; it's the pictures that got small.' Joe agrees to write her comeback script and accepts her sexual advances, but in the course of it he falls in love with a young writer, for which he is eventually shot dead by Miss Swanson. When Norma's wish for new fame finally comes true, it is in front of newsreel cameras as she is taken away to face a charge of murder. Cecil B. De Mille, Hedda Hopper, Buster Keaton and H. B. Warner all play themselves in the movie.

What the audiences – and, in fact, many in Hollywood – did not know of was the behind-the-scenes trauma that went on before and after the picture was made. First of all Wilder had approached Mae West for the part of Norma Desmond, but Miss West was shocked and hurt by the suggestion that she should play a faded star. Though by now fast approaching sixty, she considered herself much too young for the part. Wilder then tried Mary Pickford, who agreed but did not want the emphasis to rest too heavily on the has-been line; so she was out too. Gloria Swanson was the next choice and she made no pre-contract demands or conditions; she just agreed to get on with the job. Monty Clift had been signed for the role of the young writer (this was supposed to be the last in his three-picture deal with Paramount); in fact, Wilder had written the screenplay with Monty in mind. Two weeks before they were to start rehearsals, Monty was due to turn up for a run-through. Gloria Swanson recalled, 'I was sitting around waiting for Monty to show, and then somebody tells me he's backed out, and they're signing William Holden.'

In between agreeing to do the film and the rehearsal time, Monty had read the script with Libby Holman. Libby flew into a rage and said it was too close to home. She said she knew what would happen if Monty played it: she would be cast in the newspapers as the real-life fading star and Monty as the young man she had captured. Finally, Clift got on to his agents and said, 'Get me out of this.' The excuse they came up with was that Monty had decided that he could not be convincing making love to a woman twice his age. Wilder reluctantly agreed to release him and Paramount cancelled Monty's contract, withholding the final third of his fee for the trio of films. Holden was brought in – which was hardly satisfactory to Miss Swanson and the make-up people because, with his craggy features, he looked as old as the youthful Miss Swanson in real life; if realism was to be attempted, she would have to be made to look older. However, the picture was completed and, largely through Miss Swanson's performance and Wilder's direction, it had an incisiveness that few films about Hollywood ever achieved. Louis B. Mayer, who saw it before his departure from MGM, was furious. 'You bastard,' he shouted at Wilder. 'You have disgraced the industry that made you . . . you should be run out of town.' Wilder's response was brief: 'Fuck you.'

Others followed. Judy Garland found herself looking at the torment of her own life, and at the system that had produced her, as she read the script for a remake of *A Star Is Born*. Jack Warner was personally involved in casting the picture and gave Judy the part because she also agreed to sing at his daughter's coming-out party. He wanted Cary Grant to star alongside her but, as Grant was unavailable, he approached Monty Clift, who turned it down because he didn't like the ending. Once again, there were too many comparisons with his own life and he did not want to tempt fate with the prospect of seeing himself, on screen, sliding into alcoholism and ending up dead. So James Mason played Garland's husband, Norman Maine, the star who goes into decline while his wife is rising to greatness. It was a story familiar enough to those who lived under the tinsel, a candid view that did no favours to a system decaying before their eyes. Released in 1954, it was Garland's first picture since leaving MGM and her last major film for another seven years.

Meanwhile, Kirk Douglas and Lana Turner headed the cast in *The Bad and the Beautiful*, which includes portrayals of a number of easily recognisable characters from the past as the ruthless movie producer, Jonathan, callously carves his way through their lives. Lana Turner is the nobody he makes into a megastar and then forces into an alcoholic decline; around them are spun homely little Hollywood tales of lust, sex and neurotic uncertainties, half-truths and exaggerations of known case histories.

In *The Star*, Natalie Wood, still in pigtails, played the patient, loving daughter of a movie queen who had lost her throne. The film earned 20th Century–Fox heavy criticism for exploiting Bette Davis, who played the lead, because at the time she was fighting a similar battle of her own. Her looks and glamour were giving way to the first signs of the maturity and ferocity in her face that actually were to become her trademark for the remainder of her career. As Miss Davis herself said later, 'If I had had a pretty face like Elizabeth Taylor, I wouldn't have had a career left.'

Bette may have lost her youth but she had no intention of losing her status. As far as she was concerned, she was still The Star, as Natalie Wood discovered from an incident during the making of the film. Natalie, who hated water, had to jump out of a boat and swim to a raft some distance away. 'I faced the prospect of being flung into the ocean or losing the part,' she said, 'and I just went into hysterics, just howling.' Bette Davis heard the commotion and came out of her dressing room. She simply stood there looking and got the picture straight away. Then she bawled at director Stuart Heisler: 'I am not going to stand here while you throw some screaming kid into the ocean. If you want a god-damned swimmer, you should get Johnny Weissmuller.' The star insisted they use a stand-in who could swim well, and Natalie said, 'She saved it for me. I was just so terrified that day, I never forgot what she did.' Star and star-in-the-making formed a lifelong friendship.

Miss Davis was not giving way lightly to middle life and, in a way, her situation was reflected in Natalie's own position. *The Star* was shot in 1952 when Natalie was on the verge of a difficult age. She was edging towards the jump from child star to young adult which Elizabeth Taylor had achieved so successfully in one picture.

Natalie's mother could see it coming and she was scared. She had seen child stars vanish at the age of fifteen and she was determined to keep her little girl a little girl. Her only concession to her daughter's adolescence was to give Natalie her own room in the family's fine new home in San Fernando Valley – a sumptuous ranch-style house that gave the once impoverished Gurdins a status and lifestyle which once they would never have dreamed possible.

Natalie was the unblemished product of the studio. Her childhood had been spent clocking on at six in the morning, attending lessons in the studio school, and going home to bed. There is always the danger that child stars will become little monsters, but Marie did not allow that to happen. Her discipline, her routine, kept Natalie from any influences that might turn her head towards rebellion. When she began to talk about boys, and dating, and wearing lipstick, Marie hardly let her out of her sight. Natalie's younger sister Lana, recalling those days in her book *Natalie: a Memoir*, said that her mother's obsession with Natalie's career meant that the family was split; Marie was central in Natalie's life while her husband cared for Lana. They had no social life, very few friends and both girls were kept from the world outside their ranch gates or the studio. Natalie herself said, 'I was a bit like a puppet. Acting was something I did automatically, obeying the director, who pulled the strings, and my mother who ran my life.' If her mother was not around, the studio tutor or a chaperon was never far away. 'I shared a lot of the same tutors with Elizabeth Taylor; when we compared notes about our childhood, the same people kept cropping up. They were very protective and would practically follow me up into the bathroom.'

Ironically, the picture that was to be the vehicle for her move from childhood to young womanhood was so bad that it almost wrecked her career. It was her first film for the Warner studio and she was to play a young woman named Helen in a long, laborious biblical epic called *The Silver Chalice*.

A new young actor, Paul Newman, had been brought from New York for his first screen role, but the whole thing was a disaster from start to finish. They tried to change Natalie's looks and image to match Virginia Mayo, who played the same girl later in the picture, by bleaching her hair blonde and giving her contact lenses to make her eyes blue; eventually she refused to wear them and halfway through the film her eyes turn from blue to their natural black. In the promotional stills, Natalie's fans could hardly recognise her. She had been glamorised into a shapely maiden, wearing a sweater, heavy flowered earrings, eye-liner and make-up. This was no longer little Natalie. But what had they done to her in the process?

The film was a total flop at the box office. Newman suffered too and disliked being dubbed the poor man's Brando. When it was shown on television in the sixties, he ran a newspaper advertisement apologising to viewers for having to endure it.

*　*　*　*　*

In another strange twist of fate, it might have been James Dean in the role played by Newman in *The Silver Chalice*, thus casting Wood and Dean together long before they met in *Rebel Without a Cause*. Dean had been given the script to read by his agents in New York; the casting people told him the part was his if he wanted it. He read it and turned it down. He would rather wait or take something in television than accept that!

Around the same time, Dean also turned down a major role in *The Egyptian*, co-starring Michael Wilding. He had been second choice; Marlon Brando had been the original selection for the $5 million Darryl F. Zanuck production, but after first rehearsals Brando walked off the set, never to return. He told his agent, Jay Kantor, 'I just can't do that crap. Get me out of it.'

'Why is he doing this?' screamed Zanuck. 'He can't do this to me.' But Brando could and did. Zanuck sued for $2 million, which had Brando so worried that he had to resort to psychiatric help. After Dean had also rejected it, Zanuck finally got Edmund Purdom for the part but pursued his case against Brando, who settled out of court by agreeing to star in 20th Century–Fox's next big picture, *Désirée*, for no fee.

James Dean was back doing the rounds, joining the line-ups for casting directors. They were nicknamed 'cattle calls'; the queue of actors simply had to walk past the casting directors and, if they liked the look of someone, that person was called back for a reading. Grubbing around the casting calls took hours of a man's life. Some say James Dean took short cuts, using his body and attractiveness as a lure for anyone who might help him get on. He was not a homosexual, but he appears consciously to have chosen bisexuality for both professional and pleasurable purposes. He ruled out nothing in his quest to become an actor and in his search for all the experiences life can offer. When he went missing from his usual haunts in Manhattan, quite often he would come back a day or two later, grinning and cheerful, announcing that he had got a great new role; once he was gone for nearly two weeks and landed a major part. David Dalton, Dean's biographer, wrote:

> Jimmy's real sexual life had more to do with himself and the andro-gynous image he projected wandering in and out of different person-alities, than it did with his gender. . . . Jimmy's own answer to someone who asked him if he were gay was, 'Well, I'm certainly not going through life with one hand tied behind my back.' . . . Jimmy was collecting experiences and he wouldn't be prevented from trying anything.

After his first recorded television appearance in 1952 in the *US Steel Hour*, in a play called 'Prologue to Glory', Dean went on to play in twenty-three television productions over the next three years. Each time a better part; each time a better performance. Reviewers began to notice him and *Variety* observed that he stole the limelight from Sir Cedric

Hardwicke and Walter Hampden when he was cast in a play called *Danger*, delivering a 'magnetic performance' as a psychotic young janitor. Soon Broadway, and Hollywood, would notice.

* * * * *

Monty Clift had dropped out of the limelight, largely through his own doing. He had not worked since *A Place in the Sun* almost two years previously. As well as its success in the Academy Awards, the film had been given the accolade of being voted the Most Outstanding Movie of 1951 by the National Board of Review of Motion Pictures, and Charlie Chaplin called it 'the greatest picture ever made about American society'. New film scripts had been arriving for Clift almost daily; none, however, had the magnetic appeal of *A Place in the Sun* and he was adamant that the next one he did had to be just as good, or better.

His lack of employment had provided ample opportunity for Monty to slide further into lethargic ways, punctuated by his now well-known bouts of drinking and experimenting with drugs. Apart from the succession of male lovers trawled from his excursions into New York's nightlife, he was seeing more and more of Libby Holman, who, his mother said, 'just wanted to possess him'. Money was no problem. Even with the cancellation of his fee for *Sunset Boulevard*, Monty had secured a tidy nest egg (although he had entirely overlooked the need to pay tax and would soon require additional funds). Libby also had plenty. After her son's death she won the right to his $7 million fortune, although to get it she fought another terrible battle with the Reynolds family, whose money it originally was.

She and Monty were constantly in each other's company and Patricia Bosworth tells of the scene at Treetops, Libby's lavish home, where a party guest one night stumbled into her bedroom suite: 'I got the feeling Monty and Libby must have very kinky sex. Everything seemed erotic and faintly decadent, low lights, slippery white satin sheets, the overpowering fragrance of Jungle Gardenia and a huge bottle of Seconal [sleeping tablets] on the bedroom table.'

They spent the early summer of 1952 lazing around, either at her place or at his new duplex, which was being refurbished. One of its more famous inclusions was a huge medicine cabinet in the bathroom which everyone said Monty could never fill. He did – very quickly, with row upon row of bottles, phials and pill-boxes: sleeping pills, painkillers, medicine for his colitis, tranquillisers, anti-depressants, anti-sickness pills, uppers, downers and outers.

When he still couldn't sleep, he would go on to the roof and gaze endlessly into other people's bedrooms. And there were more bizarre moments: twice he was discovered hanging off the roof-ledge by his fingertips; one slip and he would have plunged to his death. His moods were variable. He swore at his mother and told her never to come to his apartment again because she was always going on about his dependence on Libby. Dr Silverberg also remained a controversial influence, now encouraging him towards a more powerful image. They had gone through attempts at heterosexual experience, but that didn't work. In the continuing analysis Silverberg counselled, 'Try aggression. Face up to people, on their own terms.' Monty's friends didn't care for it at all. Aggression brought him into face-to-face encounters, usually when drunk. Fighting would develop, and he wasn't good at that. From one bar on 42nd Street he was tossed into the gutter with a split nose and damaged eye. Silverberg was also advising Monty on which parts he should accept, which caused him further indecision and worried his friends.

In between his bouts of excess, Monty could return to his kind, generous self. Kevin McCarthy recalled:

In these moments, you could not meet a nicer guy. We'd talk for hours, at his place or ours or at the Karl Maldens. But they became fewer, particularly when he got bored. We had some great times and he was a really interesting guy, bright, funny, articulate, artistic. He spent a lot of time getting to know people like Norman Mailer, Arthur Miller and Thornton Wilder, for instance, and was always latching on to writers to write him scripts. Monty, remember, was very independent ... [he wasn't] going the Hollywood way. And then he made his big hairpin turn down skid row.

If he would just go back to work, Monty was looking at $150,000 a picture. There were a number of things in the offing and one of them he began to talk about constantly: finally the right film seemed to have come along. James Jones had sent him his novel, *From Here to Eternity*, an horrific catalogue of sadism, ill-treatment, sex and foul language in the American military, and it may be that some of his antics in real life became a way of psyching himself up for the part of Robert E. Prewitt. Norman Mailer had convinced him that he should try for it and Monty flew out to Tucson for long talks with Jones, who also wanted him. However, Harry Cohn, head of Columbia, who had bought the rights to the bestselling novel, was adamant that he wanted one of the studio stars – either Aldo Ray or John Derek – for the role of Prewitt and he would not budge, until director Fred Zinnemann threatened to quit if he could not have Clift.

There were further delays in trying to produce a cleaned-up screenplay which eliminated some of the horror of the book without losing the power, the huge emotional strength and shock of James Jones's original words – 816 pages of some of the most sexually explicit and obscene language in American fiction.

While he waited for matters to be resolved, Monty went to the opposite extreme and signed to play a priest in Alfred Hitchcock's *I Confess*. It was a role that particularly interested him. He read the screenplay, then flew up to Canada to stay in a monastery for a week. He discussed the play with the monks to discover whether the plot was feasible: the priest takes the confession of a killer and, through classic Hitchcock interaction, is eventually indicted for the murder himself and is hanged before being found to be innocent.

Clift flew to Los Angeles with Mira Rostova to begin work. He stayed sober for the filming, but at nights he drank heavily while he rehearsed into the early hours with Mira. He was uneasy, depressed and awkward, and had running arguments with Hitchcock on how a particular scene should be played or a line spoken. They were also forced to change the ending; the censors thought it would upset Roman Catholics to see a priest hanged for refusing to divulge the secrets of the confessional, and they turned it into a weaker, happier conclusion with Clift being saved at the last moment. Hitchcock and Monty parted with acrimony and the director never used him again.

Clift returned to New York. *I Confess* had taken just two months to complete and, since there was still no starting date on the horizon for *From Here to Eternity*, he went straight into a film he had promised to do for Vittorio De Sica – a prestigious situation, as the Italian director was among the leaders of his country's post-war film renaissance. The production was the result of an unusual collaboration between De Sica and David O. Selznick, producer of *King Kong*, *Rebecca* and *Gone With the Wind*. Initially called *Terminal Station*, Truman Capote was to write the screenplay. Filming was almost entirely on location at Rome's new central rail terminal, which presented its own problems. De Sica spoke hardly any English, which made life even more difficult, and David Selznick, who had put up the cash to ensure that his new wife, Jennifer Jones, got the co-starring role with Clift, had a large say in the direction, prompting Clift to describe him as an 'interfering fuckface'.

The plot, such as it was, had Jennifer Jones as an American housewife on a visit to Rome; Clift was her Italian lover. A hackneyed tale of lovers breaking up, it could never be lifted to the level of a good movie; rows on set, squabbles over the script, clashes of personality and Vittorio rattling away in French or Italian, which no one except Monty understood, spelled disaster. Selznick tried several writers as well as Capote but failed to find what he wanted. He only imagined that he wanted the Italian neo-realism and simplistic characteristics of De Sica's direction; what he really wanted was a glossy, Hollywood production of the type for which he was well known. He supervised every detail, throwing back endless words from Capote, who was running around with the script, rewriting as the film was being made, typing lines in one room of the station while actors waited to perform in another. 'Monty was right,' Capote said, 'Selznick was an interfering fuckface.' He even changed the title to *Indiscretion of an American Wife*. Then, the hours of filming they had all endured were slashed in Selznick's cutting room to a reel-time of sixty-seven minutes.

Monty became so frustrated and exhausted that he could not go for more than an hour or two without the aid of drink or pills – owing in part to the fact that De Sica could rent the Rome terminal for night filming only, which meant that Monty had to devour tranquillisers to sleep by day.

Neither did he have the calming hand of Mira to steady him. She had rowed with De Sica even before the shooting began and did not go to Rome. Instead, Monty had brought with him from New York a young Italian who was his occasional lover. That didn't please Capote, who saw him merely as an encourager of Clift's worst habits. Even Monty finally got fed up with him and ditched him when they left Rome. Capote, no angel himself, despaired of Monty but always praised his work:

He was serious about only one thing. And that was acting. He was the exception to my theory that a movie star has to be ignorant to be good. You have to be smart to be on stage, but a movie actor is just a conduit for a writer, the director and everybody else who puts him into the picture. If he's too smart he resists them and he's no good. Brando never really made it as a movie star, he's always resisted. Monty was smart and good but that was also because he was very shrewd. He knew exactly what he was doing. I once asked him why he wanted to act in movies and why he didn't want to do something more interesting and he looked at me and said, 'You don't understand. It's my life. It's all I know.' He was an artist and had all of an artist's sensibilities and flaws.

When filming ended in Rome, Monty flew back to America to begin work at last on *From Here to Eternity*. Zinnemann had finally persuaded Harry Cohn that Monty was neither too sensitive nor too frail for the part of Prewitt; in fact, he was exactly the man for it. As the calibre of the other stars became known – Burt Lancaster, Ernest Borgnine, Donna Reed and Joan Crawford (who later quit in a row with Cohn and was replaced by Deborah Kerr) – Monty grew more and more intense. He worked day and night, practising the trumpet, learning to march and drill (which he could not do because he had never been in the services) and studying boxing with James Jones, who was an expert. He walked around clutching Jones's novel and referred to it constantly, like a car mechanic studying the manufacturer's manual. Some lines, and long speeches, he practised over and over – relentlessly, for hours on end. On the set even those who weren't too keen on Monty as a person admired his dedication and his performance level, which was widely acclaimed as sheer brilliance; but also visible to most of them was the inner struggle he had to bring himself up to it.

Donna Reed, who played the hostess with whom Prewitt falls in love, recalled:

> I had never worked with any actor like him; to watch him was incredible and memorable. He had a talent and a side to our profession I had never seen before, just superb. Our scenes were lifted by Monty to the point that the impression lasted, not just on film but in my own mind, and I could go over them again and again. Then, when it was done, he would slump into a morose, quiet, almost disdainful mood and you began to wonder if you'd upset him. But that was Monty, slumping back after the great exertion of effort.

Frank Sinatra saw this picture as his chance of an acting comeback. He had gone through a lean spell; no one was calling any more, and indeed no one had when Zinnemann started casting for *From Here to Eternity*. Sinatra heard about the film and became desperate for the role of Angelo Maggio, the fast-talking Italian private; he thought it was perfect for himself and pleaded with Harry Cohn to let him do it. Zinnemann didn't want him and had already offered the part to Eli Wallach, but Sinatra did not give up easily. He begged and humbled himself, agreeing to do it for what he considered hardly any money.

'I get one hundred and fifty thousand a film . . .'

'Correction,' interrupted Cohn. 'You got a hundred and fifty thousand. Not any more.'

'OK, I used to get that. I don't want anything like that for Maggio. Just let me do it, Harry.'

'How much?'

'I'll do it for a thousand a week.'

'We'll see, we'll see,' said Cohn. 'I've got some other guys to test first.'

Sinatra flew off to Nairobi to try to save what was left of his marriage to Ava Gardner, who was filming *Mogambo* with Clark Gable, and for days he paced around, nervous and chain-smoking.

'Relax,' Gable pleaded. 'You're making us all nervous. Just take a drink and relax.' Sinatra even got Ava to call Harry Cohn, but still the word was uncertain.

Two weeks later, Wallach turned down the part after a row with Cohn, who said he didn't look like an Italian. Wallach pointed out that he had just spent fifteen months playing an Italian in a Tennessee Williams play, 'so don't try to tell me anything about acting, Harry Cohn'. But it was Clift who finally secured the role for Sinatra. Billy LeMassena explained, 'Monty loved Sinatra. We used to play his records over and over again. He was Sinatra's number one fan, and now Sinatra was out of favour and on rock bottom. Monty told me that he spoke to Cohn when all this blew up and got him the part.' There were suggestions in some quarters, however, that Sinatra got it only because of his own and Harry Cohn's mutual friendships within the Mafia. When the BBC ran the story in London, Sinatra sued and got an apology.

He and Monty hit it off straight away. It would be Sinatra's finest movie performance, and for that he had only Clift to thank. He said,

I learned more about acting from him than I ever knew before. He's an exhausting man, a total perfectionist. When I thought we'd finished rehearsing he'd suddenly get up and say 'OK, let's do it again,' until you had to plead with him to lay off.

Monty coached him and took him through his words, just as Mira had done for Monty so many times in the past.

They had little else in common, except a liking for drink, and their exploits in Hollywood and later on location in Hawaii gave Zinnemann anxious times. When they moved back to Hollywood for the final scenes, Monty took a suite at the Roosevelt. At the end of each day he, Sinatra and the author James Jones went out on the town. They all had problems and drink seemed an easy solution. Monty was suffering the anti-climax of his performance, which at first he hated and then said deserved an Oscar; Sinatra was still possessed by the thought that his marriage to Ava Gardner was on the rocks and telephoned her constantly; Jones was swearing about what they had done to his book, the strength of which had been diminished beyond what he could accept.

Nevertheless, as we now know, it was still a powerful film. It was completed in less than three months and when Harry Cohn saw the rushes he predicted that it would be a smash hit. He insisted that it should be cut and ready to go out in August, three months away. Everyone was on edge, waiting for the opening at the Capitol Theater in New York, and they sat in the restaurant afterwards waiting for the midnight editions. Critical acclaim was widespread. Lancaster, Sinatra,

Borgnine, everybody was praised. Clift too – 'another brilliant, sensitive portrayal' . . . 'his eyes and gestures unfailingly suggest the nuances of feeling that the scriptwriter dare not let him speak' . . . 'a shock absorber for the insensitivity around him'.

Harry Cohn was rubbing his hands. For an expenditure of $2 million, he had produced what is described these days as a blockbuster, taking $25 million at the box office. When the time came, Monty was nominated for Best Actor, along with Burt Lancaster; neither took the award, but *From Here to Eternity* did win eight Oscars – Best Film, Best Screenplay, Best Director, Best Photography, Best Editing, Best Sound; Frank Sinatra got Best Supporting Actor and Donna Reed was Best Supporting Actress. William Holden got Best Actor for his performance in *Stalag 17* and Monty cried his eyes out.

* * * * *

After *From Here to Eternity*, Monty did not work again in films for more than three years. He came back to Hollywood at quite frequent intervals and some of the offers he got even went to conference stage, but in the end he always dropped out for one reason or another.

His journeys west gave him the opportunity to continue his friendship with Elizabeth Taylor and Michael Wilding. He found them apparently deliriously happy, if slightly hard up, in their new-found domestic bliss with their baby and a small menagerie of assorted pets. 'I have never been so happy,' Elizabeth told Monty. 'This will be my life from now on.'

The 'bliss' following the birth of Elizabeth's first child, Michael Howard Wilding, was being carefully monitored by MGM, who were angry because she had turned down *All the Brothers Were Valiant* on a second time of asking and had also rejected *Roman Holiday*, which went to Audrey Hepburn. For this last act her suspension from the studio was extended.

Still just a few months into motherhood, Elizabeth naturally wanted to spend as much time as possible with her son. However, in early March 1953 MGM was approached by Paramount, who wanted to borrow her. Metro agreed. Loaning out was sometimes used as a form of punishment for wayward stars, since the workload could be heavy for no additional money – the actor would continue to receive the regular studio salary only, while the fee for the loan-out (which was substantially higher) went to the studio.

Paramount were producing *Elephant Walk*, co-starring Vivien Leigh, Dana Andrews and Peter Finch. They had already invested a huge amount of money in the location work in Ceylon when Miss Leigh collapsed from exhaustion. As she was flown home in a special plane, only half conscious, her husband Laurence Olivier said there was no question of her continuing; Vivien required total rest. Paramount went into a panic. They viewed the dailies to try to salvage what they could from the material already in the can and then began looking for a replacement of similar build, so that at least the long-shots of action with Miss Leigh could be saved.

Elizabeth agreed to take over, although Paramount earned some criticism for putting such a young actress into a demanding role designed for someone older and more experienced. In the film she becomes the bride of a tea-planter set in his bachelor ways, whose staff in the inherited historic mansion ignore her commands. Dana Andrews plays the obligatory lover and plantation manager who takes her away from it all.

The work on *Elephant Walk* took little more than two months and when Elizabeth returned to Los Angeles in May she faced a new trauma. During the filming a fleck of grit had become buried in her right eyeball; it had to be removed by surgery in a delicate operation during which she had to remain conscious. Her eye was bandaged for several days, then, when the gauze was removed, her doctors discovered that an ulcer had grown over the eye. More surgery was carried out immediately, but for a time it seemed that Elizabeth might lose the sight of the infected eye. After a further two weeks with her eyes in bandages, the doctors were as relieved as she was to discover that the infection had died away leaving her sight unaffected.

MGM stood by anxiously; they had already selected another movie – again in the vein that Elizabeth hated. Called *Rhapsody*, it is the story of a spoiled rich girl (Elizabeth) who falls in love with a talented violinist whose father opposes their marriage. She takes some pills, then on the rebound marries another musician, who takes to drink when he discovers that she is still in love with the violinist. The happy ending comes when Elizabeth realises that she does love her husband after all, and they sail off, hand in hand, to live happily ever after. Her sole consolation came from a reviewer who said that she was now such a talented and honest young actress that she could make the audience believe almost anything.

Next Metro rushed her into a remake of *Beau Brummel*, with Stewart Granger. Miss Taylor's own comment will suffice:

God, when I think of some of the movies I have made . . . like *Beau Brummel*. I never saw the film until after Richard [Burton] and I were married. It was on television and Richard turned it on . . . I had to change stations after five minutes . . . it was so embarrassing.

Contract actors seldom had any choice but to accept their studio's bidding; and costume roles for period pieces were very much in vogue at the time, as Hollywood tried to shake off the shackles of the blacklists. Costume films and religious epics were considered safe and entertaining; often they were unintelligent, poorly scripted and overpainted with a Hollywood gloss. Charlton Heston remembers them vividly:

It may well be that Elizabeth Taylor didn't like some of those roles, stuff like *Ivanhoe* and *Beau Brummel*, but MGM didn't do these films very well, and perhaps she wasn't equipped for them herself. A lot of actors at the time had to put up with what we called medievalese. Tony Curtis had to say one classic line in *The Black Tower* which went: 'Yonder lies the castle of my father. Gladly, will he give us shelter.' And it isn't just the Bronx accent of Curtis that spoils it; the syntax was appalling. These scripts made you talk like that. Most of the writing in these period pieces, and the epics for that matter, was pretty poor.

To Elizabeth's amazement, *Beau Brummel* was selected for the 1954 Royal Command Performance, although it was panned by the critics. Prospects looked better, however, when she was chosen for her next film. It was her fourth in a year: MGM had certainly made her pay for the misdemeanours of getting married, getting pregnant and refusing two of their productions. Now she was to co-star with Van Johnson, Walter Pidgeon and Donna Reed in *The Last Time I Saw Paris*.

With this kind of workload she had little time to devote to her new role of housewife and mother. Visitors to the Wilding home described the lifestyle as casual compared with the luxurious standards of their friends. Most of the furniture had been clawed and chewed by Elizabeth's pets; expensive wall-coverings lavished upon the property in the redecoration of not many months ago were ripped and untidy in places; and guests drinking fine champagne might discover that they were required to use odd glasses. The refrigerator invariably contained little more than a few scraps of food and even Michael Wilding admitted in one interview, 'Elizabeth can be rather absent-minded about household matters, like forgetting to organise the food for dinner.'

* * * * *

Like Elizabeth, Rock Hudson had complaints about some of the dialogue he was forced to recite, especially in dreadful lightweight films like *Taza, Son of Cochise*. He also had his personal acting difficulties to contend with, and in that film the Indian he portrayed comes on screen with a noticeable midwestern drawl. But his star was rising. As Elizabeth had recently discovered when he was introduced to her, he had a sexuality similar to Montgomery Clift's: when he walked into a room, he was noticed. Women, especially, felt his presence: he was tall, handsome, clean-cut, and his behaviour in public was generally impeccable. He seemed the total heterosexual – a Hollywood stud.

In the privacy of his own home, however, things were rather different. In the summer of 1953 he acquired a new live-in friend named Jack, who had been a fellow dinner guest at George and Mark's. He too was an aspiring actor, a handsome young man of twenty-two with blond hair and blue eyes, to whom Henry Willson immediately promised: 'I can make you a big star, just like Rock.'

But Rock wanted Jack for himself, and they moved into a new house on Grandview. Rock's finances were improving by the month. After all, he had appeared in twenty-three films by 1953; admittedly most were growing-up parts, but none the less it was an impressive list of credits. He bought a new convertible, in which he was photographed for the movie magazines, could afford to eat three steaks a day and the fan mail was flooding in.

According to the studio publicity people, he was already receiving 150 proposals of marriage a week – doubtless a slight exaggeration. One of them was made public in order to promote his sex appeal: 'Dearest, darling Rock, come and take me away where our eager lips can meet in silent vows of eternal love. . . .' One of his most persistent proposers was a rich lady from Texas who wrote every week, saying, 'If only you will give up all that Hollywood foolishness, I will make you King of the Panhandle.' Hudson was already a good actor in that he had obviously disguised his true sexuality. He gave no one in the world outside a clue that he was anything other than a wholesome he-male, while behind the closed doors of his house, he and Jack played out the role of the proverbial happy couple.

It was Rock's first real, steady relationship, but it was kept a close secret. Only George and Mark knew. Effectively, Jack fulfilled the role of a movie star's wife, although he was not camp and hated holding hands or anything effeminate. When he became bored, Rock paid for acting lessons while he was away working.

As Hudson's fame grew and he was assigned his own publicist by Universal, the fan magazines persisted with the question 'When is Rock going to choose a bride?' Always he managed to get around the question of his apparent lack of steady female companionship and Willson helped by providing him with attractive dates on special occasions.

In August, Rock was somersaulting with delight when Willson called him: 'Sirk is ready to test you for *Magnificent Obsession* with Jane Wyman. This is the one, my boy.'

Douglas Sirk, a director at Universal, wanted to do a remake of the Lloyd C. Douglas story which had made Robert Taylor a star in its original pre-war version. Hudson faced extensive testing before Sirk gave him the part, but at last he had the chance to prove himself. Almost everything so far had been costume roles, westerns or swashbuckling sword fights that had hardly given him space to show any dramatic ability if such he possessed. This one offered him scope to get into a character, playing an uncaring playboy who turns surgeon and dedicates his life to helping the widow of a doctor whose death was caused by his selfishness.

Before filming started, Hudson almost wrecked his chances. He and Jack were out swimming at Luaguna with an innertube when suddenly he was dashed against some rocks by a giant wave and broke his collar-bone. Jack called an ambulance and then the studio, who were furious. By the time he reached hospital Rock was crying, 'Does this mean I'm gonna lose it?' There were people at Universal who would use the accident to try to get him off the picture. Willson, however, had an ace up his sleeve: he enlisted the support of an executive at the studio with whom he knew Rock had had an affair and who was still keen on him.

Rock stayed. Filming began with him heavily strapped up in a shoulder bandage and dosed up with painkillers. Determination, and a lot of late-night rehearsal for the following day's lines, made him a success in the picture and turned him into a star. 'I went in later to watch them score the film,' said Rock. 'Full symphony orchestra playing Beethoven's Ninth . . . and there I am up on the screen. Well, it was overwhelming and I couldn't stop crying. Just a blithering idiot.'

At the première they laid out the red carpet for him. Rock Hudson, star, was here, beaming in a smart tuxedo and with a female date for the night on his arm. But his moment was shattered when someone in the crowd yelled: 'Faggot!'

Chapter Six

New Horizons

As Hollywood looked around for what to do next, Fred Zinnemann's direction of *From Here to Eternity* was to be one of the most influential signposts. He and other leading directors, such as Billy Wilder, John Huston, Joseph Mankiewicz, Elia Kazan and George Stevens, were desperately trying to put a spark back into the business and to get off the merry-go-round of musicals, biblicals and safe-but-sorry softies. Stevens had set the pattern with *A Place in the Sun*, challenging the Great American Dream. Zinnemann had broken new ground in a different way.

The steamy scene of passion on the beach between Burt Lancaster and Deborah Kerr was the most explicit yet seen by movie audiences; Zinnemann himself had not expected to get it past the censors. Wilder continued the trend, directing Marilyn Monroe's portrayal of sexual innocence in *The Seven Year Itch*; Kazan was even more explicit with Carroll Baker playing *Baby Doll* to the magnificent Eli Wallach's lecherous Archie. *And God Created Woman* (with a little help from Roger Vadim), while Lana Turner shocked the public with the passion in *Peyton Place*, the film adaptation of Grace Metalious's perceptive novel which homed in on small-town America and inspired the first major television soap opera.

At last the movie-makers began to look in new directions as, through its rejection of old-hat movies and its acclaim of films like *From Here to Eternity*, the cinema-going public demonstrated that it was ready for a greater maturity. And waiting with its own demands was the youth of the 1950s, the first teenage batch from the wartime baby boom, demanding more in every way than their parents had ever had.

There were those who thought that Hollywood's salvation lay in gimmicks. Fighting back against television, films became wider, longer, louder and more colourful. There came Cinemascope, and Richard Burton in *The Robe*; 3-D, with Vincent Price in *House of Wax*; biblical extravaganzas like *The Ten Commandments* with Charlton Heston; and musicals, which gave Howard Keel a career until they began to fall from fashion in the mid-fifties.

As the remnants of the McCarthy blacklists were swept away, actors, writers, and directors were discovering new freedom of expression. Kazan was a prime mover. His film *On the Waterfront* was a powerful statement against corruption, in the wake of a Senate Committee investigation into organised crime in America (which had given Hollywood more than a passing glance). When the film was finally made (for under $1 million), no one was quite sure how it would be received by the audience; even Kazan was not expecting it to be the huge box-office success that it was. Suddenly everyone wanted him. Jack Warner gave him the money to do a film of John Steinbeck's novel *East of Eden* without having read the book or even an outline for the screenplay. Kazan just described it to him, told him it would cost $1.6 million and Warner said, 'You've got it.' At the time, Kazan was considering Marlon Brando and Monty Clift as the two main leads. James Dean was nowhere in his thoughts.

That is not to say that Dean had not already made an impression. In the previous twelve months he had been seen in a number of television dramas, collected good reviews here and there, turned up occasionally at the Actors Studio. But it was jobbing work, in cliché-ridden stories of suspense and murder for thirty- or sixty-minute theatre, in which a commercial for margarine or cornflakes could be tagged on to the end of an actor's best line. All the time, though, he was developing his style, continuing to study real people and copying their characteristics. He did it on his own, secretive about his work even to his closest friends.

There were other aspects of Dean that startled those around him. Sometimes, in a crowd or during rehearsals, he would show off, pulling faces, shouting some ludicrous, half-remembered lines from another actor's part; yet he was also extremely shy and retiring, to the point that if someone said 'Hello', he could be stuck for an answer. His dress and appearance were generally untidy. His speech was slurred and his lines mumbled; and many of the actors he appeared with hated working with him because they could never get their cues or the normal signals of progression that trained players give to one another during a performance.

Mary Astor, who appeared with him in a television play called *The Thief*, wrote in her autobiography:

In the final rehearsal, Jimmy was just six feet away from me in one scene and I could barely hear what he was saying, and what I could hear seemed to have very little to do with the script. I held my palms up in a 'Help' gesture. . . . 'What's the trouble, Mary?' the director asked. . . . Paul Lukas, that excellent actor, came to my rescue. . . .

'De trouble iss dat ve don't know vat de hell he's saying, ven he's going to say vat, or vere he's going to be ven he says anything.'

Our answer came over the speaker [from the director]: 'I'm sorry people, that's the way Jimmy has to work. Do the best you can, it's marvellous in here.' The cast felt superior to this whippersnapper, or 'vippersnopper' as Lukas called him ... but the vippersnopper was the one who got all the notices and we were just lumped together as 'the cast'.

In November 1953 Jimmy achieved a breakthrough when he was offered a major role in a new Broadway play, *The Immoralist*. He wanted to tell everyone. He called Monty Clift, but all he could say was a shaky, 'Er, hello ... this is Jimmy Dean, man ...' He stuttered and stumbled, and Clift hung up. He had already seen Dean in one of his television plays and was quietly impressed but did not say as much. Jimmy had been given the role of Bachir, a devious, blackmailing, homosexual Arab houseboy in Ruth and Augustus Goetz's adaptation of an André Gide novel. Dean found the play itself confusing and eventually dubbed it 'a piece of shit'; but the character had sufficient in it to give him a good run at his store of tricks and stunts to inject between the lines, driving the rest of the cast to distraction.

The Immoralist was significant in a wider respect too: it dealt with homosexuality, which figured openly on stage. In the movies it was still a totally banned topic; in the theatre the ice-breaker had been Kazan's direction of *Tea and Sympathy*, which had opened on Broadway in the spring of 1953. Dean was slightly uneasy about that aspect of the play, especially when he considered how he would broach the subject to his aunt and uncle, Marcus and Ortense, back in Fairmount, Indiana. They would want to keep the home town informed of the latest step in the career of their local boy, and in such a town in the fifties anything sexual was scandalous; anything homosexual was simply never discussed.

In rehearsal, Jimmy got into the part in the only way he knew how, which was to delve into the character to perfect actions and movements that were neither camp nor effeminate but were still alluring. He wanted to make himself completely realistic and he searched the minds and thoughts of those of his friends whom he knew to be homosexually inclined, gleaning from them the things that they found attractive in a youth so that he could perfect his performance.

When the play opened on Broadway on 1 February 1954, Dean was singled out as exceptional. On the first night, Marcus and Ortense shuffled uncomfortably in their seats, close to the front where Jimmy had placed them with a few of his special friends. His performance that night was carefree and relaxed. At curtain-call he gave an audacious curtsey in response to the applause while the rest of the cast bowed sedately. As he came off, the director was waiting in the slips to berate him for the ad lib. Dean responded by handing him two weeks' notice.

Everyone in the cast thought he was joking. The director apologetically withdrew his admonishment, but Dean was adamant. He would leave the show in two weeks' time. *The Immoralist* was his first hit on Broadway, and his last. Louis Jourdan, who played Michel, the tormented husband in the play, could not believe it. 'What's up Jimmy?' he asked. 'You were terrific. Why are you leaving? Where are you going?' That's what everyone wanted to know.

He was going to Hollywood. Kazan had signed him for *East of Eden*, in a vital role for his film version of the complex novel. From a book of 560 pages, he had taken only the last ninety or so for the screenplay. What is not seen in the movie, but forms the bulk of the book, is the marriage of Adam Trask to a wayward beauty who is also having an affair with his brother, Charles. She visits Charles on her wedding night after slipping her new husband a sleeping powder and subsequently gives birth to twins, the implication being that they have been fathered separately, one by each brother. The film begins at the point where the boys, Aaron and Cal, are young men. The former is in his father's mould, the latter rebels against his father's authoritarian, Bible-punching ways. Adam has told them that their mother is dead, but in truth she had left him when the children were born and now Cal discovers her on the other side of the tracks, running a whorehouse.

Paul Osborn, who was writing the screenplay of *East of Eden*, was aware of Kazan's dilemma over the casting of the brothers and told him about Jimmy Dean, whom he too had seen in rehearsals for *The Immoralist*. Kazan was not enthusiastic, but he called Dean to his office. He remembered that first meeting well:

> When I walked in, he was slouched at the end of a leather sofa in the waiting room, a heap of twisted legs and denim rags, looking resentful for no particular reason. I didn't like the expression on his face, so I kept him waiting. I wanted to see how he would react. I out-toughed him, because when I called him into my office he dropped the belligerent pose. . . . we tried to talk, but conversation was not his gift . . . so we sat looking at each other.

Dean eventually asked Kazan if he would like a ride on the back of his motorbike. Kazan accepted, and at the end of it he called Osborn and agreed that Dean was Cal Trask. He sent Jimmy to see Steinbeck, who said he sure as hell was.

Richard Davalos was cast as his brother Aaron and Julie Harris as the girl in between. Raymond Massey had already been signed to play the boys' father. On 15 February they headed west for filming, which was to start in May and Kazan himself collected Dean from his apartment to escort him from New York to Los Angeles. As the limousine stopped outside, Jimmy came out carrying two parcels wrapped in brown paper and tied up with odd pieces of string – two parcels containing his worldly possessions. He looked, as Kazan described him, like an immigrant who had just arrived in poverty from Europe. During the drive to the airport, Dean confided that he had never been on an aeroplane before and for most of the way to California he sat with his face at the window.

* * * * *

In that spring of 1954, as Dean headed for Hollywood, Monty Clift was doing the reverse, looking back to Broadway for his next project. During his long spell of inactivity from films, he had been working with Mira Rostova and Kevin McCarthy on an enterprising venture: a new translation and adaptation of Chekhov's *The Seagull*, which had last been produced on Broadway just before the war. Their fellow actors in New York were full of admiration; the fact that they were writing and producing their own play in such difficult times took courage. There were many willing helpers. Roddy McDowall, although not in the eventual cast, and Bobby Lewis from the Actors Studio were assisting in preliminary readings and coaching the cast, which included Clift himself, Sam Jaffe, Maureen Stapleton, Judith Evans, Mira and Kevin.

All was not well, however. Thornton Wilder read the script and suggested some alterations, but rehearsals were uneven and in desperation Monty telephoned Arthur Miller to ask him for some direction and advice. Thornton Wilder came into rehearsal and sat there without opening his mouth. Finally, Miller turned to him and said, 'Don't you have anything to say at all?'

Wilder pondered, then in his timid staccato voice said, 'I suggest . . . you don't all just stand there like statues. And I must warn you, darlings, that when the audience can't hear you then they tend to get rather bored.'

On opening night the front stalls were crowded with Monty's friends: Marlon Brando, Richard Harris, Marlene Dietrich, Harry Belafonte, Lee Strasberg and many others. Reviews varied; Clift, Stapleton and Evans received good notices but Mira was universally criticised and Kevin McCarthy gained little comfort either. The play survived its season to the end of July, but Monty was bitterly disappointed. It was not the great success he had hoped for and, though he did not know it then, it would be his last appearance on Broadway.

He took off almost immediately to a hideaway in Maine, where he had rented a holiday cottage close to Dr Silverberg for two weeks, and, with nothing to occupy his mind, he began drinking heavily again. When the owners of the cottage came to see him off at the end of his stay, they found the house a wreck, furniture smashed, uneaten food rotting all over the place, and Monty lying in the living room, naked and surrounded by bottles.

* * * * *

Rock Hudson, meanwhile, was walking on air. With the release of *Magnificent Obsession* he had soared to third place in a national magazine poll of male stars. Suddenly he was Universal's hottest property. The film was their biggest box-office success for two years. Henry Willson moved quickly to get his protégé his own monogrammed dressing room, a complete wardrobe of clothes and a salary increase. The publicity machine began working overtime, churning out fanciful stories about their new macho-man.

Willson was worried, however, about Hudson's private life and it was his constant fear that Rock would become the subject of salacious reporting. He had visions of headlines announcing the 'Sinister Double Life of Top Hollywood Star' – and he had good reason to be concerned. Reporters from the scourge of Hollywood, a scandal sheet entitled *Confidential*, were already nosing around.

In 1954 *Confidential* was reaching its peak. It was the worst kind of gossip newspaper, running sensational stories about the rich and famous. The mere mention of its name could send shivers down the spine of any star. Its publisher, Robert Harrison, had started the paper in 1952 when he saw how riveted television audiences were by Senator Kefauver's crime investigations, which highlighted reports on vice, prostitution and gambling rackets. Under the banner motto of 'WE TELL THE FACTS AND NAME THE NAMES', *Confidential* lured its readers with headlines like: 'ERROL FLYNN AND HIS TWO WAY MIRRORS'; 'THE BEST PUMPER IN HOLLYWOOD? M-M-M MARILYN M-M MONROE'; 'DAN DAILEY IN DRAG'; 'ROBERT WAGNER A FLAT TIRE IN A BOUDOIR'; and so on. It was a magazine that everyone hated, but everyone read, usually out of fear of finding themselves in it. As it became more successful, Harrison began paying out large cash inducements for exclusives. Some journalists on respectable newspapers, and even some film stars or studio people, would ring him anonymously with a tip-off, often out of spite. Rock was a current target.

There were a few people around who resented Hudson's success, helped as it had been by at least one influential Universal man with more than Rock's career at heart. The very presence of his lover Jack was also becoming an embarrassment to Universal and whispered innuendo about their relationship was heightened by Jack's phone calls to the studio asking when Rock was coming home. It was no coincidence that soon after the première of *Magnificent Obsession* Rock was whisked out of the country to begin three months' location work in Europe for his next film, *Captain Lightfoot*, in which he was to get star billing alongside Barbara Rush.

While Rock was away, Willson had trouble with Jack. He asked his secretary, Phyllis Gates, to keep an eye on him after he had been spotted driving around in the star's easily recognisable yellow convertible. Phyllis took Jack off to Kansas to try to keep him out of sight, but the situation became increasingly difficult for her. Finally Willson called Rock and told him, 'We've got to get rid of this guy. He's going to blow it for you. The studio is getting very jumpy.'

Hudson phoned Jack and there was a row. He called Willson back: 'Do it, Henry. Get rid of the son of a bitch.'

Willson, whom Rock trusted to handle every dollar he earned, cancelled the weekly cash payments he was making to Jack on Rock's behalf, then telephoned him and said, 'It's all over between you. You'd better get out of town.' There were other implied threats that encouraged Jack to hand in his keys to Rock's house and car, and by the time Hudson returned from filming, Jack had disappeared and Willson had removed every trace of him from the house. It was as if he had never existed.

At the *Confidential* offices in New York, Harrison told his ferrets: 'Keep on that story.' It would all blow up again in a sensational manner.

* * * * * *

James Dean, too, was beginning to indulge himself in some of Hollywood's delights. He had bought himself a palomino pony, which he kept for a while in a cowboy corral on the Warners studio lot. The animal was eventually sent off to a farm in San Fernando Valley because Dean was spending too much time riding it and Kazan was now pressing hard for work on *East of Eden* to start.

The publicity people began to crowd Dean, making up stories about the boy from Fairmount, Indiana, who was really a genius actor discovered by Kazan in the outback. Jimmy's defences went up and he withdrew his co-operation with the machine; now he became the mystery boy who just wanted to be alone. When reporters pressed him he would say, 'I came here to act, not to please newspapers,' and his misery was apparent when he wrote to one of his friends back in New York, 'I don't like it here . . . wow am I fucked up!'

He did discover one familiar face. In the next studio Paul Newman was doing some retakes for the ill-starred *Silver Chalice*; Dean wandered in now and again, and met some of the young actresses Newman was working with. One was Natalie Wood, soon to be his own co-star; another was Pier Angeli, by whom he was smitten instantly.

It was part of Kazan's strategy to keep Dean moody and miserable; realism is the key to the kind of performance the director was looking for, and he fanned any spark that could engender the emotions he required at a particular moment. If, on the other hand, he felt that Dean was getting too tense through his attention to Stanislavski's Method, Kazan would take him off the lot and get him drunk. Now he allowed Dean's interest in Pier Angeli to smoulder, because he believed it would provide a further complication for his new boy to brood over.

Since meeting Pier, Jimmy had sought every opportunity to be in her company. They had to go out secretly because Pier's mother was not keen on Dean; nor would the studio wish her to become engrossed in romance at this point of her career: she already had the makings of becoming a big star and nothing should interfere with that. Born Anna Maria Pierangeli in 1932 in Sardinia, she had made her first film, *Tomorrow Is Too Late*, in her native Italy in 1949, when she won the Venice International Prize for the Best Italian Actress. Fred Zinnemann brought her to Hollywood; though she spoke only broken English, he said that she had the most spiritual face he had seen since Lillian Gish and he got her a contract with MGM.

Her mother came too, and her twin sister, also an actress, was signed by 20th Century–Fox and rechristened Marisa Pavan. Pier became an overnight star in 1951 when Zinnemann cast her in *Teresa*. When Jimmy Dean discovered her, she was on loan to Warners to star in *The Silver Chalice* with Newman – it would have been with Dean himself if he had taken the part.

Kazan began to notice that Jimmy was arriving late for work, looking tired and baggy-eyed. He couldn't fathom what was happening and began spying on him, moving into a room on the lot next to the one that Dean was using as his living quarters. Kazan recalls: 'My front door opened on to his front door, and I could hear what went on through the walls. What went on was Pier Angeli, but clearly that didn't go well for Dean . . . I could hear them boffing but more often arguing.'

What Kazan did not know – and it would at least in part have explained the bags under Dean's eyes – was that his new star had become a heavy smoker of marijuana, was taking pep pills and was one step away from hard drugs.

Dean's insecurity at the start of filming added to his performance rather than detracting from it. He became extremely intense, and initial scenes with his screen brother Dick Davalos were shot after hours of rehearsals undertaken by the two actors of their own accord. Davalos commented later:

We became so much like the characters we were playing, it was frightening; working on that movie affected all of us in it because of the depths we reached in the characterisation. In my case, it took me years to get over it.

Raymond Massey, stalwart of the American stage and films, had immense difficulty in dealing with the way in which Dean worked. In moments of despair with lines that he couldn't make work, Dean would swear violently, standing there emitting a stream of the most vile words. Massey once walked off the set, declaring that he had never experienced anything like it and that he could not work with Dean: it was impossible. 'He simply couldn't stand the sight of the kid', said Kazan, 'and dreaded every day he worked with him. He complained "You never know what he's going to say or do. Make him read the lines the way they're written."'

Dean knew that Massey hated him and did not hide his own dislike for Massey. The aggravation between them grew daily – exactly as Kazan wanted. On screen, he needed to re-create the sense of a father's disapproval and a son's antagonism. He deliberately engineered them into a state of high tension. 'Anything goes when you're directing a movie,' Kazan would say. The result was clear in the finished film: the scenes between them were electrifying.

Beneath the main theme lay the rivalry between the two brothers, not just for their father's affection but also for Abra, Aaron's fiancée (played by Julie Harris), whose pity for Cal turns to love. Their unforgettable picnic scene in the bean field conveyed a subcurrent which Kazan felt was vital to the success of the picture. Julie portrayed the epitome of goodness in a play that bristled with tautness.

Off camera, she helped Dean with his lines, going through them endlessly with him and moulding her own performance to fit his – a feat which few actors found possible with Dean. Kazan said he doubted that Dean could have completed the film without her. When it was finished, they parted and never saw each other again; but those weeks with Dean left an impression, if not a scar, on Julie Harris that she will carry for the rest of her life, and one which I found her reluctant to discuss thirty years later.

Kazan, on the other hand, has often described the trauma of making *East of Eden* and one suspects that, while he has never spoken in derogatory terms of Jimmy, he would not be a subscriber to the legend of the great James Dean.

There were several scenes with which Kazan was unhappy and which he edited out of the final version. They included in particular some moments where Dean had over-emphasised connotations of sexual am-bivalence in the relationship between Cal and Aaron. The portrayal in some of these takes was, to say the least, warped – a fact which did not go unnoticed by the rest of the cast. Whether it was Kazan's fault or the result of Dean's own plunge into the depths of his soul, or both, the camera picked up previously unseen traits in his personality which were violent and self-destructive.

Undoubtedly the storyline had some bearing on his performance because so much of it ran parallel to his own life: a mother lost in childhood, rejection by his father, a rebellious streak; even his own maternal grandfather had been named Cal. Dean himself later recognised the similarities, telling an interviewer, 'To me, acting is the most logical way for people's neuroses to manifest themselves in the great need we have to express ourselves.'

Kazan used it all. The result was a movie which was neither sensational nor considered by his peers to be among his best; but the youth of the mid-fifties identified with it immediately. To them the crescendo of the film was a statement: Cal takes his brother to meet his mother in the whorehouse; Aaron drunkenly goes off to enlist for war service, violently castigating his father for his lifetime of living a lie; rejected by his favourite son, Adam collapses from a heart attack into the arms of Cal, with whom he is reunited; finally, we see Cal sitting in a darkened room at the bottom of Adam's bed, happy to tend him with loving care. The rebel has become a kind of hero.

To millions of young people lifting their faces to the screen in cinemas around the world, that is what James Dean was about to become. In life, and in death.

Chapter Seven

The Rebels

It seems hardly feasible, looking back through the list of big names available to the major studios in the fifties, that there weren't enough stars in Hollywood. The years had taken their toll, however, and the talents of Gable, Bogart, Flynn, Cooper, Stewart, Turner, Garland, de Havilland, Garson, Swanson and Bergman had been used and abused; even their charisma could not sustain their interest for ever. A small battalion of new stars were on their way, but they had not achieved that sort of fame yet.

The *New York Times* highlighted the problem facing the casting people in an article in August 1954 when it recorded:

> The reality is that time has caught up with most of the front-line stars; middle-age paunches, disappearing or greying hair, sagging facial tissues have blunted the romantic appeal of too many top-rated stars. . . . the rapport between stars in their forties and fifties and the broad mass of film audiences, which ranges from fifteen to twenty-five, isn't as close as it should be.

The same criticism could be levelled at the type of scripts being considered for major movies – and nowhere was that crisis more acute than at the once great MGM, where, as Elizabeth Taylor described it, the 'death rattle' seemed never ending.

Pandro Berman had already seen that. One of Metro's more visionary producers, he had brought cinema-goers the light relief of Fred Astaire and Ginger Rogers in the thirties, then Elizabeth Taylor in *National Velvet* when child stars were in vogue. Now he had his eyes on the teen generation, the children of Eisenhower's comfortable fifties.

Berman had bought Evan Hunter's novel *The Blackboard Jungle*, which he saw as a statement of the day. He had to be cautious with the script: the socially sensitive plot went against MGM's current 'soft' policy. In it, a brave young teacher, played by Glenn Ford, faces a classroom full of young thugs who call him 'Daddy-O', ignore his teachings, threaten his wife and rape a woman colleague. The script was

quick to point out that this was not the state of American schools in
general, and that the vast mass of youth was polite and conforming and
did not form gangs. But in truth, by 1955 when the film appeared, the
daring scenes of classroom violence were already becoming commonplace, especially in urban schools neglected by the Affluent Society, first
in America and somewhat later in Britain.

Brando had, to some extent, stamped his style on the image of rebellious youth in *The Wild One*. Arriving leather-clad on a motorcycle,
determined to disrupt life in a quiet American town, he is asked, 'What
are you rebelling against?' and growls back, 'Whadda ya got?' Brando,
who looked a tough street-fighter, was already thirty when the film was
released, and though a thousand other actors and a few million young
men would take up his lurching, slovenly, snarling attitude, his was a
passing, personal influence, which was hardly picked up at all in Britain.

Clift, in his more sensitive and subtle approach, was another influence,
but largely on other actors, who mimicked him. Young people, and girls
especially, saw him as representing a classier image, more in line with
the less forceful youth of America's middle-classes. Their time would
come on the campuses in the sixties.

Clift and Brando gave the disorientated youth in search of idols a
whole new repertoire of sayings, postures, stances and gestures, but now
the door was wide open for a new voice and a new style.

In *East of Eden* and later in *Rebel Without a Cause*, James Dean
played characters who were crying out for parental love. Both films were
statements about parental attitudes and their consequences, rather than
about youth rebellion as such. Dean was not, in these roles, rebellious;
the characters he played were merely caught up in situations which went
against the social grain. In fact, he was more of a rebel in real life than
the characters he played in his first two films, yet in them he managed
to crystallise a vague, ill-defined mood of youth and turn it into a more
positive force.

When *East of Eden* was released in 1955, Dean was hailed as the kind
of new talent the film industry badly needed – an actor in touch with his
audience. It must be said, though, that many established actors who
came to know him neither applauded his work nor liked him as a person.
That never worried Jimmy, whose antagonism towards the Hollywood
gloss grew as each week passed.

It did, however, provide him with the means to acquire some of the
trappings and status of a new star. In addition to the palomino pony, he
bought a new heavy motorcycle, on which he could be seen roaring around
the studio lot or riding off at high speed into the desert, until Kazan warned
him that scarred or one-legged movie stars have limited appeal to casting

Starting out: Elizabeth Taylor in 1944, aged twelve. She had already appeared in four films, including *Lassie Come Home*. The one that made her a child star – *National Velvet* – was released that year. *(Metro-Goldwyn-Mayer)*

(Below) Natalie Wood, younger than Elizabeth but heading for the same dizzy heights, was already adopting the classic pose when she sat for publicity stills for her second film, *Tomorrow Is Forever*, shot in 1945.

(Below right) Rock Hudson at eighteen, when he joined the Navy for war service. Since childhood he had been fascinated by the movies and was soon hanging around the gates of Hollywood studios, making himself 'available for discovery'. *(Universal International)*

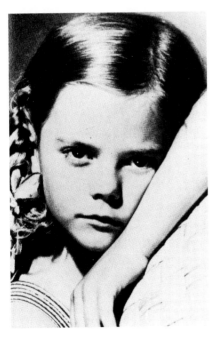

(Below and right) Montgomery Clift was a major star on Broadway and had made four films by the time he first met Elizabeth Taylor, when George Stevens cast them together for *A Place in the Sun*, released in 1951. It was here that their lifelong and devoted friendship began. *(Paramount Pictures)*

(Left) James Dean in 1947: a typical all-American boy who had seldom ventured from the town of Fairmount, Indiana. He was a quiet, athletic boy, who enjoyed baseball and made the team; but the call of the theatre was already strong.

(Above right) By 1951 Rock Hudson was already being cast as the lonely bachelor. He was photographed at his home, and the reporters were told, 'I'm too busy to think of marriage ... and anyway, I'm used to getting along on my own.' (*Universal International*)

(Above) The press, meantime, was beginning to clamour for any photograph of Elizabeth. Here she was required to do nothing but look pretty.

(Right) Opportunity came for James Dean in 1954 when Elia Kazan cast him for *East of Eden*, for which he had to dispose of his new city image and re-assume the appearance of a country boy. (*Warner–Pathé*)

(*Above*) Marriage number one for Elizabeth Taylor. The bridegroom is Conrad Nicholson Hilton, Jr, son of the hotel tycoon, and the wedding became the media event of the year. The sequel was just as big a story: when the honeymoon was over, so was the marriage. (*Syndications International*)

Julie Harris became James Dean's first screen love in *East of Eden*. Cool and collected, she helped the newcomer, tense with the pressures of Method acting, through his first major role. According to director Kazan, he might not have got through it without her. (*Warner–Pathé*)

Elizabeth Taylor's menagerie became legend; several pets were usually in tow wherever she went in the world. This off-duty moment was captured (or posed?) on the set of *The Girl Who Had Everything* – which, of course, is exactly what Elizabeth became. *(Metro-Goldwyn-Mayer)*

In four years Rock Hudson had climbed to No. 8 in the league of male box-office stars, although his roles had been lightweight. The breakthrough came with his first major dramatic performance, in *Magnificent Obsession*, released in 1954. Photographers once again found him relaxing at home alone … *(Universal International)*

Montgomery Clift had become one of the most sought-after actors in America, but he always refused to sign with one particular studio, preferring to remain in control of his own destiny. When *From Here to Eternity* was being cast, he was desperate to do it – so was his singing idol Frank Sinatra, who was going through a lean spell. Clift got his role, and was instrumental in getting Frank in the cast too. *(Columbia Pictures)*

Divorce and remarriage (to actor Michael Wilding, almost twice her age) followed quickly for Elizabeth – and so did her first child, Michael Howard Wilding, born 6 January 1953. *(Syndications International)*

Rebel Without a Cause became the focal point of youth protest, particularly after James Dean's death. Dean's principal co-stars, Sal Mineo and Natalie Wood, were also among his closest friends for the remaining months of his life. *(Warner Bros)*

A dramatic moment in *Rebel Without a Cause*: after the 'chicken run', which Dean survives but in which his rival is killed as his car plunges over the cliff. The line spoken by Dean, 'A boy was killed . . .' became a poignant focus for the critics when the film was previewed soon after Dean's own fatal car crash. *(Warner Bros)*

In *All That Heaven Allows,* Rock Hudson was cast as the outdoor he-man for a follow-up role to *Magnificent Obsession.* The film was panned, but Rock's recent acclaim made it a success at the box office (*Universal International*)

Natalie Wood was at last losing the child star image that her mother had protected for so long. After her success in *Rebel Without a Cause* she became the sweetheart of a million college boys, and got the star trappings to match. (*Warner Bros*)

Natalie had become the target of the fan magazines, and they all wanted to know the name of her current boyfriend. She obliged by giving the world a peek at the photographs around her dressing-room mirror, where James Dean clearly took pride of place. (*Warner Bros*)

Dean himself was widely photographed, and was about to age considerably as he prepared for his role in *Giant*.

As director George Stevens began casting for *Giant*, Elizabeth Taylor was determined to secure the lead. Only Grace Kelly provided real competition, but she was required elsewhere and Elizabeth got the part. *(Warner Bros)*

Rock Hudson also secured his role in *Giant*, but in the background his agent Henry Willson was laying plans to head off gossip about Rock's bachelorhood, and it was no coincidence that he was spotted having a cosy tête-à-tête with Willson's secretary Phyllis Gates. *(Jay Scott)*

(*Above*) A classic moment from *Giant*: Dean with Taylor, whom, in the movie, he secretly loved. There were sparks of emotion off screen as well. 'We were leery of each other to start with,' said Elizabeth, 'but gradually we became friends.' (*Warner Bros*)

Although he was dating Natalie Wood, James Dean never forgot his first love in Hollywood, Italian actress Pier Angeli. He wanted to marry her, but her mother insisted she marry singer Vic Damone. She did, and had a child, but the marriage was soon in trouble and Pier for ever regretted not marrying Dean. (*Warner Bros*)

Natalie Wood and Nick Adams were often together, and Adams remained a close friend of Natalie and her future husband Robert Wagner for many years. After James Dean's death, George Stevens used Adams to dub over some of Dean's lines in the final scenes of *Giant*. *(Syndications International)*

(Below) As he neared the end of filming *Giant*, James Dean talked constantly about racing his new Porsche, which he named Little Bastard. Warners banned him from driving it around the studio lot. He left for the race-track at Salinas the day after he finished shooting, but never completed the journey.

Elizabeth Taylor was reunited with her beloved Montgomery Clift for *Raintree County;* they are captured here in rehearsal. Filming was brought to a halt when Clift was badly injured in a car crash while returning from a dinner party at Elizabeth's home. *(Metro-Goldwyn-Mayer)*

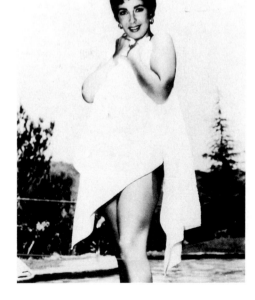

By 1955 Elizabeth had become the world's most photographed movie star and it was sometimes with reluctance that she posed for studio releases such as this.

Rock Hudson surprised the world, and shocked his millions of women fans, when on 9 November 1955 he secretly married Phyllis Gates. Years later, rumours began that it was an arranged marriage, with Phyllis the innocent party in an intricate cover-up to prevent a scandal sheet from running a story which would do more than hint at the truth of Hudson's private life. Henry Willson fixed the ceremony, ordered the cake and even booked the honeymoon. Phyllis was swept along by the glamour of it all, and at the time truly believed Hudson was in love with her. (*Universal International*)

The wedding was conducted out of sight of the media. *Left to right:* Hudson's childhood friend Jim Matteoni and his wife Gloria; the Reverend Thorpe, who married them; the happy couple; Patricia Devlin, Phyllis's best friend; and Henry Willson. (*Universal International*)

(Above) Henry Willson was anxious that his number one client should be portrayed in blissful matrimony, and Rock and Phyllis gladly co-operated with photographers. This picture was released by the studio with a caption which carefully explained that Rock had always insisted he would never marry before he was thirty. (Universal International)

In the year following James Dean's death, and in the wake of her success in *Rebel Without a Cause*, Natalie Wood was seen on the arms of many eligible young men. One brief romantic encounter was with Elvis Presley, whom she found polite, charming and virile. But she didn't get on with his mother. (Bob Williams)

Warner Brothers had the hottest teenage star of the era on their hands, and they hadn't quite realised it. They cast Natalie for some low-key productions – but someone must have spotted the potential . . . This publicity still was released to coincide with her appearance with John Wayne in *The Searchers*, but bore no resemblance to the youthful part she was assigned in the film itself. *(Bert Six, Warner Brothers)*

directors. He then bought a red 1953 MG, which pleased the studio – until they saw how fast he was driving it. He had already shown a lust for motor-racing, which had its roots in a visit to the Indianapolis 500 with the Reverend DeWeerd, and he started going to tracks in the free time he wasn't spending with Pier Angeli. In Hollywood itself, he had become a familiar sight at Googie's, a coffee-joint on Sunset Boulevard much frequented by the bohemian set (anyone who was a bit eccentric in dress or behaviour was still described as bohemian).

One of the things that upset Dean most in the surge of newspaper and magazine articles about him was the constant reference to Brando, comparing him in looks and style, voice and moods. Brando was none too pleased either, and said, 'The kid is wearing my last year's clothes and using my last year's talent.' Dean himself knew that there was a strong basis for the comparisons but, although he hero-worshipped Brando and Clift, he was now anxious to be seen as a fine actor in his own right, not merely as their shadow. He told Dennis Hopper, with whom he worked on *Rebel Without a Cause* and *Giant*:

Y'know, I've got to make it, because in this hand I'm holding Marlon Brando, saying Fuck you! and in this hand I'm holding Monty Clift saying Please forgive me! So it goes: Fuck you! Please Forgive Me! and somewhere in the middle is James Dean.

In an interview for *New Yorker*, Brando told Truman Capote:

He was always trying to get close to me. He used to call up asking for me and I'd listen on my answering service but I never spoke to him. When I finally met Dean it was at a party and he was throwing himself around like a madman and I asked him did he know he was sick and needed help?

By now, Dean's moods ranged from secretive and withdrawn to the loud, show-stopping effervescence described by Brando. With a few glasses of wine inside him, or a puff of marijuana, he could quickly take on a strange, violent tone. Kenneth Anger, in the original version of *Hollywood Babylon* published in Paris in 1959, described some of his actions as weird, giving as an example Dean's habit of stubbing out cigarettes on himself, which Anger said earned him the title of Human Ashtray. He was also seen slapping Pier Angeli in these drunken moments.

* * * * *

Dean's behaviour showed many similarities to Monty Clift's excesses, though Monty was never a violent man. Many of his closer friends, however, were beginning to give him a wide berth. Kevin and Augusta McCarthy asked him not to call again after he blacked out and fell to the floor while holding their youngest child. McCarthy also came to the conclusion that being associated with Clift was having a damaging effect on his own career. To be mentioned in the same breath as Monty these days usually meant that you were being spoken of in the latest tale of unpleasantness.

Clift's dinner parties were a sight to behold. He was adored by the New York smart set, who did not see him with the same frequency as his intimates (the small circle whom Arthur Miller referred to as Monty's 'self-appointed guardians') did and were thus able to tolerate his eccentric behaviour. 'That's Monty,' they would say. Writer Robert Thom explained, 'Even when his behaviour was abominable and his future unthinkable, he meant something to all of us.' But there was a lot to put up with; Monty could be as cruel as he could be generous. Thom recalled:

> One night the woman I was with was a young actress, well known for her beauty, who had had one enormous hit on Broadway but her career was in trouble. As we were leaving, Monty took her face in his two hands (what strange unco-ordinated hands they were) and, tears in his eyes as if he were filled with pity like a doctor recognising some incurable disease, said, 'I don't understand it . . . how can you act when you don't have any feelings?' It was some time before I saw Monty again after that and I told him my exact feelings in words that are unprintable. He apologised over and over again. . . .

The dinner parties, and there were many during the long period of inactivity after *From Here to Eternity*, started to follow a set pattern. Robert LaGuardia described a typical evening at Monty's place:

> Monty would greet his guests while his cook would prepare dinner. He might show some of the newer guests around the duplex, of which he was immensely proud. It was difficult to tell how much liquor Monty had already consumed but he would still seem sober. Then he would go to the bathroom and come back much more wobbly than before. Suddenly, he would start to slur his words and would say something about having to put a new record on. He would get up and walk across the room . . . and fall flat on his face. Heads turned in his direction . . . no one would budge. The regulars knew he wanted to be left where he was. The conversation would continue as if nothing had happened. After half an hour or so, Monty would get up off the floor and head up to his sealed-off, hell-black bedroom . . . the dinner

guests would simply continue on their own. There were variations on the basic theme. He might not keel over at all. He might make it back to the table and begin to play around with his food or the food on the plates of others, tearing at it or throwing it around. Or he might have drunk so much that he was already asleep in his coffin by the time the guests arrived, in which case one of the regulars would conduct the evening without him.

Clift's agents, meanwhile, were at their wits' end trying to get him interested in work. In a five-year period after filming *From Here to Eternity* in 1953, he was to make only one film – *Raintree County* in 1956; he rejected 143 other offers of employment in Hollywood, which included *Friendly Persuasion* (taken by Gary Cooper), *On the Waterfront* (Brando), *Cat On a Hot Tin Roof* (Paul Newman), *Not As a Stranger* (Robert Mitchum), *Moby Dick* (Gregory Peck) and many more top-drawer films.

* * * * *

James Dean, on the other hand, took no chances. In the autumn of 1954, before *East of Eden* was released, he was still a relatively unknown quantity in Hollywood and when his agents called with more television work of a fairly mundane nature, he accepted, although the price for his services had increased dramatically.

He had returned briefly to New York when filming on *Eden* finished. Now, at last, he had something big to talk about, and one of the first questions his old friends asked was: 'What's going on between you and Pier Angeli?' Not the least ardent questioner was actress Barbara Glenn, who had been 'Jimmy's girl' when he left for Hollywood and with whom he had kept up a steady correspondence, insisting that he was 'still a Hollywood virgin'.

Before he left California, the gossips were already linking Dean and Miss Angeli; there was even talk of an engagement and one columnist suggested that Jimmy was studying Catholicism to placate Pier's mother when the time came for him to ask for her daughter's hand.

Mrs Pierangeli was a widow and a strict mother who kept a close eye on her daughter's choice of boyfriends. She had already made it clear that she did not favour the untidy, moody Mr Dean. Her little Pier deserved better. She was, after all, a bigger star than Dean, with five pictures to her credit, a salary of $1000 a week, a large house in the Valley and an expensive English car.

Dean was unmoved by Mrs Pierangeli's feelings, although he did start to wear a suit when he came to call. Secretly, the relationship grew stronger and once they sneaked away for private relaxation in a cottage on the Los Angeles coast. Pier described it in an interview:

We were very much in love, two kids but sensible enough to know our own minds. Jimmy really got himself together in those days we had alone. We'd just talk and talk about what we were going to do, and lay on the beach in each other's arms and we just wanted to be together always.

By the time he was ready to leave for New York, they were talking of marriage, or at least an engagement upon his return. They reckoned without the combined forces of Mrs Pierangeli and MGM, who were united in their desire to separate them. The studio clearly did not see Dean as the perfect match for their glamorous young star and they feared that the association would affect her image. Mrs Pierangeli, meanwhile, ruled him out not simply because he was not a Catholic; more importantly, Dean had acquired a bad reputation for beating up his girlfriends when he was drunk, and Pier had already been a victim of his rages.

While he was away, Mrs Pierangeli brought matters to a head and pushed her daughter at singer Vic Damone, who had also been dating her, though lately with less frequency than Dean. As Pier acknowledged later, she allowed herself to be persuaded to drop Jimmy and she regretted it for the rest of her life. Before Dean returned from the east coast, Pier had become engaged to Damone. When he heard about it, Dean, still in New York, was unapproachable for days. The news came as a complete shock to him.

There was no turning back for Pier. The wedding had been fixed for two weeks hence, and Mrs Pierangeli wanted her family to have nothing more to do with James Dean. Pier accepted the situation, but the marriage was never a success. Some years later, after divorce and very bitter public court battles over the custody of her son, she admitted: 'Nobody knows what unhappiness I suffered by agreeing to marry Vic Damone. I only did it to please my mother; she was adamant that she would not have Jimmy as her son-in-law. But Jimmy was the only man I ever loved.'

Dean was back in Hollywood in time for the wedding. He was not invited, of course, but when the wedding party left St Timothy's Catholic Church to begin the journey to a star-studded wedding breakfast, they were met by the loud roaring of a motorcycle engine. Clad in black leather, Dean sat astride his bike right across the road from the entrance to St Timothy's, revving his engine and scowling a hatred so intense that it must have scorched the back of Vic Damone's head.

Her marriage, however, did not stop Pier seeing Jimmy on occasions, as writer Joe Hyams recalled in his book, *Mislaid in Hollywood*. Hyams described how, some months later, as he was driving up to Dean's house, Pier Angeli sped past in the opposite direction. Her face looked tear-stained and inside he found Jimmy equally distraught. Hyams continued:

> ... I asked if there was anything I could do. He [Dean] clenched his fist over and over again. 'It's already done,' he said in a choked voice. 'Pier's going to have a baby.' I was stunned by the news. I knew he had seen her from time to time since the wedding. I thought I knew what was on Jimmy's mind, that perhaps it was his baby – and there she was married to another man. I stood there at a loss, not knowing what to say. Then Jimmy started to cry. . . .

This was probably the last time Dean ever saw Pier; but her memories of him remained with her for the rest of her own short life.

* * * * *

It was no consolation to him at the time, but Jimmy was about to meet another young woman who would become an important part of the remaining months of his life. Natalie Wood was only just sixteen in the autumn of 1954. For eleven years she had been working at the rate of two films a year and she had become the nation's most famous young face. However, work had slowed up in the past twelve months and, for the first time in her life, she could spend weeks waiting for the studio to call.

In Hollywood, if you lingered too long in the powder room, you could be forgotten by the time you came out and now Natalie found herself having to look elsewhere, to television, for work. She signed with Revue Productions to appear in a series called *Pride of the Family*, playing the daughter of Fay Wray at $400 an episode. Then she found herself cast alongside James Dean in a television play called *I Am a Fool*, co-starring Eddie Albert. It was in this production that director Nick Ray saw them working together just before he began casting for *Rebel Without a Cause*.

Since Pier Angeli's marriage, Jimmy had been seen around town with various actresses, like Ursula Andress (his most regular date), Leslie Caron, and a strange television comedienne called Vampira (her real name was Maila Nurmi), who bore a remarkable resemblance to Count Dracula. (When Hedda Hopper linked her romantically with Dean, he responded, 'I don't date cartoons.') There were other enforced dates, like Terry Moore, arranged by the studio to provide an attraction on

Dean's arm at parties and functions when they thought it would be good publicity.

Natalie had vivid recollections of their first meeting:

We had been called to rehearsal for the television play *I Am a Fool* and, of course, Jimmy was late. We all sat around for ages waiting, and eventually we started without him: someone else began reading his lines. Then, we heard the roar of a motorbike engine and suddenly there was a sound behind us, and a window opened and in climbed Jimmy, exactly one hour late. What an entrance!

He was wearing an old pair of trousers with a big hole in the knee, hornrimmed spectacles, and his hair was standing on end; his sports shirt was dirty and stained, and his tennis shoes hadn't been white for a long time. He jumped off the windowledge on to a table, grabbed a script and started reading. Natalie went on:

I just couldn't take my eyes off of him, but in a peculiar way I was frightened of him, particularly when we started to do the rehearsals. He got up to all kinds of tricks; his words were slow and laborious and sometimes you could hardly hear him at all. I never ever worked with anyone quite like him. When we broke for lunch I was walking outside on my own when I heard these footsteps padding up behind me. It was Jimmy and he just said, 'Hi, where shall we go for lunch?' Just like that, as if we'd been friends for years. After that we started dating and then, suddenly we were seeing each other every night. It was always very casual. We'd go out on his motorbike, or in his sports car, drive for a while, and talk, or go for a hamburger. We became inseparable, even before we knew we were going to make *Rebel*, although that really sort of brought us together in a closer respect.

Their work together on the television play was a brief interlude that gave them a chance to study each other's techniques, which proved valuable – for Natalie at least – when Nick Ray signed them both for *Rebel Without a Cause*.

Filming on *Rebel* was not due to start until the following spring, and in November Natalie was loaned out by Warners to star with Rock Hudson and Anne Baxter in Universal's production of *One Desire*. This was the film that finally brought home to her mother that her little girl, child star and provider for the Gurdin family, had grown up. Natalie recalled the moment of her own realisation:

It was Rock Hudson who did it. In the final scenes, when I was being dressed in tight-fitting clothes, I came out of the wardrobe a grown-up young lady. Rock gave me a wolf whistle and said, 'From now on I refuse to call you a kid.' I guess I always had a soft spot for Rock after that, because he opened the door to the adult world.

It was a world that her mother had long dreaded. She had to accept her daughter's freedom – not just from the role of child actress but also in her personal life. Marie began to devote more of her time to her younger daughter, Lana, who she thought could step into Natalie's shoes; she began bringing Lana to the studio, so that she could be seen around and might catch the eye of a director.

At the same time she began to look for an 'adult' agent for Natalie. During the making of *One Desire* she met Henry Willson and, flattered by his attentions to her daughters, she was persuaded by his charm and promises of a great future to let him take over as Natalie's agent.

*   *   *   *   *

Willson still regarded Rock Hudson as his prime meal-ticket and the provider of substantial wealth in the coming years. Universal were already looking at a five-picture deal that would earn Hudson more money than he had ever dreamed possible.

His return to work after the trip abroad to make *Captain Lightfoot* was marked by a flurry of gossip-column stories about him, some of the publicity having been inspired by rumours of his activities in Europe, where he had been joined by Willson. It had not gone unnoticed by the British and continental press that he found pleasure in male companionship; in Hollywood, meanwhile, Louella Parsons was asking in her column: 'WILL ROCK PUT HIS CAREER AHEAD OF MATRIMONY?', and inference about his homosexuality was being stretched almost to libellous proportions. Willson was also worried sick by the continued interest *Confidential* was taking in Rock's single status.

It all came to a head when Jack, his cast-off lover, was offered $10,000 by *Confidential* to tell all. A panic-stricken consultation between Willson and the studio somehow squashed it; the story never appeared and Jack never got his payment – at least not from *Confidential*. Years afterwards, speculation over exactly how the story was killed seemed to point to Willson's having eliminated the threat of Rock's exposure by risking the name of another of his clients, Rory Calhoun, whose reputation Willson was apparently prepared to sacrifice to save the career of his number one star.

Certainly *Confidential* later ran a story about Calhoun, alleging a past misdemeanour. It also seems more than coincidental that, around this time, Willson was urging Hudson into some public liaison with a person of the opposite sex. The girl should be a homely sort who would not damage his career, rather than a glamorous name. Arranged marriages were certainly not unknown in Hollywood, and Willson's choice was his own secretary and personal assistant, Phyllis Gates. Willson knew he could trust her and believed she was naive enough to be manipulated into a marriage. Rock never admitted that he and Willson plotted marriage, but, in retrospect, the facts that emerged speak for themselves.

Towards the end of 1954, Willson set the scene and hoped that Cupid would do the rest. When Phyllis accepted his invitation to dinner at the elegant Hollywood restaurant, Frascati's, she was surprised to find Rock Hudson present too. There was no immediate spark of a lasting relationship, but a couple of weeks later Phyllis got a call from Rock and they began seeing each other regularly. And could there possibly have been the hand of Henry Willson behind a gossip item in the *Hollywood Reporter*, revealing a cosy tête-à-tête between Rock and his agent's secretary? Phyllis said many years later that she was completely unaware that Rock's courtship of her was being stage-managed by her boss, but she agreed that it could have been, and that there would have been some collusion with the studio, ever anxious to protect the name of a star.

Rock was now Universal's hottest property. His worth was highlighted when MGM, bereft of Gable, who had departed after making the aptly titled film *Betrayed*, and of Tracy, who had left by 'mutual consent' when he refused to make another piece of drabness called *Tribute to a Bad Man*, offered Universal $1 million for the use of Rock in a couple of pictures they were planning for 1955. Universal refused. Rock's name was gathering such momentum that they wanted to keep the benefits for themselves.

As *Magnificent Obsession* did the rounds, he had become a top-rated box-office attraction worldwide. With his new-found wealth and importance, Rock bought the first home he had ever owned, his previous apartments having been rented. It was at the expensive end of Sunset Boulevard. 'I was a bit embarrassed about living in a $99-a-month place when interviewers asked me about my lifestyle,' he said. 'And anyway, I really felt the need for a place of my own, where I could come home nights to a winding path to the front door, and a warm and welcoming hearth.' It was a two-bedroomed house, built in the style of a Dutch farmhouse, with lots of exposed timbers, and it cost $38,000. The exterior was built with automatic gates and doors to exclude the army of fans who would give chase whenever they saw Rock leaving the studio.

Early in the new year, he took Phyllis Gates to see the house and they began to spend a lot of time together there when the purchase was completed in the early part of the year. Phyllis, however, did retain her own apartment, because Rock's intentions were not absolutely clear.

* * * * *

Moving house was in fashion. Elizabeth Taylor and Michael Wilding had been hunting for a larger abode, following their announcement that they were expecting a second child, and they went further into debt to the studio to buy a magnificent white brick and weathered-timber dwelling, high in the hills, for $150,000. The house had been designed with Elizabeth in mind by an architect friend of the family and it was everything that her image required: luxuriously appointed and dramatically surrounded by lush tropical gardens. Into this domestic paradise came Elizabeth and Michael, baby Michael and their menagerie, which had now grown to consist of four dogs, four cats and a duck, all of which had the run of the house, and her pony, King Charles, which fortunately did not. A new addition, Christopher Edward, was born by Caesarian section to coincide with his mother's birthday on 27 February 1955.

Although she had no film work to promote, all this activity meant that Elizabeth remained, as ever, a regular feature of the news pages and fan sheets. She made no secret of their extravagant spending, not just on the house itself but on their lavish gifts to each other, in which she was well matched with the free-spending Michael Wilding. Financial cramp set in, and they found themselves tied to the threshold for several months to come.

* * * * *

At about the same time, James Dean was also required to move. Jack Warner discovered that his newest star was still camping out in a small room on the lot at Warners, and insisted that he should be thrown out. Nicco Romanos, *maître d'hôtel* at Jimmy's favourite restaurant, Villa Capri, rented him his first and only home in Hollywood – a log-cabin-style house on Sutton Street in Sherman Oakes, for which he paid $250 a month plus utilities. Dean soon imprinted his own identity on the house, which consisted of one large downstairs room, with a huge stone fireplace and a white bearskin rug in front, kitchen and bathroom, plus a loft for sleeping on the first floor, reached by timber stairs. In the corner of the room were his bongos, on which he annoyed dozens of people by playing incessantly. Bullfight posters and a pair of horns hung on the walls. There was a stereo set, with speakers stacked high, from which his neighbours became well versed in Bartók; and on the television he stood the fake Oscar which had been used for Judy Garland in *A Star Is Born*, given to Dean by someone who had stolen it from the set.

In January of the new year, he headed off back to New York in the company of Dennis Stock, a young photographer he had met, who was to do a picture feature on him for *Life* magazine. They stayed for two weeks, checking Dean's old haunts and old friends. He became moody again when he discovered that his former girlfriend, Barbara Glenn, was about to get married. Watching from afar his well-publicised Hollywood dates, she had decided there was no room in his life for her. Dean cried, and said goodbye.

He and Stock took off back to Fairmount, Indiana, on what was to be his last visit home. Strange photographs came out of that trip, including Jimmy playing bongos in a pigsty and one of him lying in a funeral casket in the salesroom of the local mortician. Stock did not want to take this picture, but Dean insisted; it would later be used by those who maintained that Dean was obsessed by death.

Nicholas Ray, the director of *Rebel Without a Cause*, had also been to New York to get the feel of Dean's haunts and lifestyle. Ray, a former actor himself, was an earlier version of Dean, and had similar thoughts and moods. He also enjoyed the same kind of habits, like smoking marijuana; at Hollywood parties, where it preceded cocaine as the fashionable drug, he would be among the group of people out in the garden at nights, among the bushes, where the red end of a lighted joint glowed as it was passed around.

It was important for him to study the actor, because he had no doubt in his mind that *Rebel* would be nothing without Dean; getting to know the man he was directing was as vital as the script itself. He walked the streets where Jimmy had once hung out, looked at his old, tatty living quarters, visited the seedy hotel he first stayed in when he came to New York, had coffee at Cromwell's where he used to meet his friends. Ray explained:

I wanted to find out all about this guy. I ran around with him, and met his friends, got drunk a couple of times and we were pretty close by the time we were ready to go to work. Whatever else Jimmy was, he was a searcher, ever on the look out for some trick or other he could store up and use. I could see him soaking them up and I knew he had to play that part, because he could do it like no one else I knew.

There were plenty of examples of how Dean seemed to be exactly the person for the role Nick Ray was creating. He often came roaring into the Warners lot on his motorcycle. Ann Doran, who was to play his mother in the film, described the scene:

> He was tearing about all over the place and begged me to let him take me for a ride. So I did. Well, the little stinker had gone through the entire lot and he knew every stage that had both back and front doors open and there was a place to go through. You go in the sunshine on to a stage, black, and, though he had bad eyes, it didn't bother him. We went through every one of the open stages with me screaming bloody murder.

Not long afterwards, Warners banned Jimmy once again from riding his motorcycle around the lot.

The story Ray was building centred around the topical, tense situation of juvenile delinquency. At that time in America, special police units and social analysts were being set up to monitor and counteract the increasing number of teenagers who were straying into violence and other criminal behaviour. Ray's interpretation, not just of the problems facing society but of those facing the youth of the country as well, was based on a book about a young psychopath written during the war years by Dr Robert Lindner. It was bought by Warners, but the original film script was shelved in 1947 after Marlon Brando turned it down. Neither the book nor the original script had much to do with the adolescents of the mid-fifties, but Ray and scriptwriter Irving Schulman took it and turned it into a modern story.

At issue in *Rebel Without a Cause* is the relationship between fathers and sons, mothers and daughters, and many of the movie's scenes put contemporary parents on the rack. James Dean is Jim Stark, whose father, superbly played by Jim (Mr Magoo) Backus, fails to show his son direction; Natalie Wood is Judy, whose father says she is evil for wearing tight clothes and displaying her adolescent sexuality; Sal Mineo portrays Plato, victim of a broken marriage, whose father is never around and who seeks friendship from older boys whom he sees as substitutes for his dad. The delinquents of the picture are a gang of school bullies whom Jim Stark encounters as a new boy to the area.

Nick Ray soon discovered that his studio executives did not understand what he was trying to achieve. When he was casting for Judy, among those listed for testing was Jayne Mansfield, she of the 44-inch bust. Ray did not even bother to try her out, nor many of the other familiar young faces sent over by the Warners casting people. He tested, again and again; he talked the candidates through their parts and interviewed them to obtain their views on young people, parents, teachers, drinking and social issues.

He was half-hearted about Natalie, not sure that she was right for *Rebel*; she was perhaps just too much like the girl next door. Then a surprising turn of events convinced him. He recalled:

> I still hadn't settled on her until, late one day, I got a call from Dennis Hopper, who I had already cast as one of the gang. He said there had been an auto wreck in Laurel Canyon. He was out driving with Natalie, and now she was in hospital. I went over there straight away, and when I discovered there was no family doctor available, I sent for my own. At Natalie's bedside, she was drowsy from concussion, but she indicated weakly she had something to tell me. So I bent over and she whispered: 'Nick, when they brought me in here, do you know what the cop said? He said I was a goddam juvenile delinquent. You hear me Nick? That's what he said. Now do I get the role?' I looked down at her and said, 'Natalie, you got it.'

The final crucial role to fill was that of Jim's other friend, Plato, who had to be a mild-mannered boy, showing homosexual tendencies. There in a line-up of bruiser boys auditioning for the gang was a fresh-faced youth who stood out simply because of his looks – frailish, dark and mysterious features, one of those rare actors who could go on without make-up. Sal Mineo had made it to Hollywood from the Bronx and, when Nick Ray talked to him about his background, he knew that Sal was Plato. He had just passed his sixteenth birthday and wanted the part so badly that 'I nearly threw up when Nick talked to me'.

He had got into acting three years earlier, when a dance teacher persuaded his mother that the boy should be taken off the streets of the Bronx; he had been expelled from school and was roaming with a pack of young thugs. Since then he had changed dramatically, into a sensitive, timid young actor, and the abilities he showed at the first reading settled any remaining doubts in Nick Ray's mind. Sal became Dean's friend and lover, and the two of them were joined by Natalie Wood and Nick Adams as an inseparable foursome.

As rehearsals proceeded, Nick Ray had no illusions about whose picture this was. It was Dean's, without question. The power and improvisation of his performance lifted other actors into a state of tension from which Ray could extract quality performances. He gave Dean a free hand throughout, considering it important if the film was to touch the youth of the day. Ann Doran described working with Dean:

Jimmy was a strange boy. On the first day, Jim Backus couldn't believe it. We were watching Jimmy doing his scene and someone had said, 'Quiet, we're going to shoot now.' And they got up speed and were ready for action. Jimmy went down on the floor in the foetal position for the longest time. It seemed like half a can of film . . . and finally gave this funny little [soft whistle] and Nick said, 'Action.' Jimmy stood up and went into the scene. Well, Jim [Backus] and I got hysterical. We had never seen this method of doing things. Nick seemed to be mesmerised by Jimmy. Jimmy did most of the directing. He gave us our lines; he dominated the entire thing . . . and I think that is why in the picture you will find things that do not lock together.

Behind the scenes, Dean was emerging as a boy tortured by his own image. Ann Doran's personal experience provides a revealing insight into how he was developing and changing:

When we were up in the planetarium, shooting up there, that also took forever and ever and ever. And of course we shot at nights, all night, every night. And that's where – I guess I was an innocent babe or something – but that's the first time I had been around anyone who smoked marijuana.

Jimmy had called her in and said he wanted to talk about the scene they were doing. When she walked into the trailer he was using as a dressing room, Ann immediately noticed a sickly smell, so strong that her head began to swim, and she said, 'I'm sorry, Jimmy; I've got to go outside. There's something in here that smells funny. It's making me sick at the stomach.'

Dean replied, 'It's marijuana. What's wrong?'

Doran said, 'Oh, so that's what it is. That I will never smoke, I can tell you right now, because it would make me vomit.' And they continued the conversation, at her insistence, in the cold but fresh night air outside. For ever afterwards, Ann felt that Dean, whom she believed had a good mind, was tainted by his genius. It worried her that he was smoking marijuana; later she was to discover that he had moved on to hard drugs.

Ann had further experience of Dean's eccentricities soon after the filming of *Rebel* had ended. It was two or three in the morning, and suddenly the peaceful neighbourhood where she lived with her mother was aroused by a raucous shouting; someone was yelling his head off in her front yard. Ann threw open her bedroom window and looked down. Someone was shouting: 'Mom! Mom! It's me. Jimmy.'

She could not make out who it was. 'Who is it? Be quiet!'

'It's your son, Jimmy.'

Doran went downstairs, pulled Dean across the threshold and dragged him into the kitchen. He was, to use her description, stinking drunk. She poured coffee down him and they talked for the rest of the night. Ann said, 'He was so lonesome; he just didn't know where to go or what to do. He said he had lots of acquaintances but didn't have any close friends. There was nobody he could talk to.'

Dean was searching for a mother figure, just as Monty Clift had so often done. All his insecurities came flooding out. He talked about his career; he was worried about where he was going and where he would end up. He was worried about the picture, that they wouldn't put it together the way he wanted it. He was in limbo, wondering whether he should stay out in Hollywood or go back to New York, whether he should remain an actor or become a director.

He was that lost. We talked and talked. It was dawn; I almost went to sleep on him. But it was the start of a number of similar episodes, and every two or three months we'd be up in the middle of the night. . . . Out in the front yard: 'Mom!' . . . and we'd sit in the kitchen and talk.

Anne explained Dean's reliance on her:

He used me as a substitute for his mother [she was his screen mother in *Rebel*]. You can talk to an older person . . . and I don't think anybody who is not in the business understands the responsibility of a star. They don't realise what a heavy burden it is.

Dean was not the self-assured person everyone thought he was; he had great doubts about himself, and Doran thought a lot of the trouble came from his drug-taking. She warned him that he was pickling his brain with it and he just said, 'Well, I don't know what else to do . . .'

Chapter Eight

Giants

Even before work on *Rebel Without a Cause* was concluded in May 1955, word had got around that George Stevens was casting for *Giant* and that three of the cast were likely to be tested – Dean himself, Dennis Hopper and Sal Mineo. Based on Edna Ferber's novel, *Giant* is another story of the American Dream, the quest for wealth and power, or, as George Stevens described it, 'people in a race, which is a very American thing. It presented me with the opportunity to examine the American mind.'

He had been working on the script for three years and, with writers Fred Guiol and Ivan Moffat, had finally put together an epic screenplay. In essence, it was a giant soap opera, on screen for three hours and eighteen minutes, about a Texan ranching family, the Benedicts, with half a million acres and several thousand cattle, whose power and influence matches their holding. Jett Rink, a cow-hand with a chip on his shoulder who has been brought up on the ranch, inherits 10 acres of the Benedicts' land and strikes oil. Woven into the story are the issues of civil rights for Mexicans; a wayward daughter who falls in love with Jett, who is really in love with her mother; and the dramatic transition of Texas from cattle state to oil-led economy. At the time, it was a highly important and prestige production. Half of Hollywood wanted to be in it.

The casting caused Stevens an immense headache, as during the course of the film the characters age almost forty years. Gary Cooper, Clark Gable and William Holden all wanted to play the lead, Bick Benedict, and Stevens had virtually settled on William Holden when Henry Willson and Ross Hunter (who had produced Rock Hudson in *Magnificent Obsession*) approached him. Hunter gave Stevens a private showing of *Magnificent Obsession*, which had not yet been released. Impressed, Stevens agreed to test Rock for the part. This time Universal agreed to a loan-out arrangement with Warners; their star's rating could only be enhanced by such a big-budget production, provided he could pull it off.

Stevens knew he was taking a chance because of Rock's lack of experience in dramatic roles, and Rock himself was nervous. Stevens set about building his confidence, as Hudson described:

> George Stevens . . . well, he was like God to me. I followed him around like a puppy, and his wife, to the point where he got self-conscious. I'd make him blush. 'Don't do that!' He'd get all flustered. Here was a man who had done countless times, I felt, brilliant work. He had such a richness to him; he read everything, he digested everything . . . so that when he prepared this film, he knew everything there was to know about Texas. He had me so rich, and so bigoted, I *was* Bick Benedict before we ever shot frame one.

At their first meeting to discuss the part, Stevens asked Hudson if he would like to see the Benedict house, which was being built in sections in the studio carpentry shop. They asked Rock what colour he wanted the paintwork and he chose the paint:

> Well it was my house. It was mine from then on. Don't you see what he was doing? 'Who would you like as your leading lady? Grace Kelly or Elizabeth Taylor?' Well! He was serious. So I said, 'Elizabeth.' 'Fine. We'll get Elizabeth.' I was eighteen feet tall. Now, what isn't being said here is that they probably had Elizabeth signed . . . if I had said Grace Kelly, he would have found a way to make me think Elizabeth would be better. That was the wonderful way of his direction, of making me feel it was my idea. And I was rich and strong and bigoted and powerful, so I didn't have to play it.

Hudson surmised correctly: Stevens had already signed Elizabeth Taylor. (He had approached Grace Kelly first, but she was already committed at MGM.) Elizabeth, like everyone else in Hollywood, heard about *Giant* and was determined to get the part. MGM was reluctant; they wanted her for another film, but eventually agreed. She got no extra money for it above her regular salary. MGM got the loan fee, but for Elizabeth it was another chance to work with Stevens, whom she worshipped and desperately wanted to please.

The role of Bick Benedict's wife Leslie would be difficult. Elizabeth was now twenty-three years old; she would have to age from eighteen to fifty-three, play mother to Carroll Baker, then aged twenty-four, and Dennis Hopper, then nineteen.

Now Stevens had Hudson and Taylor, Baker and Hopper, Sal Mineo as the young Mexican boy, and to that cast list he added actors like Chill Wills, Jane Withers, Mercedes McCambridge. He had selected actors who were reliable, solid, attractive, and who would never disappoint.

The part of Jett Rink was an important one, though not the central character; he was the wildcat whom Edna Ferber had controversially used as the catalyst for change in the bigoted Texas establishment, steeped in its traditions of cattle ranching. Initially, Stevens had been considering Monty Clift for the role and was on the verge of approaching him when he heard of James Dean's performance in *East of Eden*. By that time, in any case, Monty's drunken reputation was preceding him and the director could not afford to make any mistakes. So he signed Dean.

Stevens had lit the touchpaper and he stood back to watch the sparks fly. The group of leading actors he had gathered were filled with personal emotions, a nervous tension arising from the desire to meet the demands of one of Hollywood's most ambitious projects in recent years. For Stevens himself, it had also been a time of anxiety. This was undoubtedly the most important film of his career. As an independent, he had been unable to afford the rights to Edna Ferber's novel; instead he offered her a third partnership in a production company he set up with producer Henry Ginsberg, which she accepted. While Ginsberg set about raising the $5.4 million required for production – a huge budget at that time – Stevens began on the script. After more than two years' work, Stevens and Ginsberg took the package to Jack Warner in search of additional finance. Warner needed little convincing that they had a winner (he was proved right: in its first year *Giant* took $7 million at the box office in America alone and it remained Warners' biggest earner until *My Fair Lady* in 1964).

This preamble of independent achievement cast an aura of tense anticipation as they all gathered for pre-production work. For the actors and technicians it was never going to be easy working with one of Hollywood's most creative and demanding directors, who now had more reason than ever to strive for excellence. Everyone who has worked with him has a favourite Stevens story. Charlton Heston told me: 'He was a relentless perfectionist whose reputation gave him great scope. He would shoot a lot of footage, and not care too much about the budget. What he wanted from his actors was dedication, and what they needed was patience.'

Stevens was well known for stopping production, perhaps for hours at a time, while he turned over in his mind how a scene should be played or what changes he wanted to make to the dialogue. While the players sat around, drinking Coke, smoking, playing games, the only sound on the lot was Stevens, sucking away on his pipe. Nerves would fray. Carole Lombard once became so frustrated that she telephoned her agent, Myron Selznick, in the middle of the night screaming: 'Myron, I've finally worked out what that son of a bitch Stevens is thinking while sucking on that goddamn pipe.'

'Yeah? What's that?' asked a bemused and half-asleep Selznick.

'Not a goddamn thing!' Lombard shouted, and hung up, her emotions only slightly vented.

Ann Doran, who worked with Stevens on *Penny Serenade*, had similar recollections:

> Stevens was one of the kind that want to sit around and tear a character apart and put it back together until sometimes you think you are going to go right out of your mind. He wanted to delve into all sorts of strange things about the character. What did they have for breakfast? Did they wear a girdle? And so on. This could go on for hours. Yet when we started to shoot, I realised how much he had done.

Stevens had created a highly volatile scenario for *Giant*, in which would be acted out not just the storyline but also the private doubts, fears, hopes and ambitions of the actors. When filming began it would be 'murderous', to use Elizabeth Taylor's description: dogged by rows on set, personal disputes, rumours of affairs between members of the cast – all of which were picked up by an ever-present audience of reporters, who had been given *carte blanche* by Warners to come and go as they pleased, just as long as the film got publicity.

James Dean was exhausted from the rapid-fire shooting of *Rebel Without a Cause*, which had been completed in little over two months, but he desperately wanted to succeed in *Giant*. When he looked at the cast list, however, he groaned. Rock Hudson. Elizabeth Taylor. They were not on his list of most admired actors. They were experienced Hollywood people, but they also represented exactly the hype that he despised about the place. He had decided in advance that they had no depth and did not hide his feelings. Carroll Baker said:

> For a start Jimmy wasn't happy about being billed third below them. There was an atmosphere from the word go. Jimmy obviously wanted to take some of the wind out of Rock's sails and that wasn't difficult. Rock and Elizabeth weren't used to the kind of improvisation Jimmy could toss out. The Actors Studio taught us those tricks, which were very effective and Jimmy laid it on heavy. It infuriated them, but so what? He did not have that many scenes and he felt he had to make an impression.

In the preliminaries, he stayed away from the rest of the cast, driving off on his own to practise a western drawl and study cowboy techniques and styles, or working his lines with Dennis Hopper and Sal Mineo. He, Hudson and Taylor circled and sniffed each other and Hudson decided that feelings were mutual: he just didn't like the kid and that was that. He found him sulky and silent, complained that he contributed nothing to group discussions, was untidy and smelly. In rehearsals, Rock found that the normal give-and-take between actors was abolished when you worked with Dean: 'He was the taker. He would suck everything out and never give it back.'

'How are we going to work with this guy?' Hudson asked Elizabeth.

'Come over to my house for dinner,' she replied, 'and we'll talk. If we're going to be husband and wife for the next few months, we may as well get to know each other better.'

She could see that Rock was jumpy and she did her best to relax him. They dined and drank together, joking and talking in an exaggerated western drawl. Rock recalled:

We had a terrific time . . . so much so we all got smashed, and suddenly it's four in the morning. Holy Jesus! Not two hours later I have to get up and I'm half drunk and hungover, as is Elizabeth. But we had to shoot . . . between shots, we're running out and throwing up.

Elizabeth tried to get to know Dean a little better:

At first, we were very leery of each other. To him, I was just another Hollywood star, all bosom and no brains. To me, he was a would-be intellectual New York Method actor. We were not prepared to dig each other at all, but after a while we found we were just two human beings and became friends. He was a strange and fascinating man and seemed engulfed in loneliness. He lived in a little house in the San Fernando Valley, and Michael and I went over there one night, and we ate beans. We sat and talked and listened to his music. Later he came over to our house, and loved our Siamese cats. I knew he wanted something that belonged to him, something of his own, so I gave him a kitten and he cried.

The role of Jett Rink once again placed James Dean as the anti-hero, battling against the establishment. The rows between him and Stevens began almost immediately he walked on the set.

At the start of filming, George Stevens made a little speech: 'Now look, guys, I want to make this clear before we start: I want everyone on set, in costume on time and at all times. I want you rehearsed and line-perfect, and ready to go if we have to make a change in the schedules. Now I know that means some of you will be hanging around kicking your heels a lot of the time, but this picture is costing a heck of a lot and that's the way it's got to be.'

For the first three days Dean accepted the situation, turned up with the rest, sat around in costume and did nothing. On the fourth day he was late, sauntering in after 10 a.m.

Stevens shouted, 'Jimmy, where the hell have you been. You know the rules. On time, and ready to go. Where were you?'

Dean mumbled a half-heard excuse and slunk to the back of the lot, where he remained for most of the day; unwanted in any scene and quietly fuming. The row made the newspapers and Hedda Hopper came out to watch the filming.

'I understand you haven't been turning up for work,' she said.

'Right, I haven't,' Jimmy replied. 'Stevens has been horrible. I sat there for three days, made up and ready to work at nine every morning . . . by six o'clock I hadn't had a scene or a rehearsal. I sat there like a bump on a log watching that big, lumpy Rock Hudson making love to Liz Taylor. I knew what Stevens was trying to do to me. I'm not going to take it.'

'I hold no brief for Stevens,' answered Hedda, 'but don't you know there's a man on that set who put the whole deal together . . . Henry Ginsberg: he, Stevens and Edna Ferber are partners. It took Henry two years to do it. This is the first time in Ferber's life she took no money, only an equal share of the profits when they come in. If this picture goes wrong . . . two years of Ginsberg's life goes down the drain.'

Jimmy looked sheepish: 'I just didn't know.'

It didn't end there, however. Jimmy and Stevens argued over some of Dean's approaches; in a Kazan movie they would have been hailed as genius, but to Stevens they were stunts. To Hudson they were stunts too, and off-putting ones at that. Some of them were just minute mannerisms which Dean would use to end a scene; or perhaps he might stick his feet on the table and push himself back in his chair, which he hadn't done in the run through; or some other kind of totally unanticipated movement or expression.

Elizabeth reckoned Stevens had a victim or two on every film, and she also fell foul. For one scene he wanted to have her dressed in a man's slouch hat, thick brogue shoes, long skirt and thick socks. Miss Taylor thought she looked dreadful.

'I'm being made to look like a lesbian in drag,' she said, quietly but firmly. 'This girl is supposed to be utterly feminine and wouldn't put on this ludicrous get-up.'

Stevens exploded and, with the crew and everyone looking, said in a very loud voice, 'All you care about is the way you look. You will never become an actress because you are so concerned about being glamorous.'

Elizabeth wiped the make-up off her face, yanked her hair back in a bun the way he wanted it, and carried on.

Before long she was upset again. One particular scene was rehearsed over and over, from six in the morning until lunchtime. Before shooting finally began, Elizabeth's dress had to be pressed and her make-up and hair redone, after which she sat waiting in her dressing room for what seemed like hours, expecting to be called. Finally, she walked out to the set to find it in darkness, with the crew standing around. Stevens was sitting behind the cameras, puffing his pipe, and yelled at her that she had kept everyone waiting for an hour – who the hell did she think she was? She tried to explain that no one had called her, but Stevens paid no attention and continued to shout till tears were rolling down her cheeks. He gestured, the make-up girl wiped away the dampness, brushed her skin and Elizabeth walked to her spot to begin the scene. Nothing more was said.

Stevens's outbursts usually occurred like this – immediately before a scene of high drama or tension, or where he required a special look or a spark of anger. When the row was over, Stevens could be seen, sucking away on his pipe, smiling to himself, while out there under the lights and in front of his cameras the actor he had just bawled out was giving a perfect performance.

Rock Hudson was full of insecurity. In the dusty heat of the Texas desert town of Marfa, where the unit took up residence for location shooting, he became increasingly worried that Dean was stealing the picture from him. He telephoned Henry Willson and poured his heart out.

Willson put the phone down and turned to Phyllis Gates. 'Isn't that just like an actor? I get him the best role of his life and all he can do is complain. Phyllis, I want you to go down there and see if you can calm him down.'

When she arrived in Texas, Rock was tense and angry. 'Stevens is throwing the picture to Dean,' he told her. 'I know he is, dammit. He spends all his time talking to Dean and hardly tells me a thing.'

Phyllis tried to rebuild his shattered morale. 'Maybe Stevens has more confidence in you. This is only Dean's third picture; you've done thirty.'

Hudson would not have it. 'I need just as much direction as he does. I have never worked with anyone of Stevens's calibre before. I've worked with hacks mostly, and Stevens is giving Dean all the close-ups and I'm left out in the cold.'

* * * * *

Throughout the location work on *Giant* in the Texas heat, the actors suffered extreme discomfort. They couldn't get enough water; they were all given salt tablets daily; and, to add to their problems, they started to get threatening letters. The Ferber novel had created a stir in Texas, particularly over the anti-Mexican prejudices which Bick Benedict and Jett Rink display. Notes started arriving: 'Get out of Texas. Get out or you'll be shot.' A security guard was posted, but nothing untoward resulted from the threats.

Elizabeth also suffered back problems, then an infection in her leg, all of which added to the thought that this had been her toughest assignment yet. She grasped every opportunity to relax, as they all did. By now they were more comfortable in each other's company. They were all billeted in homes and hotels, rented *en masse* by the studio. Rock was sharing a house with James Dean and Chill Wills; Elizabeth was living across the street. There were plenty of parties and, with so many reporters milling around, gossip began filtering back suggesting that Miss Taylor was becoming rather friendly with one, or both, of her leading men.

Phyllis Gates said that before she left Marfa to return to Los Angeles, someone 'whispered in her ear' that there was something going on between Elizabeth and Rock, and she noticed that they were very close, talking 'baby talk' to one another. As rumours began appearing in the gossip columns, Michael Wilding suddenly turned up with the two children and that merely fanned the flames: 'MICHAEL WORRIED ABOUT LIZ AND ROCK', announced the headlines. Many years later, after Rock Hudson's death, Elizabeth admitted frankly that she had been attracted to Rock and, at the time, thought it quite possible that a romance might develop: 'I looked at Rock, so handsome and so apparently masculine ... but I soon realised that no woman would succeed in igniting his enthusiasm.'

There were also stories about Elizabeth and Dean, as well as about Carroll Baker and Dean, which upset Carroll because she had recently married New York stage director Jack Garefein, who was still back in the city. But Carroll says that Dean showed no sexual interest in women:

We became very close during the making of *Giant*, but we were never lovers. I never thought for a moment he was gay, I think women can sense these things. I think at that time he was asexual and didn't seem to me to be turned on by sex. However, despite the professional difficulties between them, he got close to Elizabeth Taylor during the shooting and became very attentive and rather sweet, which I think puzzled her. I got very jealous of Elizabeth when he switched his attentions from me to her, but she told me afterwards that he never once tried to touch her or get her into bed.

After Dean's death, in the welter of analytical descriptions of his life and times, rumours kept cropping up that he was bisexual and that he had had affairs with Hudson, Sal Mineo, Nick Adams and one or two homosexual roommates, although the 'evidence' was always rather circumstantial. However, Elizabeth Taylor was quoted in an interview for *Star* magazine in 1987:

James Dean was the cause of all the trouble [on *Giant*]. He had a subtle charm and after I found out the truth about Rock, I began to feel a strong affection for Jimmy. But my feminine intuition told me that a mysterious understanding was being born between the two actors . . . at times I felt like an uncomfortable third party.

Elizabeth covered up for Hudson by saying that he tried to woo her; what remained was a loving but purely platonic friendship between them for the rest of Hudson's life. As with Monty Clift, Elizabeth put aside the personal anguish in his life and never allowed it to affect her loyalty.

As far as Dean was concerned, Hudson did say later that Jimmy had formed an attachment to him, although it seems likely that the reverse was the case. As his close friends knew, Rock was especially adept at getting men into bed, regardless of their heterosexual or homosexual qualifications. Cameramen, tough and manly, had been charmed into his rooms on locations in Europe, and surprised even themselves by ending up having sex with him. When Hudson was on the warpath, using his well-known catchphrase 'Wanna have some fun?', he was skilful and practised at luring his quarry. Dean, in the right frame of mind, would try anything, often for sadistic or spiteful reasons.

Phyllis Gates recalled that when Dean was killed, Rock sobbed uncontrollably for hours. Hudson, however, interviewed in 1983 by Professor Ron Davis, showed no great regard for Dean:

Jimmy was certainly an effective actor. I never worked with an actor who had so much concentration . . . I mean he could think about this piece of glass and . . . nothing would interfere, which I felt was brilliant. Jimmy had a lot of faults. I didn't particularly like him but that didn't matter. What did I care? Or what does he care? He was very effective in the role, especially in the younger part. . . . he was a little guy and thought little. He didn't have an expansive [mind] . . . he had blinkers. He wasn't able to see sides . . . I don't know as I should say more . . . I don't like to talk against the dead. . . . I keep thinking that if Monty had done the part he would have acted the bejesus out of that role. Especially the older man. Dean broke down as the older man. He was brilliant in the early part . . . I keep thinking that if Monty had done that there would have been nobody else in the movie. He was such a brilliant actor.

*   *   *   *   *

When they all returned to continue filming in Hollywood at the end of August, things settled down. Elizabeth was back with her family, but the continuing work on *Giant* kept her on a very tight schedule at the studio. Michael Wilding hardly ever saw her during the day, and when she came home at nights she was exhausted. Her back pain was almost crippling her but George Stevens claimed it was psychosomatic; as events proved, it wasn't. However, it did mean that to quell the pain and obtain a decent night's sleep before the following day's rigorous work, she was compelled to consume assorted painkillers and sleeping pills.

For Rock, the return to California brought new press attention and continued innuendo about his private life, but he was thrilled when a jubilant Willson called with good news: *Life* magazine wanted to do a big feature on him and promised his picture on the front cover. *Life* was then at the peak of its popularity, with a weekly sale worldwide exceeding eight million. It was the one magazine that every gold-lamé star in Hollywood wanted to appear in, and Rock co-operated fully for pictures and the story of his life and arrival in Hollywood. Naturally, he was asked about his views on marriage, and he gave his stock reply to such questions: he was too busy even to think of getting wed. When the article duly appeared, it focused on that aspect with the headline: 'THE SIMPLE LIFE OF A BUSY BACHELOR. ROCK HUDSON GETS RICH ALONE'.

Suddenly, Rock was spurred on in his strange courtship of Phyllis Gates.

*   *   *   *   *

James Dean's return to Los Angeles was marked by his renewed interest in his cars, and the *Hollywood Reporter* noted that he intended to return to motor-racing as soon as he had finished filming *Giant*. Jimmy loved his car, and loved to take people for rides, fast and furious. Early that summer, he had bought the first of the two Porsches he owned, a white speedster which he raced at the California Sports Car Club in Palm Springs. Later that month he entered the races at Santa Barbara. Everyone who remembered him at those events said he was a fast driver, but not what you would class a good one.

Natalie Wood had visited him during the shooting in Texas, and now they were together again, along with Sal Mineo, Nick Adams and Dennis Hopper. They were in a state of high tension, awaiting the opening of *Rebel Without a Cause*, which had been scheduled for early October. Everyone who had seen sneak previews was impressed and Warners had already called Dean's agent to talk about a long-term deal for another six pictures worth a minimum of $1 million.

Jimmy showed off around Hollywood, driving his Porsche on to the Warners lot at high speed. There were still some big scenes to do on *Giant*, however, and Stevens continued to insist that Dean should not race his Porsche until his release from the picture.

Ironically, he was called by the National Highways Committee to make a television commercial with actor Gig Young to spread the message of safe driving. That minute piece of film was later used over and over again in television reconstructions of his life.

Jimmy arrived at the studio to film the commercial wearing his *Giant* costume (cowboy gear) and sat down rather awkwardly, smoking a cigarette. Gig Young began the interview: 'Jimmy, we probably have a great many young people watching us tonight, and, for their benefit, I'd like your opinion about fast driving on the highway. Do you think it is a good idea?'

DEAN   I used to fly about quite a bit, you know, took a lot of unnecessary chances on the highways, and then I started racing, and now I drive on the highways with extra caution. No one knows what they're doing and half the time I don't know what this guy's going to do, or that one. I don't have the urge to speed on the highway.

YOUNG   Tell us, Jimmy, how fast does your car go?

DEAN   Ooh, about a hundred miles an hour.

YOUNG   You've used it to race, haven't you?

DEAN   One or two times.

YOUNG   Where at?

DEAN   I showed pretty good at Palm Springs. I ran in a basic heat. People say racing is dangerous but I'd rather take my chance on the track any day than on the highway. Well, Gig, I'd better take off.

He stood at the door, swung a lasso and, looking into the camera, said: 'And remember – drive safely. Because the life you save may be mine.'

When those who had experienced some of Jimmy's antics at the wheel of his car, or on his motorbike, saw the commercial, they laughed.

As September arrived, Dean was already planning his next step in motor-racing. Warners had promised him some time off before starting his next picture, *The Left-Handed Gun*, in which he was to play Billy the Kid. The studio was also talking of teaming him and Sal Mineo again for *Somebody Up There Likes Me*, in which he was to play the boxer Rocky Graziano. (Sal eventually did the film with Paul Newman.) His finances were better than they had ever been and his agents assured him that he need have no remaining doubts about whether he was a big star now. So he bought a new Porsche Spyder for $5000; it was the most he had spent on anything in his life.

That car was his pride. It had a sleek, raw aluminium body, no top and no windshield. It was a racing thoroughbred. He drove it straight up to Beverly Hills, and then down Sunset Boulevard past The Strip, turned left up to Hollywood Boulevard and past Grauman's Chinese Theater, and back again. He told Elizabeth Taylor about it and promised to take her for a ride, but he never did.

Next day he drove to work in the Porsche and was told never to bring the car on the lot again because someone would get killed. For the rest of the month, he was preparing for the races at Salinas on 1 October, by when he expected to be released from work on *Giant*. In the meantime, his aunt and uncle, Marcus and Ortense Winslow, turned up for a visit from Fairmount and they were joined by his father, Winton, for a family reunion at Jimmy's house. Everyone was in good spirits.

Thursday, 29 September: Jimmy was getting hyped about the race meeting, now just two days away. He had had the number 130 painted on the side of the Spyder and the words 'Little Bastard' inscribed on the back. That evening, he drove over to Santa Barbara with his friend and dialogue coach Bill Hickman to give the car a final run before the races; in the two weeks he had had it, he had hardly been able to drive because of the pressure of work and there was little more than the delivery mileage on the clock. They were opening the throttle on Highway 101, but they ran into fog and had to turn back. On the way, he paid a call on his father, then returned to his house with Hickman. He telephoned Sandford Roth, a photographer who was concluding a photo essay on Jimmy for *Collier's* magazine, and then rang Rolf Wutherich, a mechanic, both of whom were to join Dean and Hickman on the journey to Salinas the following day.

Later he took his Siamese cat, the gift from Elizabeth Taylor which he had named Marcus after his uncle, over to the apartment of actress Janette Miller, who looked after the kitten while Jimmy was away. On the back of an envelope he scribbled some instructions for her:

One teaspoon, white karo; one big can of evaporated milk, equal part boiled water or distilled milk, one egg yolk, mix and chill. Don't feed him meat or formula cold; one drop of vitamin solution per day. Take Marcus to Dr Cooper for shots next week.

Then he and Hickman drove down to Villa Capri, from where he called his friend Vampira at 10.40 p.m. After a brief chat, his last words to her were: 'My dinner's here, I must go.' After their meal, Dean and Hickman stayed out late with the car, just driving around, and Jimmy did not return home until 2 a.m.

Friday, 30 September: Jimmy was woken at 7.30 a.m. by his landlord, Nicco Romanos, who often dropped by for coffee, particularly in the mornings. He also knew that today Jimmy was setting off for Salinas and came in to wish him good luck.

Dean was up and about quickly, but he was heavy-eyed; he poured some coffee and sat at the bottom of the steps to his loft, tapping away on his bongo drums with a Chesterfield cigarette dangling from his lips while Nicco attempted to make conversation.

The Little Bastard was already on a trailer hitched to a Ford station-wagon. Dean said goodbye to Nicco and drove off in the Ford, with the Spyder on tow, to pick up Bill Hickman, then on down Sunset Boulevard into North Vine Street, to Competition Motors, where Rolf Wutherich was waiting for them. Just before ten, Sandford Roth arrived to do some more pictures of Jimmy, while Wutherich gave the car a final check over. Jimmy and Wutherich drove home in the Ford, and Roth took Hickman back to his place.

Later that morning, Jimmy's father came over with his younger brother, Charles, who had come visiting with Marcus and Ortense and had stayed on, planning to continue his holiday in Mexico. Jimmy took Charlie for a ride around the block in the Spyder and then they had lunch. As they shook hands, Charlie warned Jimmy, 'Be careful: you're driving a bomb.' Dean patted the car and said, 'That's my baby.'

They loaded the Porsche back on to the trailer and drove over to Sandford Roth's house. All four of them – Roth, Hickman, Wutherich and Dean – stood outside looking at the skies and discussing the weather. It was a glorious day.

'Tell you what,' Jimmy suggested to Wutherich, 'let's drive the Little Bastard up to Salinas. It'll put some miles on the clock and loosen her up. And anyway, I don't want to sit cooped up in the wagon when we can get some breeze. Let's do it.'

'OK,' said Wutherich. He could see the logic and was already walking to the Ford to get the Spyder off the trailer. Bill Hickman and Roth took the Ford, with the empty trailer still on the back. Dean and Wutherich got into the Porsche. They faced seven hours of motoring that afternoon up the Californian coast.

'See you in Salinas,' shouted Jimmy. But he never would.

Chapter Nine

Death and Survival

In the coming days, weeks and months, George Stevens would sit in the cutting room editing the vast footage of film he had shot on *Giant*, with the face of James Dean staring back at him, defiantly daring him to cut out his little tricks. In retrospect, Stevens wished he had given Dean a freer hand to play Jett Rink the way he saw the character, retaining some of the spontaneous touches that Dean would add himself; but, for the most part, Stevens was satisfied.

The night before Jimmy's departure for Salinas, Stevens had watched the rushes on the final scene in which Dean appeared. Jett Rink is guest of honour at a banquet at which his speech is to be broadcast over the radio. The entire Benedict family is there, and it is then that Jett realises that his love for Leslie will never be returned. He fights with Bick Benedict, then gradually deteriorates into a drunken stupor. As the guests file away in disgust, we get our last ever shot of James Dean, slumped on the top table, vainly attempting to mumble his speech and calling Leslie's name.

Stevens felt that Dean had overdone the drunkenness: many of his lines were inaudible. Although he had already released Jimmy from the picture, he decided he would have to call him back for retakes. In fact, he had to use Nick Adams to dub over the lines a couple of months later; for Jimmy and Rolf Wutherich in the Porsche, with Roth and Hickman following in the Ford, were already heading north on Highway 99.

*   *   *   *   *

They stopped briefly at Tip's Diner just before 3 p.m. Jimmy had a glass of milk, Wutherich chose ice-cream soda and they talked about the race.

'Don't drive to win,' said Rolf. 'Drive for the experience.'

They talked more, then for no reason Dean suddenly said to Wutherich, 'I want you to have something,' and he slipped a cheap ring off his finger and passed it to the brawny mechanic.

'Why?' asked Rolf.

'Just to show we're friends.' Rolf tried the ring on his thick fingers. It would only fit his little finger and he forced it on.

As they walked to the door of the diner, a waitress stopped Wutherich: 'Is that Jimmy Dean?' He said it was and she ran back to tell her friends.

Before they left, Hickman, who had caught up now, told Jimmy not to drive so fast; they could barely keep him in sight at sixty miles an hour. The small convoy set off again.

Out on Wheeler Ridge, Patrolman O. V. Hunter of the Californian Highway Patrol was driving leisurely towards the Kern County line when, in the shimmering heat, he caught the reflection of the sun on a little silver car travelling down one of the hilly slopes of the highway. He looked at his watch – 3.30 p.m. – and kept the car in view for a few seconds. It was speeding: he could see that even from this distance, and he swung the patrol car across the central reservation and took off after it. Doing eighty in pursuit, he pulled close to the Ford, overtook it, got behind the Porsche and signalled both cars to stop. He gave them a ticket each for travelling at seventy in a fifty zone.

'Terrific,' said Jimmy sarcastically to Rolf, thinking that the newspapers would pick it up so soon after his drive-safely commercial.

Patrolman Hunter talked with Jimmy and Rolf for a few minutes about the car. Dean told him they were going up to Salinas for the races and he said, well, please don't race on the highway – slow down.

They travelled on, taking the patrolman's advice until he was out of sight. Then Jimmy was racing again, and on the flat, straight Highway 466 he opened her up to a hundred. Just after 5 p.m. they reached Blackwell's Corner, at the junction of Highways 33 and 466, where Jimmy spotted the Mercedes 300SL owned by Lance Reventlow, Barbara Hutton's twenty-one-year-old son, parked outside the grocery store at the side of a Richfield petrol station. He braked hard and spun the Porsche alongside the Mercedes. Lance was also heading for Salinas; they laughed and joked, boyish and bragging, and Dean said he had just clocked a hundred and thirty. Rolf stood by the roadside to flag down the Ford and, as they stood around drinking Coke, Hickman warned Jimmy that it was getting difficult to see his car at times as the light began to fade.

Back on the road, farmer Clifford Hord, his wife and two children were travelling home in their Pontiac after a day at Bonneville Flats, where they had been watching speed trials. Hord suddenly went tense as he saw coming towards him a little silver sports coupé overtaking another car; the two of them were almost upon him. He cursed them and swerved violently so that the two offside wheels of his car were off the road and bumping along the pot-holed verge. How he avoided a crash he could never work out. He looked in his rearview mirror to see the Porsche speeding away.

One mile ahead was a Y-intersection, known locally as a danger spot. Donald Turnupseed, a twenty-three-year-old student driving his cherished 1950 Ford Tudor, was heading home from the California Polytechnic in San Luis Obispo, for a weekend visit to his parents at Tulare; he was an hour away from home and had driven the road many times. He approached the intersection at around thirty miles an hour, slowed down and edged towards the white line in the middle of the road to make a left turn into Highway 41. The Porsche was heading straight towards him in the opposite direction. Wutherich said later that they were travelling at around sixty-five miles an hour at that point. Jimmy was wearing his spectacles with clip-on sunglasses; his hair was fluttering in the wind; the remnants of the evening sun were shining in their faces. Jimmy said to Wutherich, 'Everything OK?'

'Everything's OK,' Wutherich answered, half dozing. He recalled:

We were not talking now, not of Pier Angeli or of Dean's mother, or of anything. The only thought in Jimmy's mind was winning that race. There was no doubt of that. I glanced at Jimmy but could see no shadow of fear across his face. He had no premonition of death. Suddenly, the Ford was coming at us; the car swung towards the centre of the highway to turn into Highway 41 . . .

Dean's last spoken words to Wutherich were: 'That guy's gotta stop, he'll see us.'

Two minutes later, Turnupseed was sitting on the side of the road, moaning: 'I just didn't see him . . . I didn't see him.'

The Porsche had slammed into the left-hand side of the Ford, then spun off the road and landed wrapped around a telegraph pole. Jimmy's neck was broken; the pathologist's report later showed that he had multiple fractures and internal injuries. He was dead before the ambulance got him to Paso Robles Hospital, fifteen miles away. Rolf Wutherich was thrown clean out of the car; he had a broken jaw and other injuries, which he survived. Turnupseed was not injured and his car was remarkably unscathed, with damage only to the area over the left front wheel which the Porsche had struck. The whole of the left-hand side of the sports car was ripped apart and mangled; the engine was pushed almost into the driver's seat.

A crowd from passing cars had already gathered by the time Roth and Hickman caught up. Both were sick at what they saw: the Porsche crumpled like a discarded cigarette packet, Jimmy obviously dead. The impact had thrown his head back with such force that it was almost detached from his torso. Instinctively, Roth began snapping pictures, though when he developed the film he was so upset that he resolved never to release them for public showing.

* * * * *

Soon after 7.00 p.m., the duty security man at Warners' studio took a telephone call from the operator at the War Memorial Hospital in Paso Robles. She told him that James Dean was dead. Reporters were already at the scene and the news would be broadcast very shortly.

George Stevens was still on the lot with Elizabeth Taylor and other members of the cast of *Giant*; they had been watching the day's rushes in the projection room. Stevens was called to the phone and the others heard him say: 'No – oh my God. When? . . . Are you sure? Can there be any mistake?' He listened to the voice on the other end, then put the phone down, motioning to have the film stopped and the lights turned up.

'I've just been given the news. Jimmy Dean has been killed.'

Elizabeth Taylor collapsed in tears, and others broke down as the realisation sank in. Some began telephoning the police and hospitals to try to confirm the news, to see if it had not been some awful mistake. They stayed on the lot for two hours, then began to file away. As Elizabeth was being helped to her car outside, she saw a figure coming towards her in the darkness. It was George Stevens; he had just been talking to Henry Ginsberg on the telephone and was now getting into his Mercedes to drive home.

'I can't believe it, George,' Elizabeth cried. 'I just can't believe it.'

George replied, 'I believe it. He had it coming to him. The way he drove, he had it coming to him.'

Down on Sunset Boulevard, as the news leaked out first by word of mouth and then on the radio, a small group of Jimmy's friends gathered at Googie's, and the following morning, when the papers were full of it, tearful fans stood outside Warners, hoping for confirmation that it was all a mistake, that Jimmy Dean wasn't dead.

The actress Mercedes McCambridge, who had become friends with Dean while making *Giant*, was driving that morning to begin a holiday in San Francisco with her husband Fletcher. They had stayed the night with friends and were travelling, early on Saturday, along Highway 466 when they pulled in at a filling station for petrol. Fletcher heard the girl at the station telling Mercedes, 'We have Jimmy Dean's sports car inside.' He thought Jimmy must have broken down; then he heard Mercedes cry out: 'Oh my God – oh no!' She had seen the battered Porsche, still with remains of Dean's blood on the aluminium body.

Shocked, and silent, they drove to Paso Robles with half a thought that there might be something they could do. There wasn't, so they drove on to San Francisco. But Mercedes couldn't settle; she collapsed in a fever and Fletcher had to have her flown home, where she was put in hospital for two days.

Ann Doran read the news and reflected. Their last meeting had been just before he started work on *Giant*. She said later:

> It was fate; if he had not been going quite so fast, he would not have been at that spot at that time. But I always thought that somehow, his getting into drugs contributed something to his death ... because basically he was a nice kid.

* * * * *

That day, 3 October 1955, *Rebel Without a Cause* opened across the country to mixed reviews. Naturally, the death of Dean was compared with the scene in *Rebel* of the 'chicken run', in which Jim Stark and Buzz are driving two stolen cars towards the edge of the cliff; the first one to jump out is branded a chicken. Jim rolls out at the last second, but Buzz's coat sleeve is caught in the door handle and he hurtles over the cliff to his death. In the aftermath comes Dean's anguished cry: 'A boy was killed.'

Although some critics showed no great enthusiasm for the film, saying that, like *The Blackboard Jungle*, it was cashing in on juvenile delinquency, picture halls throughout the world were soon crammed with young people, who joined together in an unprecedented show of unity, in which fact and fantasy merged, to provide the beginnings of the legend of James Dean. In a town where bad taste seemingly knows no bounds, someone unkindly said, 'That auto wreck was the best career move Dean ever made.'

They buried him the following weekend in Fairmount, Indiana. None of his movie friends was at the service, though most sent flowers, and his coffin was borne to its rest by old friends from school. A simple headstone marked the spot: JAMES B. DEAN 1931–1955.

* * * * *

In Hollywood, life went on. George Stevens insisted that Elizabeth Taylor and Rock Hudson immediately resume shooting the remaining scenes for *Giant*, and Nick Adams came in to do what he thought might give a boost to his career, dubbing over Dean's inaudible lines. Stevens took a year to edit the film.

Henry Willson was convinced that *Giant* would, once and for all, establish Rock Hudson as a top star and predicted an Academy Award for his performance. There was still the lurking danger of an exposé of Rock's private life, but Willson said that marriage would dispose of the rumours for good.

In September, *Confidential* had run a story about another of Willson's clients, the handsome and rising young star Tab Hunter, alleging a minor stain on his past. Once more, there has been ample speculation that Willson sacrificed yet another good name to get Hudson off the hook. It has been one of the most widely discussed aspects of the progression of Hudson's career, but there is no way of establishing the truth. However, *Confidential* did not do its story on Rock and, whether or not Willson had a hand in that, he was certainly deeply involved in the next move, which was to get Rock married off.

Hudson's involvement with Phyllis Gates had hardly been a passionate prelude to marriage and she was as dumbstruck as anyone when Rock called her at the end of October 1955 and said: 'Let's get married.' When her shock had subsided, she agreed – only to discover with renewed surprise that Rock and Willson had all but finalised arrangements for an elopement: they would be married in secret in Santa Barbara on 9 November, with only a cameraman from Universal present, standing by to release pictures to a surprised world. From proposal to marriage took little more than a week: Rock had to be ready to start his next picture, *Written on the Wind*, by the end of November.*

The wedding was carefully planned so that not the slightest hint of the impending Hudson nuptials escaped. Willson wanted the ceremony to be held away from prying eyes and without any danger of face-to-face questioning of the bride and groom, and he was ready to whisk them away on honeymoon to Jamaica as soon as it was over. Hudson telephoned his best friend from boyhood days in Winnetka, Jim Matteoni, and asked him to be best man. Matteoni, of course, was startled by the news. Phyllis, still apparently unaware that it was all a charade, was

---

* Also starring Robert Stack, Dorothy Malone and Lauren Bacall, this picture would become something of an embarrassment to Hudson next time he met Monty Clift, because the incestuous little tale written by Thornton Wilder had been based on the real-life scandal of the Reynolds tobacco heir who married Libby Holman. Fictionalised, Libby became a central character, easily recognisable. Wilder, of course, had achieved first-hand knowledge of the situation through his friendship with Monty and, subsequently, Libby.

allowed to tell only her closest friend, Pat Devlin, who was bridesmaid, and the little party trooped out to Santa Barbara for the ceremony.

Henry had seen to everything. He had booked the preacher, a local Lutheran minister, the Reverend Nordahl Thorpe; he had ordered the wedding cake; reserved a suite at the Biltmore Hotel where the wedding was to take place; even arranged the flowers. He had also made all the arrangements for the honeymoon.

As soon as the wedding was over, Willson called Jack Diamond, Rock's publicist at Universal, who was standing by to give out the story. Meanwhile, Willson was rehearsing with Phyllis the lines that she would say when Hedda and Louella got wind of it.

'Can I just call my mother and tell her the news?' asked Phyllis.

'No, no, not yet,' replied Willson. 'You've got to speak to Hedda and Louella first. They can still make the home editions.'

Whether the Hudson marriage was an arranged one – which it certainly was – became a subject for discussion among Rock's friends for years. Once Willson went so far as to admitting, 'Well, perhaps I did play Cupid,' but Hudson himself never revealed the details. Phyllis Gates remained silent, even after the marriage foundered, and only after Rock's death did she give a clue to her own feelings when she said:

> I always believed Rock had good intentions at the start. But he was always a charmer; he was always acting. Now I don't believe it was genuine . . . he did more acting when we were together than he did when he was at the studio. He never loved me and I think that my marriage was probably arranged by the studio.

The press and the fan magazines were soon knocking on the door. From now on Rock the Lonely Rich Bachelor was portrayed as the Happily Married Star who had courted his homely, no-nonsense girl from the sticks and had won her heart. The picture features on them depicted a warm, cosy life in the Hudson household and, for the time being at least, Willson's fears of a hiccup in his boy's career could be dispelled.

* * * * *

The scandal sheets, meanwhile, had turned their attentions to Elizabeth Taylor's marriage. They had been focused upon it by an article in *Confidential* claiming that while Elizabeth was away filming *Giant* in Texas, Michael Wilding had invited a pair of strippers into his home for a poolside party. For the next six months or more the headlines became relentless, fuelled by Taylor herself when she gave a surprisingly frank statement, agreeing that it would be foolish to deny that their relationship had become frayed and had entered a stage when their arguments had become more frequent and punishing – particularly, she said, on her part, because of her temper and Wilding's reluctance to become involved in a full-scale shouting match: 'He is such a gentleman when we are rowing.'

Wilding had his say: 'Once I thought I could influence this trembling little creature and guide her along life's stoney path. Lately, I'm simply told to shut up.'

What had happened since they married was in the classic pattern of one spouse becoming more famous than the other. In the beginning Elizabeth had followed in Michael's wake. Most of the places they went to were of his choosing and with his friends; she had had no previous existence or big friendships that would enable her to bring him into her world and she had tagged along with an obvious shyness. Now he was in her shadow, and Wilding had come to the conclusion that any minute now they would start calling him Mr Taylor.

They thought they had escaped the limelight temporarily when she joined him on location in Morocco, where he was filming another instantly disposable piece of magic called *Zarak* with Anita Ekberg and Victor Mature; but *Confidential* followed them and ran some scurrilous innuendo about Elizabeth and Mature. So she returned to Los Angeles, where she was delighted to find news of her next film: *Raintree County*, and reunion with her beloved Monty.

The story of how *Raintree County* came to be made is an interesting one. In 1947, author Ross Lockridge, a young English teacher from Indiana, won MGM's annual $150,000 award for the best novel of the year. His thousand-page epic became a bestseller and MGM owned the film rights by virtue of the prize. Mr Lockridge did not remain on this earth long enough to enjoy the fruits of his arduous task; riven by depression after the long project, he killed himself, in spite of his newly acquired wealth. The book, meantime, sat gathering dust in the MGM archives until 1955, when Dore Schary was scouting around for a major property and picked it up.

Raintree County was another tale of the Civil War, but with a Northern flavour, as opposed to the Southern aspect of *Gone With the Wind*, and Metro unashamedly began to make comparisons with that classic. Unfortunately, the three-and-a-half-hour film did not match those boasts.

Elizabeth was to play Susannah, a tempestuous Southern beauty who moves north and ensnares an idealistic young schoolmaster named John Shawnessy in a complicated plot involving lots of Hollywood specialities:

hot passion, slavery, North–South politics, madness and suicide.

Schary signed Edward Dmytryk, now rehabilitated in Hollywood after his exile in Britain, as director and, after they had talked further with Elizabeth, she asked if the part of Shawnessy could be offered to Monty, who accepted even before he had read the script. He cherished the thought of working with Elizabeth again; and he was flat broke. All his money had been dwindled away by his free spending, his generosity to friends and to lovers (and blackmailers) who passed in the night, never to be seen again. He was also in debt through advances from his agents.

In the previous few months he had stormed off to Italy, where Libby Holman was on holiday, after a row with Thornton Wilder. He had been intending to do a new play for Wilder at the Edinburgh Festival, but when he received the script he started making pencil marks all over it and insulted Wilder by suggesting some rather drastic changes to his lines. Wilder angrily declared that he would not change a single word of his work, and furthermore he no longer wanted Monty to perform it. Their friendship, which had endured almost fifteen fairly turbulent years, was never the same after that.

He also caused a scene at the New York preview of *Guys and Dolls*, when he turned up half drunk, made disparaging remarks about Marlon Brando and moaned, 'Oh, my God, what have they done to Frank [Sinatra]?' well within the hearing of a good section of the audience. People began hissing him and telling him to be quiet; halfway through, he said, 'This film stinks,' and left. On the way out, he put his fist through the glass panel of the front-hall showcase where photographs of the stars were displayed. Later he became deeply apologetic to the cinema manager, who had seen him do it, and sent a cheque to cover the damage. (Clift telephoned Sinatra to commiserate. Frank did not think the film was that bad but complained about Marlon Brando, whom he believed had tried to overpower him in every scene. Sinatra also thought he should have played Sky Masterson because that role had all the best ballads.)

When he arrived in Hollywood for the beginning of *Raintree County*, Clift found himself embroiled in the death throes of the Wilding marriage. Neither party appeared to want a break-up, more out of friendship than love, but there seemed no way of stopping it.

Monty had taken a house in Dawn Ridge Road for his stay in Hollywood and the studio laid on a chauffeur-driven limousine to be on call day and night so that he didn't have to drive. (The Los Angeles Police Department had already done the studio more than enough favours in keeping Monty out of court on previous occasions.) Filming began in April 1956, and at the start Monty was as good as gold. However, as he drew more deeply on his strength for the daily performances, the pressure began to show. The script was a daunting one; Monty was to appear in almost every scene and, perhaps through the sheer exhaustion caused by his work, he began drinking again. Often he mixed drugs with his alcohol. This in itself provided the make-up people with a problem at the start of every day. The picture was being filmed in the new 65mm 'Window of the World' process, which MGM boasted would give the audiences the most crystal-clear and sharpest colour they had ever seen; the cameras would pick up the slightest blemish. Often Monty had to sit with cold pads over his eyes to try to eradicate the bloodshot and swelling which were the legacy of the previous night's drinking.

In early May, Dore Schary came down to the set and went to see Clift in his dressing room.

'I'm getting bad reports about you, Monty,' he said. 'We've got too much at stake here for problems like this.'

'What problems?' Monty asked.

'You know what. Drinking. Shooting up. That's the problem. Elizabeth is upset but she's not saying anything because you're her buddy. But everyone can see what's going on and Eddie [Dmytryk] is worried sick. You have got to stay sober, all the time, nighttimes as well.'

Clift apologised profusely and sincerely, as he always did, and said that it would not happen again. He tried to explain that the injections he was giving himself were straight vitamins.

Three days later, Schary's 'problem' became a nightmare. Monty had gone home early on the evening of 13 May, deciding that he would not go out that night. He gave his chauffeur the night off and threw himself on his sofa. At 6.30 the phone rang. It was Elizabeth, calling to invite him to a dinner party at her home that night. Monty refused, saying he was exhausted, but then Michael Wilding came on the phone and pleaded too. In the end Monty said all right, but he would come as he was, without dressing up.

With the chauffeur already gone, Clift drove himself up the winding road to the Wilding's house high on the hill. When he arrived, looking dishevelled and in sloppy clothes, Rock and Phyllis Hudson and Kevin McCarthy were already there. Michael Wilding poured everyone a drink, then slumped on to a couch where he spent half the evening, explaining that he had taken some painkillers for a sore back. They had all been there for half an hour or more before Elizabeth made her entrance in a white gown, her body scattered with jewellery.

Monty was sullen and moody. Elizabeth sat next to him to try to cheer him up and they talked together, fairly oblivious of the others. He told her he was miserable about the work on *Raintree County*, which he didn't think was going well. Rock and Phyllis chatted away to Kevin, and Michael Wilding roused himself now and again to interject in one or other of the conversations. Dinner was fairly subdued. No one was drinking much and, at the most, after cocktails they had only a couple of glasses of wine.

Soon after 10.30, Monty announced that he was leaving, then began complaining about that goddam road and how he could never find his way back in the dark. Kevin was ready to leave too, so he offered to drive ahead, allowing Monty to tail him down to Sunset Boulevard. Clift agreed and the two men set off, leaving the Wildings and the Hudsons to finish the evening together.

Kevin kept sight of Monty's car in his rearview mirror, but suddenly he got scared: Monty was coming too close and looked as if he might hit the back of his own car at any second. Kevin accelerated and had difficulty negotiating the next corkscrew bend. Monty was still right on his tail – then the headlights behind veered off, left and then right. There was a terrific bang and a cloud of dust, visible even in the dimness of the night.

McCarthy stopped and ran back. Clift's car was crumpled against a telegraph pole, badly wrecked; the engine was still running and there was a strong smell of petrol. McCarthy feared an explosion:

I looked inside the car but I couldn't see Monty. It was as dark as hell. I switched off the engine, and then I found Monty, slumped under the dash and I couldn't make out whether he was dead or alive. The doors were jammed, and I couldn't get him out.

Kevin got back into his car, drove at breakneck speed back to the Wildings' house and rushed into the sitting room. Shaking and only half coherent, he shouted, 'My God, oh my God. I think Monty's dead.'

'Oh, shut up,' said Wilding, still drowsy from the sedatives and believing McCarthy had returned at Monty's behest to play a joke on them. Almost immediately, however, he wished he hadn't said that because suddenly he could see that Kevin was serious.

Elizabeth hadn't taken it in either. 'What's happened? What's happened?' she repeated.

'Monty hit a telegraph pole. We must call an ambulance.' They phoned, then all went running down the hill towards Monty's car. Kevin tried to hold Elizabeth back, but she pulled away and kept saying, 'I must go to Monty, I must go.'

She was virtually the first to arrive at the scene, although people from nearby houses were gathering. She began tugging at the door, but it was still jammed, so she climbed in through the back and crawled over the front seat where Monty was lying. Somehow she managed to sit with his head nursed in her arms. There was blood everywhere, and her white dress was soaking it up in huge red patches.

Elizabeth realised that Monty was still alive. She described later how they sat there:

> He was breathing, and moaning. All my revulsion about blood absolutely left me. I held his head and he started coming to. I could hardly see his face, it was so smashed and cut, just a pulp and a mass of blood. He was suffering terribly, and there was a tooth hanging on his lip by a few strands of flesh. He whispered to me to pull it off, because it was cutting into his tongue.

She began screaming for someone to open the doors. Rock, Kevin and Michael Wilding were trying to force them open but it took them twenty minutes or more to get them free and gingerly lift Monty from the wreck. As they were doing it, Elizabeth screamed again: 'Get that damn camera out of here.'

Although the ambulance had not yet arrived, the photographers, alerted by the police call, had dashed to the scene and were flashing every angle. The ambulance got lost; it took forty-five minutes to arrive after the original telephone call.

A local doctor was already there, doing what he could, and when they lifted Monty into the ambulance for the journey to the Cedars of Lebanon Hospital, Elizabeth insisted on travelling with him. Phyllis Hudson also went in the ambulance. Monty's face was still bleeding profusely. His whole head was swelling, almost visibly; his eyes had virtually disappeared and it looked as if a giant red football were sitting on his shoulders.

Elizabeth and Phyllis stayed with him until he was taken into surgery, at which point Elizabeth lost her composure and collapsed into wailing hysteria. She was treated for shock, and Phyllis stayed with her until seven the following morning, when they learned that Monty's condition had stabilised. The doctor's report showed that he had suffered a fractured jaw, broken nose, crushed sinus cavity, severe facial lacerations and two teeth were missing. The remainder of his body, though badly bruised, was relatively unmarked.

The following day, Libby Holman flew out to California; so did Monty's parents and, for the moment, his mother's intense dislike of the woman was set aside. Libby and Elizabeth were Monty's most frequent visitors; but Libby in particular was always around to see to his needs and make his telephone calls for him. He was unable to speak for three weeks while his mouth was clamped by the wires holding his jaw together – but still he managed to sip Martinis through a straw.

Dore Schary and Edward Dmytryk visited regularly, putting on a brave front. Privately, they went into deep discussion about the future of *Raintree County*. It seemed hardly possible that Clift could continue in the film with his face scarred and swollen. Monty, however, insisted that he could resume as soon as he got the wires off; he was sure the make-up people could hide the scars.

Almost half the picture had been filmed, at a cost exceeding $2 million. To replace Monty now would have meant scrapping a huge footage; only the long-shots might be salvaged. Schary seemed prepared to consider that option, knowing that much of the cost could be recouped from the insurance companies if it could be proved that Monty had been injured to such a degree that it was not possible to continue filming with him as a leading player.

When Elizabeth heard that this possibility was being discussed she pleaded with Schary not to replace him; she was afraid that he might go into deep depression and kill himself. Libby Holman, on the other hand, was desperately trying to get him to give it up, take a couple of years off and go back with her to Treetops where she could nurse him back to health. He refused, insisting that he would return to the picture just as soon as he possibly could. Dore Schary finally agreed, aided in his decision by the discovery that he would be able to claim $500,000 compensation from the insurance company for the delay to production.

Monty's recovery was remarkable and, despite his broken jaw and the necessary plastic surgery to his scars, after eight weeks his face had healed sufficiently for him to discharge himself from hospital and present himself for work – against the advice of his doctors, who said he needed more time to get over the accident before putting himself through the rigours of a difficult and heavy film script.

*   *   *   *   *

The trauma of Clift's accident, the shock, the worry and the endless debates over the future of *Raintree County*, all took their toll on Elizabeth. Now she hated driving up that twisting road to their house; her stomach churned every time she passed the spot where she had found Monty. She could see his battered face every time, and it haunted her in her nightmares. She had been drained emotionally and physically, and this in turn increased the pressure on her marriage.

While they waited for filming to start again, she was pleased to receive an invitation for herself and Michael Wilding to dine with the gregarious Mike Todd, who was cruising in his yacht off the Californian coast.

Elizabeth was intrigued. She hardly knew Todd, but of late she had heard much through Hollywood gossip and the trade papers about his latest venture, the epic *Around the World in Eighty Days.*

That weekend, 29 June, he was having a party on board the yacht after filming some sequences with David Niven. Mr and Mrs Michael Wilding joined him and sailed up to Santa Barbara for dinner. Close observers might have noticed a sparkle in the eye of Mr Todd as he chatted with Elizabeth. A couple of weeks later he threw a small party – about two hundred guests – at his rented mansion in Beverly Hills in honour of the broadcaster Ed Murrow. Elizabeth and Michael were again invited. She spent three hours preparing herself and arrived in stunning elegance, wearing a magnificent white satin gown, which formed a perfect circle around her feet, and laden with diamonds.

Eyes met across the room. Mike Todd, cigar between his teeth, jostled his way over to greet her. In a moment, they both admitted later, a certain magic entered their lives. Michael Wilding left early and Kevin McCarthy brought Elizabeth home at 2 a.m. From then on, the Wilding marriage was heading fast towards the rocks.

On 19 July Hollywood was stunned by a joint announcement, issued through the MGM press office, informing the world that they had separated. The brief statement said: 'Much careful thought has been given to this step we are taking. It has been done so that we will have an opportunity to thoroughly work out our personal situation. We are in complete accord in making this amicable decision.'

They remained friends – 'I still loved him, but like a brother' – but they found no way to work out their problems and filed for divorce later in the year.

Hedda Hopper, in her column, advised caution. Miss Taylor, she said, should take stock of her life before proceeding again into matrimony. Her advice went unheeded. The day following the Wildings' announcement, the telephone rang for Elizabeth. It was Mike Todd: he would like to meet her at his office, and she agreed.

What they had in common was anyone's guess. Todd was a brash, full-of-zest producer and entrepreneur whose fortunes had alternated with alarming frequency between the possession of great wealth and being chased by creditors. A Jewish boy from the slums of Minneapolis, his rise had been startling. He made his first fortune at the New York World Fair in 1938. He brought the stripper Gypsy Rose Lee to international fame, putting her name in huge letters on Broadway hoardings to announce both her arrival and his own as a New York producer. Throughout the forties, he continued his money-making with an amazing and outrageous array of schemes.

When his romance with Gypsy soured, he became devoted to the 'blonde bombshell' Joan Blondell, whom he wanted to marry. His wife Bertha, who had borne him Mike Todd, Jr, refused to divorce him, however. Then one night, Bertha was discovered lying on the kitchen floor at her home covered with blood and died on the operating table at the local hospital as doctors tried to patch up a deep gash in her right arm. Mike Todd was arrested on suspicion of murder, but he was eventually released when Joan Blondell confirmed that he had been with her the night Bertha was found. An autopsy revealed that she had died of a heart attack while on the operating table, but whether the cuts on her arm were self-inflicted or accidental remains unresolved.

Todd resumed his commercial ventures with his usual vigour, wealthy one day, poverty-stricken the next. In 1950 he was $1 million in debt after a disastrous series of gambling losses. It took him five years to get level and make enough to surround himself with sufficient trappings of apparent wealth to arrive in Hollywood and secure the services of a dozen major international stars on the promise of excellent salaries, as well as the assistance of several banks to back his most ambitious project yet. They were unaware that his dream of producing *Around the World in Eighty Days* was little more than that – a dream, a magnificent vision. With his brimming confidence and energy, he succeeded in raising the finance and now his global journey with David Niven was nearing its end, the film almost in the can.

The headlines were still mauling the break-up of her marriage when Elizabeth arrived at MGM for her appointment with Mike Todd. She had no inkling of what it could be about. At 3 p.m. on the dot she walked down the office corridors and spotted Todd talking to Benny Thau, one of the studio's chief executives. Todd grasped her arm and ushered her into his private office, snapping at his secretary: 'No calls. No interruptions.'

Not a word had passed between them apart from greetings. Now he looked at her across his desk. She stubbed a half-smoked cigarette and sat there, tense. Todd spoke: 'I see you've ditched Michael. Well, hear this good. Don't go around looking for anyone else. There's only one guy you're going to marry. And that's me!'

Chapter Ten

Myths and Emotions

The legend of James Dean had been created and now the mythology began. Teenagers throughout the world saw him not as an actor but as one of them. As the myth grew, it generated an aura of godlike proportions around the memory of a young man who in reality was nothing special. He had provided the right personality at the right time in the right films. Perhaps even his next movie, about Billy the Kid, might have shown a changing course and broken his spell. As it was, his death at that particular moment allowed him to become a catalyst for the growing movement of youth protest that would go on for years to come.

Long before John Lennon caused so much controversy by announcing that the Beatles were bigger than Christ, Gwin Steinbeck, former wife of the author of *East of Eden*, chose a similar comparison to illustrate her thoughts on the Dean Age. 'Many young people', she said, 'had no emotional roots and were without a basic faith. Dean became a substitute Christ. As such, they even tried to resurrect him.'

As *East of Eden* and *Rebel Without a Cause* suddenly took on major cult proportions, Warner Brothers became inundated with letters from Dean's fans around the globe, many thousands of whom simply refused to believe he was dead. Groups formed outside the studio entrance, believing that if they waited long enough they would actually see him, and Warners were scared that there might be a riot or mass break-in.

Word had got around that, by some miracle, he had escaped death in the crash, or that he and the studio had masterminded a massive charade of his burial and the coroner's inquest in order to perpetuate the story that he had been killed. The theory was either that he was so disfigured by his injuries that he wanted to hide away until the scars had healed and would re-emerge later; or that he had chosen this point in his life to retire from the world and become a recluse. Those who wanted to believe this found temporary support from America's gossip of the airwaves, Walter Winchell, who was accused of hinting that Dean was still alive. Under pressure from Warner Brothers, he subsequently broadcast a denial, saying, 'I never at any time said Dean was still alive. This message is addressed to his fans who have deluged my office with hundreds of letters. The physical James Dean is dead. The memory lives.'

A denial of such magnitude, however, merely fanned the flames. Rumours continued unabated: Dean was living in a hospital; he had been transferred to a private suite on the Warners lot. They reached such proportions that Warners themselves put a complete embargo on requests for information, photographs and anecdotes about their dead star. It was difficult to put into effect because *Giant* had still not been released; however, the reaction to his death now threatened to eclipse the other stars of the film, even though Dean had not played the main character.

A formal statement was drawn up:

We are receiving around two to three thousand letters every week requesting autographed photos, mementoes and souvenirs of Jimmy. We do not betray the contents of those letters and the publicity for the forthcoming release of *Giant* will be arranged around the cast as a whole, and the various great stars who played in it together with Dean. We do not want to encourage or exploit this morbid interest in him.

The letters kept coming and, somehow or other, their contents began to appear in the media. One girl wrote: 'Dear Jimmy, All this remembrance stuff is a waste of time, because I know you are still alive. Why worry so much about the way you look, because your fans worship you however disfigured you are.' And another: 'Dear Jim, Even if you refuse to show yourself to the world, don't hold out on me. Tell those who are looking after you to send me a piece of your clothing, or a button from your leather jacket. I so long to have a lasting souvenir of your wonderful personality that makes mockery of the word death.'

The papers were full of interviews with the I-Knew-Jimmy-Dean brigade. People emerged or were dragged from past corners of his life who talked about everything from his angry devotion to the memory of his mother, to his alleged death wish. Girls he had never met, or students with whom he may have had a passing friendship, claimed passionate affairs; some said they had married him secretly, while others claimed he had left them pregnant.

Fan clubs were forming everywhere. One group called itself the James Dean Death Club and, as the cult spread, a more desperate trend emerged. In Japan *Rebel Without a Cause* was banned for a time because teenagers were reconstructing the chicken-run game and two died a similar death to Buzz in the film. The British censors cut the knife scene. In Sweden there was anguished press comment that everyone was walking around looking like Dean, in leathers and jeans, even the girls. In Hamburg two teenage girls jumped to their deaths from a fourteenth-floor apartment, leaving a suicide note to their parents explaining that Jimmy was calling them. An English postman who saw *Rebel* four hundred times changed his name by deed poll to James Byron Dean.

Poets and songwriters took up the cause and in the year after his death eight eulogising records were issued in America, ranging from 'His Name Was Jimmy Dean' to 'Jimmy Dean's Christmas in Heaven'. A morbid range of Jimmy Dean memorabilia came on sale, and a magazine called *Jimmy Dean Returns* sold half a million copies, largely on the claim that Dean had written an article from beyond the grave by communicating with a girl who had professed her undying love for him. A second-hand-car dealer bought the wreck of Dean's car and put it on public view 'in support of the campaign for road safety'; he charged 25 cents for everyone who came to look.

Then there were the 'jinx' stories and the Curse of James Dean, which gathered momentum over the years. Car-designer George Barris eventually bought the wreck of the Porsche to sell off some of the undamaged parts. When the car was delivered to his yard, it rolled off the back of the lorry and broke a mechanic's legs. A Beverly Hills doctor, Troy McHenry, who also raced cars, bought the engine from Dean's Porsche, transferred it to another car and was killed the first time he drove it. Another doctor who bought the transmission and put it in his own car was seriously injured in a crash, and a man in New York who bought two of the Porsche tyres spent weeks in hospital after they both 'mysteriously' blew out at the same time. A year later, the remaining shell of the car was being transported for a public road-safety exhibition in Salinas. The driver of the transporter was killed as the lorry skidded and crashed; Dean's wrecked Porsche was stolen and it has never been seen since. And so it went on.

By the middle of 1956, the James Dean aftermath had reached such fever pitch that an official James Dean Foundation, based at Fairmount was formed as a non-profit-making company to provide a 'living and perpetual memory' to him, to finance scholarships, encourage knowledge of the theatre arts and to give financial help to deserving young professional talent.

The pressure on the people of Fairmount became unbearable as the pilgrimage to Dean's birthplace began. At weekends especially, hundreds would arrive, just to walk around and look at his grave. Marcus and Ortense Winslow were constantly pestered by people knocking on their door and asking, 'Is Jimmy here?', but they remained passive and calm, apparently prepared to talk endlessly about the boy – to the point that even they became swept along by the torrent and changed their early view that Jimmy was 'just an ordinary boy' to the realisation that he was 'special and different, we can see that now'.

One American writer, Charles Hamblett, tried to sum up the frenzy when he wrote:

> There is a widespread guilt complex about Dean's death, partly based on America's craving for speed, for pushing ahead of the next guy, for the stepping-on-the-gas-and-to-hell-with-the-consequences outlook. . . . things are getting faster all the time. And at the end of the road is a vast atomic mushroom cloud permanently in the subconscious mind. It is the shadow that followed James Dean all his life, the pressure that seeks relief in travel, self-analysis and speed. America's young rock and rollers are obsessed by these pressures, as was their idol Jimmy Dean.

Elia Kazan, like many others in Hollywood at the time, had a more mundane reaction to the dawning of the Dean Age. Kazan said: 'Dean was the glorification of hatred and sickness. When he got success, he was victimized by it. He was a hero to the people who saw him only as a little waif, when actually he was a pudding of hatred.' Edna Ferber agreed: 'Dean suffered from success poisoning, despite all that his image stood for.'

Other actors, and especially some of those good actors in *Giant* whose performances would be overshadowed by the publicity surrounding Dean, found it difficult to comprehend this sudden adulation of the young man they had worked with; and, as professionals, they did not find it a pleasant experience. Charlton Heston put it all into perspective:

> Dean was extraordinary, there is no doubt about that. He was obviously a very gifted young man. But you can go into any acting class and find talented actors – there are a lot of talented actors around. The difference between a talented actor and a great actor is the difference between James Dean and Laurence Olivier. That's not to say he would not have become a good actor, or even a great actor. He only made three pictures; the first two were OK – not great, but interesting, and he was good in both and he played the central charac- ter. Probably only *Giant*, of the three, was a good picture and he was not the central character; there was a host of fine actors.

Dean was nominated posthumously for Academy Awards for Best Actor for his role in *East of Eden* and subsequently for *Giant*, but got neither. In France, however, he was given the Crystal Star for the Best Foreign Actor for his roles in *Eden* and *Rebel*.

He did become a prime influence on other actors and entertainers, however. Elvis Presley became obsessed; he went to see *Rebel Without a Cause* forty-four times and obtained a copy of the film script so that he could memorise every line spoken by Dean, as Natalie Wood discovered. 'I could give him a cue-line from a certain scene, and he would come straight back with the line that Jimmy spoke. It was uncanny.'

Presley began to visit the Hollywood haunts once frequented by Dean and started to edge his way into the crowd at Googie's. He deliberately sought out Dean's old buddies and became friendly with Nick Adams, who was among the host of young actors and lookalikes adopting the Dean style of speech, dress and moodiness in the vain hope that they might also achieve his success. Adams was also among the much-quoted friends of Dean who were always ready to expound upon the subject of 'Jimmy and Me' or 'What James Dean Was Really Like – by His Best Friend'. Adams, in fact, sickened many of Dean's more responsible friends by the way he prostituted himself in the aftermath, extracting as much mileage as he could for his own career. He was also at the centre of a web of homosexual intrigue, and his favours included arranging for a Dean-like young man to be available to male associates.

Adams took Elvis Presley to a preview of his new film, *The Last Wagon*. Natalie Wood went with them, and it soon became clear that Presley was intent on forming a relationship with 'Jimmy's girl'.

* * * * *

Since making *Rebel Without a Cause*, Natalie had broken free of her mother's shackles. The effect the film had on her was dramatic. She talked often of how Dean taught her to 'look inside herself' for her performance, as he himself did, unleashing personal emotions that would heighten the realism of her lines. In doing that, Natalie discovered for the first time that she was angry with her mother for the total hold she had maintained over her life and for ignoring the fact that she was now a young woman who wished to be doing the things that other girls of her age were doing. She became angry with her father, too, for failing to intervene in Marie Gurdin's domination.

Natalie also realised, while reading the lines in *Rebel* about parental weakness, that she herself held the power, the purse-strings; she was the breadwinner in the life to which her family had become accustomed – and if she wanted to go out on a date, or to drink, she was damn well going to, regardless of what her mother said.

Natalie was breaking free and, like a greedy child with a box full of presents placed in front of her, she grasped at everything. At first she was seen around a lot with Nick Adams and Sal Mineo, and they smoked marijuana together. It was the in thing to talk about teenage unhappiness. 'I loved both of them, just as I loved Jimmy,' she once said. 'And they seemed terribly glamorous, and with it. We used to talk about how unhappy we were and who came closest to committing suicide the night before. It was that kind of silly age.' After Dean died, she also had an affair with the director of *Rebel Without a Cause*, Nick Ray, who was twice her age. They were discovered in bed together by another of the film's stars. Now Natalie too was becoming a subject for the media gossips.

*　*　*　*　*

Speculation over Elizabeth Taylor's romantic intentions was also bubbling away. It escaped no one's attention that Mike Todd was sending her large bundles of flowers almost daily, in full view of everyone on the set of *Raintree County*, where filming had resumed after Monty Clift's accident. At weekends, when she was free, Todd would send a private plane to bring her to join him in New York.

Clift had discharged himself from hospital before his wounds and the plastic surgery to his damaged eye had completely healed, but the make-up people did a good job and on film the 'before and after' discrepancies were minimised. His face was thinner, however, his eyes set back, and he was constantly unsteady on his feet. The combination of strong painkillers and occasional straight doses of intravenous morphine, plus his return to alcohol in defiance of doctors' orders, meant that his abilities were often impaired. Eddie Dmytryk said:

> He was not physically different after the accident – a lot of people said he was. What happened was that because of the pain he was suffering, he started to drink and he took every known drug in the world – we searched his room one day and found two hundred and fifty kinds of drugs in there – and on top of that, the liquor. . . . I've had the same damn thing happen with several others . . . with Bill Holden, with Richard Burton, in particular, who were on the wagon when the picture started, went off the wagon and within a week, their faces were puffy, their eyes were red-ringed. Richard Burton hadn't been in an accident, yet [he] aged twenty years in two weeks. And in bad shape. The same thing happened to Bill Holden who looked like . . . a young leading man when we started . . . and after drinking, all of a sudden there he was, forty-five, or fifty. And this is what happened to Monty Clift. You cannot drink and take dope and retain your physical firmness, your muscle texture. Your face falls apart.

When filming moved out on location to Natchez, Mississippi, it became obvious to everyone that Clift was still suffering severe repercussions. He looked tired and drained. After the day's filming he would go straight to his room and swallow sleeping pills chased down by vodka to knock himself out. One morning, when he failed to arrive on set, Dmytryk sent someone round to rouse him. Monty was found in a coma from an accidental overdose of sleeping pills, with two fingers on his right hand badly burned. He had fallen unconscious with a lighted cigarette in his hand and it had burned through the flesh on the sides of both fingers.

Now he required further medical attention: bandages to the wounds on his hand and more tablets to get him back on his feet. Somehow he dragged himself into a state where he could face the cameras. Every ounce of his energy and determination was drawn upon each day. It was a miracle that he could speak, let alone act. Yet far from ruining the picture, he was helping to save it. Uppermost in his mind was the unselfish thought that Elizabeth Taylor, come what may, should be seen in a good light. They spent hours together in their hotel rooms and Clift could remain sober and sensible long enough to help her rehearse, taking her through her script, over and over until she got it right.

MGM still had great faith in the picture and, when the unit moved on to Illinois for further location filming at Danville, the studio laid on a private aircraft to bring reporters and photographers to the set. Swarming all over everywhere and carrying what they understood to be Dore Schary's personal invitation to talk to any of the stars, they all went straight for Monty, asking what was wrong with him and was there anything between him and Taylor. Out of it came not the stories MGM had hoped for – or did they? Instead of chatty pre-release news of the stars of what had been billed as 'this great movie', the media were filled with personal attacks on Clift and innuendo about his relationship with Taylor. Fortunately, the press was not around on the night when Monty suffered one of his terrible nightmares and was discovered running naked and distraught in Danville main street.

The location work was finally wrapped up and, after three weeks' more filming in Hollywood, the actors parted company at the end of October, leaving Eddie Dmytryk with the task of bringing the movie, with all Schary's great expectations, to the screen for première the following spring. It had taken 160 days to shoot, and now Dmytryk was called into the studio to discover that Dore Schary was no longer *in situ*. He, in his turn, had been removed. The new management wanted to inject major alterations and refilming, and threatened to sack Dmytryk when he disdainfully rejected huge rewrites to the script of a film which was already completed. He was saved only by Elizabeth and Monty's intervention; they both threatened to quit if Dmytryk were fired before the final edit, or if he were forced to make changes against his will. In the end, Dmytryk compromised by reshooting small sections which entailed about twenty-seven lines of rewritten material.

Privately, Clift had his own fears about the film's quality. Only Elizabeth could view it as a triumph. Her performance was widely acclaimed as her best so far, better even than *A Place In the Sun*; she dominated the screen throughout and her portrayal won her her first Academy nomination as Best Actress of the year.

The critics gave *Raintree County* a poor reception; descriptions ranged from monumentally boring to amazingly diffuse. The public, however, flocked to see it. After the incredible pre-release publicity the film had received from Monty's accident and other off-screen incidents, they ghoulishly expected to discover one of their favourite stars looking like a creation of Frankenstein.

* * * * *

During the latter part of the filming, Elizabeth spent hours on the telephone to Mike Todd; their calls might last two or three hours a day. In early October 1956, she and Wilding announced, in another joint statement issued by the studio, that they were to be divorced. Wilding openly acknowledged his wife's association with Todd; but, as Elizabeth later pointed out, he was a gentleman to the end, calmly insisting: 'They did not see one another alone until after we had separated and Todd's conduct throughout has been beyond reproach. I do not feel any bitterness towards him and I am adult enough to reconcile myself to the situation.' Wilding said that they had agreed to sell their house and share the proceeds; even the custody of the two children had been resolved amicably, with Elizabeth taking care of them for nine months of the year and he for the remaining three. After that, Mr Wilding exited stage left. MGM, who had no further use for him after his detachment from Miss Taylor, ended his contract by 'mutual agreement' and he gathered up his belongings and his father (who had been living with them since his wife's death) and moved away.

In the third week of October, Todd and Taylor went public, appearing arm in arm at the world première of *Around the World in Eighty Days*. They could not have chosen a more glamorous occasion. It was a brilliant, star-studded night for which Todd had flown in the countless famous faces who had had cameo roles, plus half the acting fraternity and celebrities of America. Broadway was his that night, and so was Elizabeth Taylor. At a lavish party afterwards they announced their intention to marry and Elizabeth told her family, 'I am passionately in love with him.' She was also quite taken with the huge rock he placed on her engagement finger: a diamond an inch wide and half an inch deep.

For Todd, it was a night of spectacular triumph. His completion of this huge adventure story had been achieved against all the odds, entirely through his personal dedication. All the stops and starts during its making, the trouble with finance, the immensely difficult location work, the creation of his Todd-AO process after the movie moguls had frozen him out of using Cinerama, and various other difficulties, would have floored a less energetic promoter.

Nor was he backward in showing his gratitude to those who had helped. He put his arm around Noël Coward, for instance, took the cigar from his mouth and kissed him on the cheek: 'I owe you a lot Noël, you know that, don't you kid?' Coward did know. When Todd was frantically looking for big names for the vital cameo parts, he had already had a number of refusals before he telephoned Coward and asked him to make a guest appearance for a fee of just £100 a day. Coward agreed and that enabled Todd, in his future calls, to say 'Noël's doing it.' Todd further showed his gratitude to Coward by giving him a Bonnard the following Christmas.

Now an ecstatic audience was applauding what Todd would claim to be the most successful picture in the history of movie-making. Elizabeth Taylor eventually received from him a forty per cent ownership of the film – one of many gifts he lavished upon her in the coming months. His frankness to reporters left no doubt about his feelings for her:

OK, so I know she's spoilt and, like my friend Nick Schenck once said, 'Who wouldn't want to indulge a girl like that?' Yeah, and I know anyone who marries an actress marries a problem. But it's a darned attractive problem to wake up to every morning, kid.

Todd whisked his future bride off to the Bahamas and a meeting with Lord Beaverbrook. While they were there, Elizabeth suffered a fall that injured her badly. She was stepping off a boat when it suddenly lurched, throwing her to the foot of the steps, where she writhed in pain. Todd hired a plane and had her flown straight to New York. At the Presbyterian Hospital of the Harkness Pavilion, X-rays revealed that she had crushed three discs at the base of her spine and an operation was necessary. For the next three weeks she endured agonising pain as doctors cut the dead bone away and built up the damaged area with bone taken from her hip and pelvis. There were fears that she might be left partially crippled.

The fall and operation paralysed the use of her legs and for two months she had to be lifted and turned on her bed to ease the constant pain.

When he discovered how long she would be confined, Todd went out and bought a few paintings to hang on the wall of her room – a Monet, a Renoir and a Pissaro; and just after Christmas, when he flew to London for a business conference, he telephoned to tell her: 'I've bought you a little present.'

'What is it? Tell me please, what is it?'

'It's a Rolls-Royce. Silver Cloud. You'll love it, kid.'

Todd could hardly wait to marry her. He was intoxicated by her beauty and head over heels in love – like a schoolboy, he kept saying. He had a roomful of lawyers working on the best way to achieve a speedy divorce and an immediate marriage. When Elizabeth was discharged from hospital in mid-January 1957, he had already made the arrangements: they would fly down to Mexico, get her divorce there and marry straight away.

The original divorce hearing had been scheduled for Santa Monica, but it had been postponed because of Elizabeth's accident. Michael Wilding had agreed to assist Todd in arranging a speedy marriage, so Todd paid for him to fly from London to join them in Acapulco, where Elizabeth would be found dining with her soon-to-be-ex-husband and he husband-to-be, happily discussing the arrangements for the wedding.

For a showman like Todd, the wedding could never be a sneaky affair. Plane-loads of guests were flown in from Hollywood, New York and other parts of the globe; he ordered fifteen thousand white gladioli to decorate the mansion he had rented for the ceremony, plus fifty cases of champagne and large amounts of lobster, caviare and turkey for the wedding breakfast; he laid on the biggest fireworks display Mexico had seen in years. Reporters, cameramen, newsreels and television took the Mexican town by siege. The Taylor–Todd wedding had all the classic trappings the gossip journalists adored, and every minute detail was recorded for an avid public.

Elizabeth took her marriage vows for the third time on 2 February 1957, twenty-five days before her twenty-fifth birthday, wearing a beautiful pale-blue cocktail dress designed by Helen Rose. The Mayor of Acapulco conducted the ceremony; Todd's closest friend, Eddie Fisher, was best man; his wife, Debbie Reynolds, was Elizabeth's matron of honour.

That night, at the reception on the terraces of the mansion, guarded against gatecrashers by fifty troops of the Mexican army, the guests were given shirts ornamented with the couple's monograms. The final scene of the fireworks display lit the skies with a huge heart of flames encircling the initials MT–ET. Francis Taylor was moved to one of his few public comments on his daughter's life: 'I hope this time her dreams will come true,' and, as she fingered the bracelet heavily laden with diamonds which Todd had given her as a wedding present – along with two cinemas in Chicago – Elizabeth purred: 'I am the happiest and the luckiest girl in the world.'

Todd whisked her out of the Hollywood life that had, despite its glamour, become ordinary and mundane to her, particularly in the last stages of her marriage to Michael Wilding. Ahead lay a new experience, filled with excitement and incident, and with supreme luxury.

* * * * *

Three weeks after their wedding, the Todds were back on the front pages again. In the Academy Awards for 1956, *Giant* had received ten nominations and *Around the World in Eighty Days* eight. It was a night of varying emotions for Elizabeth, who had starred in one film and was married to the producer of the other. She also saw bitter disappointment for Rock Hudson, who failed to get the Oscar for Best Actor that Henry Willson had so confidently predicted for him; nor was James Dean awarded Best Supporting Actor.

Elizabeth herself had moved on a long way since *Giant*. Her affiliation now lay with her husband, and when nominations for best film were read out – *Giant*, *The King and I*, *Friendly Persuasion*, *The Ten Commandments* and *Around the World in Eighty Days* – there was no question of which she wanted to win. And it did. Todd collected the Oscar for Best Film and also won five other categories. As he leapt from his seat and began running down towards the stage, he suddenly stopped, turned back and, in full view of the millions watching on television, gave Elizabeth a long kiss, saying, 'That's to show the world how much I love this kid.'

The fireside existence she had led with Michael Wilding was at an end. The house on the hill was replaced by a penthouse suite in New York (which Todd considered his spiritual home), a small estate in Beverly Hills, a house in Connecticut for weekends and a holiday home in Palm Springs. There was a private plane to ferry them around, its interior fitted in the style of a sumptuous apartment, with thick carpets, soft, lounging furniture and a huge double bedroom.

And as they began a world tour, which half resembled the film they were promoting, Elizabeth found herself caught up in a whirlwind: New York, Paris, London, Rome, even Moscow. Every week he brought her a new present, including a Degas bought from Aly Khan in Paris for $30,000.

In London, on the night of the première of *Around the World in Eighty*

Days, Todd staged the biggest party London had ever seen. He hired Battersea Fun-fair for the evening, had sixteen famous orchestras playing and flew in planefuls of exotic food, plus the chefs to cook it. Two thousand escapees from *Who's Who* rode the fairground and drank champagne until dawn. The papers described it as a wild and wonderful, mad and marvellous extravaganza. His son, Mike Todd, Jr, wired from New York to tell him that the film was making nearly as much money in America as he was spending in Europe.

In the middle of their tour, Elizabeth announced that she was pregnant; the news made Todd even more heady.

Eddie Fisher and his wife Debbie Reynolds joined the Todds on the great hype. Mike Todd would put his arms around Fisher and called him 'my pal'. Who could possibly have guessed that, in less than a year, Todd would be dead; and, not long afterwards, Elizabeth would be embroiled with Eddie in a devastating scandal?

Chapter Eleven

Hot Properties

Within Hollywood's dream factories, publicity and promotion was a major industry in itself. It had been built up since the thirties and by the mid-fifties, when cinema audiences were beginning to evaporate, the publicists were among the studios' most important employees. Around each picture a team of writers, photographers and artists would swing into action to push their film. Every possible aspect would be covered, including the personal lives of the stars. Each studio had a team of 'planters' who would feed stories to selected parts of the media – to the news agencies, the columnists and general news releases. Most publicity departments, for instance, had a specific planter for Hedda Hopper and Louella Parsons so that different 'exclusives' could be given to each, thus achieving maximum publicity. On a quiet day, no one was choosy about the kind of tips that went out.

Natalie Wood became an instant target, and a victim. She had long been the subject of publicity hype, but now it was different. Young and sexy, her private life could no longer be regarded as her own. The aftermath of James Dean and *Rebel Without a Cause* swept her off her feet and, although she had been reared on a Hollywood lot, Natalie was unprepared for it – as indeed were Warners.

She had received an Oscar nomination as Best Supporting Actress for *Rebel* (in the event she lost to Jo Van Fleet, who had played Dean's mother in *East of Eden*) and, in the volumes of idolatry inspired by Dean's death, she suddenly became the sweetheart of a million college boys and the one every other teenage girl wanted to copy in hairstyle, clothes and make-up.

Warners had not noticed, until now, that they had the biggest teenage star of the age on their hands – at least that's what Natalie could have been had the studio planned it properly. They had already cast her, however, for a movie that did little to promote that idea. She was to appear in a smallish role alongside John Wayne and Jeffrey Hunter in what became another classic western, *The Searchers*. As the child kidnapped by Indians and eventually found by her uncle, Natalie was to appear only towards the end of the film (her sister Lana played her as a young child) and, although the experience of working with John Ford and Wayne himself did her ego the world of good, it hardly fitted her image of the moment. Warners, trying to capitalise on her popularity, rushed her into two more pictures which became instantly forgettable. The first, with Tab Hunter, was *The Burning Hills*, in which she plays a Spanish half-breed set on revenge against the gang who murdered her father; she falls in love, naturally, with the character played by Tab. Her lines made her cringe: 'You dirty gringos. You're no good, none of you,' but, with the prospect of making Natalie and Tab into a new romantic team, the publicists billed her as 'the sensational girl from *Rebel Without a Cause*, flaming with the fire of her first love'. Underneath a tantalising photograph of the two young stars, which had Tab bare from the waist up, they added: 'Don't call them kids, not any more!'

For her next film, she co-starred in *A Cry in the Night* with Edmond O'Brien and Raymond Burr. Burr, twenty-one years older than Natalie and soon to find fame as television's Perry Mason, played a psychopathic kidnapper and had audiences on the edge of their seats wondering whether he was going to have his evil way with the tiny Miss Wood, playing the abducted heroine. Before long Hedda Hopper's story planter from Warners dropped her the tiniest hint that something was going on between the teenage star and the heavyweight actor.

They dated for a month or more, the budding romance gathering daily attention. The substantial Mr Burr was serious enough to consider his figure and went on a diet to shed fifty pounds. Natalie was serious enough to 'confide' to Hedda Hopper, who naturally confided the information to her millions of readers, that they had reached an 'understanding'. Years later, Burr admitted in an interview that they had considered marriage. But they had reckoned without the concerted chorus of fan magazines and gossip columns, who were branding her a wild girl and asking: 'IS NATALIE HEADING FOR A FALL?' Warners liked the publicity but not the prospect of her marriage to Burr; nor did Natalie's mother, and they joined forces to call a halt to the whole business. Raymond was warned off and Natalie was given some prudent advice about seeing someone her own age.

Snapping at her heels was a pack of young wolves, including Elizabeth Taylor's ex-husband Nicky Hilton, and Jimmy Dean's racing friend and Woolworth's heir Lance Reventlow. But Natalie's next move suited the publicity people admirably: suddenly she was crazy for Elvis Presley. In November 1956 she revealed:

When Nick [Adams] introduced us, I was quite surprised by Elvis's looks and manner. He was so clean-cut, and ever so polite, not a bit like the publicity made him out to be. He doesn't talk bop talk and he isn't hipster at all.

They went on that first night to a restaurant for dinner and afterwards drove down to Malibu beach, singing their heads off to the car radio. Elvis took her home at about 1 a.m. and didn't try to kiss her; he just shook hands. After that, she saw him almost every night.

The interview provides a rare retrospective view of Presley before he too became 'poisoned by success' and the pressures that go with it. Natalie went on:

Elvis never took me to swank places; he is unimpressed by his success and totally different to what you'd think. He's probably the most good person I've ever met and lives by a rigid set of rules. That doesn't mean he is dull, anything but that. He is also tough and virile and full of fun.

Things were getting serious for Natalie when Presley telephoned one day and said, 'I'd like you to come down to Memphis and meet my mother.' She agreed, and got into trouble with the studio because on the day that she flew down to Tennessee she should have been making a personal appearance at the Hollywood Bowl before fifteen thousand members of the Young Men's Christian Association who had wanted to make her their Harvest Queen. She planned to stay for a week with Elvis, and it was fun at first. He had just bought a huge new motorcycle and they roared around the countryside with Natalie riding pillion. It did not take her long to discover, however, that Elvis too had a domineering mother; after a few days she had had enough and telephoned her own mother: 'Get me out of here. Make any excuse, but tell me to come home.'

In comparison to James Dean, a fund of knowledge, intelligent and intense, she found Presley childlike and unsure of himself, complex and lonely. But he was handsome and extremely virile, and, as Natalie admitted, 'For a girl, that's a deadly combination.' In the end, his virility and sexual prowess were not sufficient to sustain their affair, and from Elvis she fell into the arms of the man who, for a while at least, would give her stability.

Robert Wagner – RJ to his friends – was a young, slightly struggling actor, who came up via the same type of star-creation school that produced Rock Hudson and Tony Curtis. He was a childhood friend of Elizabeth Taylor, dating from the time they first met around Roddy

McDowall's pool; RJ and Roddy were also the best of friends and they and Natalie had many mutual acquaintances. Natalie had first seen RJ on a film lot when she was ten years old and, according to the publicists, had told her mother at the time: 'One day I'm going to marry him.' That may have been another piece of Hollywood invention; what is certain is that they went out on one date together in the summer of 1956, then Natalie did not hear from RJ again until after her brief affair with Elvis had ended. After that their togetherness quickly flourished.

Towards the end of 1956, Wagner had just begun to get star billing after appearing in sixteen films, one for MGM and the rest for 20th Century–Fox. He had finally been noticed for a fleeting moment when Susan Hayward sang to him in the musical *With a Song in My Heart* in 1952, and fan mail started arriving at the Fox studios. His most recent films had put him alongside major players, including Spencer Tracy and Richard Widmark in *Broken Lance*; John Lund and Jeffrey Hunter in *White Feather*; Jeffrey Hunter again, Joanne Woodward and Mary Astor in *A Kiss Before Dying*; and Spencer Tracy again in *The Mountain*. He had just completed another fairly mundane war picture, *Between Heaven and Hell*, when he was given his next task, which would entail working with director Nick Ray. Fresh from *Rebel Without a Cause*, Ray had been signed by 20th Century for the remake of the Jesse James story, the 1939 version of which had starred Tyrone Power and Henry Fonda. He had been working on the old Nunnally Johnson screenplay for some time to make it more presentable to a fifties audience and retitled it *The True Story of Jesse James*.

Ray's drinking bouts and his affinity for the Dean-style Method approach to acting could not have suited the straightforward, slightly boring, no-nonsense approach of Robert Wagner, who was the studio's choice for the part. The result was a dull picture that made a profit but no impact whatsoever. Still, with Natalie basking in the publicity that had surrounded her affair with Elvis, plus the Raymond Burr incident and Warners' big build-up for *The Burning Hills*, anyone remotely associated with her could expect a press-tail and Wagner became an obvious candidate.

Natalie had been signed for two more films and it was clear that Warners had still failed to find the right vehicle to turn her into a top-billing star, which Nick Ray felt she was capable of becoming. The studio made a second, and last, attempt to create a hot screen duo out of Natalie and Tab Hunter in *The Girl He Left Behind*, which audiences shunned after the great let-down of *The Burning Hills*. Then she went straight into *Bombers B-52*, a smallish part in a patriotic non-event co-starring Karl Malden and Efrem Zimbalist, Jr. It was a bigger bomb than the B-52 was capable of carrying, but at least it gave the publicity people an angle: after photographic sessions in front of aircraft and promotional visits to airforce bases, Natalie became the sweetheart of the American airborne services.

Wagner, meanwhile, had been signed to play alongside Joan Collins in *Stopover Tokyo* and the gossip columns were full of rumours that they had also become involved romantically. So persistent were they that, as the cast flew off to film on location in Japan, Natalie turned up at the airport to give RJ a farewell kiss at a moment chosen deliberately to be in full view of the English actress. 'As the plane taxied down the runway,' Natalie said afterwards, 'I realised I loved him. I knew then that I would marry RJ.'

By coincidence, Nicky Hilton also had an interest in the departure of the crew and players for *Stopover Tokyo*. He had recently been dating Joan Collins and now he was lonesome. He had admired Natalie from afar for some time, and the predictable telephone call was not long in coming. Soon they were driving down Sunset Boulevard in his pale-blue Lincoln Continental and no one was fooled by the photograph of them at Roman-off's with Zsa Zsa Gabor, Nicky's ex-stepmother, apparently acting as chaperon. A couple of days later they flew down to Las Vegas, from where news of her ex-husband's latest escort in the casinos reached the ears of Elizabeth Taylor. One of the gossips was even suggesting that wedding bells were in the air, not for RJ and Natalie, but for Nicky and Nat.

Elizabeth reached for the telephone: 'I just thought I should warn you . . .' She explained what Natalie might expect of the man: he was unstable, drank heavily, gambled a lot and probably took narcotics; nor, as she had discovered, was he averse to landing his ladyfriends a slap across the mouth in moments of anger. 'Stick to RJ,' Elizabeth advised, and that, Natalie decided, is what she would do. On his return from Tokyo she tried her best to dismiss her association with Hilton as unimportant and meaningless.

At the time, Elizabeth was being offered the lead in the film version of Herman Wouk's bestselling novel, *Marjorie Morningstar*. Montgomery Clift was being approached as her co-star in the story of a rich Jewish girl from New York who rebels against the strictures of her religion and falls deeply in love with a writer, several years older than herself. The book had achieved phenomenal sales across America and was being spoken of in glowing terms; it should have been the basis for one of Hollywood's most successful films and, once again, comparisons were made with *Gone With the Wind*. Elizabeth, however, was in the hectic turmoil of her new marriage and the world tour to promote *Around the World in Eighty Days*; she was also expecting her third child. Any major new commitment was out of the question, even with the prospect that Monty might be playing alongside her.

When she heard that Warners, who were making the film, were considering a nationwide search for an unknown actress to play the lead, Natalie got straight on to Henry Willson: she *must* do *Marjorie Morningstar*; it was her part. Willson fixed a lunch for her in New York with Herman Wouk, to enlist his aid; unfortunately the author did not share Natalie's enthusiasm. In his view, she was not Marjorie Morningstar.

Willson persisted and Natalie fought. She wanted that role come what may. Finally, Jack Warner agreed and, since he was the man with the money, Wouk accepted. Monty Clift had already rejected the co-starring role because he thought the significance of the book had been virtually eclipsed in the screenplay by taking out the controversial religious elements, thus turning it into just another ill-starred love story. Paul Newman was also approached but was not available, and Warner finally cast Gene Kelly, which, years later, even he admitted was perhaps a mistake; Jewish actors might have made the production more realistic.

Warners remained convinced that they had a big hit in the making, however, and Jack was also pleased that he had cast the two leads so cheaply: Natalie was a contract player and Kelly did not cost the earth, either. They all moved east to the Adirondack Mountains for the location work, but, as they would soon discover, classic novel plus decent budget does not always equal success.

* * * * *

Rock Hudson was about to make the same discovery. As Natalie was heading across country, Hudson was flying out to Italy to begin work on the screen adaptation of Ernest Hemingway's *A Farewell to Arms*. This too had all the ingredients of a big box-office attraction; produced by David O. Selznick and directed by John Huston, with a strong cast, it seemed that it could hardly go wrong. But it did, almost from day one.

Selznick had assembled some of the team from the Monty Clift film *Indiscretion of an American Wife*, including his own lovely wife Jennifer Jones, of course, and the Italian wizard Vittorio De Sica, who had evidently forgotten the difficulties he had experienced with Selznick on the earlier film. The producer had not changed his ways. Throughout the preliminary work he fired off memos to Huston almost daily, to the point that Huston threatened violence. Also, there was soon no doubt in Huston's mind that his producer had little regard for the passion of Hemingway's words. Selznick, forever trying to re-create past glory, was

more interested in promoting on-screen passion between Hudson and
Jones, which he was convinced would be more important at the box
office than the novel itself. His defence was simple: nobody had complained when he had changed Margaret Mitchell's book and look what
he had done with Clark Gable and Vivien Leigh. This was going to be
a repeat performance, and Hudson and Jones would be the screen
sensation of the age.

Huston was fired the day before filming began. For a week or two
shooting went ahead without any director at all; a second-unit director
ran things until Charles Vidor was flown in to take over. Hudson
continues the story.

> I had these highly emotional scenes to do, crying, and carrying on, at
> the beginning of the picture. I'd never cried on screen before. And
> somebody who doesn't know how to direct anyway says, 'OK, cry
> now.' Well, it doesn't happen, does it? De Sica, who was a marvellous
> man and a hell of a director himself, was watching. . . . I had to come
> out of the building sobbing, walking right past the camera. And he
> [De Sica] saw the director didn't know how to tell me. He knew that
> I didn't know how to do anything like that, so he took me to a local
> hotel and, in his very limited English, he talked to me and talked . . .
> until I got it right.

As the shooting continued, problems got worse. Most of the unhappiness was centred around the pressure Selznick put on individuals. First,
he disliked Rock's haircut, which he wanted in the style of a First World
War soldier. Then he was concerned about the size of Hudson's Adam's
apple and kept observing that it not only protruded rather noticeably,
but constantly moved up and down (presumably as Hudson swallowed
his nerves). Eventually, he instructed the make-up department to devise
a way of shading the offending lump so that it could not be seen. For
Rock, it was a miserable experience:

> I'd say to him, 'Good morning, David,' and he'd never say 'Good
> morning'. He'd say, 'Your Adam's apple isn't made up.' He was such
> an intense man that it never occurred to him to say 'Good morning'.
> Besides, that was a waste of time. He was concerned with everything
> and everybody, to a hundred and fifty per cent, and drove everybody
> crazy, including Jennifer. There was no favouritism . . . he was con-
> cerned with her . . . with me . . . with De Sica . . . with the set, he was
> concerned with the rainbirds and with everything.

What Rock had thought would be his biggest movie to date turned
into a nightmare, but problems on the picture were not the only thing

that he had to contend with. His sham of a marriage to Phyllis was already heading for the divorce courts. In Rock's eyes, she had changed. He said of her:

> She was unbeatable. She was family. She had the greatest sense of humour and we had a ball until the day we got married. From that day, it was all over. The white piece of paper changed everything. She became the movie star's wife; she had to have a new dress for everything, and she'd have to have a mink, not fox. She wanted to know where I was every minute . . . it just didn't work.

Phyllis, on the other hand, maintained later that Rock's attitude towards her had altered with their marriage. He seemed embarrassed by her presence, particularly at parties; whenever they went out, he warned her not to talk too much, although considering the company they kept such a thing was well-nigh impossible. She countered that he bought her lots of dresses and furs simply because he wanted her to look the part for their grand entrance at whatever party they were going to that night. She also complained that Rock was mean and gave her hardly any spending money for her personal needs.

More than that, Phyllis was perturbed by Rock's disappearances, especially at nights – when he would invariably be meeting a boyfriend – and his refusal to tell her where he had been. Other odd traits – she once came home and found him performing ballet routines in the nude – made it seem impossible that they would remain married for long.

Phyllis had planned to accompany him to Italy for *A Farewell to Arms* but, when the time came for them to travel, she was taken ill. She was well enough to see him off, but was admitted to hospital almost immediately afterwards to be given the news that she had contracted infectious hepatitis, which had almost certainly been passed on through her husband's homosexual promiscuity. Rock had been ensconced in Rome for more than two weeks when word got out that he was ignoring his ailing wife. Louella Parsons ran the story, full of innuendo, that Phyllis's doctor had telephoned him in Italy to point out the serious nature of his wife's illness. Her physician was reportedly angry that, although he had cabled him a fortnight earlier, Phyllis still had not heard a word from her husband.

As always, Henry Willson stepped in to try to calm the situation before it got out of hand. He told Phyllis: 'Rock could win an Oscar for this picture. If he has to break the filming now and come home, it could ruin it for him. He'll lose the thread, and seeing you like this will really make him miserable. He's got problems enough.' In Italy, the publicity people were working overtime to put out stories to counter the effect of Louella's piece. They told how Rock was desperate to return home to see his wife, but the heavy filming schedule made it impossible for him to leave. Furthermore, he was lonely, miserable and depressed at not having Phyllis by his side.

Those with him in Italy might have been forgiven for thinking that the releases were describing a different person. Apart from whooping it up in his free-time with Elaine Stritch (with whom he had formed a close friendship) and other members of the cast, Rock had also found himself an Italian lover – a renewed acquaintance with a young actor whom he had met in Rome while filming *Captain Lightfoot*. And there were others.

In the middle of it all, Henry Willson flew in from Los Angeles, bringing with him a smart young stud whom he had just taken on to his books and whose purpose at the agent's side soon became obvious.

Willson was also carrying a new Universal contract which required Rock's signature. At the time, Hudson was considering moving studios. He had already formed his own production company and was thinking in terms of bigger money, better deals. Whatever arrangements Willson came to with Universal were never made public, but later rumours had it that he was to receive lucrative personal benefits if he could persuade Hudson to sign a new contract with the studio. His handsome young attendant had been brought as a sweetener for Rock and, this time, he succeeded in his task without unpleasantness. But few doubted his ability to resort to blackmail if the need arose.

Rock returned to Los Angeles towards the end of the summer of 1957 after five months' filming in Italy. The studio laid on a limousine to take Phyllis to the airport for a tearful, and seemingly joyful, reunion. Their marriage, however, was all but over and embarrassment was following on behind. In an intimate moment, Rock's Italian lover had captured from him the promise that he would get him started in Hollywood, and not many weeks would pass before his arrival brought renewed fear of scandal.

*   *   *   *   *

All that summer, Rock had jostled with Elizabeth Taylor in the news columns and gossip pages. The Todds' world tour had succeeded in its intention: a colossal promotion for the Todd film, in which they were the star players. They had even made capital out of the public scraps they had had, willingly answering reporters' ever-flowing questions about their marriage. During one session Elizabeth made her oft-quoted comment: 'We have more fun scrapping than most people do making love.' To which Todd added a rider: 'This kid's been looking for trouble all her life. Now she's got it. When she flies into a rage, I fly into a bigger one. We also happen to love each other very much.'

Todd's influence on her was beginning to show. He could be brash and foul-mouthed, in which Elizabeth was perfectly capable of matching him. He also, however, gave her an appreciation of some of the better things of life that she had never before experienced. He could talk on a higher plane than she was able to; his knowledge of art was immense and he liked good music; his interests were wide and varied. He showed her places, people and a style that she had never encountered – sexually, as well as in everything else. Hedda Hopper once commented, 'He taught her everything he knew about sex, good and bad.' He was protective like a father, sensitive and jealous like a lover, and as her pregnancy progressed he surrounded her like a mother hen.

As they sailed back to New York from the European tour, Elizabeth went into premature labour and had to be given anaesthetic to stop the contractions. As it was still only July and the baby was not expected until October, the columnists did their sums and surmised that she must have been pregnant before her marriage.

Doctors had already warned her that it would be dangerous to have another baby; in fact, when she first knew that she was pregnant they had suggested to Elizabeth and Todd that they should seriously consider an abortion. Her back injury had left her still wearing a brace to support her spine and they feared that the growing foetus would force the brace out of position and cripple Elizabeth for life.

She was admitted to hospital immediately on arrival in New York, although she and Mike lingered at the boat terminal long enough for rapid banter with the American press, ensuring their presence on most of the front pages the following morning. She went to the Harkness Clinic, where doctors discovered that, because of the brace, the baby had grown under her rib-cage. The pain was becoming intense. She remained under observation for a couple of weeks before being allowed to join Mike at the twenty-five-room mansion he had leased at Westport, but at the beginning of August she was rushed back into Harkness. On 6 August, surrounded by a team of nine doctors, she was delivered by Caesarian section of a daughter, Elizabeth Frances Todd. The baby, weighing a fraction over four pounds, was stillborn and, although she was put immediately on resuscitation equipment, the doctors came to tell an anxious Todd, 'We have saved your wife, but the baby is dead.' As they spoke, there was a sudden flicker of life and, fifteen minutes after her birth, the child began to breathe. She remained in an incubator for more than a month and Elizabeth herself was kept in hospital for five weeks.

This gave Todd time to plan his next publicity bonanza, which was to be a joint celebration for the safe arrival of his daughter and the first anniversary of *Around the World in Eighty Days*. He hired Madison Square Garden and sent out twenty thousand invitations. On 17 October, several hundred celebrities were flown in free of charge from around the world. A score of dance bands, led by Duke Ellington, played; there was enough champagne to float a battleship; a magnificent circus procession, headed by a bewildered but brave Sir Cedric Hardwicke sitting gamely astride an elephant and clinging as if his life depended on it to the animal's left ear, heralded the start of the party; there were dancers and bagpipes, and clowns and horses, and the *pièce de résistance* was a fourteen-storey birthday cake for which ten thousand pounds of flour, two thousand eggs and sixty-eight gallons of milk and water had been used.

This was the spectacular to end all Todd spectaculars – but it declined into a spectacular débâcle as thousands of people gatecrashed, attracted by the publicity revealing a host of free gifts to be presented to guests, including a Cessna aeroplane, four cars, a dozen motor-scooters, a hundred cameras, mink stoles and ten thousand other little trinkets. The party degenerated into a drink-sodden scrum, which reached laughable proportions when the massive cake collapsed as Elizabeth was trying to cut it and great chunks of icing clung to her magnificent red velvet gown and got stuck in her diamond tiara. Confusion reigned and tempers flared. The fleets of transporters delivering food were stripped bare in the main auditorium, leaving the folk in the other areas pleading for scraps and begging passing waiters for a drink. Top-line entertainers and bands competed with each other and with the noise of the crowd to make themselves heard. Someone started throwing doughnuts and others looted the prizes arranged on a platform at one end of the arena.

Next morning, Todd and Elizabeth were lambasted by the newspapers over the fiasco, but they laughed good humouredly and, as the showman totted up the bill, he confessed philosophically, 'I knew it would be a shindig, but I thought it would run smoother than that.'

Now recovered from the birth of their daughter, Elizabeth was ready to join her husband on another massive promotional tour, taking in Honolulu, Japan, Australia, New Zealand, then back to Europe and on to Russia. But in Japan she collapsed with appendicitis and insisted upon returning to America immediately to have her appendix removed. Rumours spread that the only reason Elizabeth wanted to return was that she had become weary of being at the forefront of Todd's publicity machine and merely wanted to go home. Whether she needed the operation or not, they returned to America where the appendix was duly extracted under the microscopic examination of the world.

*   *   *   *   *

In the relative calm of Hollywood, Monty Clift had finally come out of the hibernation into which he had retreated after *Raintree County*. His director on that film, Eddie Dmytryk, called him with an enticing offer: to star alongside his arch-rival Marlon Brando in *The Young Lions*. Even with his knowledge of Clift's problems, Dmytryk still wanted him in his pictures: 'I think Monty at his best was as good as Spencer Tracy. He was more creative; he was the most creative actor I ever worked with.'

Monty's agents, MCA, who despaired at the amount of work he had turned away, also wanted him to take the part. MCA were becoming an increasingly powerful force in Hollywood (they eventually took over the Universal studio). Brando, too, was a client, and when *The Young Lions* was first discussed the third male star was named as Tony Randall. When he dropped out it was no coincidence that he was replaced by another MCA client, Dean Martin.

Martin had made three films since the end of his partnership with Jerry Lewis in 1956, and they had gone down like lead balloons. But, just as he had done with Sinatra in *From Here to Eternity*, Clift nursed and cajoled Martin into one of his best-ever screen performances.

The film was based on the long Irwin Shaw novel tracing the wartime deeds of three very different young men. Brando plays Christian Diestl, who begins the war as a pleasant young German ski-instructor and, in the screenplay, was supposed to end up as the villain, a flag-waving Nazi conforming utterly to Hitler's regime. Clift is cast as Noah Ackermann, a Jewish soldier confronted with racist attacks, who tries to beat the system. Martin is the sly, draft-dodging, cowardly playboy who ends up a hero.

There was a lot of discussion about the script. Monty talked about it endlessly to his friends and even to his family, and Billy LeMassena recalled that he used to walk around Central Park, reading and reciting from the script. He immersed himself in the part, spending hours on Jewish research. But he was becoming more and more nervous about the whole thing and, when he compared the book with the script, he complained (as did Irwin Shaw) that the screenplay had again watered down the impact of the novel.

Marlon Brando, meanwhile, was going through the same machinations, though separately and for different reasons. He had little contact with Monty until the later part of the picture, when they appeared together. Brando wanted a new ending which put the German in a better light, believing that because the war had been over for a decade, audiences would accept the Nazi in a more sympathetic way. Clift's response was decisive: if Brando was allowed to do that, he would have nothing more to do with the picture. It was left to Dmytryk to resolve the dispute by rewriting large sections of the script, almost as the film was being shot, to reach a compromise which suited not only himself but his two stars as well. Even so, Brando's performance caused controversy. Clift was outraged by the way he tried to make the German into a more humane person. Friends joined with the critics in castigation and Maureen Stapleton was moved to tell him, 'You played the Nazi like Jesus Christ.'

Dmytryk, as usual, also had to contend with the personal traumas of his cast. Monty had worked himself into such a state that he was eventually frightened by his part, yet at the same time he was convinced it would be his best work to date if he could get it right. When the unit moved to Paris for location work, he went missing. He was eventually found unconscious through drink in a dilapidated hotel in southern Italy.

When he was brought back to the Hôtel Raphael in Paris, where the rest of the cast was installed and waiting, Brando was shocked. Clift, already thin and gaunt, had lost another fifteen pounds for the part of the Jew and now he just looked emaciated. His weight loss seemed to have made the scar from his accident more apparent. Clift himself was painfully aware of that: through all his other tensions, he was tormented over the way the world would see him on screen and all his inner demons came surging forward. Maureen Stapleton said,

His poor face looked a mess and he was very worried about it, and what the audiences would think. When the film was released he took me to the preview and people around us were saying, 'God, is that Monty Clift?' It was an awful experience.

Brando, on the other hand, looked portly and well-fed; his weight had increased by twenty pounds to 190 lb. He was not drinking at all, after a recent experience which had left him smarting. Truman Capote, interviewing him for the *New Yorker*, had managed to coax Brando into less than discreet observations about himself and others (including James Dean) by administering heavy shots of vodka. So Clift and Dean Martin were left to see the nights away together, though Martin could not keep pace with Monty's drinking.

On set, Clift now carried a cooling flask of what appeared to everyone to be orange juice. Those who took a drink from it, however, soon felt their heads swirling: it contained a home-made concoction of juice, vodka and crushed barbiturates – as Brando discovered when they were filming his last scene, in which he is shot, rolls down a hill and comes to rest in a pool of mud. As he did the fall, Brando hurt his shoulder and got up angry and in pain. 'Has anybody got a drink?' Monty handed him his flask of 'fruit juice' and Brando gulped down a mouthful. His head jerked back: 'Jesus! What the fuck have you got in that?' he cried. Monty gave a disarming smile, took back the flask and swallowed another mouthful himself.

Towards the end of the picture, when they had returned to Los Angeles for final set-work in September 1957, Brando became so concerned about Clift that he tried to straighten him out himself. Maureen Stapleton recalled:

We were all at a party, Jerry Robbins's I think, and Marlon was talking to Monty and then the two of them went off on Marlon's motorcycle for an hour. Apparently Marlon took him off for a talk about his drinking. He tried again a couple of weeks later and offered Monty everything. He said, 'I'll go with you to AA. I'll hold your hand. I'll do whatever you want.' But Monty just said he didn't have a problem. This was nine o'clock in the morning and while they were talking, so Marlon told me, Monty poured a half tumbler of vodka and drank it as they talked. Whatever Marlon offered him that day, there were no takers. But Marlon tried, he really tried.

* * * * *

In the autumn of 1957, Rock Hudson had returned moody and brooding from Hawaii after completing the location work for his next movie, *Twilight for the Gods*, which he knew full well was, once again, the usual kind of Universal potboiler in which he was not going to set the world alight. He had entered into the film with great hopes after a terrific build up from Henry Willson and the studio. It was written by Ernest Gann, who had created the John Wayne success, *The High and the Mighty*; it had a strong storyline, they said, and a good cast including Cyd Charisse, Arthur Kennedy and Leif Erickson. More than that, said Universal producer Gordon Kay, it had been bought specially for Rock. But it was not the right vehicle for him. Although he was to play the down-at-heel, often drunk, skipper of a tramp steamboat, studio executives insisted that the super-clean-cut image of their top male star must remain untarnished and the director's request to 'dirty him up a little' was refused. Rock looked totally out of place and he knew it.

Phyllis had joined him in Hawaii for part of the filming and, though he put on a smiling public face, his rows with her were becoming louder and more frequent. Their return home saw no improvement, and Phyllis didn't help by suggesting that Rock should consult an analyst about his lack of interest in sex and his torment over his career.

On the afternoon of 17 October, while Phyllis was out, Rock collected a few things and, in the best tradition of Hollywood husbands leaving their wives, took a room at the Beverly Hills Hotel under an assumed name. He left a note in the kitchen for Phyllis asking her to 'keep it quiet'. The studio had to be told, of course, and Gail Gifford, one of the senior Universal publicists, stood by to fend off press enquiries. None the less, Sheilah Graham had a piece in the first editions. A week later, the studio officially announced that Rock and Phyllis had decided to separate.

*   *   *   *   *

At the other end of the spectrum, the gossips were agog with the news that Hollywood's most attractive young couple, Natalie Wood and Robert Wagner, were to marry. The decision was made when RJ returned from a nationwide promotion tour with Joan Collins for *Stopover Tokyo*, which dismally failed to encourage audiences to turn out in large numbers to watch the film; it was flopping badly. 'Hollywood Report', the syndicated column by Charles Hamblett, recorded the news on 28 October 1957:

> Hollywood's dippiest, dreamiest, craziest teenager has said Yes to the boy she loves most . . . an elderly heartthrob of twenty-seven named Robert Wagner. At last? At a mere nineteen? Well, Natalie Wood is a special case. A true child of the Frustrated Fifties, she's the high-priestess of America's Youth Cult. In Hollywood terms she's a living doll.

The publicity people were in their element. It seemed, for them, almost too good to be true. A wedding, right on cue, which could be used to promote both Wagner's film and Natalie's latest, *Marjorie Morningstar*, which was due on the circuits early in the New Year. If the promotions department had racked their brains for a publicity stunt, they could not have come up with a better one.

Chapter Twelve

Grief . . . and Scandal

Hollywood went partying on in its inimitable way, seemingly disregarding the truth that the very foundations of the industry that kept this hot-house community in drink and caviare and limousines and mansions had all but rotted, and that the whole structure was about to come crashing down around them. Those who watched the forlorn figure of Louis B. Mayer going for a lonely stroll along Sunset Boulevard with his limousine trailing a few paces behind and laughed that 'the old grey Mayer ain't what he used to be' should have taken note: there would be many followers on the path of rejection.

Mayer's successor at MGM, Dore Schary, was back where he started, writing screenplays and producing for United Artists, and the power behind the once great studio had shifted into the hands of a hotel chain. RKO had gone completely. Howard Hughes had sold it in the mid-fifties to a consortium in Chicago which, it was later discovered, was financed by the Mafia. The deal was cancelled in a welter of publicity. The studio was then bought by the General Tire and Rubber Company, who filmed a few remakes of past RKO successes before closing it completely two years later. The studio stood empty for a time before being bought by the television partnership company of Lucille Ball and Desi Arnez – Desilu – in 1954.

Samuel Goldwyn, who had been Hollywood's greatest independent producer since his split with Louis B. Mayer in 1924, was also losing his influence (he made his last film in 1959 but did not finally retire until 1965); Darryl F. Zanuck was heading for a fall at 20th Century–Fox (although he would return later); and Harry Cohn was in his last months as head of Columbia. Of the original moguls, only Jack Warner and Barney Balaban, head of Paramount, remained in total control of their empires.

Harry Cohn voiced the opinion held by many: 'The lunatics are trying to get control of the asylum'; he often accused actors and their agents of attempting to increase their power. Jack Warner, loud, flashy and addicted to a sumptuous lifestyle, had the same thought about his stars and was renowned for the running battles he had with some of his famous names. 'I pay 'em, and they do what I tell 'em,' was his motto. Those who challenged his ability to run their lives would be taken to the window of his office, overlooking what was then the vast acreage of the Warners' studio, and, with a wave of his hand, he would ask, 'Would all that be there if I didn't know what I was doing?' Humphrey Bogart, who had an epic contractual fight with Warner, called him the Governor of San Quentin, and he remained the great dictator of his studio until the last. Like Bogart, Natalie Wood came up against Warner's autocratic stubbornness towards the end of 1957, and it became a cloud over her happiness in the new year.

* * * * *

The gossips quickly tagged Natalie and Robert Wagner 'the new Debbie and Eddie', comparing their love to the much-publicised togetherness of tinsel town's most charming and romantic couple of recent years, Debbie Reynolds and Eddie Fisher. The public was in love with them, the newspapers projected them as the ideal couple, and they were almost forced into an immediate marriage by the clamourings of the press and their fans. When Wagner joined Natalie for some location work on *Marjorie Morningstar* at Schroon Lake, New York state, he was followed by several thousand anxious fans, who crowded around as soon as the two young idols met.

While public interest in the couple heightened in the autumn of 1957, Frank Sinatra added to the excitement by asking Warners to loan out Natalie to star with him and the equally hot Tony Curtis in *Kings Go Forth*, a Second World War drama in which she was to play a half-French, half-black girl who is the subject of the romantic inclinations of her two male leads. Sinatra was desperate to sign Natalie, not the least of his reasons being that he personally wanted to work with her. He also had an interest in the film, which was being independently produced for United Artists. Natalie was keen to do the movie, but Jack Warner did not share her enthusiasm and initially gave a firm refusal.

Sinatra persisted and Warner eventually relented, but he set down some extravagant terms. 'I want a hundred and fifty thousand dollars for Natalie Wood to star,' he said, 'plus you, Frankie. I want your signature on a picture deal for Warners.' They eventually settled on $75,000 for Natalie and Sinatra accepted a film deal to co-star in the Dorchester production of *Ocean's Eleven* with the rest of the Rat Pack – Sammy Davis, Jr, Peter Lawford and Dean Martin – which was released through Warners and grossed millions. Jack Warner came out well on top.

Natalie was delighted when the deal went through, but she was furious when she discovered that, although Warners were getting a huge payment for her services, her salary remained unchanged. In the event, it did her no good at all. A running battle with Jack Warner had begun, and the film was laughed off the screen by the critics. Even Tony Curtis was moved to remark, 'Kings go backwards.'

Filming for the movie was under way when Natalie and RJ decided on a prompt and quiet wedding. On 30 December 1957 they slipped off to Scottsdale, Arizona, where Wagner's parents lived, accompanied by a hastily assembled group of relatives and close friends, and declared their undying love for each other before a Methodist minister in the humble local church, thus depriving the Hollywood community and press corps of a fanfare of nuptials. There were less than a dozen people present to witness the twenty-minute ceremony and the wedding breakfast at the only decent hotel in town. The only 'star' present was their mutual friend Nick Adams, who was one of the witnesses. And when Natalie and RJ went on to Miami for their honeymoon in the Keys, Adams went too. He was there waiting when they arrived.

By this time, they had been tracked down by the newspapers. Also, a photographer friend of RJ's who had taken some nice pictures of the wedding on the understanding that they would be for the personal albums of Natalie and RJ only, had already discovered that he was sitting on a potential gold mine and had sold them to an agency, and then on around the world, so that the wedding was served with the cornflakes the next morning. This, of course, prompted an invasion of photographers, who began camping outside the bridal suite. The presence of Nick Adams in a nearby locale had not gone unnoticed, either, and, much to RJ's annoyance, New York writer Dorothy Kilgallen, in her syndicated column, made some sarcastic suggestions about a charming threesome.

They all transferred to New York for the continuation of the honeymoon before they were required for filming. RJ, who had done nothing except a publicity tour in the last seven months, was informed that he had been cast in a supporting role to Robert Mitchum in *The Hunters*, his performance with Joan Collins in the Japanese fiasco having failed to cause any major stir at the box office, and he was apprehensive and gloomy. Natalie's own career prospects looked bright as *Marjorie Morningstar* opened in New York to packed houses and she looked gleefully at the queues of people waiting to get into the Radio City Music Hall on première night. Before long her joy turned to deep despondency. The critics were not complimentary about her or the film, and several

made the point that there seemed to be no romantic fire between her and
Gene Kelly. Audiences inspired by the success of the book soon discovered that the Jewish aspect of the story had vanished and, as this had
been a major selling-point of the novel in the first place, the box-office
queues quickly evaporated. Although the film made money, it was not
the runaway success Warners had expected. Far from providing Natalie
with a turning-point that would project her from the role of nation's
sweetheart into major stardom, it proved to be a significant setback.

Despite continued press interest in them, neither she nor RJ had yet
reached the big league of earnings. As contract players, they were netting
little more than $100,000 a year between them, which, by Hollywood
standards, and after tax and agents' fees, meant that they were confined
to a relatively modest lifestyle. It was a state of affairs that did not
improve, for Natalie's contribution to the household expenses was about
to dry up altogether.

After the disappointment of *Marjorie Morningstar*, she became deeply
depressed, and only Wagner's support kept her intake of sleeping pills
and white wine down to manageable proportions. The pressures increased when Warner called her to the studio for her next project. She
was to be loaned out to United Artists again, this time for the production
of George Bernard Shaw's *The Devil's Disciple*, with Laurence Olivier,
Burt Lancaster and Kirk Douglas. Warners were to receive $100,000 for
her services; she would continue on normal salary. When she discovered
that the film was to be shot almost entirely in England, Natalie threw
up her hands in despair.

'I can't do it,' she said, in tears. 'I can't. I don't want to be separated
from RJ. We've only been married three months.' Warner did not see
her point, and her friends insisted that she must be crazy, turning down
the chance to play alongside three of the best male actors around; but
in spite of her limited financial resources, she would not budge. Warner
responded by placing her on immediate and indefinite suspension, which
meant that, if she persisted in refusing to do the film, she would not
work at all until he said so – and he would not say so for many months
to come.

*   *   *   *   *

Elizabeth Taylor was having similar, though less dramatic, problems.
She had been talking for some time about retiring. All through the past
year, when she had been trailing around the world with Mike Todd,
the thoughts kept coming back and her comments in that direction had
not gone unnoticed at MGM. The studio decided as 1958 began that

she should be invited back to work, and in that they had an unexpected ally. When director Richard Brooks sent her the script for the Tennessee Williams play *Cat on a Hot Tin Roof*, which was to co-star Paul Newman and Burl Ives, producer Pandro Berman had already called Mike Todd to enlist his support and Mike had agreed that it would be a great part. Berman said that, at the time, all contact with their star had to be made through Todd; she was under his spell and nothing and no one came between them. 'You must do this film,' Todd told his pondering wife. 'It could win you an Oscar.' Elizabeth agreed on condition that she had a reappraisal of her contract with MGM, which still had thirty-two months to run. She wanted to cancel her remaining commitment and, at a conference, Metro executives threatened to put her on suspension if she did not continue to work. When Miss Taylor pointed out that she would simply retire completely, they agreed to release her after she had completed *Cat on a Hot Tin Roof* and one more film.

Shooting for the new movie began in early March. That weekend, Mike Todd threw a small barbecue party for himself and Elizabeth, Debbie and Eddie Fisher, and David and Hjordis Niven. They talked about their various projects; Todd had already started work on his next movie, *Don Quixote*, and his biographer, Art Cohn, was just finishing his book, *The Nine Lives of Mike Todd*. He was enthusiastic about everything, but especially his wife's new film. The following week, he began making arrangements to attend a Friars' Testimonial Dinner at the Waldorf Astoria in New York the next Sunday, at which he and Elizabeth were to be the principal guests. He had been named Showman of the Year, and the award was to be presented to him. Elizabeth had even rearranged her filming schedule to be by his side.

On the Wednesday, Elizabeth was ordered to bed by her doctor. She was running a high temperature and suffering from bronchitis and by Friday, 22 March, it was clear that she would be unable to travel to New York, although she begged her physician, Dr Rex Kennamer, to let her go. He talked with Todd and both insisted she was too ill to venture out of her bedroom, let alone get on a plane. Mike began making telephone calls to find someone to join him for the flight in place of Elizabeth. He fancied a game of poker with friends on what was then a ten-hour flight. He tried Kirk Douglas, but he was busy. He called Joe E. Lewis, and his pal, director Joseph Mankiewicz, but both said they couldn't go. So Todd kissed his wife goodbye and set off in his private twelve-seater, twin-engined plane, *Lucky Liz*, with only his crew and Art Cohn for company.

He telephoned Elizabeth when he got to the airport and said he would call again when they touched down in Albuquerque to refuel. The plane was last seen taxiing down the runway in heavy rain at 10.20 p.m.

Elizabeth slept fitfully, still with a high temperature even though a nurse had rubbed alcohol into her body to try to break the fever. When she awoke at six in the morning, Mike still had not called. She waited. Seven o'clock came and went. Eight o'clock, still no call.

By now, Rex Kennamer and Dick Hanley, Mike's private secretary, were heading towards the house in Schuyler Road, Beverly Hills.

'How's she going to take it, Rex?' Hanley asked over and over. 'How are we going to tell her?'

Elizabeth was still in bed when the two men walked in, stern-faced, wishing they could put the moment off but knowing they had to tell her before she heard it on the radio. They stammered to break the news: *Lucky Liz* had crashed from the skies at seven thousand feet in a storm while crossing the Zuni Mountains in New Mexico. The remains were scattered over two miles, and the passengers could be identified only by dental records. One of the few items found in the wreckage was Todd's gold wedding ring, twisted and charred, which was eventually taken to his widow.

Elizabeth screamed: 'No, it can't be. Please God, no.'

Hanley tried to put some words together: 'Liz, I'm so sorry . . .' But she bolted from her bed and ran through the house, screaming so loudly that she could be heard outside. She went downstairs, moaning and screaming, and out into the street, as if she were trying to get away from the news. Kennamer chased her and tried his best to calm her, edging her back through the front door. She was still screaming: 'It can't be, it can't be. He'll call me any minute now.' The doctor managed to administer sedatives to quieten her, and soon friends began arriving with their condolences. Debbie Reynolds was among the first there, to take Elizabeth's children back to her house. Michael Wilding himself came and spent hours trying to calm her. She kept repeating, 'Why didn't I go with him. Why? Why? We had planned to do so much together. I wish I had been with him.'

The house was ringed with security men from MGM, and studio publicist Bill Lyon set up a link with the newsreel and television cameramen and the reporters who were already parking their equipment outside in Schuyler Road. Visitors came and went, all recorded on film. Telegrams of sympathy began pouring in from all over the world; more than three thousand wires were received, including one from Mamie Eisenhower expressing the condolences of herself and the President. Rock Hudson sent a hand-written note, as did Natalie Wood and Robert Wagner, but Elizabeth was seeing only her closest relatives and rejecting most calls.

Monty Clift telephoned but was not able to speak to her because of her sedated state.

Even those in Hollywood who did not like Elizabeth felt for her. Everyone knew the sorrow could destroy her. When Richard Brooks, director of *Cat on a Hot Tin Roof*, came to offer his condolences, she yelled at him to get out: 'You bastard, you've just come to see when I'll be back at work. Well, screw you and your movie. I'm never coming back.'

She was inconsolable, and Dick Hanley was worried that she would not be in sufficient control to go to the funeral, which Todd's brother, David Goldenbogen, had arranged to take place at the Jewish Waldheim Cemetery in Zurich, Illinois, just outside Chicago. With the aid of Kennamer's medication, however, she was able to make the journey, for which Howard Hughes placed one of his TWA airliners at her disposal. At the airport, she was assisted down the steps in a state of near collapse by her brother Howard and Eddie Fisher; Debbie had stayed in Los Angeles to look after the children. They were met by Mike Todd, Jr. Crowds of fans were already there, shouting and screaming as Elizabeth walked unsteadily to the car that was to speed her away to the Drake Hotel, where a suite had been reserved for her.

Her car led the funeral cortège. All along the route, and at the cemetery, crowds had been forming since early morning to see the twenty-six-year-old widow, draped in a black veil. They were jostling and pushing for a better view; the noise was incredible and unbearable for the mourners. Some had children in arms; many were eating snacks and drinking; some were taking photographs. Discarded rubbish and drink-containers littered the road. The crowds surged forward as Elizabeth reached the cemetery, clutching pieces of paper and trying to get autographs. A wandering gypsy band playing guitars and mandolins was entertaining the assembled onlookers. But always, the centre of attraction, the reason they were all there, was Elizabeth, and wherever she went they screeched and called her name as if she were arriving for a star-studded première.

Monty Clift had flown in from New York and tried to get close to Elizabeth; but he had to stand on the periphery of the ceremony, to which only closest friends and family had been invited. Monty was sickened by the crowd scenes and said later, 'It was hateful, awful. Those people were so noisy. I saw jealousy and envy in their faces. It was so bleak.' Rex Kennamer, who was also Clift's physician when he was in Hollywood, saw that he was in a poor state and stayed with him for a while to try to console him. Monty was distraught at not being able to get near his best friend and watched from a distance as the funeral party retreated and she stayed, alone for a minute or two, weeping at Todd's graveside, which had been surrounded by a tent to protect the mourners from the sightseers.

Even then, there were appalling scenes as photographers argued with members of Todd's family over where they should stand, insisting that they should be allowed to take shots inside the tent. Meanwhile, the crowds were becoming more restless, chanting, 'Liz, Liz. Come on Liz,' and when she emerged from the tent, the police lost virtually all semblance of control as dozens of people broke through their cordon and dashed forward towards the desperate widow.

She was helped back into her black limousine by Eddie and Howard, surrounded by a thick band of police trying to push their way through the spectators. Overhead, a photographer's helicopter dived low to get better pictures. Elizabeth collapsed into the car, sobbing deeply, and began screaming as the crowds pressed forward again, jostling to get a closer view of her and shouting, 'Liz. Liz. Let's see you, Liz.' Faces were pressed at the windows and she began banging at them on the glass with a clenched fist. They swarmed all around, rocked the car from side to side and climbed on the front so that the funeral party was trapped for almost ten minutes before the police were able to clear a way through. She returned to Los Angeles in a state of total collapse. Monty went back to New York. What he had witnessed had affected him deeply and he could speak of nothing else for days.

Two nights later, the Academy Awards proceeded as normal, with David Niven as the host and Natalie Wood and Robert Wagner among the stars handing out the awards. The names called for nominations included Elizabeth's for her appearance in *Raintree County* and Mike Todd's for his technical achievement with the introduction of Todd-AO. The seats reserved for the two were vacant. Elizabeth was watching the ceremony on television. Todd-AO took the technical award and Jennifer Jones, who was standing in for Elizabeth, collected it on her behalf. Elizabeth edged forward in her chair as the nominations for Best Actress were called: it was won by Joanne Woodward.

'I knew she would win it,' wailed Elizabeth. 'Nothing will go right for me now Mike is dead.' Later, at the awards gala, Joanne was presented with a bouquet of white orchids which carried a note saying, 'I am so happy for you. Elizabeth Taylor Todd, and Mike, too.'

Elizabeth was carried upstairs to bed that night and there she remained for a week or more, sedated for most of the time, until gradually she began to think about getting back to work.

In mid-April she returned to the set to resume filming. It was difficult enough for her to make that decision; what made it even more agonising was the intensity of the drama of *Cat on a Hot Tin Roof*, dealing as it does with death. Rex Kennamer was constantly on call to soothe her, but she cracked up when Judith Anderson had to say to her, 'I guess things never turn out the way you dream they are going to turn out.' Richard Brooks had to ease her into the shooting schedule, arranging the scenes so that the heavier parts were left until later. Slowly, she began to fight off her depression and started eating for the first time since Todd's death when in one scene she had to consume a plate of baked ham and cornbread. She recalled: 'They had to do the scene over and over again, and each time I just ate and ate.'

For the next six weeks, she was tied up with filming. The play is a demanding one, moving without pace through the story of Big Daddy (Burl Ives), the hard, irascible master of all he surveys, who is dying of cancer. Elizabeth plays his daughter-in-law to Paul Newman's Brick, the heavy-drinking son who shows no particular interest in his forthcoming inheritance. Typical of Williams's plays, there are long speeches; Elizabeth delivered hers in one take, giving a memorable performance, rated as her best to date.

* * * * *

Rock Hudson too was depressed and seriously worried about his career, which had come to a sudden halt, he thought. His last two movies had done nothing for him; indeed, they had pegged him back a pace or two. Far from earning him an Oscar, *A Farewell to Arms* had brought nothing but consternation. He was also deeply tormented by his personal problems.

On 22 April Phyllis filed for divorce, entering sworn statements alleging extreme mental cruelty by Rock and testifying that he had on occasions beaten her. She said that he often stayed out at nights and, when she tried to question him about his movements, he would swipe her across the face. One of her friends also testified that she had seen Rock beat his wife. The divorce had the makings of one of the most sensational Hollywood cases of the age, but behind the scenes a great deal was being done to prevent a scandal.

The prospect that the truth of Rock's phoney marriage and his real sexual inclinations would leak out sent a shudder down Henry Willson's spine. He told Rock, 'We've got to keep that dame quiet, whatever it costs,' and at the same time he launched his own propaganda, aimed at discrediting Phyllis. If he had his way, her name would be mud, and he tried his best to make it stick with stories that she was just a gold-digger and a lesbian. The fear that she might be beaten up, or worse, had also crossed Phyllis's mind, knowing the tricks her former boss had been capable of in the past (which had apparently included paying gangsters to frighten off anyone who threatened to tell all about his star).

Willson was especially scared when he heard that Phyllis had hired Jerry Giesler, one of Hollywood's most successful lawyers, who had defended Errol Flynn in his infamous rape case and had acted for Marilyn Monroe when she left Joe DiMaggio. Willson's fears were well founded: it did not take Giesler long to discover the hidden facets of this extraordinary marriage; nor was it long before he found out the name of the Italian lover Rock had taken during the filming of *A Farewell to Arms*, and who had followed him back to Hollywood. He suggested that Phyllis might name the man as co-respondent. He found out things of which even Phyllis herself had been unaware, and now it finally dawned on her that she had been set up as the little wife at home, purely as a front for Hudson's homosexual activities.

Had she revealed all in the divorce papers, Rock's career would have ended, and even Giesler could see that Phyllis's best interests might well be served by not pursuing some of the more dubious associations in Hudson's immediate past. Willson himself would certainly have figured large if the case had ever become a bitter public slanging-match, and he wanted to avoid that at all costs. Rock, on the other hand, kept insisting that he was not going to allow Phyllis to take him for all he had and he promptly closed her credit accounts. Giesler leaked that to the gossip columns and the following day Phyllis had a surprise visitor. Marlon Brando, whose wife Anna was one of Phyllis's best friends, had brought her a cheque for $1000 to tide her over.

The case was developing into a legal wrangle in which both sides knew the implications for themselves if the truth came out, and gingerly the lawyers toyed with each other. They eventually agreed alimony of $250 a week, plus the house the couple had shared as man and wife, which Rock had bought for $38,000, and a new Ford Thunderbird car. Phyllis also retained a five per cent share in Rock's production corporation. Later, as Hudson began stripping the assets of this corporation to make her holding worthless, and perhaps realising that she had sold herself short, Phyllis returned to court and won a further lump-sum award of $130,000. She also agreed privately to a condition that she would never speak of or write about her marriage, or any of Willson's private business. She kept her part of the bargain, refusing all requests for interviews until after Hudson died, when she wrote her book *My Husband, Rock Hudson*, with Bob Thomas.

On the surface, little of the background to the Hudson marriage and divorce emerged other than Phyllis's testimonies about Rock's occasional violence and the mental cruelty she had endured. But it was publicity enough, of the wrong kind, to keep Hudson in the headlines as he prepared for what would become a major step in his career.

That summer, producer Ross Hunter, who had steered Rock towards some of his best work, was working on a script for a new comedy called *Pillow Talk*. Rock was apprehensive; he was unsure about playing comedy, and when he skimmed through the words he was not keen on them either; he thought they were too modern for his style. But Willson and Hunter both implored him to consider the role; they were agreed that he needed a new style of film if he were to progress into the superstar bracket and not end up a has-been. Apart from *Giant*, his dramatic roles had not been hugely successful, and he was criticised for a wooden, placid tone. He wasn't rugged enough for character parts and, if anything, was suffering from the clean-cut, all-American image that the studio had built for him. This screenplay, by Stanley Shapiro and Maurice Richman, was in fact nothing more than a light comedy with classy sexual undertones. *Pillow Talk* and its follow-ups are the sort of films that today are shown on late-night television as mild and harmless, but at the time they represented a new, sophisticated image for light comedy.

Rock plays a womanising composer who gets his prey to his apartment by writing a song just for her. Doris Day is a career girl, and her more orthodox suitor is played by Tony Randall. In *Pillow Talk* Hunter established the pattern for which they would be typecast in their successive movies: Doris was the independent, modern woman, sexy and slightly sexist, who always kept at least one foot on the floor in love-scenes; Hudson became the romantic male lead for which he was clearly best suited; and Tony Randall was for ever more the sullen, neat-and-tidy and terribly annoying bore.

Like Rock, Doris also had her inhibitions. She was no stranger to movies, of course, or to very feminine roles, but she didn't think she was sexy. Under contract to Warners she had completed seventeen films since 1948, and had done another seven as a freelance since her departure from the studio in 1955. Her last two films, *Tunnel of Love*, with Richard Widmark, and *It Happened to Jane*, with Jack Lemmon, had flopped and her husband, Marty Melcher, who also managed her and handled the finances, was concerned that his breadwinner could slip out of sight. Ross Hunter, however, could see the way forward:

Doris hadn't a clue as to her potential as a sex image and no one had realised that under all those dirndls lurked one of the wildest asses in Hollywood. I came right out and told her: 'You are sexy, Doris, and it's about time you dealt with it.' I felt it was essential for her to change her image if she was going to survive as a top star.

Doris accepted, adapted and discovered that Hunter was right. Marty liked the sound of it too, because Hunter was amenable to his suggestion that, if Doris did *Pillow Talk*, he, Marty, should get a $50,000 payment as co-producer. Like Rock Hudson, Doris was in the hands of a devious plotter, only in her case she was married to him. He also tried to get his hands on Rock's share of the proceeds from the film and began telling him how wealthy he had made Doris by buying into oil-wells and bonds. He could do the same for Rock, he said, if he turned all his earnings over to him. Rock promised to think about it, but never took up Marty's kind offer. What no one knew at the time was that Marty was filching his wife's funds; when he died in 1968 she was left with debts of half a million dollars after a lifetime's work.

Rock and Doris hit it off straight away. 'We became great friends,' said Rock, 'and the whole thing became one big continuous laugh. Doris gave the best acting lessons I ever had; her sense of timing and instincts were terrific. I just kept my eyes open and copied her.' Rock also got a part in the film for Nick Adams, whom he had first met with Jimmy Dean while filming *Giant*.

Production on *Pillow Talk* was delayed because Hunter had problems getting final approval from the studio to make the film. He discovered even greater problems trying to sell it; it was such a departure from what was doing the rounds towards the end of the fifties that no one, including Universal boss William Goetz, thought it stood much chance. However, the film became a huge success. Theatre owners discovered that their audiences had been starved of a light, romantic comedy team, and Hudson and Day were soon being compared to Gable and Lombard, Tracy and Hepburn. Doris Day, especially, found a new career as the whiter than white, professional virgin of the sixties, and for *Pillow Talk* she was nominated for an Academy Award.

The film gave Hudson's confidence a boost. He emerged from the celibate lifestyle he had pursued for the past few months, out of fear that one more setback would finish him in Hollywood for ever, and returned to his stridently sexual ways.

* * * * *

Elizabeth Taylor had also come out into the sunlight again and resumed life with her usual gusto in that summer of 1958. Friends had rallied round: Eddie and Debbie called regularly; Monty Clift telephoned often and in June she flew out to New York for a brief stay with him, returning to make her first appearance in public since the funeral when she joined Debbie for Eddie's first-night appearance at the start of a season in Las

Vegas. Rock Hudson also invited her to dinner. Paul Newman and Joanne Woodward asked her over, and she dined several times with Natalie Wood and Robert Wagner.

Arthur Loew, Jr, the theatre-chain heir, also helped out. The house in Beverly Hills she had shared with Todd was only leased and Elizabeth had moved temporarily into a bungalow at the Beverly Hills Hotel. Her children and their nurse had moved into the Loew household and Loew also took them all for a holiday to his home in Arizona. It soon became obvious that he had fallen deeply in love with Elizabeth. The gossips began penning a budding romance, with an eyebrow raised here and there that Elizabeth's new association should come so soon after her husband's death.

By July her depression had begun to disappear. Hedda Hopper took her to a lavish party at Romanoff's and she made her entrance in a stunning red dress, decorated with some of the diamonds Todd had bought for her. It was like an opening night; friends gathered around her and treated her like a long-lost duchess. She told everyone she was planning a long holiday in Europe and in August she went back to New York to prepare for her departure, leaving her children still in the care of Arthur Loew. By coincidence, Eddie Fisher was also in the city to film a television show, leaving Debbie behind in Los Angeles. He and Elizabeth went out to dinner a couple of times but no one paid much attention. Eddie, after all, had been her husband's best friend.

Then she joined Eddie for a weekend on a benefit trip to Grossinger's, the Catskills resort which had very special connections for him: he had started his singing career there and married Debbie Reynolds at the same spot. Over a thousand guests were waiting to see their favourite son, and Elizabeth made no attempt to make herself scarce. On Monday, back in New York, they embarked on a social whirl in which they must have known that they would be noticed and that it would set the gossips writing. First they dined at Quo Vadis, then they were seen at the Harwyn Club, then they were dancing cheek to cheek in the Blue Angel. They turned up together at a cocktail party given by Nicky Hilton, and by now the wires between New York and Los Angeles were getting hot.

Debbie was on the phone regularly and knew that something was wrong. When the first stories broke on 10 September that Eddie and Elizabeth were in love, she stood by with a firm denial. 'It's ridiculous,' she said. 'Eddie and Liz are very good friends. What's wrong with that?'

The following day there were more headlines and Eddie flew home to try to head off a scandal. By the time he arrived, reporters and photographers were camping outside his house and in that day's afternoon editions Elizabeth was quoted as saying, 'You know that I'm a friend of Eddie and Debbie, everyone knows that. I can't help what people are saying.' Was she going back to California? 'Of course I am. I've got three children there.' The fact that she had not seen them for more than three weeks, and that Arthur Loew was still running her crèche, was not pursued.

Elizabeth arrived back in Los Angeles the following afternoon and hardly had time to unpack before Hedda Hopper came on the telephone. While other journalists were laying siege to the Beverly Hills Hotel, Hedda had discovered that the star had taken refuge at the home of her agent, Kurt Frings.

'Elizabeth, you've got to level with me,' said Hopper. 'What's going on with you and Eddie?' The whole town was saying that she had broken up the best marriage in Hollywood, the columnist told her.

'It's a lot of bull. I don't go about breaking up marriages,' Elizabeth replied. 'Besides, you can't break up a marriage. Debbie and Eddie's never has been.'

Hopper: 'I hear you even went to Grossinger's with him?'

Taylor: 'Sure, we had a divine time.'

Hopper: 'What about Arthur Loew? You've known he's been in love with you for six months and your kids are still living in his house.'

Taylor: 'I can't help how he feels about me.'

Hopper: 'Well, you can't hurt Debbie like this without hurting yourself more, because she loves him.'

Taylor: 'He's not in love with her and never has been. Only a year ago they were about to get a divorce but stopped it when they found out she was going to have another baby.'

Hopper: 'What do you think Mike would say to this?'

Taylor: 'He and Eddie loved each other.'

Hopper: 'You're wrong. Mike loved Eddie. In my opinion, Eddie never loved anyone but himself.'

Taylor: 'Well, Mike's dead and I'm alive.' (Miss Taylor later disputed that quote and claimed that what she really said was, 'I loved him more than my life. But Mike is dead and I'm alive and the one person who would want me to be happy is Mike.')

But the most telling quote Miss Hopper left out of the story and revealed only in her memoirs. She claimed Elizabeth ended the interview by saying: 'What do you expect me to do – sleep alone?'

Hopper's story ran on the front page of the *Los Angeles Times* that night, and then throughout the world. The result was astonishing, far worse than Elizabeth had ever expected. The whole of Hollywood, it seemed, was on Debbie's side and Elizabeth was immediately branded the scarlet woman who had come between what, on the surface at least, was one of show business's happiest unions. The balloon finally went up in a big way three days after Eddie's return from New York. A terse press statement from Debbie's studio, MGM (where once again the publicity department was on hand to deal with such a delicate situation), said simply: 'A separation exists between Debbie and Eddie. No further action is being taken at this time.'

Eddie moved out of the matrimonial home and borrowed a bedroom at the house of his friend, the comedian Joey Forman, while Debbie took the children to stay with friends. Metro press people took over their house, still besieged by reporters. There were so many outside that ice-cream and hamburger pedlars set up stalls.

On one occasion when Debbie returned to the house, she commented, 'I'm hoping Eddie and I can sort this out . . . do not blame him for what has happened.' By now, however, the lawyers had entered the fray and from Eddie's came the statement that Fisher accepted sole responsibility for the failure of his marriage. It would have come to an end even if he had not known Elizabeth Taylor.

Debbie's legal advisers countered that there was nothing magnanimous in Fisher's assuming responsibility for the break-up, because that's exactly where the responsibility rested. Debbie added:

> It seems unbelievable to say that you can live happily with a man and not know that he doesn't love you. That, as God is my witness, is the truth. We have had our difficulties . . . but for the past year and a half I truly believed we had found our happiness.

In a later interview, she pointedly remarked that she and Elizabeth had never really been friends; Eddie and Mike were friends and the four of them went about a lot together, but, she said, the two of them were never close.

The squabbling continued through the headlines for weeks. In the middle of it all, Elizabeth's baby Liza, now eighteen months old, was found unconscious by her nurse and was admitted to the UCLA Hospital on 14 November with double pneumonia. For three days it was touch and go whether she would survive. Even that brought no movement of sympathy to Elizabeth's side. The way the whole Eddie and Debbie separation had blown up shocked her beyond measure; never had she imagined that it would escalate into such a furore. What she and Eddie had overlooked was Debbie's popularity, both in Hollywood and with her fans; the fact that there may have been problems in her marriage hardly mattered to the commentators and Elizabeth was made to pay. When she and Eddie finally ventured out together in public after Debbie filed for divorce early in December, she found herself snubbed by old friends. They were shunned by acquaintances as they walked into

Romanoff's; people she knew well crossed the street rather than face her; conversations in restaurants stopped if she walked in; and few would even acknowledge her. Her closest friends, like Monty Clift and Rock Hudson, were sympathetic, but, ironically, some of her strongest support came from Hollywood's newest sweethearts, Natalie and RJ, who had replaced Debbie and Eddie as the town's happiest young couple. Elizabeth recalled: 'I don't know what I would have done without them. Natalie and RJ were just about the only people in the industry who would talk to me.'

The final humiliation came when the influential Theater Owners Association rescinded the award they had given her upon the release of *Cat on a Hot Tin Roof*. No longer was she Star of the Year.

Chapter Thirteen

Suddenly One Summer

Of all Hollywood stars, perhaps the most unlikely for the role of agony aunt was Montgomery Clift. Towards the end of 1958, however, here he was, cast as a young newspaperman who spends his life writing a lonelyhearts column, giving advice to the afflicted and tormented.

Monty was desperate to make a good movie, though when he read the script of *Lonelyhearts* he soon realised that this might be rather difficult. It was Dore Schary's first independent production since leaving MGM. He had been given limited financing by United Artists and was filming entirely inside the Goldwyn studios. Schary himself had written the screenplay, based on Nathaniel West's bestseller, *Miss Lonelyhearts*, and he had gathered together some of his best acting friends and explained that he personally had a lot resting on the success or failure of his picture.

As well as Clift, he hired Maureen Stapleton, Robert Ryan, Myrna Loy, Delores Hart and Jackie Coogan. Myrna Loy was another of Monty's conquests; she fell in love with him and was captivated by his wit and charm. Like the other women in his life, she tried in vain to steer him from his course of self-destruction.

On the set of *Lonelyhearts*, Maureen Stapleton noticed that Monty's stamina and ability to withstand hours of filming, which had once astounded his fellow actors, had diminished to a pathetic level.

Once, we were sitting in my dressing room waiting for our call and he was laying with his head in my lap. He had always suffered from insomnia, now it was worse. I looked down, and found he had fallen asleep, and I began to cry as I looked at this childlike figure before me and I just held him there until he woke up.

The passion with which he had always used to argue against any aspect of a film he disliked was drifting away. Everyone in the cast realised that the power of West's book, which so emphatically highlighted the plight of those lonely people who, at their wits' end, write to newspapers with their problems, had been lost in its transfer to the screen. Perhaps the most dramatic change was the ending. In the book, Monty's character becomes romantically entangled with one of his correspondents, the wife of a cripple, who eventually kills him. In the film he is allowed to live and goes off happily with his girlfriend. Maureen, who played the cripple's wife, read her words and warned Monty that they had problems:

> I called him and said, 'Monty, you can't possibly live at the end. I'm so disappointed with it.' And he replied, 'Maureen, my darling, I am used to being disappointed,' which struck me as a strange thing to say. I could never have imagined him ever saying that, this man we all once saw as an idol. It was very sad.

Dore Schary was even sadder. In spite of the talent he had around him, the movie was a disappointment and, when it was released in 1959, received little critical acclaim.

After forty days of shooting, Monty and Maureen headed back to New York. Monty was depressed. Not long afterwards, Maureen was at one of his dinner parties when he collapsed head first on to the table. Maureen cried. 'What can we do with him?' she asked Roddy McDowall.

'All we can do', said Roddy, 'is hold his hand to the grave. Just hold his hand to the end.'

Roddy remained close by whenever he was in New York, but by now many of Monty's friends had deserted him. He had become deeply attached to his latest lover, a young Frenchman named Jacques (not his real name; he is still alive and living in Paris), who had virtually thrown himself at Monty, writing him a stream of explicit love-letters and finally presenting himself at the actor's front door. He moved in towards the end of 1958. He was certainly no stabilising influence, for he aped Monty in whatever he did. When Monty got drunk, Jacques got drunk; when Monty took pills, Jacques took pills.

Monty tried to keep his lover hidden from his friends for some time, even to the point of booking him into a hotel whenever he was having visitors around, but Jacques' presence in the apartment finally became common knowledge one night when fire broke out. Libby Holman arrived at about the same time as the fire brigade. Monty and his friend, apparently unaware of the smoke, sat up in bed in amazement as everyone forced their way in.

After so many years, Libby was one of those who were drifting away from the actor. She had recently become engaged to painter Louis Schanker and, although she kept up her vigil of observation, her friendship with Monty had begun to fade.

Against this background of sexual involvement, at a time before the world was ready for confessionals, Tennessee Williams giggled at the thought of Monty playing the lead in another of his sexually adventurous creations. Based on a one-act play by Williams, *Suddenly Last Summer* was almost pornographic in its mix of homosexuality, incest and even cannibalism. Sam Spiegel was producing it for Columbia and had already talked to Elizabeth Taylor. Could she possibly be interested in such a script, considering the scathing publicity surrounding her romance with Eddie Fisher? Then Spiegel approached Katharine Hepburn to play the other leading lady. Could she, renowned for her choosiness, be remotely interested? And Monty? Wasn't the subject matter of Tennessee's latest attack on the bounds of decency too close to home?

Elizabeth ignored her agent and advisers and said yes, she would do it. She had been nominated for an Academy Award for *Cat on a Hot Tin Roof* and Tennessee had brought her good fortune. She rang Monty and pushed him into accepting. Surprisingly, Miss Hepburn also agreed – perhaps because she was not at all sure what homosexual men did in private. (Spencer Tracy literally had to sit her down and explain it to her; she was absolutely aghast and said, 'I don't believe it. I just don't believe that,' but by then she had already signed.)

* * * * *

In preparation for her marriage to Eddie, Elizabeth had completed her Jewish studies and was claiming that she had now been accepted into the Jewish faith, for which she had taken the names Elisheba Rachel. She was hoping for an early marriage, which she rather optimistically believed would dispel the continued press harassment and hostile crowds. Wherever she went, she was greeted by chants of 'Homewrecker', or 'Give him back to Debbie', or 'Husband stealer'.

Debbie was granted her divorce in February 1959 before a Los Angeles judge, who, in less than five minutes, awarded her a $1 million property settlement covering the Fishers' two homes in Hollywood and Palm Springs, custody of their two children, plus an unusually large alimony of $10,000 a year for twenty years. There was, however, one major setback to Elizabeth's plans. The divorce would not be finalised for a year, which meant that, in the state of California, Eddie could not remarry until that time.

He was due to open for a season at the Tropicana in Las Vegas at the beginning of April and they decided that, if they took a house there now to qualify under the residency rules, they could obtain a quick Nevada divorce and be married before Elizabeth was ready to go to Europe in May to begin filming *Suddenly Last Summer*. Miss Reynolds, however, had no intention of allowing the situation to be resolved quite so easily. 'We are already divorced', she told reporters, 'and I don't approve of the Nevada kind. And what shall I tell the children when they learn their daddy had two wives?' The bitterness between them mounted daily, but in the end Debbie announced that she would, after all, give her consent.

Elizabeth, meanwhile, had been displaying some rather nice diamonds which Eddie had been lavishing upon her. For her birthday at the end of February, he gave her an evening bag adorned with one diamond for each year of her life, and invited those friends who were still on speaking terms to a party, including Rock Hudson, the Wagners, Tony Curtis and his wife, Peter Lawford and his wife, and Ronald and Nancy Reagan. There was another present still to come: on their engagement he gave her a bracelet studded with fifty diamonds.

With the wedding now certain, they appeared together before the press for the first time and agreed to answer 'reasonable' questions, hoping to enlist a less hostile media coverage than they had received of late. 'We are very much in love,' Elizabeth assured everyone. 'Now I just want to devote my time to being an adoring wife and mother.' She brushed aside another questioner who asked, 'Isn't that what you said before?'

On 12 May 1959, Eddie obtained his Nevada divorce and later that day, before a small group of friends and relatives, they were married at the Temple Beth Shalom in Las Vegas. Mike Todd, Jr, had flown down to be best man and Mara Taylor, wife of Elizabeth's brother Howard, was matron of honour. The bride, in a magnificent Jean Louis green chiffon dress, arrived twenty-five minutes late and stunned everyone by her beauty.

A honeymoon cruise in the Caribbean preceded their trip to London, where the rest of the cast was gathering at Shepperton Studios to begin work on *Suddenly Last Summer*. Mike Todd's old friend Joe Mankiewicz was directing. As the three principal players arrived, he must have realised that he had a lot to contend with: a rattled star who had just come through the most horrendous inquisition into her personal life; a male lead whose personality swung violently from the extremes of goodness and charm to half-raving drunkenness; and the *grande dame* of Hollywood, who also had her problems.

Apart from the constant worry she endured over Spencer Tracy's health, and her vigilance to keep him from drink, Katharine Hepburn felt that she had been misled by Sam Spiegel over the script of *Suddenly Last Summer*. He had told her that Williams's original story would be toned down; but when she finally got the screenplay, written by Gore Vidal with Tennessee's collaboration, it was far more explicit than Spiegel had said and she was not at all happy with the way her character was to be portrayed. She even considered backing out, particularly since Tracy was ill and could not join her immediately for the journey to England. Tracy himself, however, persuaded her that she should honour her contract.

The original play had been acclaimed in its off-Broadway première as one of the best, and certainly most talked about, productions of the 1958 season. Sam Spiegel had paid Williams $50,000 for the rights, with a twenty per cent share of the profits. The Gothic story contained some extraordinary elements and was based, in part, on experiences from Tennessee's own life. In his memoirs, he admitted that some of the scenes were inspired by the violence he had suffered in the course of his own homosexual pursuits, others by a lobotomy performed on his adored sister at the instigation of their mother, who 'was offended by her disturbed daughter's obscene speech'.

Katharine Hepburn is cast as the rich and eccentric Mrs Violet Venables, who takes her niece Catherine (Elizabeth Taylor), branded as insane, to an asylum, where she tries to bribe Dr Cukrowicz (Montgomery Clift) to perform a lobotomy which she believes will relieve Catherine's madness. The doctor, a psychosurgeon, begins to probe his patient's mind and falls in love with her; he administers a truth drug to reveal the hidden horrors of Catherine's life (thus instigating the film's flashback sequences). He discovers that for years she travelled the world with Mrs Venables and her son Sebastian, a homosexual poet who had persuaded his beautiful mother to lure young men for his sexual satisfaction. As Violet began to age, Catherine was substituted as the decoy. But, suddenly last summer . . . Sebastian died, supposedly of a heart attack, although his death certificate records that his body had been somewhat damaged.

In the film's hysterical finale, Dr Cukrowicz extracts the full, despicable story of Sebastian's death, which had become locked in Catherine's amnesia. She had been used to attract a gang of starving Spanish adolescents, some of whom Sebastian tried to seduce. They turned on him and attacked him, tearing his body apart and devouring parts in an orgy of frantic cannibalism (an aspect of the film which caused the Spanish government to ban it).

Katharine Hepburn was repulsed by the whole thing. Her struggles with the dialogue, and with Mankiewicz, began almost from the first day of filming. In one difficult scene, she asked for changes. 'If only you knew what it means to me when I have to say those things,' she said, to which Mankiewicz replied, 'That's the play, and that's what we have to do.'

Mankiewicz's problems with Katharine Hepburn became eclipsed by his confrontations with Monty Clift, who was having difficulty in remembering lines and hitting his marks. Mankiewicz asked one of his friends to go into Clift's dressing room to talk to him and try to discover whatever it was that Monty was taking to get into such a condition. The inquirer returned mystified. 'I can't see anything,' he told Mankiewicz. 'All he does is drink orange juice from a flask.'

Once or twice Monty passed out in the director's suite at The Dorchester. In a way, it was a re-run of some of the problems Mankiewicz had experienced with Spencer Tracy in the past, as Hepburn well knew. The difference was that Tracy, and other heavy drinkers like Clark Gable, generally kept their playtime off the set. Monty's drug-taking, however, brought the added complications of personality changes. Mankiewicz openly admitted that he was 'saddled with Monty' to appease Elizabeth; at one stage Sam Spiegel, who had just viewed the early rushes, said, 'We've got to get rid of him,' to which Taylor replied, 'Over my dead body.'

The animosity and acrimony grew worse. The gulf between Hepburn and Mankiewicz widened, and the arguments over the interpretation of certain scenes and his rough treatment of Clift continued almost to the end. Hepburn's revenge was not long in coming, however. When Mankiewicz closed down the production, she walked across to him and said, 'Are you absolutely sure you won't need my services any more?'

'Yes, I am.'

'Absolutely?'

'Absolutely.'

She leaned towards him, looked him straight in the eye, and spat in his face. Then she swung around, stormed into Spiegel's office and gave a repeat performance. She vowed that she would never watch the film and her friends say that she never did.

What Mankiewicz had created as he had guided, cajoled and pushed his stars through the powerful script was obvious perhaps only to those who understood the problems that had faced him. He praised Elizabeth's performance as 'probably the best she ever gave'. In the final scene, Elizabeth had to read a twelve-page monologue, stopping at various points to repeat the words for different camera angles, and at each stopping point would have to beat herself back up to the emotional pitch she had just achieved. It was one of the most difficult long speeches Mankiewicz had ever seen accomplished on screen, and Elizabeth called it 'the greatest, most draining, the most emotionally stimulating experience of my life'.

The reviewers agreed that the performances of Taylor and Hepburn were miraculous and both received Academy Award nominations as Best Actress. Monty Clift, in spite of everything, also came out well. The film was steeped in controversy, but the critics were undecided; comments ranged from 'ludicrous claptrap' to 'malignant masterpiece'. Tennessee Williams was seen giggling at the previews, but this was put down to the fact that he was drunk. In his memoirs, he said that the film made him 'throw up'.

Sam Spiegel wasn't interested in the views of the intelligentsia. With the public uproar over Elizabeth's private life still very much to the fore, he knew exactly how to target his film. He instructed Columbia's promotions people to draw up a massive advertising campaign centring around her. She was photographed in a low-cut white bathing suit, the words underneath her designed equally for titillation: 'Suddenly last summer, Cathy knew she was being used for evil.'

The film took almost $7 million in American cinemas and doubled that with foreign sales. Mankiewicz, whose rating had suffered after some disastrous movies in the fifties, was back in demand; soon he would be teamed again with Elizabeth for what would prove to be the greatest fiasco in the history of Hollywood.

The film also re-established Elizabeth as one of the world's highest paid and most sought-after actresses. She received $500,000 for appearing in *Suddenly Last Summer*, which she had been allowed to do by MGM provided that she made one more film for them before her contract was terminated. She shot back into the top ten box-office stars (where she was joined by Rock Hudson and Doris Day after the release of *Pillow Talk*). The prospect of the kind of money she could now demand was intoxicating. She had talked of retiring, but before they left England, out of the blue came another milestone for Elizabeth and for Hollywood.

It was Walter Wanger on the telephone to their suite at The Dorchester Hotel. Spyros Skouras, president of 20th Century–Fox, had given the go-ahead for *Cleopatra*, which Wanger had been trying to get into production for two years. Elizabeth had already seen a draft screenplay and was half interested, but thought the script was appalling.

'What about it?' asked Wanger. 'Will she do it?' He put the question to Eddie, who, like Mike Todd before him, had assumed the mantle of mouthpiece.

Elizabeth reflected and was still unconvinced. Then she said, 'Tell him I'll do it for a million dollars.'

Wanger picked himself up off the floor and said he would get back to her after the studio had been informed of her requirements.

One million dollars was a stunning figure in 1959; it would buy half a dozen Beverly Hills homes and still leave change. But suddenly that summer a new era of high-paid stars was born – an age which, ironically, would help to put a few more nails in the coffins of the dying studios.

*　*　*　*　*

Back in Hollywood, the first six months of 1959 were unhappy ones for Natalie Wood. Her battle with Jack Warner, in which she was being helped by Ronald Reagan, then president of the Screen Actors' Guild, showed no sign of ending; she was unemployed and unemployable, because Warner refused to allow her to work for another studio. She was seeing her psychiatrist three times a week and Robert Wagner was concerned that she found it necessary to seek help so soon after their marriage. But for the first time since she was five, Natalie was not working, and she did not know how to cope.

She spent many of her days watching Robert Wagner working and found herself face to face with Elizabeth's recent arch-enemy, Debbie Reynolds, who was co-starring with Wagner and Bing Crosby in the 20th Century–Fox film *Say One For Me*. Natalie's constant attendance on the set appears to have annoyed Debbie, and director Frank Tashlin probably noticed some needle. He politely informed Natalie that it was not his practice to allow wives to give acting lessons to their husbands from the wings, and would she kindly not come again.

At last she resolved to end her feud with Jack Warner, not least because of their financial position. During the fourteen-month lay-off, she had been forced to cash in $27,000-worth of government bonds which had been invested for her by law when she was a child star. In the current climate in which stars and their agents were beginning to dictate the pace, however, she would not go back to the studio on the terms of her original contract, which provided her merely with a straight salary. After protracted negotiations, Warner finally agreed to her return with substantially improved conditions. She would receive a new contract worth $1000 a week, rising to $7500 over five years, and there was one other very important concession: for every film she made for Warners, Natalie was free to make one for any other studio.

So the prodigal daughter returned, and Warner laid on a public 'welcome back'. He gave her the big-star dressing room, which she had redecorated in beige and gold. It had once belonged to Joan Crawford and she sent Natalie as note, hoping that the room would be as lucky for its new occupant as it had been for her. She had won an Oscar for *Mildred Pierce* while using it.

Natalie's first film, however, was hardly the one to restore her to public acclaim. She was cast alongside the latest hot male lead, James Garner, who epitomised the changing times by becoming a star on television first, through *Maverick*, a western series produced at Warners. Entitled *Cash McCall*, the film was a weak story of a Wall Street tycoon, and Natalie's role as his lover was undemanding. Warners billed it as a fascinating insight into the world of big business, but it failed to inspire any great audience interest, despite Garner's small-screen popularity. Natalie would have to wait.

* * * * *

As soon as he had completed *Suddenly Last Summer*, Montgomery Clift was called to star in Elia Kazan's latest project, *Wild River*. He promised Kazan he would stay sober, cut down the pills and give him a good performance. The film was important to Kazan, who had spent five years working on it; it was his concept of a tribute to his hero, President Roosevelt, and the New Deal. Initially he was not keen on casting Monty, who had been forced on him by Spyros Skouras at 20th Century–Fox. However, he began to see that he could use the actor to his advantage, playing him as the weak against the strong in the role of a government official who is sent to a remote part of Tennessee to persuade an obdurate old lady who lives on an island that she must leave her home so that the area can be flooded. The little old lady was Jo Van Fleet, whom Kazan had last used as James Dean's mother in *East of Eden*. He said of her: 'She was one of the great character actresses of the day, and difficult and as dear a woman as a director in need of a performance could hope for . . . full of constrained violence, she'd eat Clift alive and I was prepared to let her.'

Lee Remick was cast as Monty's lover. Fresh from her success in *A Face in the Crowd*, she too was a powerful, confident actress. So the two female leads dominated and Kazan was able to contrast them with excellent effect against Monty's personal insecurities and his weakness as a screen lover. Remick, in the love-scenes, instinctively drew him to her rather than the reverse – an accident of personality which the director exploited.

Wild River was one of Kazan's favourite films and Monty too had high hopes for it, but it failed at the box office. Fox took it off the cinema circuits after a few weeks; it disappeared into the studio vaults and has never been seen again.

* * * * *

The film that MGM selected as Elizabeth's last picture for them threw her into a rage. It was easy to see the cause of her anger. *Butterfield 8* was a strange, wicked story with a high sex content. She hated the script, which she thought pornographic, and she hated the part she was expected to play, which was that of a nymphomaniac who becomes a prostitute but doesn't charge for her services. If there was thought at MGM of getting revenge on their star for walking out on them, this was the movie to do it. And there was nothing that Elizabeth could do, as the posse of lawyers she hired soon discovered. If MGM wanted to get really difficult, they could hold her to fulfilling the remaining part of her contract, which still had two years to run, as Sol Siegel, Metro's head of production, was quick to point out. There was nothing on paper which legally required them to let her go.

Siegel instructed Pandro Berman, who had produced four of Elizabeth's previous pictures, to get her to work. Berman had his own reasons for wanting Elizabeth. The John O'Hara novel on which the film was based, first published in the mid-1930s, had lain gathering dust ever since. Berman personally owned a share of the rights and would receive forty per cent of the profits after the film had made $2 million. He recalled:

> I particularly enjoyed the fact that I got it made with Elizabeth Taylor. She didn't want to make the picture under any circumstances; she and her agent went crazy. They said she wouldn't touch it. Well, for once in my life I was lucky because somebody in the company – I don't know who – really wanted that picture made and Metro said to her, at my instigation, 'You will never make *Cleopatra* until you make *Butterfield 8*. So stop refusing to make it; you're only delaying your million dollars. We never quit!'

There were further meetings with lawyers, but Sol Siegel stood firm. Elizabeth stormed out and said she would never make the picture. Siegel promptly put her on suspension, effectively preventing her from working anywhere until she had resolved her differences with MGM. After a week, she gave up the fight and returned to the studio with a list of demands, which included finding a role for Eddie Fisher and changes to the script. Berman threw her script changes in the wastepaper basket and initially refused to give Eddie a part. He admitted later, 'We forced her to make that picture, very much against her will.'

Elizabeth was at her wits' end. When finally she agreed, she spat her anger at Berman. According to him, she shouted, 'You will regret this. I will never come to the set on time. I will give you trouble. I will make it very hard for you.'

Berman, ruffled but calm, replied, 'I'll take my chances. And I'll remind you that you are a member of the Screen Actors' Guild and you will have five or six of the Guild members working with you on this picture, and I don't think you will want to go through trouble with the Guild if you don't behave.'

Elizabeth cursed him and walked out. But at least she won one battle.

The year 1956 saw Elizabeth Taylor's marriage to Michael Wilding collapse. On hearing the news, showman *extraordinaire* Mike Todd called her to his office and said: 'There's only one guy you're going to marry. And that's me!' Miss Taylor became more stunning than ever, adorned with all the jewels, finery and publicity that Todd could lavish upon her. *(Syndications International)*

Robert Wagner first came into Natalie Wood's life when she was ten. According to studio publicity, she saw him on the lot one day and said to her mother, 'I'm going to marry him.' She did – twice – after a series of highly publicised romances which earned her the title of 'wild girl' of Hollywood.

Monty Clift and his friend and longtime rival Marlon Brando came together for the first time in *The Young Lions*. They argued over the script: Clift, who played a Jew, took it to heart when Brando wanted to give his Nazi character a touch of humanity. While they were at loggerheads, Dean Martin slipped in his best-ever film performance. *(20th Century–Fox)*

It was an embarrassing moment for Rock Hudson when he read the script of *Written on the Wind*, co-starring Lauren Bacall and Dorothy Malone. The plot was a thinly disguised real-life love story involving a 1930s scandal surrounding actress Libby Holman *(right)*, one of the women closest to Rock's friend Monty Clift. Libby married the homosexual heir to a tobacco fortune who died from gunshot wounds. His family accused her of murder, but the case was dropped. *(Universal International)*

(Above) Elizabeth Taylor was in the middle of making *Cat On a Hot Tin Roof* when the news came that her adored husband Mike Todd had been killed when his private plane, *Lucky Liz,* crashed. After a traumatic four weeks, during which friends feared she would retire from acting, she returned to give the best performance of her life. *(Metro-Goldwyn-Mayer)*

When Monty Clift appeared in *Lonelyhearts* with his good friend Maureen Stapleton, she found him 'as lovable as ever', but concerned over his facial appearance; the scar left by his accident was more noticeable because he had lost some weight.

Mike Todd was still sharp in Elizabeth's memory in the summer of 1958 and perhaps that was why she turned to his best friend, Eddie Fisher, for moral support. Elizabeth and Eddie became lovers, and Hollywood's most revered marriage between Fisher and Debbie Reynolds was over. Elizabeth was denounced as a 'homewrecker', but she had claimed husband number four, and Eddie became Mr Taylor. *(Syndications International)*

(Below) Elizabeth had already been offered $1 million to star in *Cleopatra* when MGM insisted that she made one last film for them: *Butterfield 8*, an appalling tale of a nymphomaniac prostitute who doesn't charge for her services. Elizabeth steadfastly refused, but MGM said 'No *Butterfield*, no *Cleopatra*.' She had the last laugh – she won an Oscar for her performance. *(Metro-Goldwyn-Mayer)*

(*Above*) Warren Beatty was living with Joan Collins when he was cast alongside Natalie Wood in *Splendor in the Grass*. Director Elia Kazan noticed that something was going on between his two young stars and felt sorry for Robert Wagner, watching from the wings. Miss Collins wasn't very happy either, and eventually suggested that Beatty might care to leave her house. (*Warner Bros*)

Splendor in the Grass was Natalie Wood's best film so far, but she was deeply depressed over her career. The pressure, and new acquaintances, also put a strain on her marriage, and she and Wagner separated a few months later.

(*Right*) Elia Kazan, enigmatic director and co-founder of the Actors Studio, responsible for some of Broadway's most renowned plays of the forties and Hollywood's best films in the fifties. His technique was to exploit the deep-down tensions of his actors, and they were usually better for it. (*Warner Bros*)

(*Left*) Montgomery Clift was a character Kazan enjoyed studying. Monty had come through a bad time after his accident, with his growing addiction to prescription drugs and his drinking. Elizabeth Taylor was one of the few who would not desert him in his last years. Monty was also captivated by her daughter, Liza Todd, who was just two in this picture. (*Ken Danvers: Horizon Pictures for Columbia*)

(Above) Rock Hudson struck gold when he was teamed with Doris Day for *Pillow Talk*, released in 1959. Today the film is viewed as a mild romantic comedy, but at the time it represented a major departure from the usual type of film being shown. It made Rock the number one male star in the world. *(Universal International)*

(Below) Arthur Miller got the idea for his classic screenplay *The Misfits* while awaiting a divorce from his first wife. In the film his second wife, Marilyn Monroe, was cast alongside Monty Clift and Clark Gable. Miller later denied that he had written references to the 'scarred face' of the cowboy with Monty in mind. *(United Artists)*

Marilyn Monroe was reaching the height of her problems during the filming of *The Misfits* and was missing from the set through 'illness' or arrived late on many days. She and Monty Clift *(right)* were kindred souls in their addictions and inner torments. Gable, who died of a heart attack soon after the film was made, despaired of them both. *(United Artists)*

After months of setbacks, delays and the near death of Elizabeth Taylor, Cleopatra is rolled out among a cast of thousands in the greatest movie fiasco ever, which all but sent 20th Century-Fox into bankruptcy. It also became famous for other reasons, and soon after this photograph was taken on the mammoth set in Italy, Eddie Fisher flew off to America to resume his own career with the song 'Arrivederci Roma'. *(20th Century-Fox)*

'Well,' mused Richard Burton, 'I suppose I've got to put on my breastplate once more and play opposite Miss Tits.' Initial apprehension by both, however, quickly evaporated and very soon what Burton termed 'Le Scandale' was up and running. It overshadowed any previous aspect of Elizabeth's well-publicised life. *(20th Century–Fox)*

Many scenes from *Cleopatra* contained lines which bore an uncanny resemblance to real life. This might not have been accidental; director Joe Mankiewicz was still writing the script as filming proceeded, and behind-the-scenes developments in the Taylor–Burton romance could be detected in the looks and loving gazes flashing between them on screen. *(20th Century–Fox)*

Natalie Wood was among those who followed Elizabeth Taylor's lead in achieving higher salaries. It came at a time when Natalie was also being offered roles with a greater sex content, such as *Gypsy*, in which she starred as the stripper Gypsy Rose Lee. Released in 1962, it was followed by perhaps her most highly acclaimed performance, in *Love with the Proper Stranger*. (*Warner–Pathé*)

The most demanding role of Montgomery Clift's entire career came, tragically, at a time when his personal problems made him most vulnerable. Cast as Freud *(left)*, he became locked in battle with director John Huston *(above)* over the way the part should be played. Some of Monty's friends believe that it was his experiences while making this film that finally broke him.

Stanley Kramer selected Clift for *Judgment at Nuremberg (below)* because Monty's own condition related, in a way, to the part he was to play. He had difficulty in remembering his lines until Spencer Tracy finally said, 'Monty, look into my eyes . . . play to me.' He did, and afterwards the whole crew applauded.

The switch from the most glamorous star in the world to a rather raunchy, middle-aged actress came in what was viewed as Elizabeth Taylor's best-ever performance in *Who's Afraid of Virginia Woolf?* Her life with Richard Burton continued to be a daily ingredient of newspaper and magazine columns. It was perhaps here that Elizabeth began her physical decline, which, through illness and excess, resulted in less attractive portraits of her *(top right)*.

In the eighties she re-emerged in classic matronly beauty *(left)*, although her problems were by no means at an end. Here she appears in 1985 with Liza Minnelli and Rock Hudson, already ill. *(Syndications International)*

The final tragic days of Rock Hudson first became public knowledge after his appearance at a special television tribute to Doris Day *(below)*. Soon questions were being asked, and then came the admission that he was dying of AIDS. There followed the sensationally reported revelation of Rock's secret life as a homosexual, which he had fought for three decades to keep hidden. Ironically, his last lover, Marc Christian, sued Rock's estate for part of his fortune. *(Associated Press)*

Berman relented over a role for Eddie Fisher, on the advice of one of the MGM bosses, who thought that their star would cause less bother if Eddie was around. It would also be an added bonus for the promotions department, who could bill a first-time appearance on screen of the world's most famous lovers. Eddie duly became a piano player in the film, a role which Berman had reserved for David Janssen.

In January 1960, Elizabeth and Eddie moved to New York to begin shooting *Butterfield 8*, Elizabeth still smarting. She told reporters it was rubbish and dirty, and that she was doing it under protest. It was snowing in New York and bitterly cold. Elizabeth went down with flu. In fact, during the entire production she was afflicted by a number of illnesses, which, judging by the memos flying between New York and Los Angeles, Berman felt were imaginary, put on purely to cause him aggravation. Doctors came and went, and both Elizabeth and Fisher were prescribed a variety of medications.

In the middle of filming, the production was halted by a strike which affected all studios. During the shut-down, Elizabeth secretly hired a team of professional authors to rewrite the script and improve what she considered lousy dialogue. She presented the revisions to Berman on her return. He discarded them, saying brusquely, 'Let's leave the writing to the writers.'

The critics found little good to write about *Butterfield 8*, except that Miss Taylor had risen above a script which *Time* magazine suggested might have been copied from a lavatory wall. However, the publicity and scandal which had surrounded Elizabeth during the last year or more made the film hugely successful. It took $8 million at the box office and Pandro Berman became a very rich man. To her astonishment, Elizabeth won her first Oscar for the role – although she always maintained that she got the award out of sympathy from her colleagues, for, at the time of the nominations, she had just come through the illness that almost killed her.

*   *   *   *   *

Coincidentally, at Christmas 1959 Natalie Wood and Robert Wagner were also about to start work on a new film produced by Pandro Berman at MGM. The Wagners had just gone deep into debt to buy their first real home together, a $150,000 mansion on the prestigious Beverly Drive, in the heart of Beverly Hills. Spurred on by the thought that Natalie's new freedom to offer her services elsewhere meant that they could now make serious money, they borrowed heavily against their contracts and began ripping the innards out of the colonial-style property, transforming it at huge expense into something reminiscent of a Greek temple. A small army of decorators and builders remodelled it with garish marble-and-gilt trimmings. Natalie scoured antique shops, while RJ purchased rows of new and secondhand books for his library. The new swimming pool that they had installed was divided into two sections, his and hers, and when the gossips commented on the Wagners' extravagance in having two pools, Natalie replied wearily, 'It's just not true. We only have one pool, like everyone else.'

With such extravagance, they needed to replenish their dwindling fortunes quickly and, though when they married they had declared that they would never work together on a film, Natalie discovered that they could get another $50,000 between them as a husband-and-wife team. MGM kindly came up with a $100,000 package which would promote them as the Hollywood sweethearts, together on screen for the first time.

Pandro Berman was producing a Robert Thom screenplay of Rosamond Marshall's bestselling novel *The Brixby Girls*. The studio, in its wisdom, changed its title to the unappealing *All the Fine Young Cannibals*. It was, as the studio put it, a glimpse into the love-hungry world of sophisticated young moderns. George Hamilton and Pearl Bailey would be their co-stars. The Wagners looked at the script and Natalie announced their acceptance: 'We believe this is a challenging film which will help both our careers. It is a serious, unusual drama.' Later, she wished she had never said that. The film vanished from sight the moment it was released and was a financial disaster. Both she and RJ would regret for ever that the only film they made together was so bad.

Chapter Fourteen

Cleopatra's Needle

The year 1960 is considered by many to be the one in which old Hollywood died, but nobody noticed. A survey that year showed that there were now forty-four million television sets in America, compared with four million exactly a decade earlier, and more than half the two hundred million people worldwide who had once paid each week to see their favourite stars on the silver screen were staying at home. Control of the dream factories had all but fallen to an assortment of conglomerates, hotel owners, soft-drink purveyors, lawyers, bankers, a handful of agents and stars.

Elizabeth Taylor had become the first million-dollar actress, to be followed by others demanding similar recompense plus a share of the profits. The trend continued throughout the sixties and seventies, reaching what seemed incredible heights in 1978 when Marlon Brando was paid $3.7 million for twelve days' work on *Superman*, and proceeded into the eighties when Sylvester Stallone was guaranteed $20 million for *Rocky IV*. In the wake of a handful of mega-earners were dozens of struggling actors who would never see the opportunities that the studio system had once offered to new faces.

The great autocratic showmen who had created the stars, and Hollywood itself, had gone forever. In their place were the deal-makers, ready to shower big money on the big names, whom they saw as their salvation against the onslaught of television. The gimmicks had failed: they had tried every trick in the book; they had filmed every book. The new hype would centre around the two dozen or so most popular actors and actresses, who would be projected into even greater stardom.

*　*　*　*　*

After the runaway success of *Pillow Talk*, which had taken over $8 million at the box office and had become one of Universal's all-time highest earners, Rock Hudson had been earmarked for three follow-up films. He and Henry Willson decided to follow the pack and secure a bigger share of the take for themselves. They formed their own film company, Gibraltar Productions, whose purpose was not to make movies but to purchase a share in those in which Rock starred. In that way, he could begin to make real money instead of just the contract salary that Henry had pushed him into signing a couple of years earlier and which now looked dismally low compared with what was on offer elsewhere. Willson also saw this as an opportunity to feather his own nest and, having seen how easily Doris Day's husband took $50,000 from Universal as a so-called assistant producer, he wanted the same deal. Unknown to Rock, he negotiated his own payments from the studio by getting himself on the payroll as an assistant producer.

In the summer of 1960, Rock went to Mexico to make *The Last Sunset* with Kirk Douglas and then on to Italy for a comedy, *Come September*, with Gina Lollobrigida. His new production company benefited with a share of the profits from both films. His next picture with Doris Day, *Lover Come Back*, which was already being discussed, would put Rock too in the million-dollar earnings bracket.

*   *   *   *   *

In May, Natalie and RJ took off for New York, where Natalie was to begin filming *Splendor in the Grass*; the film was scheduled to take three months and to be shot entirely on location in the city. Elizabeth and Eddie threw a party for them and bought them a portable hi-fi as a going-away present. Natalie was overjoyed at the chance of doing the film, in which she was to co-star with Shirley MacLaine's younger brother, Warren Beatty.

Neither of the young stars was the original choice of the director, Elia Kazan. He said:

> When Natalie was first suggested to me I backed off. I didn't want a washed-up child star (as the sages were then calling her). But when I saw her, I detected a twinkle in her eyes. I knew there was unsatisfied hunger there . . . she reminded me of the 'bad' girls in High School who looked like 'good' girls. . . . I could see that the crisis in her career was preparing her for a crisis in her personal life. She told me she was being psychoanalysed. That did it. Poor RJ, I said to myself.

Warren Beatty was suggested to Kazan by the homosexual playwright Bill Inge, writer of *Come Back Little Sheba*, *Picnic*, *Bus Stop* and *Dark at the Top of the Stairs*, who had written the novelette on which Kazan had based his screenplay for *Splendor in the Grass*. Beatty, who had never previously appeared in a movie, was Inge's protégé. He had come along the James Dean route – stage work off Broadway and some spasmodic television work in the Kraft Theater and Studio One. Natalie and RJ were on nodding terms with him after meeting him at various Hollywood parties, where his party-piece was to play jazz-piano, at which he was highly talented. He had a defiant streak similar to James Dean's, and a fiery temperament that could explode in the face of anyone who taunted him; but as an actor he also possessed some of the sensitivity of Monty Clift. In fact, *Time* magazine made exactly those comparisons in a description of Beatty in 1961:

> With a facial and vocal suggestion of Montgomery Clift and the mannerisms of James Dean, he is the latest incumbent in the line of arrogant, attractive, hostile, moody, sensitive, self-conscious, bright, defensive, stuttering, self-seeking and extremely talented actors who become myths before they are thirty.

Beatty was, above all, ambitious and intended to get to the top, fast. Now here he was, staring opportunity in the face, and with the benefit of love-scenes with one of Hollywood's most beautiful young actresses.

It was Warren's sexual qualities – and his piano playing – which had endeared him to the twenty-four-year-old Joan Collins, whose romances even then were sending flutters to the hearts of the gossip columnists. After her divorce from English actor Maxwell Reed (who created history and headlines by suing her for alimony of $1250 a month), Joan had had a long-standing relationship with Arthur Loew. He turned his attentions to Elizabeth Taylor when Joan found someone new. Then Elizabeth went off with Eddie Fisher, and Loew began dating Debbie Power, the young widow of Tyrone. At a party in the Power mansion in Beverly Hills in the summer of 1959 Joan spotted Warren Beatty: it was love at first sight and soon they were living together in a tiny apartment at Chateau Marmont, which was in a shabby location but out of sight of prying eyes. In her autobiography, *Past Imperfect*, Miss Collins spoke highly of Beatty, adding that he had an insatiable appetite for love-making – three, four, sometimes five times a day.

Joan became pregnant and broke the news to Warren at the end of April, just a couple of weeks before he was due to start filming *Splendor in the Grass*. Recalling the scandal surrounding Ingrid Bergman, who became a Hollywood outcast when she had Roberto Rossellini's illegitimate child, Joan and Warren decided that there was only one course of action to save both their careers and, after a great deal of heart-searching on Joan's part, she had the pregnancy terminated.

As Beatty began work on the film, they rented a small apartment on Fifth Avenue and often Joan would wander into the Filmways Studios to watch her lover at work. Robert Wagner, who was similarly at a loose end, did the same. Both shuffled uncomfortably as Warren and Natalie prepared for the clinch.

The two were thrown together by the very nature of the plot. They play a couple of sweethearts hemmed in by the morals of an American midwestern town of the 1920s, though the story could easily have been transposed to the sixties. When Natalie's character refuses Warren's sexual advances, he drops her and promptly dashes off to bed with a schoolfriend of easy virtue. Natalie dates another boy, who tries to rape her, and she ends up in the local mental asylum.

Wagner was wary of Beatty, and there was certainly no love lost between Joan and Natalie. Towards the end of filming in August, there was just the slightest hint of a forthcoming scandal when Dorothy Kilgallen, in her syndicated column, noted that Beatty and Wood had been seen together in Manhattan without their respective escorts. Lawyers for Natalie and RJ immediately demanded a retraction; they said the story was defamatory and untrue.

But something was happening amongst all that splendour as they rolled around in the grass. Elia Kazan spotted it: 'All of a sudden they became lovers. When did it happen? When I wasn't looking, and I wasn't sorry. It helped their love-scenes. My only regret was the pain it was causing RJ.'

Mr and Mrs Wagner returned to Los Angeles to resume an apparently blissful existence, but it would not last much longer.

*　　*　　*

Joan Collins, meanwhile, had been put on standby in case she was needed by Fox for the role of Cleopatra. In July 1960, Elizabeth Taylor still hadn't signed her contract and Spyros Skouras kept telling Walter Wanger that they could make the film much more cheaply without her. 'Anybody can play Cleopatra,' said Spyros, 'Hayward, Collins, Woodward . . . any one of them, and they cost us nothing' (they were all contract players). Wanger disagreed, insisting that the picture needed the biggest box-office draw in the world: the most beguilingly beautiful actress available – and there could be no question about whom he was talking. And the studio boss knew that he was right. Skouras was staking the future of Fox on the picture. The studio was teetering towards bankruptcy; in the past five years, it had lost $70 million on a succession of flops. Only three of its films were in the list of top earners for that period: *Peyton Place*, *The King and I* and *The Seven Year Itch*. The situation was desperate. At the end of July, Spyros told Wanger to get Elizabeth at all costs.

Like Rock and Natalie, Elizabeth had formed her own company, MCL (her children's initials), with a base in Switzerland to get the best tax advantages. After dangling Wanger on a string for months, finally she was ready to sign. Her agents negotiated the following terms: $125,000 for the first sixteen weeks' work; $50,000 a week for every week thereafter; $3000 living expenses a week; round-trip expenses for herself, Eddie and her three children to England, where the film was to be shot; one all-round trip for her agent Kurt Frings; and a 16mm print of the film. There were also subsidiary terms, such as Rolls-Royce transport, which eventually added up to well over a million.

Fox, meanwhile, was spending what little money the studio had left in preparation for the film they thought would get them out of trouble. Skouras agreed to pay $500,000 to an Italian film company who had been planning a rival version of *Cleopatra*. Then they began building work to re-create ancient Alexandria over eight acres of Pinewood Studios in England. The set was gigantic: palaces and temples sprouted from the 80,000 cubic feet of timber and 750,000 feet of steel tube. The cost for this alone had already reached $600,000. Eighteen major actors had been signed, including Peter Finch to play Julius Caesar and Stephen Boyd as Mark Antony. Shooting was due to start in September 1960.

Eddie was at Elizabeth's side constantly, and his own career had now been set aside to take care of her and the entourage, which consisted of her three children, seven animals, her hairdresser, children's nanny, secretary and occasionally her doctor. Apart from his demanding role as Elizabeth's lover, for which he might be required at any hour of the day or night, he had also assumed that of general dogsbody, attending to all the whims and fancies of his bride. His tasks were numerous: answering her telephone calls, supervising the meals, caring for the children, walking the dogs, calling for the car, checking the temperature in the swimming pool, reassuring her over her acting performances, soothing her after her numerous rows, organising parties, talking to her friends when she was too busy and planning her future arrangements. Fisher had hardly worked since he became Mr Taylor. The only way he could resume his own career was by leaving Elizabeth to continue working alone, but she could not manage without him. The most sensational Hollywood marriage of the day, hastily constructed on their joint grief over Mike Todd's death, already seemed to be under pressure that August as Eddie herded everyone on board a cruise ship to go sailing round the Greek islands before their journey to London to begin work on 'the most spectacular picture of all time'.

* * * * *

Monty Clift, in August, was down in Reno, Nevada, preparing for his latest role in Arthur Miller's screenplay of *The Misfits*, which John Huston was directing for United Artists and Seven Arts. Clift's co-stars were Miller's then wife, Marilyn Monroe, Clark Gable, Eli Wallach and Thelma Ritter. Once again, the script, on which Miller had been working for months, bore many uncanny resemblances to the real lives of the actors assigned to the film.

The idea came to Miller when he was living in a cabin in Quail Canyon, Nevada, to establish residency for his divorce from his first wife. He met three cowboys who made their living tracking and catching wild horses, which they sold to a pet-food cannery for 50 cents a pound. He wrote a short story about them, which was published in *Esquire*. Back in New York, and married to Marilyn, he was walking in a park near Doctors' Hospital, where his wife had just had another of her pregnancies terminated, when the idea came to him to turn the story into a screenplay, his first.

Clark Gable was cast as the tough, heavy-drinking cowboy whose life takes on new purpose and stability when he meets a voluptuous beauty, played by Marilyn Monroe. Gable's own life had followed a similar course. After his bitter exit from MGM, years of drink-laden depression over the death of his beloved Carole Lombard and the countless dud films that he had had to endure, he married actress Kay Williams and reached perhaps the happiest stage of his life. He was even talking of retiring to his ranch to enjoy his remaining years with Kay and her two children, who adored him. When the script for *The Misfits* landed on his desk, Gable read it and knew that he had to do the film. He and Kay moved to the desert location well ahead of the shooting date and he began to get into trim for the physically demanding role. He played golf, went on a diet and cut down his drinking to virtually nil.

Monty Clift was to play the younger cowboy and rodeo rider. In his opening scene, he is shown talking on the telephone to his mother, whom he idolises. He is telling her that he has recovered from a rodeo accident, but that his face has been so badly scarred that she won't recognise him. Writer Robert Thom later accused Miller of being 'ghoulish and cold-blooded' to have written this line, knowing full well that Monty was a mother's boy and that his face had been smashed by his accident. Miller denied it, claiming that, although he had always thought of Monty as a prospect for the part, he did not write the lines with him specifically in mind. It all seemed too coincidental to be true, however, and the script was certainly not concluded by the time Monty was cast: Miller was rewriting almost until the start of filming, and then Huston was rewriting the rewrites.

Marilyn Monroe also had many lines which were incredibly close to home. She plays the bubbling, sensitive, heavy-drinking young wife who arrives in Reno to get a divorce from her husband (Kevin McCarthy, in his briefest ever screen appearance) and joins up with Gable. At the time, Marilyn's own life was beset with the same kind of troubles – drink, drugs and tremendous insecurity over her career.

She was also rumoured to be on the verge of divorce from Miller, and reporters were swarming all over the place, eager to get the low-down on her and Miller, or to catch Monty in one of his traumas, or to see Gable get drunk. Of all those possibilities, problems with Gable were the least likely. He was determined to prove something and worked as if this were going to be his last film. He and Monty got on well together; Gable admired Clift's work and his style.

The problems began with Marilyn, who failed to show up on the first day of shooting. A telephone call to New York established that she was feeling unwell and would come down to Reno the following day. Huston, who also had something to prove after two or three recent failures, took the opportunity of tinkering further with the script. Marilyn finally breezed in, hours late and in a state of high tension. On the flight, she had changed her dress, which carried an unsightly period stain at the rear, tidied herself up and did the best she could to disguise the bags under her eyes before stepping from the plane to be met by the Governor of Nevada, carrying flowers from Arthur Miller. She brought with her drama coach Paula Strasberg, upon whom she relied totally to get her through a day's filming; a hairdresser and her masseur were also in tow.

The pattern continued. Marilyn was constantly late, sometimes not turning up at all. Gable complained, 'I like this kid. In fact, she's damned good. But what the hell is her problem? She's so goddamned unprofessional. It's driving me nuts waiting for her to show.' The question 'Is Marilyn working today?' became commonplace.

Gable and Wallach sat around impatiently as the desert sun scorched down upon them; for most of the day, temperatures were well in excess of 100 degrees. It was all too much for Monty, who was soon drinking his mixture of vodka and barbiturates, missing his start times or disappearing altogether. One night he was found slumped naked in the lift at the Mapes Hotel, where they were all staying, and sent the guests who discovered him scattering. Libby Holman didn't help matters by turning up halfway through the filming and inviting everybody to a party.

Mainly, though, the delays centred around Marilyn. Huston said:

Sometimes, she'd be in her dressing room for hours, a whole morning maybe. Occasionally, when she came out, she'd be practically incapable of work and I said to Arthur once, 'At this rate she's going to be in an institution or dead in three years. Anyone who allows her to take narcotics should be shot.' I suppose that was an indictment against Arthur, in a way, but then I discovered he had no power over her. I think he had done everything he could to make the marriage work but she humiliated him in front of everyone. One time, she drove off in her car, leaving him standing in the middle of the desert.

Miller was working constantly on the script, and eventually cleared out of their room with his typewriter. Paula Strasberg moved in with Marilyn.

The whole production was shut down on three occasions because of her 'illnesses'. The first, on 26 August, came after a scene with Gable in which he had to say the lines, 'Honey, we all got to go sometime, reason or no reason. Dyin's as natural as living. The man who is afraid to die is afraid to live. . . .' That night, Marilyn took an overdose of Nembutal capsules and word got out that her life had been saved by a stomach pump. She was flown immediately to Los Angeles, where she remained in hospital for ten days under the care of her personal psychiatrist, Ralph Greenson. Louella Parsons revealed the secret in her column, saying, 'Marilyn's a very sick girl who needs help; she's much worse than was at first thought.'

Monty and Marilyn stood side by side in their insecurities, emotions and addictions, and their similarities probably helped draw them together. They spent hours in Marilyn's dressing room with Monty giving her additional coaching, and they worshipped each other. Marilyn knew that Monty was homosexual, but she would tantalise him with her body, rubbing her nipples across his nose. She was determined to get him into bed for the sheer hell of it. He later admitted that they had one abortive attempt at love-making but they were both too drunk. Still, said Monty, 'we fooled around a lot', and he and Marilyn were often seen in quiet corners. As her rows with Miller became more frequent, she increasingly turned to Monty for companionship, and to join her in drink and pills. With so many reporters around, rumours that Monty and Marilyn were having an affair did not take long to spread.

Elizabeth Taylor was said to be furious when she heard; the word was that she hated Monroe and she did not like Monty socialising with her. (In Norman Mailer's biography of Marilyn, he quotes Eli Wallach's version of a meeting between Taylor and Monroe after *The Misfits* had been filmed. They came across each other in the Polo Lounge in Beverly Hills and Elizabeth was alleged to have said, 'Get that dyke away from me,' which seemed to imply that she thought Marilyn was a lesbian. When she heard that Mailer was going to use the quote, her lawyers threatened to sue for $6 million, but Mailer got Wallach and several other witnesses to confirm that she had said it and the action was not pursued.)

In the film, these behind-the-scenes activities were never noticeable. Monty often appeared wide-eyed on screen, but intelligently worked his way through the picture. Marilyn's performance was fascinating, especially considering that for long stretches she was simply incapable of working. Arthur Miller said of them in an interview:

> Neither of them was able to deal with the situations they found them-
> selves in. Monty was a little better capable of running his life than Mari-
> lyn and could continue to work. . . . her performance was extraordinary
> but I'm not sure if it was worth all that torture, all that agony . . .

Clark Gable did many of his own stunts in *The Misfits*, partly out of boredom while waiting for Marilyn and partly to meet Huston's quest for realism. The film crews marvelled at his ability to rope a wild horse and then allow himself to be dragged along the desert floor at twenty or thirty miles an hour, which, at sixty years old, was no mean feat; there was no question that he suffered great emotional and physical strain. He was pleased with the picture, and delighted when Kay informed him that she was expecting their child.

He would never see either. A week after filming ended, forty days late and ahead of budget by $500,000, Kay found Gable sitting by the bed, his face white as a sheet. 'I've got this terrible pain . . .' he told her, rubbing his hand across his chest. It was the onset of a massive heart attack, and the film that he thought was his best since *Gone With the Wind* was indeed his last. He died in hospital ten days later.

Shortly afterwards, Marilyn re-enacted the initial scenes of *The Misfits* by flying down to another divorce town, Ciudad Juarez in Mexico, to end her marriage to Miller. A judge opened his office specially for her at eight o'clock in the evening and she emerged after six minutes clutching a single piece of paper which granted her divorce on the grounds of character incompatibility, with which a local lawyer for Miller concurred.

All that remained was to await the critics' verdict. Huston was proud of his film, and in spite of the problems praised Marilyn's contribution. 'She went deep down into her own personal experiences', he said, 'and pulled out something that was unique. It was all the truth, it was Marilyn.' Perhaps because of that, the critics made some hurtful observations when the film was released, describing her performance as one of neurotic individuality that symbolised nothing. The next day, she was admitted to a mental hospital.

* * * * *

Filming for *Cleopatra* should have started at the end of September, but Elizabeth Taylor had been struck by fever and was ordered to remain in her hotel room. Director Rouben Mamoulian, his long-awaited first day with his million-dollar star in front of the cameras aborted, amused himself by taking exterior shots of the temples and palaces and pools, which looked dismal in the dull English autumn.

The telephone lines between Walter Wanger and Spyros Skouras were hot and, as Elizabeth remained in her hotel suite and production expenses mounted at the rate of $130,000 a day, Skouras got on a plane to London. Two dozen other actors and five hundred extras sat around wondering when they would be called. Two strikes by technicians interrupted what little filming could be done. Parts of the set remained unfinished and began gathering rust and damp in the October drizzle. The script was a disaster, and still they were writing major scenes, then rewriting again, which meant that sets could not be finished.

By the end of October, under pressure from the insurance companies who examined the books and discovered a $2 million loss caused by the halt in production, Lord Evans, personal physician to the Queen, was called in to examine Elizabeth, whose temperature still fluctuated around fever point. On 31 October he ordered her into the London Clinic for further tests, and she made an ignominious exit from The Dorchester on a stretcher with flashbulbs popping all around. Her own doctor, Rex Kennamer, flew in from Los Angeles to join the frenetic medical activity around the star. A huge crowd of fans and a large gathering of journalists stood at the doors of the clinic waiting for news.

Ten days after she was admitted, the medical team announced that they had found the cause of Elizabeth's illness – an abscessed tooth, which they extracted, expecting the patient to return to good health and fitness within a few days. She was brought back to The Dorchester and Fox joyfully put their languishing cast back on the alert.

Four days later, Elizabeth was again carried from The Dorchester on a stretcher, moaning and weeping and clutching her head. Eddie told waiting reporters that she had gone through twelve hours of excruciating pain. Lord Evans diagnosed an inflammation of the spinal cord and brain which produced symptoms similar to meningitis, and on 18 November she was pronounced too ill to resume work.

As autumn gave way to freezing fog swirling around the set at Pinewood, Wanger and Mamoulian despaired. Even if they had a star to perform, there was no way they could create an atmosphere remotely resembling ancient Egypt. Every time someone spoke, vapour from their mouth was visible. The insurance companies at Lloyd's of London, who already faced a pay-out exceeding $3 million, insisted that Skouras cast another Cleopatra and even suggested names: why couldn't the part be played by Kim Novak, or Shirley MacLaine or Marilyn Monroe? Skouras himself was inclined to agree and screamed at Wanger: 'If you had done what I'd suggested in the first place, we wouldn't be in this mess.' Wanger would not be moved from his stance: 'No Taylor, no Cleo'; and so, without a star, they had no option but to close the production down. Wanger called the crew and actors together at Pinewood and announced: 'I'm sorry guys, there is nothing more we can do for the moment. We are closing the production down until 3 January. Go off and have a good Christmas, and we'll see you all back here in the New Year.'

Back at The Dorchester, where the penthouse suite was showing signs of wear and tear from the Taylor traumas, the succession of visitors, doctors, children and so on, Elizabeth and Eddie planned a holiday to allow her to recuperate. Before setting off, however, they called a council of war to fight back against the newspapers and magazines that had written unkind things about them in the past few weeks; she was especially annoyed at one report in the *Daily Mail* suggesting that there was nothing wrong with her, but that she had been hiding away in her hotel room because she had grown too plump. Others, in America, had made some startling allegations: that Elizabeth had taken Stephen Boyd as her lover; that she and Eddie had neglected their children; that their marriage was all but over. In early December, in consultation with lawyers, she issued libel writs amounting to $7.5 million against seven newspapers and eventually collected substantially from them.

By now she had recovered sufficiently to fly to Paris, then on to Palm Springs for a Christmas holiday and to regain some of her strength. She told reporters as she left, 'I've never been so glad to be alive. There were moments when I thought I'd never live to see another day.'

At the beginning of January 1961, she was back at The Dorchester, ready for work when filming resumed on 3 January. Her first task was a nude scene, about which she had protested until Wanger and Mamoulian convinced her that it was historically accurate: Cleopatra is rolled in a rug to be presented to Julius Caesar. The scene required six takes and she insisted that the set be cleared of everyone except the essential people. In another scene, where Cleopatra is dining with Caesar, production once again came slithering to a stop; the script was simply unplayable. It was obvious to the actors and to the production staff. Author Nunnally Johnson was paid $100,000 to fly immediately to England to help the scriptwriters, who were by now demented by the daily rejections of their words.

Then everything stopped again. Rouben Mamoulian threw his arms in the air and screamed, 'I cannot stand this another minute.' He walked off the set and never came back. He had been working on the film for fifteen months; the costs to Fox so far amounted to $7 million and Mamoulian had managed to get ten and a half minutes of usable material on film. He had frequently tendered his resignation as the fiasco progressed; this time it was accepted. What he did not know was that, on 18 January, Skouras had privately contacted Taylor, who was screaming publicly for her own release. She suggested that perhaps the only salvation would be to hire a new director, like Joe Mankiewicz with whom she had worked the previous year on *Suddenly Last Summer*.

At the time, Mankiewicz was holidaying in the Bahamas. He leapt at the offer but his agent, Charles Feldman in New York, sensed that big money was about. This was confirmed when Skouras rang back to plead with him to get his client to New York for a meeting. They lunched at the Colony Club and Skouras talked money, plus other gifts like a villa in the south of France or a yacht at Antibes. Joe's lawyer, Abe Bienstock, was consulted. 'No yacht and no villa,' he ruled. 'You'll be in the federal penitentiary for tax fraud if you accept.'

Skouras persisted and the stakes rose. They would pay Mankiewicz $1.5 million for the production company he owned jointly with NBC, which had only one film in progress. Mankiewicz agreed to sell, but his advisers pushed it further, pointing out that NBC would be entitled to half the payment. Finally, Skouras offered $3 million, half to Mankiewicz and half to NBC: 'Now is it a deal or not?' Mankiewicz said yes, thank you, it was. On top of the $3 million, he would also receive a full salary and expenses, becoming the highest-paid director ever.

Mankiewicz flew to London on 1 February, had a private showing of the remnants of filming bequeathed by Mamoulian and declared it to be wondrous rubbish. He read the script and tossed it aside. He walked around the sets and pronounced them a garish disaster; they would have to be rebuilt. Skouras, meanwhile, was trying to explain to Fox shareholders how on earth he had got into such a mess. With the payment to Mankiewicz and the continuing daily costs at Pinewood, Fox had now invested $11.5 million and had absolutely nothing to show for it, with the exception of a few weather-beaten temples and seven thousand feet of unwanted celluloid. Insurance companies were also contesting his claims. Wringing his hands, Skouras tried to reassure his anxious bankers, and himself, that 'all is now well and we start filming on April 3.'

While Mankiewicz suspended production to rewrite the script, Elizabeth, who was now entering the $50,000-a-week segment of her contract, flew to Munich with Eddie in the middle of February for a weekend of relaxation at the pre-Lenten Karnival. While they were dining on 16 February, Eddie collapsed with appendicitis and was hurried back to

London, where he went into the London Clinic for an immediate operation. The following week, Elizabeth began to run a temperature and was confined to bed for her twenty-ninth birthday. On 4 March, the penthouse suddenly took on the appearance of an emergency ward. The star collapsed, clutching her throat; she was unable to breathe and her face was turning blue. A frantic nurse on duty at The Dorchester found her unconscious and choking to death. By chance, a well-known London anaesthetist, Mr J. Middleton Price, was at a party in a nearby suite and was summoned. He struggled for ten minutes to correct her breathing; he shook her violently and hit her chest to try to relieve her congested lungs and he constructed a makeshift oxygen tent while an ambulance hurtled towards The Dorchester. Mr Middleton Price knew that only a tracheotomy would save her. Ten minutes later, she was being wheeled into the London Clinic and doctors put her chances of survival at less than 50–50; they reckoned that had she been any later arriving at the hospital, she would have had no chance at all, and certainly had Mr Middleton Price not been in The Dorchester at the time, she would not have left there alive. The headlines rang out around the world: 'LIZ TAYLOR FIGHTS FOR HER LIFE'. Physicians confirmed that she had acute Staphylococcus pneumonia and was gravely ill.

Outside the clinic, the crowds gathered. Worried fans joined the horde of cameramen and reporters as day by day for the next week her condition lunged from 'improving' to 'worsening' to 'fears for her life'. Mail and goodwill cards poured in by the sackload from all parts of the globe.

Joan Collins, asleep in bed with Warren Beatty in their new rented home on Sunset Plaza Drive back in Los Angeles, answered the telephone in the early hours. It was her agent: Liz Taylor was dying and they wanted Joan to take over if she did. Joan said that she couldn't possibly do that; it would be ghoulish. Her agent replied, 'I hope she doesn't die, but if she does . . . think of your career.'

Joan hung up and turned to Warren. 'That's shitty. Really shitty,' she said.

Beatty replied, 'Showbiz, baby – but don't worry about it. She's got nine lives.' And she had.

The bulletins from the London Clinic became more hopeful and on 10 March Elizabeth's six doctors released this tribute to her:

She has made a very rare recovery. Much of it can be attributed to the special drugs but of course she herself, with a remarkable will to live, was the biggest factor in overcoming the illness. She has put up a wonderful fight.

Towards the end of March, she was almost completely recovered –

though still very weak. When Truman Capote visited her in hospital, she was laughing and joking; she pulled the rubber patch over the hole caused by the tracheotomy and said, 'Look, Tru, when I pull this off, my voice disappears.' She pulled it off and her lips moved without sound. She remained in the London Clinic until 27 March, when her doctors declared her well enough for the journey back to America and, amid jostling crowds so large that she was almost lost in the crush, she was taken in her wheelchair first from the clinic and then through the airport terminal; in each place she was surrounded by a dozen policemen to protect her from the masses of well-wishers.

Similar sympathy and acclaim for her courage were bestowed upon her, along with the Oscar for *Butterfield 8,* by her Hollywood colleagues, who clamoured to wish her well. She was back in the bosom of her peers, who but a few weeks earlier had still been admonishing her for running off with Eddie. In the Academy nominations she had received support from an unexpected quarter. MGM, who had let her go without so much as an official goodbye after her eighteen years with the studio, launched a $250,000 advertising campaign to help her secure the award. Hedda Hopper wrote: 'She didn't get it for *Butterfield 8*; she got it for nearly dying,' and Elizabeth agreed.

Spyros Skouras announced hopefully that he expected to resume filming *Cleopatra* towards the middle of 1961 and that this time it would be shot 'right here in Hollywood'. He had already ordered the huge sets constructed at Pinewood to be dismantled and packed in crates for shipment to the United States. Some were already on the way when a Fox executive pointed out to Skouras two problems that he had overlooked. First, all studio space at Fox large enough to accommodate the sets was committed; second, there was a binding commitment in Miss Taylor's contract that the picture should be shot outside America so that her company, MCL, could take advantage of the tax situation. Skouras turned a lighter shade of grey and ordered a survey of Rome to discover the possibilities of shooting the film there. What about the sets, someone dared to ask, on their way from England? 'Tip them over the side, as far as I care,' said Skouras, now totally at his wits' end. He had a tiger by the tail, but he could not let go.

* * * * *

Natalie Wood had also been in hospital; she too had had pneumonia and she too had been on the critical list. In her case, it began with a plan which got out of hand.

After *Splendor in the Grass*, she was offered two new films at the same time. One was *Parrish* for Warners, and Jack Warner was insisting that she did it; the other was *West Side Story* for United Artists. She read the script of *Parrish* and tore it up in a rage. 'It's crap,' she screamed. 'I'm not doing it.' *West Side Story* was another matter; she would do anything to get the role of Maria, but she knew that if she started up her feud with Warner again she would simply be placed on suspension and that would be that.

The ploy she used to get out of *Parrish* sounds like something only Henry Willson could dream up. Natalie suddenly went down with tonsillitis and an operation to remove her tonsils put her out of action just long enough to get her out of doing *Parrish*, thus leaving her clear for the musical. But immediately after being released from hospital she contracted an infection; it turned to pneumonia and she was on the critical list for three days. Fortunately, she recovered sufficiently quickly to start work on *West Side Story* in April 1961.

United Artists, who were financing *West Side Story*, had offered Natalie $50,000 and a share of the profits or a one-off payment of $250,000. She took the latter; with Wagner's career still in the doldrums they needed the money. It proved to be a mistake, however: *West Side Story* made huge profits and a percentage deal would have given her substantially more. She would not make that mistake again.

Natalie had begun to model herself on Elizabeth. She wafted around with an air of elegant importance, wearing sunglasses from her collection of two hundred pairs, with her fur draped around her shoulder over spectacular skin-hugging dresses and a long, diamond-studded cigarette-holder held at shoulder height. Thus did she arrive on the set of *West Side Story*, with her newly acquired entourage in tow: her secretary, her hairdresser and her dresser, with RJ trailing behind pulling a reluctant miniature poodle named Gigi.

Only her psychoanalyst knew that Natalie's air of total confidence masked deep fears and emotions, which ranged from the basic insecurity about whether she could do justice to the demanding singing-and-dancing role of Maria, to the developing crisis in her marriage arising from the secret contact she had maintained with Warren Beatty since finishing *Splendor in the Grass*.

Filming the hit Broadway musical was always going to be difficult. Choreographer Jerome Robbins was an exacting task-master who strove for perfection. Robert Wise, the director, said:

The major problem was that film and stage are such different mediums. Our biggest problem was how to translate all the highly stylized and theatrical poetic moments and scenes from stage into the reality of the screen. And that's what we struggled and worked with more than anything else on the picture. The collaboration with Jerry was difficult, but very productive.

It soon became clear that the intricate operatic requirements of *West Side Story* were beyond Natalie. Robbins worked her sixteen hours a day, and weekends, to try to get perfection. Robert Wise recalled, 'She really tried hard; she did all her tracks and then sang back to them. They were good, but not good enough.' The solution was for Natalie to continue to do the songs, but to have them dubbed over by Marni Nixon, who had sung for Deborah Kerr in *The King and I*.

Natalie also had difficulty in maintaining a consistent Puerto Rican accent, and in this she was coached heavily by her friend Rita Moreno, who saw that Robbins was giving her a hard time over this aspect of her performance. Her dancing also lacked the polish Robbins was looking for, and she rehearsed and rehearsed until she got it right, step by step. But Robbins fell victim to his own perfectionism; the relentless search for the best possible performance from the entire cast drove Natalie to make lunch-break appointments with her analyst to get her through the day. United Artists, worried about both schedule and budget, eventually forced Robbins out, though, fortunately, he had rehearsed all the songs and his assistants stayed on to help Wise finish.

Natalie had problems too with her co-star, Richard Beymer, who was cast as her lover. They just did not get on. She thought he was weak in both singing and dancing and eventually tried to get him off the picture. George Chakiris, who played Bernardo, remembered:

Natalie didn't like Richard Beymer . . . she was going with Warren Beatty at the time, while still married to Robert Wagner. . . . anyway, evidently she played sick for a couple of days because she really didn't want Richard Beymer; that's what the grapevine said. But she didn't win that one. Richard Beymer stayed and certainly seemed talented enough to me.

Warren Beatty came back on the scene towards the end of filming *West Side Story*. He had been to England and Rome to star in another of Bill Inge's screenplays, *The Roman Spring of Mrs. Stone*, opposite Vivien Leigh. Although neither of his pictures had yet been released, the columnists were talking of Beatty in big-star terms; so was his agent, who was demanding $300,000 a picture. He and Joan Collins had planned to marry when they returned from Europe and she had already bought her wedding dress. When she discovered he was secretly seeing Natalie Wood, she kicked him out.

Robert Wagner had at last been cast for a new movie, *Sail A Crooked Ship*. It could not have come at a worse time. No longer able to be at Natalie's side, Wagner left the path open for Beatty. Suddenly the gossips were ablaze. Hollywood's most idyllic marriage since Eddie and Debbie was on the rocks. The final humiliation for RJ came when Natalie turned up at a party for him at the end of filming with Beatty at her side. The following day the Wagners issued a joint statement that they were to begin a trial separation.

Elizabeth Taylor was as shocked as anyone. 'When I heard the news', she later told Natalie, 'I took two tranquillisers and went to bed.' Rumours abounded, the most popular opinion being that Natalie was about to get a Mexican divorce and rush into marriage with her new lover. Instead, she leased a house in Bel Air and Beatty moved in.

* * * * *

In June 1961, Spyros Skouras began negotiations to sell off 250 acres of the massive Fox studio complex in Beverly Hills to a property-development company, who later turned it into the Century shopping plaza and business centre. *Cleopatra*, Skouras announced, would go ahead and the entire production would now be shot on location in specially built sets in Rome. He enquired of Miss Taylor if she were sufficiently recovered to resume filming. Her doctors gave an emphatic no, and Spyros meekly agreed to postpone the start until September.

He was surprised, therefore, to see her back on the front pages on 11 July, when she and Eddie caught a plane from New York to make the arduous journey to Russia for the Moscow Film Festival, as official representatives of the United States. The previous day, she had been guest of honour at a fund-raising banquet for a new medical centre and had sat next to Senator Robert Kennedy. Some of her audience wept as quietly she took them through her recent drama in a speech Joe Mankiewicz had helped compose, and for which Eddie had rehearsed her:

I have had more than a passing acquaintance with death. Too close. Close enough to know what death is like, and that is far too close. Throughout those many critical hours in the operating theatre of the London Clinic, wanting to live was so strong within me, so overpowering, so consuming, that I remember it, strangely perhaps, as an incredible and agonizing pain. As if every nerve, every muscle in my whole physical being, was strained to the point of torture, by this insistence on life, to the last ounce of my strength, the last gasp of my breath. But then gradually and inevitably and finally, that last ounce of strength was drawn. I remember I had focused desperately on the light hanging directly above me. It had something I needed almost fanatically to continue to see; that light had become my vision of life itself. But yet slowly, as if its source of power were my own fading strength and inability to breathe, it faded and dimmed, ironically enough, like a well-done theatrical effect, to blackness. I have never known, nor do I think there can be, a greater loneliness. Then it happened. When I say 'it' I do not know how long, or when, it was. I can only recall my awareness of it. First there was the awareness of the hands. Pushing, pulling, pressing, lifting; large rough hands, and smaller gentler ones, incessantly manipulating my body as if to force it to respond in some way, in any way, even as a reaction to discomfort or pain. I can only forgive, I bless all those hands for the beating they gave me. And then the voices. From a great distance at first, so far away they seemed forgotten voices I had once heard and which now I seemed to remember. But ever so slowly they grew louder. . . . I was to do what they said, somehow I was to bring myself to do what they demanded of me – to cough, to move, to breathe, to live. . . . That hanging lamp, that most beautiful sight my world has ever known, began faintly to glow again, to shine again. . . .

Miss Taylor was back. On top of the world. And ready for her next brilliant performance, for which Spyros Skouras would pay her another $1 million.

Chapter Fifteen

Trial and Judgment

It has never been a secret, as we have seen, that directors often indiscreetly choose their actors for the parallels between their own lives and the parts they are to play, and Stanley Kramer knew exactly why he wanted Monty Clift and Judy Garland as he began casting for his classic *Judgment at Nuremberg*. They were kindred souls, whose lives had been wrecked by their excesses and addictions and when Kramer was challenged about his reasons for choosing two such difficult actors for two such crucial roles, he replied, 'Because I will get from them the performance of their lives.'

Kramer had already signed Spencer Tracy, Burt Lancaster, Marlene Dietrich, Richard Widmark and Maximilian Schell for the leading roles. When he approached Monty's agents, they said that he would want $200,000; Kramer pointed out that he would be on screen for only seven minutes, but the agents countered that he would want that figure whatever the length of time. That was too much for Kramer, who went direct to Clift and asked for a meeting. When he came face to face with the actor, even he was shocked by the extent to which Monty had deteriorated since last he saw him. He was unsteady, his hands were shaking, he was chain-smoking and looked jaundiced and gaunt. He was exactly what Kramer wanted for the role of a tortured Jew who has been sterilised by the Nazis.

Kramer explained, 'This isn't an attractive part. You won't be the sensitive young and handsome guy. It will strip you bare.'

Monty replied, 'It intrigues me. I like it, I like the sound of it. I want to do it.' Kramer mentioned that his agents were still asking big money, but Monty said, 'Leave them out of it. I'll do it for nothing. Just pay my expenses.' Clift explained later that he did not want to set a precedent by taking a lower fee and thought it more practical to do it for nothing than reduce his asking price. His agents did not see it that way at all, but by then he had already signed on the basis of Kramer's footing the bill for Monty's stay at the Bel Air Hotel, plus first-class travel from New York for himself and Jacques.

Kramer's second cameo appointment, Judy Garland, came at a time when she, like Monty, was considered by many in Hollywood to be unemployable. Little more than a year before, she had been admitted to hospital in a disastrous state, with cirrhosis of the liver, an enlarged spleen and her whole body poisoned from chronic alcoholism and pills. Her liver was four times larger than normal, her weight had ballooned to 11 stone 2 lb, which was enormous for her tiny frame. At any moment she could have sunk into a coma, and her husband Sid Luft was warned by her doctor, 'I have to tell you the truth. I don't think she is going to make it.'

But Judy didn't give up easily. Seven weeks later, she was discharged from hospital. Her weight was down to 8 stone 8 lb after doctors had withdrawn forty pints of fluid from her body. She was confined to a wheelchair and had been told that she must accept that she was an invalid and could never work again. It was shocking news, not just from the medical point of view, for at the time Judy was deeply in debt. Just about everything she owned was mortgaged and every day brought threats of foreclosure and bankruptcy.

In the middle of the year, five months after leaving hospital, she was back, heading for Europe, where she gave some highly acclaimed concerts before her most critical audiences, in London and Paris. Before she left, Roddy McDowall gave a little farewell party for her in New York and her closest friends came to say goodbye. In England, she rented a country house and among her first visitors were Elizabeth and Eddie. She was overwhelmed by her reception, particularly in London, where Dirk Bogarde led a small army of her theatrical fans in tumultuous cheers. In Paris she was met by similar warmth and entered a social whirl which included dinner at the home of the Duke and Duchess of Windsor. The Duke loved her, and once again she had to sing 'Somewhere Over the Rainbow', which she hated.

It was the beginning of her third comeback. Now Kramer wanted her for *Judgment at Nuremberg* as the German woman, Irene Hoffman, whom the Nazis accused of intimacy with an older Jewish man.

Their interview was similar to the one Kramer had had with Monty Clift. Judy came to his office, dressed entirely in black, with deeply tinted sunglasses that hid the puffiness of her eyes. She was still a little overweight, trembling heavily, but cheerful. Kramer told her, 'I can't pretend your role is anything more than a cameo part . . . but this is a big thing for me. I want you to do it and I'll tell you right off, if you won't it will break my heart.'

Judy sat for a moment in silence, and her answer was surprising. 'Mr Kramer, haven't you heard about me?'

'Haven't you heard about me, Miss Garland?' he replied. He explained that she would not come out of the picture as the most attractive woman in the world. 'This woman has had it . . . she's been through it and I feel you'll be able to reach everything in her character.'

'Goddam it, you believe in me don't you?' said Garland.

'Goddam it, yes I do,' said Kramer. 'How much do you want?' Like Monty, Judy would also have done the part for nothing. This was her first picture since *A Star Is Born*, seven years ago, and she had been through hell and back since then.

The very real personal experiences of Garland and Clift gave Kramer the performances that he wanted. Monty had only three pages of heavy dialogue, then eight pages of questioning in the courtroom drama of the Nuremberg Trials. Even so, he had difficulty in remembering his lines; Kramer did his scenes six or seven times, and still he hadn't got it. Always he stopped somewhere in the monologue, or couldn't remember the answers to the questions. As each take was halted, Clift disintegrated into a shaking, nervous wreck, unable to go on, until one afternoon Spencer Tracy, who was playing the chief judge at the trial, came over to him and took him by the shoulders. Tracy, who was himself seriously ill and who, of course, knew as much as anyone about the sort of problems Monty faced, said to him quietly: 'Monty, just look at me. Look into my eyes. Stanley doesn't care about the lines. You know what it's about. Just look at me and play it. It doesn't matter about the lines. Do it to my eyes and you'll be perfect.' Clift did just as Tracy told him, stammering and pausing, and, half acting and half simply being himself, he produced a performance that the whole cast and crew stood to applaud. Kramer had no illusions:

His own condition and mental state contributed greatly to that performance. The way the lines came out, in bursts of lucidity and mumbling, was classic. I don't think anyone, and certainly not a more orthodox and stable actor, could have done it better.

Those seven minutes brought Monty his fourth and final Academy nomination for Best Supporting Actor.

Monty sat watching Judy Garland's heartrending performance, huddled in his foetal position, holding his knees, with tears streaming down his face. Judy also won an Academy nomination for Best Supporting Actress, but in the event neither she nor Monty won the awards.

After this, Clift was full of renewed hope and, when John Huston cast him for the prestigious leading role in *Freud*, he saw it as a potential breakthrough; perhaps it would be his route back to major screen performances. Instead, it would destroy him.

* * * * *

In the summer of 1961, Robert Wagner flew to Europe to appear in Darryl F. Zanuck's prestigious film, *The Longest Day*, joining a cast that included John Wayne, Robert Mitchum, Henry Fonda, Richard Burton, Sean Connery, Robert Ryan, Stuart Whitman, Red Buttons, Curt Jurgens, Sal Mineo and many other American and European stars. Before he left, the Fishers threw a farewell party for him. Natalie was not present. She had gone off to Florida in a blaze of publicity with Warren Beatty, who was filming the final scenes for *All Fall Down*, for which his friend and mentor Bill Inge had once again written the screenplay.

Wagner, who had not seen Natalie for three months, had no intention of providing her with an immediate divorce after his very public humiliation, even though he had struck up a new friendship of his own with Stanley Donen's estranged wife, Marion, whom he eventually married. Lack of divorce, however, did not stop Natalie and Beatty becoming engaged, a fact duly reported in the newspapers, where it was noted that Warren had bought her a chihuahua puppy instead of an engagement ring. Their wild activities in New York, where Beatty had been filming, had brought them constant press attention. Their love affair had the highest of profiles.

Wagner discovered his own name in the papers when he got to London. Joan Collins had moved there temporarily and one day Wagner, who was at a loose end, called her. They went together to Anthony Newley's West End show, *Stop the World, I Want to Get Off*, and immediately the headlines proclaimed them a twosome, consoling each other because their respective partners had run off together.

Joan was bitter about the implications that the foursome had changed partners, insisting that she and Wagner were just friends – a fact with which RJ's friends would certainly have concurred. Later she was polite in her description of Wagner: 'He was a kind and gentle person who was just too sweet for me to be involved with sexually. But the tabloid press found it hard to believe.'

Ironically, on the night that caused the press to pair them off, RJ took Joan backstage to Newley's dressing room. The outcome was that Joan married Newley.

* * * * *

Even before they began filming *Freud*, Monty Clift had upset director John Huston by bringing his friend Jacques with him to stay at Huston's home in Ireland, where they had all met for a pre-production conference. When they moved to Germany to begin filming, the relationship between the director and his leading man deteriorated into violent rows, in which Huston all but struck his star, over how the part should be played.

Before Monty left New York, he had long conversations with his analyst, Dr William Silverberg, who by the sixties had gained an international reputation as a proponent of many of Freud's theories. From these conversations, Monty had worked out in his own mind, as far as he could, how he was going to approach his monumental task.

However, he was completely unaware of the background to the screenplay. It was the result of a four-year collaboration between Wolfgang Reinhardt and Jean-Paul Sartre and, when they presented Huston with the script, it was enough to film a movie eight or nine hours long. Furthermore, Huston seemed to have been totally unaware that the main theme running through Sigmund Freud's professional life was sex. As he read the script he became more and more perplexed: virtually every scene had some sex content and the script dealt with the full range of Freud's work – homosexuality, masturbation, incest, paedophilia, even sex with animals.

In the meantime, another problem had arisen. Huston had wanted to make the film independently but, as the costs mounted to over $2 million, he had been forced to sell the rights to Universal, who agreed to put up the finance based on Huston's own budget figure but gave him strict instructions that it should not be exceeded. Sartre immediately pulled out, and Reinhardt was also unhappy; they accused Huston of sacrificing their highly accurate portrayal of history's most controversial medical mind on the altar of Hollywood razzmatazz. Their opinion was re-affirmed when Huston revealed that he had been trying to sign Marilyn Monroe to co-star with Clift, thus re-creating the intriguing partnership – and presumably the agonies – of *The Misfits*. Miss Monroe was not available; her psychiatrists required her continued treatment for mental disturbances (using, no doubt, some Freudian techniques).

Huston took over the script himself. Despite Sartre's accusation, he still saw it as a most important work, probably the most important of his career, and he reacted accordingly. He began paring down the Sartre tome, hacking huge sections away and rewriting almost everything else, to bring the words into manageable proportions. The new script still included long and difficult passages for Monty, which Huston insisted were an accurate re-creation of Freud's speeches and lectures. Monty spent hours and days memorising his lines, but if he took the slightest wrong turn, Huston would yell 'Cut!' and he would have to start all over again. Hours and hours of filming were scrapped, and Monty was sweating and nervous as he tackled each new day and the prospect of more rows with Huston.

There was a brief respite when Judy Garland arrived in Germany with Spencer Tracy and Richard Widmark for the première of *Judgment at Nuremberg*. But that film only aroused hostility towards Monty in the German press and soon newspapers were attacking him, homing in on his private life and his exploits with the bottle. He was also linked to the publicity surrounding Judy Garland, who suddenly took off from Germany, announcing that she was going to Rome to visit her friends Elizabeth and Eddie Fisher and Roddy McDowall. On her arrival, Judy collapsed and Elizabeth's doctor treated her for what he thought was the onset of pneumonia. She was put on the next plane back to America but got lost during a stopover in Paris, and Sid Luft, who had flown in to escort her home, eventually found her huddled and shivering alone in another airport building miles from where she should have been.

Back on the set of *Freud*, Monty's problems intensified and Universal ordered him to have a complete physical and mental examination by a psychiatrist. Into this mêlée came the calming influence of the beautiful British actress Susannah York, whose role did not require her presence until later scenes. She was playing an amalgam of Freud's many cases, the part which Huston had originally offered to Marilyn Monroe. Miss York's description of what she encountered sums up the difficulties:

> My schedule was originally for three months, but it turned into six, because John was continually rewriting the script. Sometimes we would shoot a scene and come back the next day and find he had rewritten it, and we'd have to do it again. It is very difficult, because you are trying to create a subject that is very complex around a scene that would be rewritten. It is much harder to relearn. The language [John wrote] was also quite purple and for a truthful actor like Monty, this was a problem to handle.

What Huston despised most was what he saw as Monty's weaknesses, his whole build, his whole nature, which were the complete opposite of Huston's idea of manhood. His treatment of Monty on set, however, aroused suspicions among the cast that his anger was inspired by fear of his own latent homosexuality, a subject dealt with in the *Freud* screenplay. Susannah York said:

> By the time I arrived on the set, there had been a month of shooting, and a pattern had been set and tensions were apparent. For example,

there was a scene where Freud is giving a lecture to about two hundred students. There were three sides of foolscap notes and the subject matter was complex. Naturally, you would expect an actor to refer to the notes from time to time; you would also expect the scene to be shot in sections. John didn't want this, and he didn't want Monty to refer to his notes. It was a very humiliating three days for Monty, with John making him do it over and over again. Monty was too much of a stoic, too much for his own good. It wasn't that he didn't stand up to John, but he bent like a fine wire that bent and bent but was never broken. John was like a huge Corinthian figure, embellished, florid, grandiose, magnificent, weighty and threatening. But he wasn't solid right the way through. There was a lot of hot air inside that column. I hate bullies and it was terrible to see the way John bullied Monty, but I can also see Monty could be a pain in the neck. It was terribly depressing to work with a director who wasn't watching a scene but doodling on a piece of paper, then being demoralised by having to do the scene all over again. It was horrendous.

Susannah worked with Monty almost every evening in the hotel on scenes they would be doing the next day, often working until two or three in the morning.

Monty was drinking a great deal and, I suppose, taking drugs, but I didn't know anything about drugs then. He would be drinking six, seven nights a week. He had a friend, Jacques, who was around to keep things running smoothly, but there were obviously a lot of tensions between them, although I don't know what they were; I think Jacques was jealous of me. I loved Monty. I found him generous, excessive, totally truthful and very courageous as an actor, but I can imagine he could be maddening for the wrong sort of director, one who didn't have empathy with him, and of course his drinking didn't help.

Susannah always thought that Monty inspired her to good performances; in fact, she went so far as to say that he would never let her get away with anything but the best.

His drinking became more of a problem as Huston taunted him. After the day's filming, he would relax and was excellent company, with a wicked, devilish sense of humour. Gradually, as he drank more vodka, he would become incoherent, slowly disintegrating before Susannah's eyes. Then she would leave him, all chances of getting any further work done evaporated with his alcoholic dementia. One day, Monty disappeared from the set. It followed a scene in which an extra had to call him a dirty Jew and knock his hat off. The extra accidentally hit him across the eyes. Monty held his hands to his face, worried about the effect on his cataracts, and that night took off to London to be examined by a specialist. When he returned, Huston said loudly in front of the crew, 'I suppose we'd better have a collection to buy him a guide dog.' Susannah went berserk:

> I just set upon him, big as he was. It was just the sort of thing he would do to alienate you, but then he was just as capable of some grandiose gesture. I returned to my dressing room to find it was stuffed with dozens and dozens of red roses. Monty was tough, too, and had this enduring quality. I thought he would recover from this experience, but the confrontation between two personalities like John and Monty was enormous. I'm sure it contributed to, and hastened, Monty's decline.

The film was finished, and Monty joined Susannah in London for a few days before returning to New York; but his battles with Huston and Universal over *Freud*, which had exceeded its budget by over $1 million and came in three months behind schedule, were far from over. Soon, a nasty and very bitter legal tangle involving Monty, Universal and their insurers developed over who was to blame for the delays and extra costs, and everyone seemed intent on laying the blame at Monty's door.

*   *   *   *   *

While Monty faced the relentless struggle to meet John Huston's demands, Elizabeth Taylor was at last embarking on the most Gargantuan, spectacular, bizarre and outrageously expensive piece of film entertainment ever made, and Richard Burton said, 'Well, I suppose I've got to put on my breastplate and play opposite Miss Tits.'

Spyros Skouras was still signing cheques, much to the chagrin of his bankers, and behind the scenes they were trying to oust him from 20th Century–Fox. He had scrapped the two boatloads of sets which had been sent from Pinewood to Hollywood and invested almost another $1 million rebuilding the palaces, temples and pools in Italy. Filming was scheduled to start on 1 September 1961, although less than a third of the building work had been completed.

Elizabeth swept into Rome with her ever increasing accumulation of people, animals and luggage trailing along behind, carefully supervised by her dutiful minder, Eddie. Apart from their three children, there followed the children's nanny; Elizabeth's secretary; her wardrobe man; Dr Rex Kennamer, who stayed to see her settle in; fifty-two pieces of luggage; Eddie's St Bernard dog, Elizabeth's collie, three terriers and two Siamese cats; and Eddie's chauffeur. Home for the duration was to be a magnificent house called Villa Pappa (rechristened Casa Taylor), just a few minutes' drive from the *Cleopatra* sets at Cinecittà, with fifteen rooms, a swimming pool and tennis courts, and complete with a butler, four maids, three manservants, a chef and a houseboy. Elizabeth also had her private chauffeur and twenty-four-hour use of a Cadillac provided by the studio, while Eddie had the green Rolls-Royce given to him by Elizabeth.

Her co-stars for the new *Cleopatra* were all new faces. The original company had been disbanded and now Rex Harrison was cast as Caesar, receiving all the personal trappings befitting a Roman emperor. Skouras had also paid out $50,000 in compensation to the producers of the Broadway production of *Camelot* so that he could sign Richard Burton for the role of Mark Antony. Burton, who won acclaim and the 1961 Tony award for his performance as King Arthur, was half-hearted about *Cleopatra* until he heard that the fee for three months' work would be $250,000, and more if he went into overtime, plus a superb villa for himself and his family, a Cadillac, a chauffeur and servants. It was the biggest money he had ever earned. He had been commuting between Britain and America for a number of years and had been a contract player at Fox; although the money had been good, it was nothing to compare with this. The only other time he had even come close was when he had walked out on Fox to return to England for another of his beloved Shakespearean stage roles. On that occasion, the head of production instructed one of his minions, 'Who is this Old Vic? Find out what he's paying Burton, and I'll pay him double.'

Burton enjoyed fame and the good things in life that went with it, especially the money. 'Of course,' he observed, 'the girl [Elizabeth] is getting more.' With him from *Camelot* came Roddy McDowall, for whom Elizabeth had secured the role of Octavius, and he and a friend moved into Burton's villa.

Richard was not required for the early scenes and languished around local bars with other unwanted members of staff. In fact, there was a good deal of languishing, owing to the unusually inclement weather for the time of year. Just as the fog had impeded them a year ago at Pinewood, now torrential rain dampened the spirits of the hundreds of extras who lined up each day for their calls, at enormous cost. On the instruction of the bankers back in America, Walter Wanger was called upon to work out the daily expenditure; it came to $70,000 whether they filmed or not. And at the moment it was not.

Days rolled into weeks; and by the end of October Mankiewicz had secured very little in the way of usable footage. It did give him a chance to continue writing the script, of course, which was still unfinished and was changing almost as dramatically as the weather. To complete this mammoth undertaking, he was being injected with Benzedrine stimulants three times a day to keep him awake, and was working well into the night. By 22 October, he had completed two hundred pages of script, which amounted to exactly half; he still had the other two hundred pages to write, as well as directing the film and dealing with the other production problems into the bargain. Everything fell on Joe's shoulders; Skouras had long since lost faith in Walter Wanger and went directly to Mankiewicz.

In desperation, the director appealed to Fox to postpone production so that he could finish writing the words. Skouras was aghast: 'Are you mad? We're paying Elizabeth Taylor fifty grand a week and you want to stop production?' Mankiewicz countered that it would be cheaper to pay Miss Taylor half a million for hanging around than to go blindly on with the picture without knowing what sets, costumes and extras would be required for the second half. Skouras contemplated ending the film at the first half, which would have left it hanging as 'Cleopatra Meets Caesar', thus deleting the requirement for Antony and Richard Burton. The Welsh actor heard the rumour and threatened to sue the pants off Skouras if he tried.

In October even the sets for the first half were still having the finishing touches put to them; filming began before they were complete, and no wonder. They were gigantic monstrosities which would have dwarfed the original buildings they were supposed to represent. Even Elizabeth's dressing room was five times bigger than normal. By November, Mankiewicz had agreement from Fox to allow him to work the cast to French hours – midday to 8 p.m. – which would allow him to spend more time on the script and production meetings during the mornings; it would also cut out lunchtime drinking, thus giving him a sober cast to work with, which was not a small consideration.

Before he was required for major scenes with Elizabeth, Burton had been in Italy for nineteen weeks and had spent only five days on the set. By this time he was into lucrative overtime. He had been drinking heavily, often leaving his wife, Sybil, in the villa at nights while he went off prowling on his own. She was used to such behaviour; it had been going on for years. He would come back drunk and crawl into bed beside her in the early hours. One night he got into bed fully dressed with a lighted cigarette and Sybil awoke to find the room full of smoke. Burton had dropped his cigarette into the bedclothes and was in a drink-induced coma. She could not rouse him, and had to dash through the house to wake others to help her put out the smouldering linen and bring their handicapped daughter Jessica, aged two, from the smoke-filled rooms.

Elizabeth and Burton came face to face for their screen parts on 22 January 1962. Elizabeth recalled:

I had known Richard for about nine years. I'd first met him at Stewart Granger's house and I didn't care for him much. In fact, I kind of resented him and I was certainly determined not to become another notch on his belt.

But by the time they began filming, she had already fallen for his Welsh charm and the poetry of his voice and his sparkling blue eyes. She went on, 'Well, on the first day we were filming together, he was hung over and his hands were shaking so badly that he asked me to hold his coffee cup to his lips. That did it, I was gone.'

Burton took a little longer to acquire a taste for Miss Tits. At the start of filming he was moaning to Mankiewicz about her acting. 'She's useless,' he said. 'I can't work with her. I can't hear what she's saying half the time. She is nothing; just dull.'

Mankiewicz, who was an out-and-out Taylor fan, said, 'Dick, come with me and watch the rushes.' They went through to the viewing room and Burton sat with Mankiewicz through the day's filming. At the end of it, he sat back and pulled on his cigarette: 'Incredible. She's incredible.' The camera had picked up visuals that Burton could not see, and the sound men had captured her voice so that it was heard, and it mattered.

Rumours often start before anything untoward has actually taken place. Observers noticed the sparks generated between them; the meeting of eyes; the fire and responses to each other's lines; there was more in it than just acting. Joe Mankiewicz said, 'I could see it happening, and I said to Elizabeth what's going on between you two? And she said, "Nothing, Joe. Nothing at all. We're just friends."' Joe murmured: 'Oh yeah?' and let the subject drop. Yet, in a way, Mankiewicz was inadvertently encouraging a budding romance by the words he was writing for Elizabeth and Burton to say to each other on screen. Eddie became noticeably uncomfortable over some of the dialogue as he watched the two go through their performances.

One night, Elizabeth and Eddie invited Richard and Sybil, and Roddy McDowall and his friend, over to the Villa Pappa for dinner. It was a very formal affair; the Fishers used the free facility of servantry to their full advantage. They had the finest foods and the best champagne, served in impeccable style. Burton gradually became more and more drunk as the evening wore on and went off into long, laborious Shakespearean monologues. It was a familiar sight to many of his acquaintances, but totally new to Eddie and Elizabeth. She was enthralled. It was this kind of excitement in his personality that struck a chord with her, and at dinner that night she told Eddie to be quiet when he began talking over one of Burton's drunken recitations.

In the middle of it all, Elizabeth had just completed the formalities to adopt a child. She had said publicly that she and Eddie wanted children but she was unable to become pregnant again on health grounds. They had discovered a nine-month-old girl in Germany whose parents had put her up for adoption because they could not face the cost of the extensive surgery required for the child's deformed hip. Elizabeth said, 'She was covered with abscesses and had severe malnutrition when we saw her, and I wanted to help all the more because she was ill.' They called her Maria and the child from poverty became part of the life of the world's most famous woman.

Towards the end of January, as their film sequences became more intensive, there was a hint of impending scandal in two newspaper reports suggesting that Elizabeth was gazing into Burton's eyes rather longer than the script required, and Mankiewicz told Walter Wanger that he thought there was something going on between them.

The new complications were a terrific strain on the director, who was already in a state of near exhaustion from his workload. One night he was called to the Casa Taylor by a frantic Eddie Fisher. Elizabeth had taken some pills, on top of alcohol, and had passed out. Joe managed to bring her round and she admitted to him that she had taken four tablets. Word got out, and rumour of a serious split between Elizabeth and Eddie began to circulate. The whole thing exploded in their faces at the end of the second week of February.

Amid all the rumour and speculation, Sybil Burton, who had suspected for some time that her husband was having an affair, gathered up her belongings and took off for New York, ostensibly to visit Burton's ailing surrogate-father, Philip Burton. Richard himself flew off to Paris, where he was required for further filming on *The Longest Day*. Eddie drove off in the Rolls and was reported to be looking at property in Switzerland.

On 18 February the headlines bellowed the news: 'LIZ TAYLOR IN HOSPITAL'. And now the world's press was descending at Rome airport at the rate of several a minute. Elizabeth was variously reported to have been struck down by food poisoning from bad beans, bad oysters, bad chilli or bad beef; or by a throat infection, a fever, nervous breakdown, exhaustion, overwork . . . ; and finally, as the accusations over Burton became more strident, it was alleged that she had taken an overdose of sleeping tablets.

It quickly became a sensational story, outdoing Elizabeth's previous scandal with Eddie by miles and providing more front-page headlines than Edward and Mrs Simpson. The Rome offices of Reuters and Associated Press, the international news agencies, were inundated with demands for more and more immediate information; reporters and gossip columnists in America and Britain got out their passports and leapt on the next planes to Rome; others went to buttonhole Burton in Paris. He was deluged; never in his life had he been involved in such a furore, and the following day one of his aides issued a statement:

For the past several days, uncontrolled rumours have been growing about Elizabeth and myself. Statements attributed to me have been distorted out of all proportion and a series of coincidences has lent plausibility to a situation which has become dangerous to Elizabeth. Mr Fisher, who has business interests of his own, merely went out of town to attend to them for a few days. My foster-father Philip Burton has been quite ill in New York and my wife Sybil flew there to be with him for a time. Elizabeth and I have been friends for twelve years . . . and I would certainly never do anything to hurt her. . . . in answer to these rumours my normal inclination is to say 'No comment.' But I feel that in this case things should be explained to protect Elizabeth.

The statement did nothing to quell the growing storm. In fact, it gave reporters the chance to put some flesh on the story. They ferreted around the sets, talking to anyone who would talk, and putting together 'incidents' from the past few weeks which demonstrated that the Taylor–Burton affair was true. Philip Burton sent his foster-son an admonishing cable; they did not speak to each other again for more than two years.

Burton flew back to Rome, continuing his denials; furious and totally floored by the extent of the publicity, he returned to the set. Sheilah Graham arrived from Hollywood and wrote a piece suggesting that Elizabeth's affair with Burton was punishment to a recalcitrant admirer. Joe Mankiewicz also found himself blown into the scandal when Italian newspapers reported that the whole thing had been a cover-up to hide his own affair with Elizabeth. Mankiewicz retorted, 'No, actually it's to cover up my affair with Richard Burton,' then walked over to Burton, kissed him on the lips and stormed off.

Eddie tried to paper over the cracks and threw a birthday party for his wife at one of Rome's most elegant nightspots, attended by Roddy McDowall, Mankiewicz and others from the cast. Needless to say, he did not invite Burton. But the headlines continued, and Mankiewicz battled to settle them all down to continue filming. Spyros Skouras flew in from America, ashen-faced. Surveying the scene of his ill-starred but very famous movie, he turned to Walter Wanger and said: 'I wish I'd never met you.'

In the third week of March, all semblance of trying to cover up what Burton termed 'Le Scandale' vanished when Elizabeth was handed a note while performing a scene with Burton. It was from Eddie. He had instructed that it should be delivered to her at a specific time – half an hour after he had left for America. Now the headlines screamed: 'LIZ AND EDDIE SPLIT'. Within days, Burton and Taylor were openly and publicly going around together. Burton explained, 'I got fed up with everyone telling us to be discreet so I said to Liz: "Fuck it. Let's go to fucking Alfredo's and have some fucking fettucini."'

Public condemnation came rapidly from all quarters. The po-faced Ed Sullivan commented on his top-rated Sunday night show: 'I hope youngsters will not be persuaded that the sanctity of marriage has been invalidated by the appalling example of Mrs Taylor-Fisher and married man Burton.' The Vatican accused them of erotic vagrancy and castigated Elizabeth over the adoption of her new child, who would innocently be brought into their tawdry world. Hollywood trade papers poured sympathy on Skouras and Wanger over 'Taylor's antics', and suddenly she had become the centre-piece, and the cause, of all *Cleopatra*'s problems. Eddie, in New York, found himself in demand for television and night-club performances, and put together a new act which began with 'Arrivederci Roma', while back in Los Angeles Groucho Marx quipped at a benefit dinner: 'Spyros Skouras faces the future with courage, determination and terror.'

Elizabeth was being named by some as the villain of the piece, digging her claws into Burton and refusing to let go until she had him in her pocket, while others said that Burton was to blame because of his total lack of control when a beautiful woman came within his grasp. Mankiewicz had his own theories on how and why the affair blew up into a thunderstorm. Elizabeth, he said in a television interview, was totally incapable of dishonesty:

> For years she had been brought up in the confines of her studio; she belonged to that generation of stars who grew up in an atmosphere that resembled a nunnery. Morals had always been drummed into her and she could never get involved in a backstreet affair, absolutely not. Everything had to be out in the open and she fully realised that in those situations you stand hand-to-hand and take whatever comes, and she believed that.

Burton's womanising was legend, but for him Elizabeth Taylor was different. Many years later, his daughter Kate confirmed:

At the outset, I don't think he knew what he was getting into. Here was the most famous actress at that time, beguiling and beautiful beyond words, very different to the women Dad had come across, and she just knocked his socks off. But he hadn't thought it through; he'd never imagined himself in a crazed obsession with someone like this. Not only that, what it did to him in terms of publicity was incredible.

Burton had obviously given some thought to the ramifications of the publicity as it rumbled on. In fact, Mankiewicz challenged him when the affair became public: 'I spoke to Richard about his intentions, and I shall be this indiscreet: he was very drunk and he said, "I'll use her. She is going to make me millions." And of course she did.'

Sensational it may have been, but Mankiewicz managed to continue filming and that, at least, had its lighter moments. In the great and horrendously expensive scene where Cleopatra enters Rome in her huge chariot, wearing a $7000 dress swathed in 24-carat gold, she is surrounded by several elephants, six black panthers, sixteen dwarfs riding mules painted as zebras, thirty-six trumpeters on white horses, a twenty-piece Egyptian band, thirty guards of honour on sorrel horses, seven acrobats, twenty-six snake dancers, eight chariots pulled by sixteen black horses, sixteen fan-bearers, six white oxen, sixty black slaves, two thousand white doves, plus four thousand costumed extras and dozens of other sundry players. It took five hours to assemble them, but finally: 'Action' – the procession began to roll. Then Joe Mankiewicz bellowed 'Cut!' Through his spy-glass he had spotted in the middle of it all an enterprising Italian selling ice-cream. Other unexpected incidentals, such as a cat chasing a bat during a love-scene between Taylor and Burton, held up production at a cost of several thousand dollars.

There was a halt to all scenes involving Elizabeth at the end of April. She and Burton had rented a villa for the weekend high in the hills overlooking the sea and they drove off to escape the pressure of the world and the paparazzi. In their isolation, they played around like newly-weds, but as their discussions about the implications of their affair became deeper, they were both consumed by guilt and began to drink heavily. Torn by the crisis, Burton eventually told Elizabeth that he would return to Sybil when she came back to Rome; they must end the affair. Elizabeth said she would kill herself if he did and went to get a box of sleeping pills. Burton, in his haze of drink, said, 'Go ahead, if that's what you want to do. Go ahead,' never believing for a moment that she would. Soon he was driving at breakneck speed to get her to a hospital in Rome to save her life, while she lay unconscious in the back of the car.

When she returned to her own villa, Elizabeth sent for Mankiewicz and took off her heavy sunglasses to reveal a black eye and a badly bruised nose, caused by the hospital staff's desperate attempts to revive her with oxygen masks and stomach pumps. Mankiewicz declared her unphotographable for two weeks, even with the aid of make-up.

Unaware of these events – as was the rest of the world – Sybil Burton returned to Rome the following week, with an attendant posse of reporters who had followed her from New York to London and on to Italy. She steadfastly refused to accept that her marriage was over, insisting that her relationship with Richard had been built over fourteen years and that they had a perfect understanding. At the same time, Burton was headlined in the Sheilah Graham column as saying, 'It's a nine-day wonder. By the time the picture is released everyone will have forgotten about it, unless something new happens, like me divorcing my wife to marry Elizabeth. But darling, there's no chance of that.'

As Le Scandale rumbled on, Fox bankers and top executives came to Rome at the beginning of June to examine the books. Immediate economies were ordered, such as cutting down on paper cups, which were being used at the rate of 2500 a day. Meanwhile, Rome burned, and Walter Wanger was fired. (He sued Fox for $2.6 million for wrongful dismissal and eventually settled for $100,000 plus his ten per cent share of any profits from *Cleopatra* which was part of his original deal.) They found Mankiewicz all but collapsing through sheer exhaustion. They ran through the remaining script with him, cut some of the major battle scenes that still had to be filmed, ordered that the picture must be completed by 30 June – and instructed that Elizabeth's salary should cease immediately.

She had indeed cost them dear, but so had others. Burton's overtime had run his payment up to $750,000; Rex Harrison had been signed for $100,000 and ended up with four times that figure; John Hoyt was hired for eleven weeks, stayed for seven months and worked on fourteen days.

At the month's end, Spyros Skouras was forced to quit 20th Century and Darryl F. Zanuck made his triumphant return as head of the studio. But, at the end of all this mess, Fox had to have several scapegoats. Not the least of the objects of Zanuck's venom was Elizabeth herself. She, he claimed, should shoulder some of the responsibility for the astronomical costs of the film, which were now being put at $35 million. Mankiewicz was quick to defend Elizabeth and himself:

Cleopatra was conceived in emergency, shot in hysteria and wound up in blind panic, but any effort to saddle blame on Miss Taylor is wrong ... she may have had problems of illness and emotional problems, but she didn't cost Twentieth any $35 million.

When Mankiewicz finally presented his film after 215 days of actual shooting, there were eight hours of celluloid ready for editing to a manageable length. Zanuck then fired Mankiewicz, informing him that he would be allowed no part in the final cut. Just to rub it in, Zanuck issued a public statement:

> In exchange for top compensation and a considerable expense account, Mr Joseph Mankiewicz has for two years spent his time, talent and $35 million of 20th Century–Fox shareholders' money to direct and complete the first cut of the film *Cleopatra*. He has earned a well-deserved rest.

Mankiewicz was furious, and received public support from Elizabeth – 'it's disgraceful, degrading and humiliating' – and from Burton – 'it is appalling and vulgar'.

The rows had developed into a public slanging match and observers were startled to discover new facts: Zanuck revealed that, to date, Elizabeth had been paid $2 million and was due to receive much more by virtue of a thirty-five per cent share of the profits, through the deal she had negotiated at the start of the second attempt to film *Cleopatra*.

When she complained that Fox planned to offset an unfair proportion of the initial box-office income to meet the costs, Zanuck promptly settled upon Taylor and Burton writs totalling $50 million, alleging that they had damaged the film's commercial impact by their immoral conduct, and had added to the costs by causing delays through their late arrivals on set and the period when Elizabeth was unable to be photographed because of her black eye. Certain commentators made the point that if Zanuck were successful in his legal action, he would make an instant profit of $15 million for Fox, since the cost of the film was now put at $35 million.

Zanuck gave a revised figure of $44 million as the break-even point – at which Elizabeth would begin to receive her share – and battle-lines were drawn for *Cleopatra* to become a courtroom drama. However, after lengthy and expensive legal exchanges, the cases were eventually settled quietly out of court with Elizabeth's fortune still intact, and everyone ended up making a profit. (Later, four cinema chains based in San Francisco joined the fray and filed a $6 million suit claiming that they had been sold an inferior product and that vital details about the script being written on a daily basis had been withheld. Another cinema in Oregon sued Burton and Taylor for anticipated lost revenue caused by their scandalous behaviour. Neither case came to court.)

When *Cleopatra* opened for previews in 1963, it had been reduced to four hours, and was sliced to three hours after a poor reception. Burton's role was heavily cut, as was Roddy McDowall's, and Mankiewicz publicly stated that his carefully structured work had been progressively butchered to the point where it was meaningless. In that he was supported by the notoriously savage *New York Times* critic Bosley Crowther, who saw the first version and described it as 'one of the great epic films of our day'. When he saw the cut print, he announced that he was shocked by its mutilation.

In the trade, Zanuck had his supporters. Some who saw the full version agreed that the first half of the film, in which Rex Harrison was dominant, was stylish and witty, whereas the second half, with Burton, became duller by the minute. The script was banal in parts and the pressures on Mankiewicz and the leading actors showed. Also obvious were Elizabeth's weight fluctuations as she proceeded from one trauma to another, and the blotchy, blue patches on Burton's face, evidence of alcoholic 'night befores'. The debate about the quality of the film continued for many years – as did Le Scandale.

As filming came to an end, Burton was riven with guilt over what he had done to his wife and family. His friend since university days, actor Robert Hardy, said,

He shook himself very dreadfully by what he did and, in a way, never quite recovered from it; and having dealt so destructive a blow to his marriage and to Sybil, he then had an element of 'I don't care what I destroy, including myself'.

Burton and Taylor agreed to part. Elizabeth headed for her house in Gstaad with the children and her parents, who had flown in from America to give her moral support. From there she wrote letters to the adoption agency in Germany and to the parents of little Maria, assuring them that the child would have her undying love and devotion for the rest of her life. She remained in seclusion for two months. She called Eddie a couple of times, but he was off-hand and insisted on going ahead with a Nevada divorce; he wanted a $1 million settlement.

In August, Elizabeth's affair was temporarily set aside by the media after the discovery of Marilyn Monroe's nude body, sprawled across her bed, beginning an everlasting debate – which in the long term would eclipse even the Burton–Taylor saga – over whether she had committed suicide or had been murdered.

At the end of that month, however, Le Scandale started up again. When newspapers reported that Elizabeth was planning to return to New York, Burton called her from his villa at Lake Geneva. Could they meet for lunch? It was a tense and tearful rendezvous, during which Elizabeth, by her own account of the meeting, said, 'We needn't get married. In fact, I don't want to get married. But if you want me to be your mistress, then I will.' And that's how it was left.

Back in Los Angeles, Elizabeth's former employers at MGM were surveying the wreckage of *Cleopatra* and scheming. Producer Anatole de Grunwald had in his hand a script by Terence Rattigan entitled *The V.I.P.s*, which, by chance, is all about a jet-setting love-triangle of a millionaire, his wife and her lover. It was so close to home that no one thought Taylor and Burton would even look at it – but it was worth a try, said Grunwald; think of the publicity value. The scripts went off – and Elizabeth jumped at the chance of being back with her man. She promptly replied yes, she would do it for $1 million. Burton agreed, for half the price. And the lovers were reunited . . .

Chapter Sixteen

'Never happier . . .'

Pinnacles are reached and passed, and, as a new era of movie-making came with the sixties, the status of the five subjects of this book had risen, for different reasons, to a level from which there could be only one eventual route. James Dean's death left an immortalised image, untarnished by the vagaries of age and of life itself; the four who remained faced the plain fact that the glamorous icons of Hollywood, bejewelled and adored, were going out of fashion. It would be a few more years before they became extinct, but by the mid-sixties the writing was on the wall.

* * * * *

Despite his own troubles, Monty Clift always showed great concern over what was happening to Elizabeth Taylor. As the onslaught of headlines about her affair with Richard Burton continued unabated, he would wander around, clutching his newspapers, amazed, amused and distraught, depending on the tenor of the piece. 'Bessie Mae has become the world's most famous woman,' he said. He called her to tell her as much and then waited, like the rest of the world, for the next instalment.

With Elizabeth and Richard back together again in the autumn of 1962, professionally and otherwise, Sybil Burton had to face the inevitable fact that she had lost her husband. She did not give up easily, and among her last public utterances was an interview with Sheilah Graham, whom she told: 'I shall never allow the father of my children to become the fifth husband of Elizabeth Taylor.' Burton, however, had already instructed his lawyers to begin drawing up separation papers, in which he signed over to Sybil the best part of his fortune and a commitment from his future earnings. Then he took off for Mexico to begin filming *The Night of the Iguana*, followed by stage performances in *Hamlet* in New York and Canada. Elizabeth was now constantly at his side – and in his bed – though both consistently declared that they had no intention of getting married.

In December, Sybil gave up the fight. She flew down to Mexico to obtain a quick divorce and then took up permanent residence in New York, where she married a youthful pop singer and adopted a zestful but more settled life, ignoring press requests and large amounts of money for exclusive interviews, and disregarding the continuing shenanigans of the man with whom she had shared her life for fifteen years.

Eddie and Elizabeth's forthcoming divorce had developed into a more public display of hostilities, each berating the other through their lawyers and through the press. Fisher had moved to Nevada to complete his residency qualifications and when he was told by reporters that Elizabeth was becoming impatient, he mustered the best venom he was capable of and said:

I am certainly not standing in the way of this earth-shattering, world-shaking romance. I have tried for months to get Elizabeth on the phone to talk it over and now I am supposed to be hindering the marriage of this lovely young couple. . . . well, the great lovers will just have to stay in their playpen for another few weeks, these things take time. I am just as anxious as Sir Richard the Lionheart to get it over and done with.

Eddie wanted to talk money. He felt he was entitled to some of the funds Elizabeth's company, MCL, had accumulated during the latter stages of their marriage, not to mention the small mountain of jewellery that he had bought her. There was also the question of Maria, whom Elizabeth had left in London with a nurse for another round of expensive operations: what was to be her future? There were other incidentals, such as the Rolls-Royce and their houses.

Maria was the problem that lay most heavily on Eddie's mind. An innocent child had been brought into a marriage which was broken almost before the ink was dry on her adoption papers. However, since Elizabeth had been the instigator of the adoption in the first place, he eventually agreed, with some reluctance, to drop claims over her, to allow Elizabeth total custody and to clear the path for her formal adoption by Elizabeth and Burton when they married. This aspect remained a matter for private discussion, while Le Scandale itself was battled out publicly.

Burton accused Fisher of 'living in the realms of fantasy' over his intolerable demands, to which Fisher replied, 'Burton should get an Oscar for his sheer gall. I am not demanding money with menaces, but I have no intention of giving up property which I own. Mr Burton is in no position to lecture on morals.'

Burton and Taylor left Mexico and moved into the royal suite at the

King Edward Hotel in Toronto, while he played Hamlet. In March, Elizabeth obtained an instant Mexican divorce on the grounds of 'abandonment' by Eddie. She married Burton secretly in Montreal ten days later. When the newsreels caught up with them, she stood in front of the cameras and obligingly gave out the words everyone had been waiting to hear.

Interviewer: 'How do you feel, Liz?'

'I've never been happier in my whole life.'

'It will last this time, will it?'

'You better believe it!'

'How do you feel, Dick? Will it last a while?'

'I feel —' but Burton's answer remains unheard as Elizabeth interrupts indignantly: 'A while? Watch it!'

Similar recitations of their undying love and devotion came at various stages on their route through life together. Burton came out with some profound statements about her being his everything, 'my breath, my blood, my mind, my imagination. I cannot see life without her'; to which Elizabeth would respond in words that cynical observers noted had something of a familiar ring: 'I love him dearly and deeply and I plan to stay married.' Burton was honest enough to point out the advantages of the new-found fame and wealth that came through his love for Taylor. He said:

> I became a far more important actor than before; and after that stupid and stupendous publicity, we could pick and choose our work. Furthermore, I liked it. I liked being famous, and I liked being given the best seat in an aeroplane, or in a restaurant.

His friends feared that he would decline into just another 'Mr Taylor', herder of the entourage; but he did not, and indeed positively fought against it. Sir John Gielgud remarked, 'When he became surrounded by the glamour of Hollywood and Elizabeth's showy personality, it infected him, and in fact he learned to do it much better than she did.'

* * * * *

Interspersed with the Taylor–Burton affair, the gossip columns had been laying bare the emotions of Elizabeth's best friends, Natalie Wood and Robert Wagner. Natalie filed for divorce in the summer of 1962, then dashed off to the Cannes Film Festival with Warren Beatty, where they were photographed everywhere. Someone dubbed them 'the poor man's Taylor and Burton', and, by coincidence, all the protagonists of the two romantic sagas ended up in Rome at exactly the same time.

Beatty and Natalie travelled there from France. Wagner was already there with Marion Donen, and RJ had a brief reunion with Elizabeth one evening in a Rome night club. 'She walked in, and the whole place went wild,' he recalled. A few nights later, RJ and Marion were dining in the same club when Beatty and Natalie came in. There were cool hellos, Wagner invited them to his table and the evening passed with a politely subdued air. It was this scenario, plus Joan Collins's romance with Anthony Newley in London, which prompted Dorothy Kilgallen to suggest a likely outcome: Beatty would run off with Marion, Natalie would steal Newley from Collins, Joan would go for Burton and Elizabeth would walk off into the sunset with RJ. Anything seemed possible.

The Wagners' divorce was finalised in the spring of 1963, which gave RJ and Marion the all-clear to marry. Natalie and Beatty had not discovered the same kind of togetherness. The ever active Mr Beatty found it difficult to restrict his attentions to one woman; quarrels became more frequent, and public, and, since the main bond between them at the outset had been sexual lust, when that diminished so did the relationship. Beatty vanished to pastures new, and Natalie was left alone.

She went through another series of highly publicised romances, including one with Arthur Loew, Jr, one-time protector of both Elizabeth Taylor and Joan Collins. (He had married Debbie Power and adopted the son born three months after Tyrone died, but they divorced in 1963.)

Natalie had all the aspirations of becoming a star in the same league as Elizabeth and, after her success in *Gypsy*, the film story of Gypsy Rose Lee, her status rose again in the widely acclaimed *Love with the Proper Stranger*, co-starring Steve McQueen. But she achieved her greatest success so far at the end of 1963 when Jack Warner agreed to pay her $750,000 for *Sex and the Single Girl*. Her importance to Warners can be seen by comparing her salary for that picture with those of her co-stars. Tony Curtis, who was also a big star, commanded just $400,000; Henry Fonda received $100,000; and Lauren Bacall got $50,000. *Life* magazine voted her Screen Personality of the Year, and Arthur Loew bought her a diamond boulder to mark their engagement. They were due to marry in three months' time, during the spring of 1964, but Natalie called it off a few weeks later.

A certain sadness came into her life when, one night in La Scala, she saw RJ handing round cigars to celebrate the birth of his first child with Marion. She knew then that she still loved him, and suddenly she wanted to be alone.

With her new wealth and good fortune, Natalie established herself in a sombre-looking mansion in Bel Air, and with the continued advice and help of her analyst she became what her Hollywood comrades termed a culture vulture. As a millionairess in her own right, she could afford to indulge herself. She toured galleries and bought paintings by the score; she built up an enviable collection of pre-Columbian art, enrolled for courses at UCLA to further her knowledge, and would say to friends, 'Darlings, you simply have to see my super Bonnard and I've picked up this marvellous Courbet and a divine sculpture and this exquisite painting by Boris Pasternak's father and, well, I'm a collector now . . .' She also began delving into English literature, and in an interview at the time revealed:

> Do you know, it occurred to me that I had never read *Hamlet*. I have been making movies since I was five; forty of them. So I've never had time for the ordinary sort of schooling. There are, shall we say, some gaps in my education. Now I'm into Burns, Shaw, Eliot and many others. It is the first organised reading I have done in my entire life.

She drew heavily on the cigarette perched precariously at the end of a twelve-inch holder and continued:

> My analyst has made me realise this. He has played a big part in bringing this out. He has made me realise that I lacked the ability to enjoy myself, enjoy being alone. As a child, I was always surrounded by people, and chaperons. Now I have had to learn to be alone. My analyst has helped me learn this and has brought out my latent interests and I am able to put my work into perspective.

Natalie went off skiing to Switzerland and on the piste she met a handsome blond and very wealthy shoe manufacturer from Caracas, Ladislav Blantik, whom she noticed one evening in the *après-ski* bar doing his party trick of munching a wine glass and swallowing it. Ladislav followed her to Los Angeles, and in the coming months darted frequently between her house and his. They became engaged in April 1965, then disengaged four months later. This fairly wanton behaviour masked an emptiness in Natalie's life that her new financial security could not fill.

*   *   *   *   *

Rock Hudson had reached similar heights of financial reward after *Lover Come Back* and, with his co-stars Doris Day and Tony Randall, was promptly cast in another comedy, *Send Me No Flowers*. He had become Universal's biggest star. The box-office clamouring for his films had made the studio millions at the very stage when Hollywood was going through its most difficult time; many have said that Rock's films during that period saved Universal from financial ruin.

With his wealth came a parting of the ways with Henry Willson, who had become increasingly demanding over his share of the star's fortunes, insisting on bigger and bigger back-handers from each film Hudson made. Towards the end of 1962, Rock wanted to buy himself a new house, which was being sold for $167,000, but he discovered that, absurdly, he did not have enough cash to pay for it. It finally dawned on Hudson, who had never taken a great interest in his own finances, that the man who had discovered him and had steered him by devious means to become the world's top-rated male box-office attraction, had also been lining his own pockets and spending Rock's money freely.

The extent of Willson's underhand dealings never became public, but it was serious enough for Rock never to speak to him again for the rest of his life. With that, Willson's career as an agent was all but over. His other major stars also began to drop him; doors began to slam in his face and Willson increasingly sought comfort from the bottle. When he died nine years later, a penniless alcoholic in the Motion Picture Home, people said 'Henry Who?' His funeral was sparsely attended and Rock sent no flowers.

Hudson still managed to buy the house he wanted on Beverly Crest Drive; Universal put up the money on condition that he signed a new contract with them and the house deeds were passed to him when the contract ended five years later. He called it his castle and it remained his home until he died. He threw a party there for Elizabeth and Burton as soon as they returned from their travels, and indeed the Hudson parties became legend. He said that the acquisition of the house gave him a feeling of inner security that he had lacked in the strange existence he had been confined to under Henry Willson, a man who had been his mentor, his lover and, in a way, his captor. Equally, his search for sexual companionship became more relaxed, and soon after moving to his castle, he formed several long-term relationships, the first with a young actor several years his junior named Lee, who stayed with him for more than three years.

* * * * *

Conversely, over in New York, Monty Clift's career problems had plunged him to the depths of despair. After the release of *Freud* in 1962, for which he received some surprisingly good notices – Bosley Crowther described his performance as 'illuminating' – he became embroiled in a long legal argument. Universal decided to sue Monty for what they claimed was his deliberate action in delaying production. The studio was battling with insurance companies to try to recoup some of the additional costs caused by the problems during filming, not the least of which had been Monty's eye injuries. Universal served Monty with a writ for $600,000 and charged him with refusing to learn his lines, which he admitted had been true, but claimed he had not done so because he knew they would have to be rewritten anyway. The studio also used against Monty the psychiatrist's report they had ordered during filming because of his problems. They had withheld payment of the balance of the salary still owed to him for the picture – $175,000 – and for months the legal wrangle lurched on. In the end, the evidence supported Clift; he was exonerated and Universal had to pay the money they owed him.

The case had begun in 1962 and dragged on for more than eighteen months. For all that time, no new work came along. By now the damage was done. In Hollywood terms, Monty was finished. He was uninsurable, anywhere, and that meant no offers. The only headlines he was getting were bad ones.

His life was a total mess, and his relationship with Jacques had descended into constant rows and fights. Jacques began to find his own friends and lovers, while Clift himself often went out in search of company and drugs. These excursions took him increasingly to the seedier sections of New York, placing him in constant danger of being attacked and robbed. Time and again he came home blood-spattered, more often than not too drunk or drugged to notice. There were times when, even in his own home, he was beaten up by a lover he had picked up in a bar somewhere; others tried blackmail and occasionally he had to get his lawyers to pay them off.

His physical and mental state had reached such a pitch that in the autumn of 1963 his mother, Ethel, contacted Monty's old friend Billy LeMassena and pleaded with him to help her try to stop Monty from destroying himself. Billy described one horrifying episode:

I called around at Monty's place one evening, and Monty was out cold; Jacques had just put him to bed. So I didn't disturb him. Jacques really still worshipped Monty, adored him and had become his nurse as well as his lover, although he too had his problems with drink, but they were nowhere near as bad as Monty's. Anyway, Jacques left the living room where I was sitting, and had been gone for some time. When he returned, he looked pale and I asked him what was wrong. He said, 'Billy, I can't stand it any longer. I've just taken a whole bottle of sleeping pills.' I couldn't believe it, because although he was obviously upset, he was also calm, and I said, 'Are you sure? The whole bottle?' And I was already reaching for the phone to call an ambulance. But then Jacques said, 'No, no – I was only kidding. It's a joke.' I wasn't sure, and I questioned him some more and he kept insisting that he hadn't taken the pills, so eventually I got up and left.

The next morning, Monty called Billy quite early, and he asked how Jacques was. Monty replied, 'I don't know, I haven't seen him yet. He's still zonked out.'

'Oh my God!' cried Billy and he told Monty what had happened the night before. Monty let the phone drop and went dashing off to him; a minute or two later he was back on the phone, screaming, 'Come quickly, Billy. I think he's dead.' Billy told him to call an ambulance and he would get there as soon as he could.

Jacques wasn't dead, but in a deep coma. When Billy arrived at the house, he expected to find it swarming with medics and police; in fact, Monty had called one of his personal doctors and they arranged to have Jacques admitted to a private clinic, where Monty himself had secretly been a patient several times after overdoses. Jacques stayed there for several weeks and recovered, but when they were ready to discharge him the doctors insisted that he and Monty should be split up, for both their sakes.

Jacques went to stay with Billy for a time, and in consultation with the doctors, LeMassena and Mrs Clift found a young black boy, Larry, to move in with Monty and take care of him. 'There was no doubt', said Billy, 'that Monty needed someone around to take care of him twenty-four hours a day. It had reached that state. Larry stayed with him for the remainder of his life, caring for him, watching over him, even sleeping in the same room.' Larry's role was to be not so much nurse as minder, and for weeks after his arrival he had to stand firm and refuse Jacques' many attempts to see Monty.

Billy LeMassena blamed Monty's decline partly on his associations with some strange medical people, by whom he was fascinated. The renowned Dr Silverberg seems to have done nothing to alleviate Monty's problems; rather, he encouraged them through his own homosexual involvement with his patient. Another who became a particularly bad influence in the later stages of Monty's life was a bogus plastic surgeon who also practised satanism and the occult and who became famous when his heiress bride of three weeks died mysteriously; a murder charge against him was dropped because he had embalmed the body himself before investigators were able to carry out an autopsy. He later operated on Monty to remove bags from under his eyes, which subsequently turned septic and threatened his sight. Billy said:

Some of these so-called doctor friends, I think, weren't doing him any good at all. They prescribed stuff for him that got him hooked and

God know's what they were pumping into him. Monty came round to my house for dinner one night with Larry and a doctor. Just before dinner, the doctor gave Monty a shot in the ass. He told me it was vitamins. But who knows? His mother was desperate about the drugs; she knew he was into hard drugs and it was tearing her apart.

His disintegration continued, and when Elizabeth Taylor saw him again in the spring of 1964, she was appalled. Burton was playing Hamlet in a production directed by John Gielgud in New York and they invited Monty to the opening night. He went, but wished he hadn't. Monty, the veteran of Broadway, said Burton had turned serious theatre, and Shakespeare no less, into a freak show. The audience came not to see *Hamlet*, but Taylor and Burton. Outside, before and after the performance, newsreel cameras and photographers, plus hordes of sightseers and fans, screamed and shouted for Liz and Dick; the party afterwards was a sycophantic display of cheek-kissing and hugging and champagne toasts, and Monty left in disgust.

They met frequently for the duration of the play, however, and Elizabeth decided that the only thing to save Monty was to get him back to work. She had two films in hand herself, after a long period of inactivity. She had not worked since completing *The V.I.P.s* and admitted that both she and Burton were getting panicky that no big offers were coming in. When MGM presented them with Dalton Trumbo's screenplay of *The Sandpiper*, they looked at it with trepidation. The plot looked as if it had been specially written to capitalise on Le Scandale, centring on an illicit romance between a bohemian artist and a minister. The script had been around for years but MGM, never backward at missing a trick, dusted it down, made some pertinent additions and presented it to the Burton–Taylor household. They talked about it and eventually Burton said, 'Oh, fuck it. Let's do it.' So Elizabeth said yes and charged MGM another $1 million.

After that, they went straight into *Who's Afraid of Virginia Woolf?*, which many see as their best work together, and for which Elizabeth won an Oscar, plus another huge fee and a share of the profits. In the meantime, she had been approached to play the nymphomaniac wife in *Reflections in a Golden Eye*, another Gothic story of mixed sexuality, in which her screen husband is a latently homosexual army officer; they both fall in love with the same young soldier. It was almost perverse even to consider Monty for the role of the homosexual husband, but Elizabeth thought that at least it would get him back to work.

She called him and asked him to do it with her. He accepted without even reading the script and she told Warners that she would do the film if Monty could be her co-star. They balked. Monty was uninsurable, everyone knew that. Elizabeth insisted and even went as far as guaranteeing his insurance out of her own fee. 'I can get him back to work,' she said. 'He'll do it for me.' Warners finally agreed, but filming would be delayed until she had completed her outstanding commitments.

* * * * *

While he was waiting for Elizabeth, Monty was approached by Raoul Lévy, who had found fame a decade earlier when he directed the Brigitte Bardot film *And God Created Woman*. He wanted Monty to star in a cheap spy thriller called *The Defector* – also for Warners – which would be shot in Munich. There was a part in it for Roddy McDowall too. The script was a godsend: both Clift and Warners saw it as a chance to warm-up before *Reflections in a Golden Eye*. Monty had not worked for more than four years; with the exception of Elizabeth, no one had called him with a decent offer in many months, and, though he realised when he read it that this one was rubbish, he went ahead. He even called Mira Rostova, whom he had not seen professionally for five years, to ask if she would travel with him and coach him. He told her that he was deeply worried that he could no longer act. Mira agreed, and at Christmas 1965 Monty began to prepare himself for the part.

Script revisions and difficulties with the cast delayed the start of filming, but in late February 1966 Monty flew to Europe with Roddy and Larry. He was desperate for everything to work, but there were problems from the outset. Leslie Caron, who was to have co-starred, pulled out even before filming began when Raoul Lévy refused to make adjustments to a script which she said was 'unactable' in parts. Monty, Leslie and Warren Beatty, who was by then a close friend of Miss Caron, tried rewriting the words in a hectic session, but Lévy refused to budge; he replaced Caron with the French actress Nicole Courcel.

Monty's moods ranged from anger at what Lévy had done to total nervousness. But he worked hard, leaning heavily on Mira and Roddy for support throughout, and remained determined enough to do his own stunts, which included falling into the ice-cold waters of a river – a scene he had to repeat four times before the director thought it was right.

Warners were taking a keen interest; they would finally decide on Monty's ability to play *Reflections in a Golden Eye* on the strength of the reports back. Monty knew that, and he behaved himself. But he was in severe pain with his back and carried syringes of Demerol with which he injected himself. The strain on him was immense. He blew scene after scene because he couldn't remember his lines, in spite of endless rehearsing with Mira and Roddy. He was well aware of his problems but tried to pass them off as something that happens when you're making movies. 'Jesus, what a day!' he said after a gruelling attempt to complete a particular scene. 'That was a hell of a day – but it wasn't all down to me. The camera blew it as well.'

And it wasn't all Monty's fault. Once again he was caught up in a directorial fiasco, described by one of his co-stars as a catastrophic joke. It was largely due to Raoul Lévy's personal life. Apart from being on the verge of a mental breakdown, he was locked into a heated and adulterous affair with a script-girl, who had suddenly rejected him. One night, after filming had finished, he went banging on her hotel-room door with a shotgun in his hands. The gun went off; Lévy was carried away with a large hole in his chest and died. By then, the film had already been wrapped up, and Monty had moved on to London for a week of parties and seeing old friends. He did the rounds with Susannah York and got drunk with Richard Harris.

As he returned to New York, Elizabeth and Burton were heading for Europe. Richard was to appear in *Doctor Faustus* in Oxford, and then they were going on to Rome to make *The Taming of the Shrew* together. Monty kept calling Elizabeth to find out if Warners had given a starting date for *Reflections in a Golden Eye*, and on 15 July they were told that the film had been scheduled for a September start. Monty's emotions were mixed. He was anxious and worried about the job, especially when he learned that John Huston was to direct, but at the same time he was relieved that, at last, he had been given the go-ahead.

He was on edge, but cheerful. He called a couple of friends and arranged some dates for the following week. On Friday, 22 July, he spent most of the day at home and went to bed at a reasonable hour. Larry stayed up to watch the late-night movie; by chance, it was one of Monty's. When he went to bed himself just before 5 a.m., he found Monty sprawled across the covers, naked but for his spectacles. He appeared to be comatose, which in itself was not unusual, but Larry sensed that something was wrong. He grasped Monty by the shoulders with the intention of rousing him to get him off the bed and walking. Then Larry noticed that the actor's body was cold, and the truth dawned: Montgomery Clift was dead.

Stunned and crying, Larry tried to raise Monty's personal physician, but he was out of town; an associate came over and pronounced that he had died two or three hours earlier. An autopsy showed that his heart had simply given out. He had severe arteriosclerosis of the main arteries, but there was no sign of a drug overdose.

Monty's mother was informed, and Larry telephoned Billy LeMassena and other close friends. Roddy McDowall cried when he heard the news. He immediately phoned London, where Elizabeth and Richard Burton had just given a party at their suite in The Dorchester. Burton took the phone call from one of their aides, who had received Roddy's message. Elizabeth broke down when Burton told her, but later said she was not surprised. Reporters from around the world called for her reactions and she told them all, 'I loved him deeply. He was my brother, my dearest friend.'

Monty, only forty-five, was buried three days later in the Friends Cemetery in Prospect Park, Brooklyn, where the Clifts had bought their own plot. Few of his friends attended the funeral: Billy LeMassena, Mira Rostova and Libby Holman were the last representatives of his so-called guardians. Elizabeth, Roddy McDowall, Kevin McCarthy and Myrna Loy all sent flowers. In London, *The Times* gave one of the most generous of all the tributes paid to him under the headline: 'MONTGOMERY CLIFT: A LEADING FILM ACTOR OF HIS GENERATION'. A month later, a memorial service was held in a Quaker meeting house. It would have been an opportunity for many writers, actors and theatre people to show their respect for a man who had once been a generous, witty, charming and talented friend, but not many did. Monty left $500,000, the bulk of which went to his twin sister and his mother, with smaller bequests for Mira, Larry and others who had helped him in various ways.

Warners brought out *The Defector* soon after Monty's death. It fared better than it would have done under normal circumstances, but the audiences came out of morbid curiosity and the critics were over-generous. Monty's performance was a shadow of his former talent; he deserved a better memorial than this.

Ironically, he might have been equally disappointed had he lived to make *Reflections in a Golden Eye*. When Monty died, Elizabeth rang Marlon Brando and he agreed to take the role of the homosexual army officer. Some thought that he agreed to it as a last tribute to Clift, but when asked why he was doing the film, he replied bluntly, 'For seven hundred and fifty thousand dollars, plus seven and a half per cent of the gross receipts.'

* * * * *

The summer of 1966 was a depressing time for Natalie Wood too. In the last eighteen months she had made three films on which she had placed high hopes and for each she had commanded a huge fee. The first was *Inside Daisy Clover*, in which she co-starred with Robert Redford and Roddy McDowall. Her salary was $30,000 a week plus a percentage of the profits, compared with Redford's $6500 weekly. Next she went into *This Property Is Condemned* for a fee of $600,000; it had been offered first to Elizabeth Taylor, but she was still engaged on *Who's Afraid of Virginia Woolf?* Based on a Tennessee Williams play, it should have been a winner; however, a poor script from a succession of writers meant that they were making it up as they went along, and the film itself was condemned by the critics. Tennessee Williams insisted that his name should be taken off the credits, since it bore no relation to his original play. By then, Natalie was already heavily involved in *Penelope*, a so-called comedy about a middle-class wife who turns to crime for excitement when her banker husband neglects her. For this, she accepted a flat fee of $750,000 from her former fiancé Arthur Loew, Jr, who was the producer.

None of the three films made any great impact. Natalie was rich but desolate, convinced that her career was in ruins and her superstardom at an end. She put on a brave face when she went personally to accept the Harvard Lampoon Award for the Worst Actress of Last Year, This Year and Next Year (Brando was voted worst actor). Natalie seemed to make light of the jibe and was the first actor ever to go to Harvard to collect the award. The event attracted enormous publicity and her student audience cheered her wildly. Afterwards, she became very depressed when she read in *Time* magazine that the Harvard people had not been joking when they awarded her the Lampoon; the organisers thought she had reached the pinnacle of her career and was on the way down. 'We wanted to let her know she wasn't the greatest actress around,' said one of them.

Behind her public façade, Natalie was scared and lonely. Writer Tommy Thompson, who was her friend and unofficial press-liaison man for many years, said:

> I remember evenings when she would disappear into her bathroom and take sleeping pills and then beseech me to sit beside her until they took effect. Had the headline writers found the same tragic words for her as they had for Marilyn Monroe, it would have saddened but not surprised her friends.

Her analyst remained an important prop in her life; she saw him almost every day and scheduled her engagements around the visits. She believed that he was helping her to find her own identity, to distinguish her real life from the fantasy one portrayed in the magazines and gossip columns. Natalie's screen image and her real self had become hopelessly confused in her own mind – a state tellingly illustrated by her favourite and most prized possession: a huge oil painting of herself in which she posed as a twenties movie siren, displaying self-confidence, sophistication, belligerence and a large bust. In reality she had none of those things.

She turned occasionally to Arthur Loew for companionship, and sometimes Frank Sinatra escorted her. At other times she would veer violently into weird relationships. One with a young writer whose answer to everything was an LSD trip caused Sinatra to become so concerned that he rang to implore her not to see this man again, and even had the writer followed to make sure that Natalie was not seeing him.

Warren Beatty drifted by now and again and, like many of her friends, was worried about her depressed condition. He wanted her to do his next film, *Bonnie and Clyde*, but she turned it down because the filming, in Texas, would have taken her away from her analyst for two months and she couldn't bear the thought of it. Apart from her work, her life was empty and she spoke with the sanguine experience of a woman twice her age. Tony Curtis quipped, 'I met her in her middle age, twenty-eight going on ninety.'

Towards the end of 1966, Natalie was talking about 'giving it all up'. She said, 'I want to get married again, and have children. I won't say I won't act again but I'll certainly give up my career. My personal life is much more important to me.' It was a phase she had seen Elizabeth Taylor and countless other stars go through, but her thoughts became more painful, more dramatic as reviewers panned her latest film, *Penelope*. Soon after turning down Beatty's offer, she sank into another deep depression and her friend Mart Crowley found her one day slumped on the stairs of her home. She had tried to commit suicide with an overdose of pills and was unconscious. She was rushed to the Cedars of Lebanon Hospital under an assumed name and given a stomach pump. When she came round, she whispered to her sister Lana, 'I just didn't want to live any more.'

Natalie made no more films for three years. When she recovered, she became intent on putting her personal life in order. In 1967 she began a relationship with British theatrical agent Richard Gregson, head of the American end of London International Artists, who had been separated from his first wife for some time. He arrived in Natalie's life at a time when she sought peace and tranquillity, and she found in him a stability and friendship completely out of the Hollywood male mould she had so far experienced. They lived together for almost two years while Gregson awaited the settlement of an acrimonious divorce, and on 30 May 1969 they married with a lavish family wedding at the Holy Virgin Mary Church, Los Angeles. Robert Redford was best man.

Her life more settled, Natalie decided to go back to work and accepted a co-starring role in the sex comedy that summed up the dying years of the swinging sixties, *Bob and Carol and Ted and Alice*, with Robert Culp, Dyan Cannon and Elliott Gould. Reviews were mixed – 'Natalie's resources as an actress are skinny and she has nothing to draw upon but the same desperate anxiety and forced smile agitation she's always drawn upon,' said the New York *Saturday Review* – but the film was a huge financial success for Natalie as well as for the studio. She accepted a low salary of $250,000 on the basis that her box-office appeal had declined; but she negotiated a percentage of the gross receipts after profit and subsequently earned $3 million from the picture.

Within a year of her marriage to Gregson, Natalie became pregnant with her first child, Natasha, who was born in September 1970, and she was 'deliriously happy'. Then, at a party at producer John Foreman's house while Gregson was away on business, she ran into Robert Wagner. RJ was also alone; his marriage to Marion was on the verge of collapse. Natalie said later:

> We found ourselves in a corner talking together, and remembering our happy times, our boat, our private moments, what few of them there were, and he followed me home. . . . it was awkward . . . but the next day he sent me flowers and it totally dissolved me.

Wagner and Marion separated early in 1971, and the alimony requirement for his ex-wife and their daughter Kate hit RJ at a bad time. For two years he had been starring in his first television series, *It Takes a Thief*, and in the spring of 1971 Universal scrapped the show. At the time, he was comforted by Christina Sinatra, who had co-starred in an episode of the show. She had always called him 'Uncle Bob' because of his friendship with her father, but now she was twenty-one and friends expected them to marry.

They had reckoned without an emotional explosion at the Gregson household in August. Natalie and her husband parted bitterly when she accused him of having an affair with his secretary. She even put security guards on the front gate to prevent him calling. The divorce was conducted, as usual, through the gossip columns. Friends pleaded with Natalie to reconsider but she insisted: 'How can I live with the man and not communicate my antagonism?', while Gregson explained:

> I was totally unprepared for living with an actress. I got very upset by her temper tantrums and I couldn't cope with her ego. Natalie was selfishly concerned with herself and I couldn't handle it. She'd get

angry and pout for a day or two until she realised that I wasn't her enemy and that I loved her.

Natalie was escorted by Mart Crowley as she began re-entering the Hollywood social whirl, but soon she began seeing RJ again, and they 'went public' in the spring of 1972 when they appeared arm in arm at the Academy Awards ceremony. They remarried six months later on board a yacht moored off the Malibu coast, and managed to keep it secret for a whole twenty-four hours. Immediately they were reinstated as Hollywood's happiest couple.

* * * * *

It was a shocking but unsurprising irony in the pattern of life for this highly volatile group of people that, as she wired congratulations to the Wagners, Elizabeth Taylor's own marriage was heading for the rocks.

Since Le Scandale, she and Burton had become the most expensive and expansive acting duo in the history of entertainment. They made eleven films together, some brilliant, some dismally poor, which earned them million upon million. They remained the most adored, admonished, acclaimed, criticised, hedonistic, excessive, extravagant, chronicled couple in the world, and they played their parts in a way that eventually isolated them from many of their friends. With an ever increasing entourage, they progressed through the continents of the world like a Byzantine court, moving in a circle of similar affluence. With wealth he had never imagined possible, even married to Elizabeth, Burton lavished upon his wife gifts so outrageously expensive that their very purchase attracted media attention. The most famous was his much publicised presentation to her of the 33.19-carat Krupp diamond, once owned by the wife of the Nazi steel magnate, which cost Burton $305,000. It was followed by many others: pearls, rubies, diamonds, and finally the most superb of all – the 69.42-carat Cartier Taylor–Burton diamond, which cost more than $1 million plus another $100,000 for a necklace to hold it. Only the Duchess of Windsor could outshine Elizabeth with her jewels and, at their various social encounters in the sixties, she made a point of doing so.

The couple's lack of concern over money was also apparent in other areas. When they were filming in England, Elizabeth's animals were refused entry because of the quarantine laws, so they moored a yacht in the Thames estuary to accommodate the animals and 'Yes, love, it did cost us twenty-one thousand dollars a month,' said Burton, 'but Elizabeth will not be separated from her pets.' They paid $190,000 for their own yacht, which they named *Kalizma* after their three daughters, Kate (Burton and Sybil's), Liza (Elizabeth and Mike Todd's) and Maria (their adopted daughter). They overlooked Burton's other daughter Jessica, Kate's sister, who was in a special nursing home for the mentally handicapped in America.

On their yacht, and at their house in Gstaad, Lafite-Rothschild was served at breakfast, lunch and dinner. Parties captured an intimate group of the world's most famous people. Money came rolling in; at one party, attended by a group of Burton's relatives, he was gathering up some papers from the top of a piano and picked up one of them. 'Look at this,' he said, waving around a cheque for $2 million which had arrived for Elizabeth as part-payment of her share of the profits of one of her films.

And so it was Hollywood, New York, London, Mexico, Rome, Paris or the south of France. It was the yacht, or the house in Gstaad, or the lodge at Céligny, or their two houses at Puerto Vallarta. (Elizabeth owned one but it was considered too small, so Richard bought the one next door and they connected them by building a bridge. When they rowed, Richard would storm off across the bridge and lock his doors to keep her out.)

It was this period that brought perhaps the most vitriolic criticism of their lifestyle, both from their friends and from the press. As Lauren Bacall said, 'Who the hell lives like that? It was obscene.' *Look* magazine described Elizabeth as 'a fading movie queen who has much and wants more'; Sheilah Graham said she looked like 'a woman who has everything and is wearing it all'; the *New York Times* was even moved to a leader article:

> The peasants have been lining up to gawk at a diamond . . . it is destined to hang around the neck of Mrs. Richard Burton. As somebody said, it would have been nice to wear in the tumbril on the way to the guillotine. In this age of vulgarity, marked by such minor matters as war and poverty, it gets harder every day to scale the heights of vulgarity. But given some loose millions it can be done, and worse, admired.

Burton, at least, had something of a conscience about it, and he became increasingly generous to others besides Elizabeth. He gave handsomely to UNICEF and there are many other examples. Once, he heard that a script-girl he knew had hit hard times; her husband had left her and the house was about to be repossessed. Burton paid off the £27,000 owed as soon as he heard about it. He put several children of less well-off friends through school. Many of his gifts were never publicised, and he continued to make them for the rest of his life. A large portion of his fortune was simply given away.

But this could not salve Burton's conscience; nor could it obliterate his deep personal unhappiness. There were aspects of his life which he hated, and of which some of his less sycophantic friends, like Welsh actor Stanley Baker, reminded him frequently; and he turned increasingly to drink. Kate Burton said of her father:

The problem was that Dad always needed a woman who would take care of him; Elizabeth had always been used to being taken care of as well. They both wanted the same thing, and they couldn't provide it for one another. He had his drink problems, and so did she, and pills, but Dad didn't take pills, except painkillers for his back complaint. But basically, Dad was a very insecure person, insecure about himself. In fact, he was very lonely. He got to the point where he lost touch with people, and was repeatedly thrust into situations he couldn't cope with or couldn't handle.

Mike Nichols, who directed Burton and Taylor in *Who's Afraid of Virginia Woolf?*, said:

There are great dangers in the acting profession, and he fell into one of them by confusing seeming with being. When he took the leap with Elizabeth, he left the world of being and was surrounded by seeming. He became a prisoner of fantasy, and he believed he had sold his soul to the devil.

As Burton began striving to break free from the fantasy world that had enveloped him, Elizabeth found she could no longer control him or his drinking; nor could she retain his attentions exclusively for herself. As the gossips began to sense a marriage in difficulties, they continued to make statements of their unquestionable love for one another. 'I never knew what love was until I met Elizabeth,' Burton said in 1973.

Yes, of course we have rows; but we battle for the exercise. I will accuse her of being ugly, and she says I'm a talentless son-of-a-bitch and this sort of frightens people. I love arguing with her except when she's in the nude . . . it is quite impossible to take an argument seriously with Elizabeth naked, flailing about in front of you. She throws her figure around so vigorously she positively bruises herself.

With another touch of irony, they agreed to make a film for Harlech Television, in which they were shareholders, called *Divorce His, Divorce Hers*, about the break-up of a marriage from each partner's point of view. As so often before, the script became crossed with real life. As the

Burtons began filming, there were tales of drunken lunches, late arrivals, ugly, public squabbles and the leading man's unruly temper. When they went back to Hollywood, there were reports of a major bust-up that sent Elizabeth off into the night to stay with a friend; when she discovered Burton next day in the bar of the Polo Lounge, she whacked him across the face, then sat down and had a drink with him.

Other personal upsets had affected them both deeply. Burton's older brother, Ifor, died in particularly traumatic circumstances. Ifor, Burton and Kate were travelling to the Burtons' home in Céligny for a short holiday. Ifor went on ahead to open the house while Burton and Kate stayed for lunch at the station buffet. When Ifor failed to return, they went to look for him and found him lying in the snow outside the house; he had fallen and broken his neck. Elizabeth also had family difficulties. Her son Michael, who had married at the age of seventeen while the Burtons were in London, was living in the Welsh mountains in a hippy commune which had been raided by police searching for drugs. Michael's 'den mother' at the commune was pregnant and his wife had left him, taking with her their baby, Elizabeth's first grandchild.

On 3 July 1973, Elizabeth issued a statement announcing to the world that they were to separate temporarily; they had been constantly in each other's pockets, she said, and she was convinced that the separation would bring them back together. There were a couple of brief reconciliations, then a divorce went ahead.

They had come the full circle in ten tumultuous years, which had left them both with deep emotional scars. Now there seemed to be a prophetic note to the words with which Elizabeth had ended her first autobiography, published shortly after they were married: 'I treat the happiness I have now with great respect, great appreciation, because I know how fragile and precarious it is . . . how easily it can go.'

Chapter Seventeen

Endings

The tide had already turned against Rock Hudson. By 1973 he had appeared in sixty movies, but the seventies had ushered in the age of the anti-hero, embodied by actors like Al Pacino, Dustin Hoffman, Jack Nicholson, Warren Beatty and Steve McQueen. Rock's day had come and gone. Though still a 'star', he would make only five more films, plus some uninspiring television specials, in the remaining twelve years of his life.

The switch into television was a difficult decision to make, and it bore heavily on him. 'I turned it over in my mind for a long time,' he said. 'After all, I'd come up in the movies and I kept thinking to myself, "Shit, it can't be over, it can't be all over yet. That can't be all there is." I mean, I'm still comparatively young.' But it was over, virtually. Rock's fears that his days as a famous actor were drawing to a close had been growing as the telephone calls and script offers became less frequent. At the same time, he began to drink heavily, and his personal relationships suffered. Two resident lovers came and went in the space of three years; he was becoming more difficult to live with as he sank deeper into depression. *McMillan and Wife*, the television detective series with Susan Saint James, was a route out and, more than that, it paid handsomely. As Rock wavered about accepting, NBC upped their offer to $120,000 an episode and he agreed.

The series gave him regular work, but it did not help his moods and he went through one of the worst phases of his life psychologically. He was drinking a bottle of Scotch a day, sometimes two. He explained frankly:

There were certain aspects of my life I was deeply unhappy about, and not the least was my work. When you have been there, at the top of the tree, and number one male actor against people like Cary Grant, it sure isn't easy to accept that people are not calling any more. I think I did too many comedies, and the scripts got repetitive, and not very funny. So there I was doing less and less. My drinking became a real bad habit, and it went on for a long, long time, too long in fact. I wasn't an alcoholic, but pretty damn close. It's pretty easy for someone to say 'one for the road' but usually it was me who was saying it. Then, when I was doing *McMillan*, I'd get home at nights after six or seven hours in the studio and all I wanted to do was take a stiff drink. The trouble was I had another, and another . . .

Around the time he went into television, Rock formed a relationship with Tom Clark, a former actor and studio publicist, who moved into the castle in 1973 and remained for more than ten years. He took over the management of Hudson's household, his work, his engagements, his travel, his parties and helping to care for their seven dogs. It was a long and stormy relationship; Clark could keep pace with Hudson's drinking and it often became a match to discover who would pass out first. In a way, Rock resented Clark's eventual control of his life, but on the other hand he desperately needed the companionship and the organisational skills Tom brought into his affairs. He also brought a better social atmosphere into the castle, arranging small dinner parties and inviting people like Roddy McDowall, Elizabeth Taylor when she was in town, William Holden and Stephanie Powers, Fred Astaire, Bette Davis, Danny Kaye and his wife, Carol Burnett and many others. It did not stop Rock's drinking, but his life took on added interest.

As he advanced in years, Hudson's sexual drive had not diminished and he was still an active predator. He would cruise the bars of San Francisco, New York, London – anywhere that he might discover an exciting new lover; he was quite capable of sex two or three times in a single day, with different people. But still he remained protective of his macho image and believed that he had successfully camouflaged his homosexuality from the rest of the world. In interviews, he continued to deny that his bachelorhood had any odd implications – 'I go around with lots of girls,' he would lie – and threatened legal action when writers came too close to revealing to his public what half of Hollywood had known for years.

*   *   *   *   *

Like Rock's, Elizabeth Taylor's film work had virtually dried up by the early seventies, and with her separation from Burton came the fading of her stardom. In the five years after their divorce she made only two major films: *The Blue Bird* in 1975 and *A Little Night Music* the following year. Her life had changed as dramatically as her appearance had in the transition from the glamorous beauty of *Cleopatra* to the almost raunchy, plump, middle-aged star of *Who's Afraid of Virginia*

Woolf? Emotionally she was drained, and leaned heavily for support on her new boyfriend, Henry Wynberg, a forty-year-old car salesman she met through Peter Lawford; but Burton still remained constantly in her thoughts. He had found new lovers, and in October 1974 he became engaged to Princess Elisabeth of Yugoslavia. When news of his admiration for the beautiful black model Jeanne Bell, of *Playboy* centrefold fame, reached the Princess's ears, however, she promptly dumped him and Jeanne moved in with Richard.

The reunion of Burton and Taylor in August 1975 surprised even their families. They were both in Switzerland, he with his playgirl, she with her car salesman, and Burton called her for a meeting to discuss their still-intertwined business affairs. The very next day, Miss Bell was departing Switzerland, followed shortly by a despondent Henry Wynberg, and the press surged forward breathlessly to reveal a reconciliation. Later Burton and Taylor even publicised letters to each other, in which Elizabeth had written: 'Fear and doubt. Will marriage spoil our confident love, make us overconfident and smug and taking for granted all the lonely awareness again? I love you Richard, and I leave it up to you. Please answer.' His response was affirmative, though tinged with doubt. 'I could elaborate endlessly on why we should marry and why we shouldn't. But it is as you say a piece of paper. Paper can be torn up. True promises cannot. Any road, I love you.'

They remarried in a jungle in Botswana, surrounded by monkeys, on 10 October 1975, and very soon Burton wished that they hadn't. By Christmas, the cracks had appeared. He met Suzy Hunt, the wife of racing-driver James, while skiing in Switzerland. A month later, when Burton flew to New York to open on Broadway in *Equus*, it was Suzy at his side, not Elizabeth. She stayed at their home in Gstaad, fuming, then flew back to America and friendships new.

After a brief resumption of her affair with Wynberg, she found herself alone and miserable but sitting next to a multi-millionaire politician and divorcee, John Warner, at a banquet in Washington. They were married on 4 December 1976 in the Episcopal Church of Middleburgh, and the superstar began her new life as mistress of the magnificent 2700-acre Warner estate and, more significantly, as a politician's wife. As she emerged from the church, in a scene reminiscent of her role in *Giant*, she told anxious reporters: 'I am really so much in love with John. I don't think I have ever felt this good and lucky about being in love before. I am so happy.' Burton, meanwhile, had married his Suzy, whom he later credited with 'saving my life'.

* * * * *

The autumn of 1975 saw the reawakening of the James Dean cult with the twenty-first anniversary of his death, and there was much speculation on his likely status in the movie world had he survived. Would he have become a truly great actor? Or a fine director? Or would he have experienced the eclipse suffered by some of his contemporaries? It matters not; at each major anniversary of his death, the image Jimmy Dean had so carefully and skilfully invented for himself has been projected for commercial gain. The industry built up around him has earned as much as he might have done had he lived.

Of the original Dean 'gang' from *Rebel Without a Cause*, none was able to maintain the image they created in that picture and, uncannily, like Dean himself, few survived to maturity. The early deaths of almost all those who were with him at that time brought new speculation about the Curse of James Dean.

Nick Adams, who drifted away from Natalie's circle, though he remained friends with RJ and Rock Hudson, tried for years to emulate Jimmy in his looks, friendships and behaviour. He remained a second-string actor in films, although he achieved success in a television series called *Saints and Sinners* and became very wealthy through his part-ownership of the rights to that and to some of his films. However, there was always an underlying bitterness in him over his failure to make it to the top. He died of a drug overdose in 1968 at the age of forty-one.

Pier Angeli, Jimmy's former lover, who once had all the makings of a great star, also fell from sight. As we have seen, her marriage to Vic Damone ended in acrimonious custody battles over their son, and later she repeated the performance when she married an Italian composer, Armando Trovajoli. Her life sank into drug addiction and a succession of drink-induced dramas, and on 10 September 1971 she killed herself with an overdose of pills. She was thirty-nine. A series of letters she left to a friend described her loneliness, her fears that she had failed as an actress, a wife and a mother, and revealed that her memories of Dean had never left her:

> Today, I am alone. I have always been alone. Always, except with Jimmy. . . . I don't think a man could save me now. It is too late. I believe I was meant to be alone and die alone. Love is far behind me; it was killed at the wheel of a Porsche. . . .

Sal Mineo, who won Oscar nominations for *Rebel Without a Cause* and for his 1960 performance in *Exodus*, never fulfilled the early promise of greater things. He dropped out of Hollywood and went to live for a time in London, where he became a close friend of Ava Gardner. He returned to Los Angeles in 1976 to start work on a play and on the night of 21 February he was stabbed to death in an alley outside his west Hollywood apartment; police said that the killing had homosexual overtones. He was thirty-seven.

Nick Ray, who directed this band of kids in *Rebel*, also failed to settle or find the kind of work he wanted. He travelled abroad, worked in England for a time, lost an eye in a bar-room fight in Madrid and returned to Hollywood in the early seventies, penniless. Elia Kazan remembered him as a great attender of Hollywood parties, where he could get cocaine free. Ray's addictions to drink and the white powder were overtaken only by a more serious problem; he died of cancer in 1979.

The producer of *Rebel Without a Cause*, David Weisbart, had also died, as did Dean's photographer friend Sandford Roth at the age of forty-five. Next, tragically and mysteriously, Natalie Wood herself was taken.

* * * * * *

Since her remarriage to Robert Wagner, Natalie's life had become almost idyllic. She took the advice of her therapist and put her career into perspective. Whereas up to the age of thirty-two (in 1970) she had completed forty-one films, she now began to pace herself and in the remaining twelve years of her life she made only six. She and Wagner also reformed their production company, called Rona II, which went on to make many millions through co-ownership of television series such as *Charlie's Angels* and Wagner's own long-running show, *Hart to Hart*.

Natalie had her second child, Courtney, in 1974 and turned down an endless stream of scripts in order to remain with her family. She passed up films like *The Towering Inferno* and *The Great Gatsby*, but unfortunately the ones she did choose to appear in were, in the main, mediocre. Wagner, meanwhile, at last entered the superstar bracket through television. He had made over thirty movies, but none had brought him the recognition or financial security that came with *Hart to Hart*.

In the seventies, the Wagners once more became Hollywood's most popular couple; the community adored them, their parties were relaxed and pleasant, and Laurence Olivier, who appeared with them in a television revival of *Cat on a Hot Tin Roof*, filmed on location in Manchester in 1977, found them 'delightful and charming' and remained a good friend. Maureen Stapleton, who was also in the cast, said: 'Natalie was so beautiful; she had matured into a divine creature, stunningly attractive and, with those big black eyes, she could captivate anyone. They were so dear, and obviously very much in love.'

Natalie gave another highly successful television performance in a remake of *From Here to Eternity* two years later, but she reckoned she had got her priorities right at last: family first, work second.

She and RJ gave ample displays of their affection for each other, and Wagner said:

> With Natalie, I am utterly fulfilled. She is my wife, my lover and my friend. She keeps our marriage together, because the pressure – the peer pressure, as Natalie calls it – is worse on a woman than on a man. Unhappy people try to make victims of others by spreading their unhappiness. If it leads to divorce, they get a perverse pleasure out of it. Never does a day go by without my feeling grateful at having Natalie back. I am truly a happy man.

In 1979 Natalie appeared with George Segal in *The Last Married Couple in America* and, as the eighties began, she started to think that the time was right to step up her now spasmodic screen appearances. She signed for *Brainstorm*, with Christopher Walken, the handsome New Yorker who had won an Oscar for his role in *The Deer Hunter*. As she went to work on location in North Carolina in the summer of 1981, Wagner was tied up filming episodes of *Hart to Hart*. The scandal sheets used the couple's first professional parting in years to reactivate earlier rumours of Wagner's friendship with his beautiful co-star in the television series, Stephanie Powers. Then, as filming progressed on *Brainstorm*, they turned their attentions to Natalie and Walken. 'Are they having an affair?' asked the gossips, ignoring the fact that Walken's wife Georgianne was living with him for the duration of the filming.

The Wagners' marital bliss was further challenged by events on 16 November, when Stephanie's famous lover, William Holden, wearing only his pyjama jacket, tripped on a rug while drinking heavily, hit his head on a table and was dead by the time he was discovered. Miss Powers was inconsolable. She collapsed in a nervous state, and RJ spent several days doing his best to help her through this traumatic time; he was photographed with her leaning on him for support. Certain 'close friends' quoted in newspapers suggested that Natalie was angry at Wagner's insistence on comforting his screen wife. As true confidants well knew, Wagner's helping hand was purely an act of friendship; he was not seeking new female companionship and any discomfort Natalie might have shown was blown out of all proportion.

The headlines over Stephanie and Holden had hardly died down before new tragedy struck. The following week, the Wagners threw their traditional Thanksgiving party on the evening of Thursday, 26 November

1981. Christopher Walken was there, but his wife had returned to their home in Connecticut. The following day, he joined Natalie and RJ on their yacht, *Splendor*, at the Marina del Ray, a bustling leisure area on the southern reaches of Los Angeles. Their skipper, Dennis Davern, was waiting for them on the pier where their boat was moored.

Natalie made some drinks, and the four of them set sail for Catalina Island, the tiny palm-tree haven twenty-eight miles from the Californian coast across the San Pedro Channel. The local community was well used to famous visitors: it had been a favourite get-away for stars like John Barrymore, Errol Flynn, Humphrey Bogart and John Wayne, who all moored their yachts there, and was the setting for a number of films, including the original *Mutiny on the Bounty*, *Treasure Island* and *MacArthur*. It was a special place for Natalie and RJ, who were married there in 1972.

On Friday evening, they tied up at Avalon, the main town in Catalina, went ashore, and had dinner at the El Galleon restaurant. By the time they were ready to return to the yacht, the sea had become choppy and Natalie, who still suffered from sea sickness in spite of all the years they had owned their boat, said she did not want to go back on board that night. Instead, she booked two rooms at the Pavilion Lodge Motel. Wagner returned to the *Splendor* with Christopher Walken and Natalie went to her room; she had trouble with the gas fire and telephoned reception, who sent a maintenance man to light it for her.

The second room was for their skipper Davern. For a long time, the question of exactly who remained on shore with Natalie was the first of the mysteries in this tragic tale. Various newspapers came out with the theory that everyone had been drinking heavily and that it was Walken who stayed at the motel, and, furthermore, that his bed was not slept in. Later reports, quoting eye-witnesses, said that it was Davern who stayed behind because he was so drunk. Two years later, Davern claimed in a newspaper article that it was indeed he who stayed at the Pavilion because he often acted as Natalie's bodyguard; he said that he slept in her bedroom 'but nothing happened because I promised to be good'.

The following day, Natalie and her companion went back on board *Splendor*, and they set sail once again for Two Harbors, their regular mooring on Catalina, the tiny seaport with a local community of around fifty people whose lives are generally involved in tending to their yachting visitors. They went ashore and spent most of the evening on the wooden decks of Doug's Harbor Reef Restaurant.

Another party became spirited, laughing and dancing to the music. Natalie and Wagner clapped along; someone from the adjoining tables recognised them and sent over a bottle of champagne. Later, Wagner sent for more wine from their yacht and they spent about two hours at the restaurant, leaving around 10 p.m. Some reports suggested that they left after a row between Wagner and his wife, but according to the restaurant manager, Don Whiting, Natalie was just having a good time and was in a 'skittish and flirtatious mood'. She slipped and fell on the dock as they went out to the mooring.

The events that followed became the subject of the most intense and sensational reporting witnessed in recent times, even by Hollywood standards, and any coherent account of what happened was overpowered by the sheer mass of speculation. However, Dr Thomas Noguchi, Los Angeles County medical examiner and coroner, did establish beyond question that once aboard the *Splendor* a 'non-violent' row developed. This was borne out by Davern's later article, in which he claimed that when they returned Natalie lit some candles on the table in the saloon and they sat drinking. He said she began flirting with Walken, which he did not encourage, and Wagner became so angry that he smashed a bottle on the table. Natalie stormed off to the master bedroom, leaving the two men together.

Walken retired to his cabin on the port side, Davern climbed the four steps to a cabin on the starboard side and Wagner eventually went into a forward cabin. About an hour after Natalie had gone to bed, Wagner went to her cabin to make up. She was gone. It was past midnight. He called Davern and they checked everywhere on the boat, even Walken's cabin; he was asleep. Davern noticed that the inflatable dinghy, which had an outboard engine on the back, was missing.

Davern wrote later, 'RJ didn't believe Natalie was in trouble; he thought she had just gone off to shore because she was mad at him for what happened. He wasn't too worried.' But as time wore on and there was still no sign of Natalie, Wagner became increasingly concerned. At 1.30 a.m. he called Don Whiting at the restaurant on the yacht's radio telephone and Whiting organised a search for Natalie, but there was no sign of her. The local Bay Watch and private harbour patrol were alerted and the Los Angeles County lifeguard was called to join the search at 5.15 a.m.

At 7.44 a.m. a Sheriff's Office helicopter radioed in. They had seen what appeared to be a woman's body, floating face down near a deserted cove called Blue Cavern Point, a mile from where the *Splendor* was moored. Washed up on the sands barely a hundred yards away was the dinghy. The oars, it was later discovered, did not appear to have been used; the engine was cold and the switch was in the off position.

The body was brought to Los Angeles. Dr Noguchi recorded that Natalie was dressed in only her blue flannel nightgown, knee-length woollen socks and a red jacket, which was half off her shoulder as if she had been struggling to get free of it in the water. Bruises on her legs, her left wrist and forearm indicated that she had fallen at some time, perhaps when she got into the dinghy from the yacht, or that it had capsized. Medical examiners estimated that she could have survived for three to four hours in the waters off Catalina. If, somehow or other, she had fallen off the yacht, or had got into the dinghy and then fallen out of it, she would have been fighting for her life for up to four hours before she drowned through sheer exhaustion. A woman from a nearby yacht told investigating officers that she had heard a woman shout 'Help! Please help me!' No one did.

After a superficial examination, the coroner concluded that there had been two contributing factors to Natalie's death:

> The reason she drowned was the great weight of the jacket. If she had taken it off, she might easily have pulled herself into the dinghy. The alcohol was a deadly factor; if she had been thinking clearly, she would have taken it off at once.

As he proceeded through the autopsy, Dr Noguchi noted that Natalie's blood-alcohol content was 0.14 per cent, higher than the legal limit for driving, though not excessive. He also found evidence of her having taken a sea-sickness pill and a painkilling drug called Darvon. Noguchi's investigators discovered from pill bottles on the yacht that she had taken twenty-eight Darvon painkillers in the previous thirteen days; they had been prescribed for a sprained wrist. In another bottle of Placidyl, prescribed six weeks earlier, there was one tablet left out of thirty. Again, such usage was not excessive, though the tablets were clearly taken regularly. Also in her medical supplies were Synthroid slimming pills, Bactrim painkillers and Dalman sleeping pills. On the night she drowned, however, she had consumed only one sea-sickness pill and one painkiller.

Noguchi also took the controversial and unexplained step of ordering Natalie's body to be checked for cocaine and other narcotics; he himself took swabs from her nose but no trace of any other substance was found.

High drama and speculation took over. Newspapers put forward theories ranging from murder to suicide to accidental death; press conferences reached fever pitch and the whole business developed into a distasteful and frenetic contest of luridity between the tabloids. Dr Noguchi was suddenly hit by the wrath of the Screen Actors' Guild, who accused him of 'taking great glee in taking advantage of the misfortune of our members in a most unseemly and inappropriate manner', citing his handling of both Natalie's death investigation and William Holden's two weeks earlier, in which the coroner had concluded (rightly) that the

actor had been drunk at the time of the accident which killed him. The
Guild complained that Noguchi had sensationalised and trivialised their
deaths, to which claim Frank Sinatra added his own personal support.
Noguchi was subsequently demoted, and began a long legal battle to
regain his former status.

Robert Wagner, meanwhile, was joined by Christopher Walken in
maintaining silence, other than in their official statements, in the days
following Natalie's death. Davern also said nothing, and kept quiet for
two years, during which time he remained in Wagner's employ. But
reporters continued their quest for answers. How did Natalie get into
the water in the first place? Did they have a violent row? Did she storm
off to bed? Did she try to get ashore? In an attempt to quell the
storm of speculation, Wagner's lawyer Paul Ziffren issued a statement
describing the likely sequence of events: Natalie could not sleep because
the dinghy was banging on the side of the yacht close to her cabin; she
went on deck to move it, and may have slipped on seaweed or algae and
fallen overboard. Wagner and Walken did not hear anything from their
cabins at the other end of the boat. Ziffren also denied that there had
been any row between Natalie and RJ. Some years later, Walken broke
his silence and said: 'Those people who are convinced that there was
something more to it than what came out at the investigation will never
be satisfied with the truth; because the truth is that there is nothing more
to it. It was an accident.'

Hollywood tried to comfort Wagner in his grief. Thousands arrived
to see the funeral procession and to watch the celebrities who arrived at
Westwood Memorial Park to pay their last respects: Elizabeth Taylor,
Rock Hudson, Frank Sinatra, David Niven, Laurence Olivier, Fred
Astaire, Gene Kelly, Stephanie Powers (still shocked from her own loss)
and Christopher Walken all joined Natalie's family for the service. Three
of her closest friends, Roddy McDowall, Hope Lange and the writer
Tommy Thompson (who himself died a year later) read eulogies. Among
the many tributes came a call from President Reagan, who had worked
with Natalie many years ago; and a telegram from Queen Elizabeth II
summed up everyone's feelings:

> On behalf of the Crown and Commonwealth of Great Britain, I send
> heartfelt condolences to the family and friends of Mrs Wagner. The
> tragic loss of great persons is felt the world over. However, loving
> memories of Mrs Wagner will live with us always.

Wagner took Natasha, then eleven, and Courtney, aged eight, to
Gstaad for Christmas, where they were supported in their continuing
sorrow by David Niven and his wife Hjordis. When he returned to Los

Angeles, RJ sold the yacht *Splendor*, which he never visited again, and put their house up for sale for $3 million. He went back to work on *Hart to Hart* and slowly, with the help of a therapist, began picking up the pieces of his life.

A lingering bitterness, however, developed in the family. In her will, Natalie left all her clothes to her younger sister Lana, who collected them from the Wagner household, making six trips in a rented van. She later sold most of the vast wardrobes of gowns for $15,000 and Wagner was furious. He asked Lana if he could keep all Natalie's furs, which he wanted for his daughters, and gave her a cheque for $20,000 in settlement. The gulf between them was only widened when Lana wrote her book, *Natalie: a Memoir*, in which she openly speculated on her sister's affair with Walken, then dismissed it as being 'all in her mind and perhaps she was only wishing it to be so'. She also wrote that, in the years before she died, the pressures on Natalie had mounted and she had responded by occasionally drinking too much. Her final comment alleged that perhaps the dewy-eyed romance of Natalie and RJ was not all it seemed: 'They had to live out the dream the world imagined for them, whether or not it had gone sour.' Wagner, alone with his grief, was incensed and hardly spoke to Lana again.

Chapter Eighteen

The Last Survivor

For almost five years, Elizabeth Taylor set aside her career to be the dutiful, if slightly bored, wife of a politician, whose own star had risen with the new conservatism that eventually elected Ronald Reagan to the White House. After John Warner became a Senator in 1978, his demands on Elizabeth's time increased greatly and her presence was required in an endless political round. This life of dancing attendance on Warner's supporters and electors was far removed from that which she had known as a movie star – and certainly a total contrast to her marriage to Burton.

For the first time in all her marriages, she found herself in the shadow of her husband and she was angered by reporters who constantly queried her intentions: 'No I haven't gone out to pasture. I have no problem with my identity.' But clearly there were difficulties in the marriage, and they both knew it.

One way in which Elizabeth's problems manifested themselves was in her weight. By 1979 she had ballooned to 182 pounds due to an insatiable appetite for junk food such as French fries, popcorn and chilli-dogs. The famous unflattering photographs of her, with earlier comparisons, began appearing in newspapers and magazines until, finally, she decided that she must do something about it. She checked into the Palm Aire Spa at Pompano Beach, Florida, and lost twenty pounds during a three-week stay. While there, she was informed of the death of her second husband, Michael Wilding, at the age of sixty-six; he had suffered head injuries from a fall at his home in Chichester.

Back in Washington in 1980, Elizabeth dismissed newspaper rumours that she and Warner were splitting up, but coincidentally she was offered a role in a television film version of Agatha Christie's *The Mirror Crack'd*. Newly slimmed and looking good again, she joined an all-star cast including Rock Hudson, Kim Novak, Tony Curtis and Angela Lansbury. Apart from a cameo role in *Winter Kills* in the previous year, it was her first movie since 1976. It gave her a taste for acting again and she began looking around for work, something different – a play, perhaps. Mike

Nichols, who had directed her in *Who's Afraid of Virginia Woolf?*, warned her against the idea. 'What about your voice?' he said. 'You haven't had the training, you won't be able to project.' But Elizabeth insisted and selected Lillian Hellman's *The Little Foxes*, which had not been performed on Broadway since Tallulah Bankhead's smash-hit success in 1939. Maureen Stapleton was signed as co-star and Elizabeth said, 'I wanted a good actress, but not that good.'

They opened in Florida for a trial in May 1981, which also allowed her more time to spend on her weight-loss programme at the Palm Aire Spa, before moving on to Washington, New York and then a daunting nationwide tour. (By coincidence, Richard Burton was also returning to Broadway at the same time, in a revival of *Camelot*.) Columnists galore had scorned Elizabeth's move into the theatre, suggesting that she was incapable of stage work. Others thought that she would call it off at the last moment, or be struck down by some 'illness', or that it was a joke. If it was, Elizabeth had the last laugh. Good reviews in Florida guaranteed a sell-out for forty-seven performances in Washington and by the time they reached New York, the Martin Beck Theater sold $1 million-worth of tickets in the first week.

A successful run in New York, and then New Orleans, was to be followed by a limited engagement in Los Angeles, where Rock Hudson was planning to throw a big party for Elizabeth and Maureen Stapleton, but by the time they arrived Rock was in hospital, undergoing major bypass surgery. He had just finished *The Martian Chronicles*, a three-part mini-series for television with Roddy McDowall and was about to begin filming another, *The Devlin Connection*, when Tom Clark found him sitting in the kitchen at the castle, deathly white and complaining of chest pains. They went immediately to the Cedars–Sinai Hospital for tests, and Dr Rex Kennamer gave him the bad news: there were blockages in three main arteries and he would have to undergo a triple bypass. He survived, and recovered with surprising speed. Elizabeth and Maureen went to see him in hospital and Maureen joked, 'You'd do anything to avoid giving us a party.' To recuperate, Rock went on a cruise with Tom, Ross Hunter and other friends, while Elizabeth headed off to London with her play, to perform to more packed houses.

She was also embarking on another highly stressful and emotional period of her life, which would bring fresh drama and more unhappiness. The strain of her stage appearances, night after night for eighteen months, was beginning to show; and her marriage to John Warner was under pressure. Her weight had risen again. During her London tour, she was photographed at her fiftieth birthday party, dressed in white and still wearing her stage make-up; she was not a pretty sight. She herself admitted that her eyes looked as if 'they had disappeared into suet . . . I looked for all the world like a drag queen.' She was also drinking again, and in the wings someone would be waiting with a large glass of Jack Daniels as she took her final curtain.

Richard Burton came to see her while she was in London. His marriage to Suzy was over and now he was with Sally Hay, a charming, unmarried and unsophisticated thirty-four-year-old television production assistant he had met at the BBC. Elizabeth herself was also on the verge of another separation. She discovered that John Warner had sold the house and bought an apartment in Watergate; her animals would have to go. 'Well if that's the case,' said Elizabeth, 'I go too.' When she returned to America from London, they parted, and in the early summer of 1982 she headed back to Hollywood alone.

When they last met, she and Burton had talked vaguely of doing something together again and, now free of Warner, she began thinking seriously of continuing her stage success with another theatrical project. She had formed a production company with Zev Bufman and they went through a list of possibles. She considered Tennessee Williams's *Sweet Bird of Youth*; someone else suggested that she and Burton should make a stage revival of *Who's Afraid of Virginia Woolf?*, but they both agreed that they could never repeat the success of the film. Then, towards the end of 1982, they came up with the idea of doing Noël Coward's *Private Lives*, which had a plot not dissimilar to their own situation: a divorced couple meet by chance while on honeymoon with their new spouses and run off to Paris, leaving their partners wondering what has happened.

By coincidence, Elizabeth was now in the initial stages of her much-publicised engagement to the Mexican lawyer Victor Luna – 'Whatever does she see in him?' asked Joan Collins – and there was much speculation over Burton's marital intentions. Would be knock Victor sideways and marry Elizabeth for the third time? During the preview performances of *Private Lives*, as thousands of fans besieged the theatre in West 46th Street, an enterprising local television station conducted a phone-in poll of viewers on whether or not they should remarry. Seventy-three per cent said yes. That prospect was shattered, much to the newsmen's chagrin, when Burton and Sally Hay nipped down to Las Vegas for a quick wedding.

But the Liz and Dick Show was back on the road, however, and from the publicity point of view *Private Lives* was initially a winner. By the first night, advance ticket sales had reached $2 million. After that, it was all downhill. Critics universally castigated both Burton and Taylor, and even Elizabeth agreed later that they were both badly miscast. But bad reviews didn't matter: the show was still selling out. As she correctly perceived, the crowds were not there to see a polite little English drawing-room comedy. They wanted high-camp Taylor and Burton, and that's what they got. However, it was a degrading sight to watch – Burton, once talked of as the natural successor to Laurence Olivier as Britain's foremost stage actor, and Elizabeth, veteran of fifty-four films and formerly the most sought-after, highly paid actress in the world, hamming it up before an audience who had little interest in their art.

Backstage, all the old fiery exchanges soon re-emerged, peppered with insults and the foulest language. 'The experience for me was devastating,' Elizabeth said, 'and I am sure it was for Richard.' Burton's dressing room was filled with an array of painkillers for his back; Elizabeth had her Jack Daniels, her pills and her food binges. Her regular medication, Percodan, was mixed with liquor – the road to oblivion and escape. She was out of the show for a week in July with a throat infection, and again later with hyperventilation. As the weeks wore on, she wanted to put an end to the torture of going out there night after night, but she risked being sued for millions if she backed out of the contract before the show ended its tour of major cities.

After each night's performance, she would muster company from the cast or stage crew and go off into the night, drinking until three or four in the morning. Richard was out with his own crowd and they seldom met socially. The play was killing them and the production looked increasingly limp. Audiences lost interest, and finally it closed in Los Angeles on 6 November 1983. Elizabeth simply collapsed; she was overweight and shattered, emotionally and physically.

A month later, after much pleading from some of her closest friends, she finally accepted that she was an alcoholic and a drug addict and went to the Betty Ford Center to begin a long course of treatment to cure her addictions and initiate her rehabilitation. She admitted in a later interview:

Drunk is a hard word, but I've got to be hard with myself to face it. A drunk is somebody who drinks too much. A junkie is someone who takes too many pills. There is no polite way of saying it. I've always been an insomniac, and I've been taking sleeping pills for the last thirty-five years. I've also had nineteen major operations and I've always had a lot of medication; but steadily I began to depend on drugs. They were like a crutch. I was taking a lot of Percodan, which I took with a couple of drinks before I went out. I just felt I had to get stoned to get over my shyness and face the world.

Elizabeth's admission to hospital was the first stage in a two-year struggle to regain her health and get her weight to an acceptable level, and in that she needed the help of her friends and family. She said:

I was in such a drugged stupor that when they filed into my room, I
thought 'Oh, how nice. My family has come to visit.' But they all sat
down and read from papers they had prepared; each said they loved
me and each said that if I kept on drinking and taking drugs the way
I had been doing, I would die.

Burton took off to Haiti for similar recuperation; he was in great pain
from his back and, approaching fifty-eight, he looked twenty years
older. Sally was good for him, and clearly loved him dearly; his friends
considered it fortunate indeed that he had someone of her strength and
stability to help him through the pain of his final months.

Less than nine months later, Richard Burton was dead. On the night
of 4 August 1984 he slipped into a deep coma while taking a break at
his chalet in Céligny. Sally called the ambulance, but it was too late. He
died at 1.15 p.m. the next day in Geneva Hospital. In the masses of
obituaries from around the world, the *Daily Telegraph* perhaps summed
up his career most aptly: 'He threw away greatness like an old sock.'

Elizabeth had survived four of her husbands – Nicky Hilton (who had
died from drugs in 1969), Michael Wilding, Mike Todd and Richard
Burton; three of her dearest friends – James Dean, Monty Clift and
Natalie Wood; and several others who had been her great supporters
over the years, including her personal assistant and organiser Dick
Hanley. Now she was about to lose another.

* * * * *

Rock Hudson, in 1984, already had AIDS. His weight loss was
noted by Nancy Reagan on 15 May when he sat beside her at a dinner
at the White House. He explained it away by saying that he had been
dieting, and it was an ironic truth that, after the bypass operation, he
had forced himself into better shape than he had been in for years. He
had started jogging and weight training and cut down on alcohol,
eliminating the bloated look that came from several years of excess in
the seventies.

By 1983, he looked a very fit man for his fifty-seven years. That was
the year in which he parted from Tom Clark. Mark Miller, who was
still with George Nader, had taken over the running of Rock's business
affairs and the two men, who had remained his best friends for nearly
thirty years, had his complete trust and confidence.

With Tom's departure, Hudson brought a new young lover into his
household. He had struck up a relationship with Marc Christian (real
name Mark Christian MacGuinnis), a tall, handsome blond of twenty-

nine whom he had met the previous year at a political fund-raiser and later at a bath-house which he visited regularly for a sauna and a massage. Very soon Marc moved into the castle, and they were indiscreet enough to be seen kissing and cuddling by other members of Hudson's staff. Marc cared not at all about the fifties' strictures of love-in-a-closet and was all for coming out, but Rock still feared the very thought of it. Although they went out together to gay restaurants and bars, by and large Rock tried to keep Marc out of the limelight when he went out publicly.

Hudson's friendships were not confined to Christian and he maintained an active sexual life elsewhere. Rock brought another young man to the house in early 1984, Ron Channell, an actor and gym instructor, to help him with his exercises, but soon he was accompanying Rock on his travels too. There were two other men whom he saw regularly, one a long-standing friend, the other a recently met young blond in his twenties whom Rock took to Mexico for a week.

Towards the end of May 1984, Hudson went to see Dr Rex Kennamer about a recurring sore on his neck. He was referred to a skin specialist, who took a biopsy. A week later, he was called back to the specialist's office and was told: 'Rock, you have AIDS.'

Hudson could not believe it – nor did he want to believe it. His reactions were those of a man who had just been given a death sentence. Stories of AIDS victims, of their slow, painful, unstoppable decline were now beginning to fill the newspapers and television documentaries; he was stunned by the horror of what lay before him, and Dr Michael Gottlieb, the AIDS specialist, told him, 'You had better put your affairs in order.'

He decided immediately on a cover-up to make sure that the news did not leak out, and he maintained the secrecy almost to his death, confiding in only three of his closest associates, Mark Miller, George Nader and another friend. Marc Christian was not to be told, he insisted, and he wrote anonymous letters to other people with whom he had had sex in the last few months to suggest that they had check-ups.

He even worked out a plan to hide the fact of his AIDS if the worst happened and he died. He believed it would be possible for his death to be certified as cirrhosis of the liver, which would not surprise anyone after his recent history of heavy drinking. His image must be protected above all else, and he fought almost to the last to make sure that his lifelong sexual preferences were not revealed.

For weeks, he remained a virtual recluse at the castle while his doctors pursued every avenue of enquiry for medical treatment. Money was no object, Rock had told them. He would go anywhere in the world, whatever the cost; but they all knew, as he must have done, that there was no known cure for AIDS. The only clinic which had had some success in prolonging the life of AIDS victims and delaying the onset of the worst symptoms was the Percy Clinic in Paris, where Dr Dominique Dormont was treating patients with a new drug called HPA-24. In September Rock travelled by Concorde to France, on the pretext of attending a film festival. With him went Ron Channell; even he had not been told the purpose of the mission. They remained in Paris for almost four weeks while Rock underwent a course of injections. Dr Dormont wanted him to stay for three months but Rock declined; his work commitments were already scheduled for later in the year and, secretly, Hudson feared that news of his treatment in Paris would leak out.

An example of how well he managed to continue as if nothing had happened came when Esther Shapiro, who with her husband Richard was co-producer of the highly popular television series *Dynasty*, flew to Paris. She brought with her the contract for him to play a new character they wanted to introduce into the show. They had discussed it briefly before Rock left America, but he was uncertain. They dined together at the Ritz and Esther implored him to join *Dynasty*. The money was good, and at the time the show was at the top of the television-ratings charts. When she left that night, she had talked him into it. 'Well, what the hell,' he told her. 'I think I'll do it.'

His treatment at the Percy Clinic over, Rock prepared to return home. At his final consultation, Dr Dormont gave him some good news: the drug had temporarily eliminated the virus from his blood, but he warned that it was likely to reappear; certainly, he should not consider himself cured. Rock, however, was euphoric and began to reject the possibility that he would die. His doctors back in Los Angeles tried to make him face the truth, but Rock ignored them and went ahead with the plans to begin filming for *Dynasty*.

He was welcomed to the set by John Forsythe (who played Blake Carrington), Linda Evans (Blake's screen wife) and, of course, Joan Collins. Everyone said how pleased they were to have him in the show; it was an honour and a privilege. In not many weeks, some of them would be cursing him for putting their lives at risk.

Towards the end of the year, his weight loss became more dramatic and the remorseless progression of AIDS symptoms began: loss of appetite, nausea, uncontrollable diarrhoea, night fever that forced him to change his bedclothes twice each night, and extreme tiredness. It was becoming evident to everyone that Rock was ill; most of all, it must have been obvious to Hudson himself that the AIDS virus was still present in his body and was now attacking his whole system. His back was covered with sores.

Then he found himself confronted with a dreadful decision. The script of *Dynasty* called for a long and passionate kiss between Rock and Linda Evans, with whom he was supposed to be having an affair in the story. He looked at it, re-read it and faced the dilemma. Should he now tell everyone he had AIDS? Should he find some excuse not to kiss Linda? Or should he just go ahead and do it? He had already been assured that AIDS could be passed on only through semen or blood, so he made his decision: he did the scene and kissed Linda. When the truth about his illness was finally revealed, that act brought him hostility rather than sympathy. He was castigated by the press and by *Dynasty* fans for what many considered to be a ruthless, dangerous decision, putting his co-star at too great a risk. Furthermore, at the time he had sores on the inside of his mouth.

Perhaps if Rock had turned down the series and remained reclusive until the seriousness of his illness had been clarified, he would have died a more revered person. But the dying star, progressing through the classic reactions of AIDS patients – fear, denial, anger and acceptance – insisted on keeping up his front of deception.

He and Ron Channell went on holiday after completing the episodes for *Dynasty* in February 1985. Marc Christian was still at the castle, although he and Rock had drifted apart.

Rock's decline was becoming more rapid and his skin eruptions more noticeable. As friends who saw him began to say 'Rock's dying', whispered rumours that he had AIDS began. Increasingly, he was in pain, unable to eat or to do anything that required much energy. In June, he was approached by producers putting together a televised tribute to Doris Day; everyone around him implored him not to accept, but he insisted – 'I must do it; I want to do it for Doris' – and on 15 July, he flew up to Carmel for the show. Everyone was deeply shocked by his appearance, especially Doris, who had not seen him for some time. Gaunt, white and stooped, he weighed little more than 140 pounds, and those who had heard the rumours sometimes turned away, embarrassed, rather than face him.

Rock was in poor shape for the television appearance, shaking badly, and when Doris hugged him he staggered, almost falling backwards. She kissed him on the cheek and said, 'You're still my buddy.' Tears welled in her eyes; the thought suddenly struck her that she would never see him again. 'I didn't even know what was wrong with him,' she said. 'All I do know is that he was determined to do that show for me . . . and I hoped and prayed for him . . .'

The famous photograph of Doris and Rock together was flashed around the world on the wire service and would be in all the newspapers the next day, exactly as Rock was returning to Paris in a final desperate bid for more treatment, and now his world caved in.

Within three days, the news was out. The *Daily Mirror* broke the story in London. Having seen the photograph, reporters began to piece together Rock's life over the past few months and discovered his attendance at the clinic in Paris, which had become famous for its work on AIDS. Then it was established that he was heading for further treatment there, and the following Tuesday morning editions revealed all: 'ROCK HUDSON AIDS FEAR'. Reporters from all over Europe were despatched to the Paris hospital; others began camping as near as they could to Rock's home in Los Angeles. Next day his illness was officially confirmed in a public statement, and telegrams and letters from fans around the world began to arrive, wishing him well. In the course of the next few weeks tens of thousands were delivered; but they were kept from him.

He returned to Los Angeles at the end of July, the only passenger in a specially chartered airliner. There was no hope of recovery and he slumped into a reclusive existence: acceptance at last. Good friends streamed in to see him; others shunned him and the *National Enquirer* lead a chorus of criticism over his continued television and public appearances even when he had known he had AIDS. The cast of *Dynasty* rallied to his support, however, and even Linda Evans was moved to announce, 'Medical evidence tells us you cannot get AIDS through kissing. I am not worried.' She had a test, all the same. Marc Christian was flown to Paris for medical tests and was given the all-clear. Other members of Rock's household were also tested, but no others were found to have the virus. Tom Clark put the bitterness of their earlier parting aside and returned to give his friend the support he would so badly need in the coming months.

Elizabeth Taylor visited Rock often – just as he had been one of her most ardent supporters in her fight against her addictions. She would sit and hold his hand as he sat crumpled and skeletal in a chair in his bedroom. She talked about old times, about Marfa in Texas where they had drunk chocolate Martinis together; but as the weeks went by he began to fade into unconsciousness even while she was there. The visits became more painful. She persisted, but wept uncontrollably when she left his room.

Even before she knew about Rock, Elizabeth had been working with other celebrities on the creation of an AIDS Foundation to fund research and the care of victims. In September she hosted a star-studded gala, at which she read what she said was a message of thanks from Rock, though in fact his contribution had been a mumbled approval when she wrote it. Linda Evans was also there and declared: 'Like everyone here . . . I would like to express my love and support for Rock Hudson.'

A few days later, at 8.30 a.m. on 2 October 1985, he died.

Elizabeth was among the first to be told. She realised only too well the crescendo of media interest that Rock's death would cause, and immediately arranged for security guards to be posted at the castle. Later, she worked with Tom Clark and Mark Miller on the funeral arrangements; his body was to be cremated and his ashes scattered in the Catalina Channel. Elizabeth suggested a Quaker memorial service, chose the flowers and the food, and checked the guest list, eliminating those whom she did not want to attend. The service was held in a marquee in the castle grounds. Elizabeth led the proceedings with reminiscences of one of her oldest friends and she was joined in the eulogies by Carol Burnett, Roddy McDowall, Tab Hunter and others. As the service drew to a close, Elizabeth said, 'Rock would have wanted us to be happy . . . please, let's raise our glasses to him.' And outside on the terraces they drank margueritas and ate Mexican food, Rock's favourites, while Mexican music played softly. They drifted away; the magnificent mansion that Rock had worked on since he had bought it in 1962, and which had been the setting for some of the last great Hollywood parties, was left silent and empty.

The house was by now worth at least $5 million; but in an age stricken by the fear of AIDS, no one wanted it and it stood vacant for eighteen months, with its price being reduced dramatically. It was finally sold for $2.9 million. Rock's possessions were sold by auction, including a stool carrying the inscription: 'ET stood here, she had to because she couldn't reach the sink. RH is a love and I thank him always – even though he is one foot taller. Your always friend Elizabeth.'

Although the full extent of the publicity surrounding Rock's illness was kept from him in his final months, he died with the knowledge that the story of his AIDS had leaked out. But he was saved the sickening aftermath. All efforts to reduce the media impact of his death were destroyed when Marc Christian sued Rock's estate for $14 million. Marvin Mitchelson, then acting for Christian, made the sensational accusation that Rock had conspired with Mark Miller to endanger his client's life by not revealing that he had AIDS.

Christian spelled out the detail of his involvement with Hudson, insisting that eight months had passed from the point at which the star had become aware of his illness before Christian learned of it. He alleged that, despite this knowledge, Hudson continued to have 'high-risk' sex with him. Lawyer Mitchelson charged that Hudson's despicable act had placed his client in extreme jeopardy.

Until the suit was filed, the details of Christian's homosexual relationship with Hudson had remained unreported and his real reason for being at the castle untold. Now his name and role became public and the tabloids rushed into print their lurid accounts of: 'ROCK'S BOYFRIEND: WHY I'M SUING' and 'ROCK SCANDAL EXPOSED'.

Lawyers for Rock's estate issued a counter-suit, claiming that Christian had blackmailed Hudson not only into allowing him to stay at the castle but also into paying him $70,000. They further accused him of stealing various items from Rock's house and of accepting money for sex from other homosexual men while Rock was abroad. Christian's lawyers denied the allegations as 'scurrilous'.

Claims and counter-claims went back and forth, and the legal activity dragged on for more than three years. When the case finally came to court, the Hudson story unfolded over seven weeks of evidence and dramatic submissions. Christian's lawyers said that Hudson had had a duty to warn their client that he had AIDS and that Mark Miller, one of the chief beneficiaries of Hudson's will, conspired to keep it a secret. When the trial ended on 17 February 1989, the jury upheld Christian's claim that Hudson had been guilty of outrageous conduct and awarded him not just $14.5 million damages for his life having been endangered, but an additional $7 million for emotional distress. (Later, on appeal, the award was reduced to $5.5 million.) The verdict enraged the leaders of America's gay community, who claimed that it would lead to an unprecedented harassment and embarrassment of homosexuals; they also pointed out that in the three years since Hudson's death, Christian had had repeated AIDS tests which had proved negative. The case was the first of its kind in which the plaintiff had not contracted AIDS.

The public airing of the whole business finally laid bare Rock's life. For more than thirty years he had fended off scandal so successfully that, although there had been some obvious hints, particularly in the British press, the revelations of his homosexuality and his, often seedy, double life, which included involvement with boys and young men, left the public astonished, even unbelieving. The secret that he and Henry Willson had fought so hard to keep hidden was out at last, his image shattered and shamed, and a large part of his fortune passing into the hands of a lover who, it was said, he ended up hating.

*   *   *   *   *

Elizabeth Taylor had by now completed her own recovery and looked sensational; there was no other word for her appearance and her re-emergence in low-cut gowns made the front pages around the world. She was off alcohol, taking no pills, and the super-inflated, blubber-like figure of 1983 had been transformed into an astonishingly svelte, clear-eyed example of wholesomeness. Writers speculated on which plastic surgeon she had used, but Elizabeth steadfastly denied that she had been under the knife.

She had pulled her life back together, and now she embarked on re-establishing herself as the undisputed Queen of Hollywood. Nolan Miller, designer of the *Dynasty* wardrobes, ran up some stunning creations which highlighted her rediscovered twenty-two-inch waist. Her romantic life was also full of excitement. After ending her betrothal to Victor Luna, she became engaged to burly film consultant and ex-jeans manufacturer Dennis Stein. A former escort of Joan Collins, Mr Stein presented his fiancée with a 20-carat oval sapphire ring set with diamonds, but two months later it was all off and Elizabeth was back on the arm of her regular escort and close friend, George Hamilton.

She began writing her book, *Elizabeth Takes Off*, in which she gave a detailed account of her recent traumas and her diet regime; she went into perfumes and cosmetics, from which she earned several million dollars; and Robert Wagner brought her back to the screen in a television movie, which his company co-produced and in which he co-starred. Entitled *There Must Be a Pony*, the plot had a remarkably familiar ring: it centred around a faded movie star (Elizabeth) trying for a comeback with the help of a new love (Wagner). It was her first screen role since *The Mirror Crack'd* with Rock Hudson in 1980. Other scripts came rolling in and Elizabeth was back at the top.

In February 1987, one hundred and fifty of her friends came to the Bel Air home of Carole Bayer-Sager and Burt Bacharach for a party to celebrate Elizabeth's fifty-fifth birthday and she made her entrance in a superb white silk gown designed by Nolan Miller, with a suitably plunging neckline to show off her figure. The assembled company applauded and flocked around. Arthur Loew, still slightly smitten, kissed her and remembered days gone by when he had loved and lost. Bette Davis puffed on another cigarette and said mischievously, 'Well, you gotta hand it to the kid . . .' And Michael Jackson cried. At the end of the evening, each woman present was given a glass reproduction of the famous Cartier Taylor–Burton diamond inscribed with her initials. For a moment, the glamour of old Hollywood reigned – but now it looked unreal and out of place.

When Elizabeth's book was published in the autumn of 1987, it became a worldwide bestseller. She embarked on a gruelling round of press interviews, television chat shows and photographic sessions. She talked as she had never done before, with remarkably frank recollections about the passion of her marriages to Todd and Burton, about her hollow legs and how she could drink anyone under the table, about the men in her life and how she expected to be sexually active well into her sixties. She was in full bloom and loving it. She gave them everything they wanted to hear. She continued her work for the AIDS Foundation and for other charities, particularly those for needy children, and raised millions of dollars. The new Elizabeth was busier than ever.

Could it last? She knew so well from her life of incredibilities that total happiness never stayed around too long and in the summer of 1988 she was struck down again with the back problems which had dogged her for so many years. Doctors did not understate the seriousness of her troubles, warning that she could become crippled for the remainder of her life. She was forced back on to prescription drugs, and everything that she had worked so hard to achieve in the past four years seemed to be slipping away. As ever, the snipers were quick to stick the knife in with claims that she was returning to her bad habits. Indeed, in the autumn she was re-admitted to the Betty Ford Center with recurring addictions, and returned there again in January 1989.

But Elizabeth Taylor is a fighter, and on 23 February 1989 she re-emerged, glistening and glamorous, for a star-studded gala organised in her honour by Bob Hope at Palm Desert, California. Surrounded by dozens of Hollywood stars, applauding and weeping, she received America's Hope Award for her outstanding and lifelong contribution to the film industry and for all her charitable work. It was a fitting tribute.

For forty-five years she has been making pictures and headlines, and, as Montgomery Clift once said, she is the most famous woman in the world. She has survived amazing pressures, unbelievable dramas, agonies and self-inflicted bodily abuse, and has managed to set aside the wounding words of those critics who have said that her suffering is no more than she deserves from a life full of excesses and over-indulgence. As the years of joy and entertainment she gave to her fans – for which, admittedly, she was handsomely rewarded – now fade into the distance, with occasional reminders on television, she insists that she is not finished. In a letter in 1988 she defiantly told the author: 'I've got a few more chapters left in me yet!'

No doubt she has.

Appendix

Film Lists

The Films of Elizabeth Taylor

There's One Born Every Minute, Universal, 1942 (Harold Young).
Co-starring: Peggy Moran, Scott Jordan, Alfalfa Switzer.

Lassie Come Home, MGM, 1943 (Fred M. Wilcox).
Co-starring: Roddy McDowall, Donald Crisp, Edmund Gwenn, Dame May Whitty, Nigel Bruce.

Jane Eyre, 20th Century–Fox, 1944 (Robert Stevenson).
Co-starring: Orson Welles, Joan Fontaine, Margaret O'Brien.

The White Cliffs of Dover, MGM, 1944 (Clarence Brown).
Co-starring: Irene Dunne, Alan Marshal, Dame May Whitty, Gladys Cooper, Roddy McDowall, Peter Lawford.

National Velvet, MGM, 1944 (Clarence Brown).
Co-starring: Mickey Rooney, Donald Crisp, Angela Lansbury.

Courage of Lassie, MGM, 1946 (Fred Wilcox).
Co-starring: Frank Morgan, Harry Davenport, George Cleveland.

Cynthia, MGM, 1947 (Robert Z. Leonard).
Co-starring: George Murphy, S. Z. Sakall, Mary Astor, Spring Byington.

Life With Father, Warner Brothers, 1947 (Michael Curtiz).
Co-starring: William Powell, Irene Dunne, Edmund Gwenn.

A Date With Judy, MGM, 1948 (Richard Thorpe).
Co-starring: Wallace Beery, Jane Powell, Robert Stack.

Julia Misbehaves, MGM, 1948 (Jack Conway).
Co-starring: Greer Garson, Walter Pidgeon, Peter Lawford.

Little Women, MGM, 1949 (Mervin LeRoy).
Co-starring: June Allyson, Peter Lawford, Margaret O'Brien, Janet Leigh, Rossano Brazzi.

Conspirator, MGM, 1950 (Victor Saville).
Co-starring: Robert Taylor, Robert Fleming, Marjorie Fielding, Thora Hird.

The Big Hangover, MGM, 1950 (Norman Krasna).
Co-starring: Van Johnson, Percy Waram, Edgar Buchanan, Gene Lockhart.

Father of the Bride, MGM, 1950 (Vincente Minnelli).
Co-starring: Spencer Tracy, Joan Bennett, Don Taylor.

Father's Little Dividend, MGM, 1951 (Vincente Minnelli).
Co-starring: Spencer Tracy, Joan Bennett, Don Taylor.

A Place in the Sun, Paramount, 1951 (George Stevens).
Co-starring: Montgomery Clift, Shelley Winters, Anne Revere, Raymond Burr, Keefe Brasselle, Shepherd Strudwick, Frieda Inescort, Ian Wolfe, Herbert Heyes.

Callaway Went Thataway (cameo), MGM, 1951 (Norman Panama, Melvin Frank).
Co-starring: Fred MacMurray, Dorothy McGuire, Howard Keel.

Love Is Better Than Ever, MGM, 1952 (Stanley Donen).
Co-starring: Larry Parks, Josephine Hutchinson, Ann Doran.

Ivanhoe, MGM, 1952 (Richard Thorpe).
Co-starring: Robert Taylor, Joan Fontaine, George Sanders, Emlyn Williams.

The Girl Who Had Everything, MGM, 1953 (Richard Thorpe).
Co-starring: Fernando Lamas, William Powell, Gig Young.

Rhapsody, MGM, 1954 (Charles Vidor).
Co-starring: Vittorio Gassman, John Ericson, Louis Calhern.

Elephant Walk, Paramount, 1954 (William Dieterle).
Co-starring: Dana Andrews, Peter Finch.

Beau Brummel, MGM, 1954 (Curtis Bernhardt).
Co-starring: Stewart Granger, Peter Ustinov, Robert Morley, James Donald.

The Last Time I Saw Paris, MGM, 1954 (Richard Brooks).
Co-starring: Van Johnson, Walter Pidgeon, Donna Reed, Eva Gabor.

Giant, Warner Brothers, 1956 (George Stevens).
Co-starring: Rock Hudson, James Dean, Carroll Baker, Jane Withers, Chill Wills, Mercedes McCambridge, Sal Mineo, Dennis Hopper.

Raintree County, MGM, 1957 (Edward Dmytryk).
Co-starring: Montgomery Clift, Eva Marie Saint, Lee Marvin, Rod Taylor, Nigel Patrick, Agnes Moorehead, Walter Abel, Jarma Lewis, Tom Drake, Rhys Williams, Russell Collins, DeForest Kelley.

Cat on a Hot Tin Roof, MGM, 1958 (Richard Brooks).
Co-starring: Paul Newman, Burl Ives, Jack Carson, Judith Anderson.

Suddenly Last Summer, Columbia–Horizon, 1959 (Joseph L. Mankiewicz).
Co-starring: Katharine Hepburn, Montgomery Clift, Albert Dekker, Mercedes McCambridge, Gary Raymond, Mavis Villiers, Patricia Marmont, Joan Young.

Scent of Mystery (Holiday in Spain) (unbilled cameo), Michael Todd, Jr, 1960 (Jack Cardiff).
Co-starring: Denholm Elliott, Peter Lorre, Beverly Bentley, Paul Lukas.

Butterfield 8, MGM, 1960 (Daniel Mann).
Co-starring: Laurence Harvey, Eddie Fisher, Dina Merrill.

Cleopatra, 20th Century–Fox, 1963 (Joseph L. Mankiewicz).
Co-starring: Richard Burton, Rex Harrison, Pamela Brown, Roddy McDowall.

The V.I.P.s, MGM, 1963 (Anthony Asquith).
Co-starring: Richard Burton, Louis Jourdan, Elsa Martinelli, Margaret Rutherford.

The Sandpiper, MGM, 1965 (Vincente Minnelli).
Co-starring: Richard Burton, Eva Marie Saint, Charles Bronson.

Who's Afraid of Virginia Woolf?, Warner Brothers, 1966 (Mike Nichols).
Co-starring: Richard Burton, George Segal, Sandy Dennis.

The Taming of the Shrew, Columbia, 1967 (Franco Zeffirelli).
Co-starring: Richard Burton, Cyril Cusack, Michael Hordern.

Doctor Faustus, Columbia, 1967 (Richard Burton & Nevill Coghill).
Co-starring: Richard Burton, Andreas Teuber, Elizabeth O'Donovan.

Reflections in a Golden Eye, Warner Brothers/Seven Arts, 1967 (John Huston).
Co-starring: Marlon Brando, Brian Keith, Julie Harris.

The Comedians, MGM, 1967 (Peter Glenville).
Co-starring: Richard Burton, Alec Guinness, Peter Ustinov, Lillian Gish.

Boom!, Universal, 1968 (Joseph Losey).
Co-starring: Richard Burton, Noël Coward, Michael Dunn.

Secret Ceremony, Universal, 1968 (Joseph Losey).
Co-starring: Mia Farrow, Robert Mitchum, Peggy Ashcroft, Pamela Brown.

The Only Game in Town, 20th Century–Fox, 1970 (George Stevens).
Co-starring: Warren Beatty, Charles Braswell, Hank Henry.

Under Milk Wood, Altura Films International, 1971 (Andrew Sinclair).
Co-starring: Richard Burton, Peter O'Toole, Glynis Johns.

Zee & Co (X Y & Zee), Columbia, 1972 (Brian Hutton).
Co-starring: Michael Caine, Susannah York.

Hammersmith Is Out, J. Cornelius Crean Films, 1972 (Peter Ustinov).
Co-starring: Richard Burton, Peter Ustinov, Beau Bridges, George Raft.

Divorce His, Divorce Hers, ABC-TV, 1973 (Waris Hussein).
Co-starring: Richard Burton, Carrie Nye, Barry Foster.

Night Watch, Avco Embassy, 1973 (Brian Hutton).
Co-starring: Laurence Harvey, Billie Whitelaw, Robert Lang, Tony Britton.

Ash Wednesday, Paramount, 1973 (Larry Peerce).
Co-starring: Henry Fonda, Helmut Berger, Keith Baxter.

That's Entertainment, MGM, 1974 (Jack Haley).
Co-starring: Fred Astaire, Bing Crosby, Gene Kelly, Peter Lawford.

Identikit (The Driver's Seat), Avco Embassy, 1974 (Giuseppe Patroni-Griffi).
Co-starring: Ian Bannen, Guido Mannari.

The Blue Bird, 20th Century–Fox, 1976 (George Cukor).
Co-starring: Jane Fonda, Ava Gardner, Patsy Kensit, Robert Morley.

Victory at Entebbe, David L. Wolper Production, 1976 (Marvin J. Chomsky).
Co-starring: Kirk Douglas, Richard Dreyfuss, Burt Lancaster.

A Little Night Music, A New World Picture, 1977 (Harold Prince).
Co-starring: Diana Rigg, Len Cariou, Lesley-Anne Down.

Repeat Performance, NBC-TV, 17 November 1978 (Joseph Hardy).
Co-starring: Joseph Bottoms, Peter Donat, Allyn Ann McLerie.

Winter Kills, Avco Embassy, 1979 (William Richert).
Co-starring: Jeff Bridges, John Huston, Anthony Perkins, Eli Wallach.

The Mirror Crack'd, EMI Films Ltd. 1980 (Guy Hamilton).
Co-starring: Rock Hudson, Tony Curtis, Edward Fox, Geraldine Chaplin, Kim Novak, Angela Lansbury, Wendy Morgan, Margaret Courtenay.

Television Features

Between Friends, 1983 (Lou Antonio).
Co-starring: Carol Burnett, Barbara Rush, Stephen Young.

Malice in Wonderland (the story of the rivalry between Louella Parsons and Hedda Hopper), 1985 (Gus Trikonis).
Co-starring: June Alexander, Richard Dysart, Joyce Van Patten.

The Films of Natalie Wood

Happy Land (uncredited bit-part), 20th Century–Fox, 1943 (Irving Pichel).
Co-starring: Don Ameche, Frances Dee, Harry Carey, Ann Rutherford, Cora Williams, Dickie Moore.

Tomorrow Is Forever, RKO, 1946 (Irving Pichel).
Co-starring: Claudette Colbert, Orson Welles, George Brent, Lucile Watson, Richard Long, Ian Wolfe.

The Bride Wore Boots, Paramount, 1946 (Irving Pichel).
Co-starring: Barbara Stanwyck, Robert Cummings, Diana Lynn, Patric Knowles, Peggy Wood, Robert Benchley, Willie Best.

Miracle on 34th Street, 20th Century–Fox, 1947 (George Seaton).
Co-starring: Maureen O'Hara, John Payne, Edmund Gwenn, Gene Lockhart, Porter Hall, William Frawley, Jerome Cowan.

The Ghost and Mrs. Muir, 20th Century–Fox, 1947 (Joseph L. Mankiewicz).
Co-starring: Gene Tierney, Rex Harrison, George Sanders, Edna Best, Vanessa Brown, Anna Lee, Robert Coote, Isobel Elsom.

Driftwood, Republic, 1947 (Allan Dwan).
Co-starring: Ruth Warrick, Walter Brennan, Dean Jagger, Charlotte Greenwood, Jerome Cowan, H. B. Warner, Margaret Hamilton.

Scudda-Hoo Scudda-Hay!, 20th Century–Fox, 1949 (F. Hugh Hubert).
Co-starring: June Haver, Lon McCallister, Walter Brennan, Anne Revere, Henry Hull, Tom Tully.

Chicken Every Sunday, 20th Century–Fox, 1949 (George Seaton).
Co-starring: Dan Dailey, Celeste Holm, Colleen Townsend, Alan Young, William Frawley, Connie Gilchrist, Veda Ann Borg.

The Green Promise, RKO, 1949 (William D. Russell).
Co-starring: Marguerite Chapman, Walter Brennan, Robert Paige, Ted Donaldson, Connie Marshall.

Father Was a Fullback, 20th Century–Fox, 1949 (John H. Stahl).
Co-starring: Fred MacMurray, Maureen O'Hara, Betty Lynn, Rudy Vallee, Thelma Ritter, Jim Backus.

No Sad Songs for Me, Columbia, 1950 (Rudolph Mate).
Co-starring: Margaret Sullavan, Wendell Corey, Viveca Lindfors, John McIntire, Ann Doran, Richard Quine, Jeanette Nolan.

Our Very Own, RKO, 1950 (David Miller).
Co-starring: Ann Blyth, Farley Granger, Joan Evans, Jane Wyatt, Donald Cook, Ann Dvorak, Gus Shilling, Phyllis Kirk, Martin Milner.

Never a Dull Moment, RKO, 1950 (George Marshall).
Co-starring: Irene Dunne, Fred MacMurray, William Demarest, Andy Devine, Gigi Perreau, Jack Kirkwood, Ann Doran.

The Jackpot, 20th Century–Fox, 1950 (Walter Lang).
Co-starring: James Stewart, Barbara Hale, James Gleason, Fred Clark, Alan Mowbray, Patricia Medina, Tommy Rettig.

Dear Brat, Paramount, 1951 (William Seiter).
Co-starring: Mona Freeman, Billy De Wolfe, Edward Arnold, Lyle Bettger, Mary Philips, Lillian Randolph.

The Blue Veil, RKO, 1951 (Curtis Bernhardt).
Co-starring: Jane Wyman, Charles Laughton, Joan Blondell, Richard Carlson, Agnes Moorehead, Don Taylor, Audrey Totter, Cyril Cusack, Everett Sloane, Vivian Vance.

Just For You, Paramount, 1952 (Elliot Nugent).
Co-starring: Bing Crosby, Jane Wyman, Ethel Barrymore, Robert Arthur, Cora Witherspoon, Ben Lessy, Regis Toomey.

The Rose Bowl Story, Monogram, 1952 (William Beaudine).
Co-starring: Marshall Thompson, Vera Miles, Richard Rober, Keith Larsen, Tom Harmon, Ann Doran, Jim Backus, Clarence Kolb.

The Star, 20th Century–Fox, 1953 (Stuart Heisler).
Co-starring: Bette Davis, Sterling Hayden, Warner Anderson, Minor Watson, June Travis, Barbara Lawrence.

The Silver Chalice, Warner Brothers, 1954 (Victor Saville).
Co-starring: Paul Newman, Virginia Mayo, Pier Angeli, Jack Palance, Walter Hampden, Joseph Wiseman, Alexander Scourby, Lorne Green, E. G. Marshall, Ian Wolfe, Albert Dekker.

One Desire, Universal, 1955 (Jerry Hopper).
Co-starring: Anne Baxter, Rock Hudson, Julie Adams, Carl Benton Reid, William Hopper, Betty Garde.

Rebel Without a Cause, Warner Brothers, 1955 (Nicholas Ray).
Co-starring: James Dean, Jim Backus, Ann Doran, Rochelle Hudson, William Hopper, Sal Mineo, Corey Allen, Dennis Hopper, Virginia Brissac, Ian Wolfe, Nick Adams, Edward Platt.

The Searchers, Warner Brothers, 1956 (John Ford).
Co-starring: John Wayne, Jeffrey Hunter, Vera Miles, Ward Bond, John Qualen, Olive Carey, Henry Brandon, Harry Carey, Jr, Antonio Moreno, Dorothy Jordan, Lana Wood, Pat Wayne.

The Burning Hills, Warner Brothers, 1956 (Stuart Heisler).
Co-starring: Tab Hunter, Skip Homeier, Eduard Franz, Earl Holliman, Claude Akins, Ray Teal.

A Cry in the Night, Warner Brothers, 1956 (Frank Tuttle).
Co-starring: Edmund O'Brien, Brian Donlevy, Raymond Burr, Richard Anderson, Irene Hervey, Anthony Caruso.

The Girl He Left Behind, Warner Brothers, 1956 (David Butler).
Co-starring: Tab Hunter, Jessie Royce Landis, Jim Backus, Henry Jones, Murray Hamilton, Alan King, James Garner, David Janssen, Vinton Hayworth.

Bombers B-52, Warner Brothers, 1957 (Gordon Douglas).
Co-starring: Karl Malden, Efrem Zimbalist, Jr, Marsha Hunt, Don Kelly, Nelson Leigh, Robert Nichols.

Marjorie Morningstar, Warner Brothers, 1958 (Irving Rapper).
Co-starring: Gene Kelly, Claire Trevor, Ed Wynn, Everett Sloane, Martin Milner, Carolyn Jones, George Tobias, Martin Balsam, Jessie White, Edward Byrnes, Paul Picerni, Alan Reed, Ruta Lee.

Kings Go Forth, United Artists, 1958 (Delmar Daves).
Co-starring: Frank Sinatra, Tony Curtis, Leora Dana, Karl Swenson, Anne Codee, Jackie Berthe.

Cash McCall, Warner Brothers, 1960 (Joseph Pevney).
Co-starring: James Garner, Nina Foch, Dean Jagger, E. G. Marshall, Henry Jones, Otto Kruger, Roland Winters.

All the Fine Young Cannibals, MGM, 1960 (Michael Anderson).
Co-starring: Robert Wagner, Susan Kohner, George Hamilton, Pearl Bailey, Jack Mullaney, Onslow Stevens, Anne Seymour, Virginia Berman.

Splendor in the Grass, Warner Brothers, 1961 (Elia Kazan).
Co-starring: Warren Beatty, Pat Hingle, Audrey Christie, Barbara Loden, Zohra Lampert, Fred Stewart, Joanna Roos, Gary Lockwood, Sandy Dennis, Jan Norris, Crystal Field.

West Side Story, United Artists, 1961 (Robert Wise and Jerome Robbins).
Co-starring: Richard Beymer, Russ Tamblyn, Rita Moreno, George Chakiris, Tucker Smith, Tony Mordente, Eliot Feld, David Winters, Simon Oakland, John Astin.

Gypsy, Warner Brothers, 1962 (Mervyn LeRoy).
Co-starring: Rosalind Russell, Karl Malden, Paul Wallace, Betty Bruce, Ann Jillian, Harry Shannon, Faith Dane, Roxanne Arlen.

Love with the Proper Stranger, Paramount, 1963 (Robert Mulligan).
Co-starring: Steve McQueen, Edie Adams, Herschel Bernadi, Tom Bosley, Harvey Lembeck, Penny Santon, Virginia Vincent, Nick Alexander.

Sex and the Single Girl, Warner Brothers, 1964 (Richard Quine).
Co-starring: Tony Curtis, Henry Fonda, Lauren Bacall, Mel Ferrer, Fran Jeffries, Leslie Parrish, Edward Everett Horton, Larry Storch, Stubby Kaye, Otto Kruger, Max Showalter, Count Basie and His Band.

The Great Race, Warner Brothers, 1965 (Blake Edwards).
Co-starring: Jack Lemmon, Tony Curtis, Peter Falk, Keenan Wynn, Arthur O'Connell, Vivian Vance, Dorothy Provine, Larry Storch, Ross Martin, George Macready, Marvin Kaplan.

Inside Daisy Clover, Warner Brothers, 1966 (Robert Mulligan).
Co-starring: Christopher Plummer, Robert Redford, Roddy McDowall, Ruth Gordon, Katharine Bard, John Hale, Harold Gould.

This Property Is Condemned, Paramount, 1966 (Sydney Pollack).
Co-starring: Robert Redford, Charles Bronson, Kate Reid, Mary Badham, Alan Baxter, Robert Blake, John Harding, Dabney Coleman, Jon Provost.

Penelope, MGM, 1966 (Arthur Hiller).
Co-starring: Ian Bannen, Dick Shawn, Peter Falk, Jonathan Winters, Lila Kedrova, Lou Jacobi, Norma Crane, Jerome Cowan, Arlene Golonka.

Bob and Carol and Ted and Alice, Columbia, 1969 (Paul Mazursky).
Co-starring: Robert Culp, Elliott Gould, Dyan Cannon, Horst Ebersberg, Greg Mullavey, Celeste Yarnall.

The Candidate (unbilled cameo as herself), Warner Brothers, 1972 (Michael Ritchie).
Co-starring: Robert Redford, Peter Boyle, Don Porter, Allen Garfield, Melvyn Douglas, Karen Carlson, Michael Lerner.

Peeper, 20th Century–Fox, 1976 (Peter Hyams).
Co-starring: Michael Caine, Kitty Winn, Thayer David, Liam Dunn, Dorothy Adams, Michael Constantine, Liz Renay, Guy Marks, Margo Winkler.

Meteor, American International, 1979 (Ronald Neame).
Co-starring: Sean Connery, Henry Fonda, Trevor Howard, Brian Keith, Karl Malden, Martin Landau, Richard Dysart, Joe Campanella, Bibi Besch.

The Last Married Couple in America, Universal, 1979 (Gilbert Cates).
Co-starring: George Segal, Richard Benjamin, Arlene Golonka, Alan Arbus, Marilyn Sokol, Dom De Luise, Valerie Harper, Bob Dishy, Oliver Clark, Priscilla Barnes.

Willie and Phil (cameo as herself), 20th Century–Fox, 1980 (Paul Mazursky).
Co-starring: Michael Ontkean, Margot Kidder, Ray Sharkey, Jan Miner, Tom Brennan, Julie Bovasso, Louis Guss.

Brainstorm, MGM/United Artists, 1983 (Douglas Trumbull).
Co-starring: Christopher Walken, Louise Fletcher, Cliff Robertson, Jordan Christopher, Donald Hotton, Allan Fudge, Joe Dorsey, Georgianne Walken.

Television Features

The Affair, Spelling/Goldberg, 1973 (Gilbert Cates).
Co-starring: Robert Wagner, Bruce Davison, Jamie Smith Jackson, Kent Smith, Frances Reid, Pat Harrington.

Cat on a Hot Tin Roof, Granada TV Ltd, 1976 (Robert Moore).
Co-starring: Robert Wagner, Laurence Olivier, Maureen Stapleton, Jack Hedley, Mary Peach, Heidi Rundt.

From Here to Eternity, Columbia Pictures, 1979 (Buzz Kulik).
Co-starring: William Devane, Steve Railsback, Roy Thinnes, Joe Pantoliano, Kim Basinger, Peter Boyle, Salome Jens, Andy Griffith.

The Cracker Factory, Roger Gimbel Productions/EMI, 1979 (Burt Brinckeroff).
Co-starring: Perry King, Peter Haskell, Vivian Blaine, Juliet Mills, Marian Mercer.

The Memory of Eve Ryker, Irwin Allen Productions, 1980 (Walter Grauman).
Co-starring: Ralph Bellamy, Robert Foxworth, Roddy McDowall, Bradford Dillman, Jean-Pierre Aumont, Peter Graves, Mel Ferrer, Morgan Fairchild.

Television Series

Pride of the Family, Revue Productions/ABC Network, 1953–4 (Bob Finkel).
Co-starring: Paul Hartman, Fay Wray, Bobby Hyatt.

The Films of Montgomery Clift

The Search, MGM–Loew's International, 1948 (Fred Zinnemann).
Co-starring: Jarmilla Novotna, Alina MacMahon, Ivan Jandll, Wendell Corey, Mary Patton, Leopold Borkowski, William Rogers.

Red River, United Artists, 1948 (Howard Hawks).
Co-starring: John Wayne, Walter Brennan, Joanne Dru, Noah Beery, Jr, John Ireland, Coleen Gray, Harry Carey, Harry Carey, Jr, Paul Fix.

The Heiress, Paramount, 1949 (William Wyler).
Co-starring: Olivia De Havilland, Ralph Richardson, Miriam Hopkins, Vanessa Brown, Mona Freeman, Ray Collins, Betty Linley, Selena Royle, Paul Lees, Harry Antrim, Russ Conway, David Thurdby.

The Big Lift, 20th Century–Fox, 1950 (George Seaton).
Co-starring: Paul Douglas, Cornell Borchers, Bruni Lobel, O. E. Hasse, Danny Davenport.

A Place in the Sun, Paramount, 1951 (George Stevens).
Co-starring: Elizabeth Taylor, Shelley Winters, Anne Revere, Raymond Burr, Keefe Brasselle, Shepherd Strudwick, Frieda Inescort, Ian Wolfe, Herbert Heyes.

I Confess, Warner Brothers, 1953 (Alfred Hitchcock).
Co-starring: Anne Baxter, Karl Malden, Brian Aherne, O. E. Hasse, Roger Dann, Dolly Haas, Charles Andre, Judson Pratt, Ovila Legare, Giles Pelletier.

From Here to Eternity, Columbia, 1953 (Fred Zinnemann).
Co-starring: Burt Lancaster, Deborah Kerr, Frank Sinatra, Donna Reed, Philip Ober, Mickey Shaughnessy, Harry Bellaver, Ernest Borgnine, George Reeves.

Indiscretion of an American Wife, Selznick–Columbia, 1953 (Vittorio De Sica).
Co-starring: Jennifer Jones, Dick Beymer, Gino Cervi.

Raintree County, MGM, 1957 (Edward Dmytryk).
Co-starring: Elizabeth Taylor, Eva Marie Saint, Lee Marvin, Rod Taylor, Nigel Patrick, Agnes Moorehead, Walter Abel, Jarma Lewis, Tom Drake, Rhys Williams, Russell Collins, DeForest Kelley.

The Young Lions, 20th Century–Fox, 1958 (Edward Dmytryk).
Co-starring: Marlon Brando, Dean Martin, Hope Lange, Barbara Rush, May Britt, Maximilian Schell, Dora Doll, Lee Van Cleef, Liliane Montevecchi.

Lonelyhearts, United Artists, 1959 (Vincent J. Donehue).
Co-starring: Robert Ryan, Myrna Loy, Dolores Hart, Maureen Stapleton, Frank Maxwell, Jackie Coogan, Mike Kellin, Frank Overton, Onslow Steven.

Suddenly Last Summer, Columbia–Horizon, 1959 (Joseph L. Mankiewicz).
Co-starring: Elizabeth Taylor, Katharine Hepburn, Albert Dekker, Mercedes McCambridge, Gary Raymond, Mavis Villiers, Patrick Marmont, Joan Young.

Wild River, 20th Century–Fox, 1960 (Elia Kazan).
Co-starring: Lee Remick, Jo Van Fleet, Albert Salmi, J. C. Flippen, James Westerfield, Barbara Loden, Frank Overton, Malcolm Atterbury, Robert Earl Jones, Bruce Dern.

The Misfits, United Artists–Seven Arts, 1961 (John Huston).
Co-starring: Clark Gable, Marilyn Monroe, Thelma Ritter, Eli Wallach, Estelle Winwood, Kevin McCarthy, Dennis Shaw, Marietta Tree.

Judgment at Nuremberg, United Artists, 1961 (Stanley Kramer).
Co-starring: Spencer Tracy, Burt Lancaster, Maximilian Schell, Richard Widmark, Marlene Dietrich, Judy Garland, William Shatner, Ed Binns, Kenneth MacKenna, Werner Klemperer, Torben Meyer, Alan Baxter.

Freud, Universal International, 1962 (John Huston).
Co-starring: Susannah York, Larry Parks, Susan Kohner, Eric Portman, Eileen Herlie, Fernand Ledoux, David McCallum, Rosalie Crutchley, David Kossoff.

The Defector (released posthumously), Warner Brothers–Seven Arts, 1966 (Raoul Lévy).
Co-starring: Hardy Kruger, Macha Meril, Roddy McDowall.

The Films of Rock Hudson

Fighter Squadron, Warner Brothers, 1948 (Raoul Walsh).
Co-starring: Edmond O'Brien, Robert Stack.

Undertow, Universal, 1949 (William Castle).
Co-starring: Scott Brady.

I Was a Shoplifter, Universal, 1950 (Charles Lamont).
Co-starring: Scott Brady, Mona Freeman.

One Way Street, Universal, 1950 (Hugo Fregonese).
Co-starring: James Mason, Marta Toren, Dan Duryea, William Conrad.

Winchester '73, Universal, 1950 (Anthony Mann).
Co-starring: James Stewart, Shelley Winters, Dan Duryea.

Peggy, Universal, 1950 (Fred De Cordova).
Co-starring: Diana Lynn, Charles Coburn.

The Desert Hawk, Universal, 1950 (Fred De Cordova).
Co-starring: Yvonne De Carlo, Richard Greene.

Shakedown, Universal, 1950 (Joseph Pevney).
Co-starring: Howard Duff, Peggy Dow, Brian Donlevy.

Tomahawk, Universal, 1951 (George Sherman).
Co-starring: Van Heflin, Yvonne De Carlo, Preston Foster, Jack Oakie.

Air Cadet, Universal, 1951 (Joseph Pevney).
Co-starring: Stephen McNally, Gail Russell, Richard Long.

The Fat Man, Universal, 1951 (William Castle).
Co-starring: J. Scott Smart, Julie London.

The Iron Man, Universal, 1951 (Joseph Pevney).
Co-starring: Jeff Chandler, Evelyn Keyes, Stephen McNally.

Bright Victory, Universal, 1951 (Mark Robson).
Co-starring: Arthur Kennedy, Julie Adams.

Here Come the Nelsons, Universal, 1952 (Fred De Cordova).
Co-starring: Ozzie, Harriet Rick, David Nelson.

Bend of the River, Universal, 1952 (Anthony Mann).
Co-starring: James Stewart, Arthur Kennedy, Julie Adams, Lori Nelson.

Scarlet Angel, Universal, 1952 (Sidney Salkow).
Co-starring: Yvonne De Carlo, Richard Denning.

Has Anybody Seen My Gal?, Universal, 1952 (Douglas Sirk).
Co-starring: Piper Laurie, Charles Coburn.

Horizons West, Universal, 1952 (Budd Boetticher).
Co-starring: James Arness, Robert Ryan, Julie Adams.

The Lawless Breed, Universal, 1953 (Raoul Walsh).
Co-starring: Julie Adams.

Seminole, Universal, 1953 (Budd Boetticher).
Co-starring: Barbara Hale, Anthony Quinn, Richard Carlson, Hugh O'Brian, Lee Marvin.

Sea Devils, RKO, 1953 (Raoul Walsh).
Co-starring: Yvonne De Carlo, Dennis O'Day.

Gun Fury, Columbia, 1953 (Raoul Walsh).
Co-starring: Donna Reed, Lee Marvin, Neville Brand.

The Golden Blade, Universal, 1953 (Nathan Juran).
Co-starring: Piper Laurie, Gene Evans.

Back to God's Country, Universal, 1953 (Joseph Pevney).
Co-starring: Marsha Henderson.

Taza, Son of Cochise, Universal, 1954 (Douglas Sirk).
Co-starring: Barbara Rush, Gregg Palmer.

Magnificent Obsession, Universal, 1954 (Douglas Sirk).
Co-starring: Jane Wyman, Agnes Moorehead, Barbara Rush.

Bengal Brigade, Universal, 1954 (Laslo Benedek).
Co-starring: Arlene Dahl, Dan O'Herlihy.

Captain Lightfoot, Universal, 1955 (Douglas Sirk).
Co-starring: Barbara Rush, Jeff Morrow, Dennis O'Day.

One Desire, Universal, 1955 (Jerry Hopper).

Co-starring: Anne Baxter, Julie Adams, Natalie Wood, Carl Benton Reid, William Hopper, Betty Grade.

All That Heaven Allows, Universal, 1956 (Douglas Sirk).
Co-starring: Jane Wyman.

Never Say Goodbye, Universal, 1956 (Jerry Hopper).
Co-starring: Cornell Borchers, George Sanders.

Four Girls in Town, Universal, 1956 (Jack Sher).
Co-starring: George Nader, Julie Adams.

Giant, Warner Brothers, 1956 (George Stevens).
Co-starring: Elizabeth Taylor, James Dean, Carroll Baker, Jane Withers, Chill Wills, Mercedes McCambridge, Sal Mineo, Dennis Hopper.

Written on the Wind, Universal, 1957 (Douglas Sirk).
Co-starring: Robert Stack, Dorothy Malone, Lauren Bacall.

Something of Value, MGM, 1957 (Richard Brooks).
Co-starring: Sidney Poitier, Dana Wynter, Wendy Hiller.

Battle Hymn, Universal, 1957 (Douglas Sirk).
Co-starring: Martha Hyer, Dan Duryea.

A Farewell to Arms, 20th Century–Fox, 1957 (Vittorio De Sica).
Co-starring: Jennifer Jones, Vittorio De Sica, Mercedes McCambridge.

The Tarnished Angels, Universal, 1958 (Douglas Sirk).
Co-starring: Robert Stack, Dorothy Malone, Jack Carson.

Twilight for the Gods, Universal, 1958 (Joseph Pevney).
Co-starring: Cyd Charisse, Arthur Kennedy, Leif Erickson.

The Earth Is Mine, Universal, 1959 (Henry King).
Co-starring: Jean Simmons, Dorothy McGuire, Claude Rains.

Pillow Talk, Universal, 1959 (Michael Gordon).
Co-starring: Doris Day, Tony Randall, Thelma Ritter.

The Last Sunset, Universal, 1961 (Robert Aldrich).
Co-starring: Kirk Douglas, Dorothy Malone, Joseph Cotten.

Come September, Universal, 1961 (Robert Mulligan).
Co-starring: Gina Lollobrigida, Sandra Dee, Walter Slezak.

Lover Come Back, Universal, 1962 (Delbert Mann).
Co-starring: Doris Day, Tony Randall, Edi Adams.

The Spiral Road, Universal, 1962 (Robert Mulligan).
Co-starring: Burl Ives, Gena Rowlands.

Marilyn, 20th Century–Fox, 1963 (Pepe Torres).
Hudson narrated this documentary film.

A Gathering of Eagles, Universal, 1963 (Delbert Mann).
Co-starring: Rod Taylor, Barry Sullivan, Kevin McCarthy, Leif Erickson.

Man's Favorite Sport?, Universal, 1964 (Howard Hawks).
Co-starring: Paula Prentiss, Maria Perschy.

Send Me No Flowers, Universal, 1964 (Norman Jewison).
Co-starring: Doris Day, Tony Randall.

Strange Bedfellows, Universal, 1965 (Melvin Frank).
Co-starring: Gina Lollobrigida, Gig Young, Terry Thomas.

A Very Special Favor, Universal, 1965 (Michael Gordon).
Co-starring: Leslie Caron, Charles Boyer, Walter Slezak.

Blindfold, Universal, 1966 (Philip Dunne).
Co-starring: Claudia Cardinale, Dean Stockwell.

Seconds, Paramount, 1966 (John Frankenheimer).
Co-starring: Salome Jens, John Randolph.

Tobruk, Universal, 1967 (Arthur Hiller).
Co-starring: George Peppard, Nigel Green.

Ice Station Zebra, MGM, 1968 (John Sturges).
Co-starring: Ernest Borgnine, Patrick McGoohan, Jim Brown.

A Fine Pair, National General, 1969 (Francesco Maselli).
Co-starring: Claudia Cardinale, Thomas Milian.

The Undefeated, 20th Century–Fox, 1969 (Andrew McLaglen).
Co-starring: John Wayne.

The Hornet's Nest, United Artists, 1970 (Phil Karlson).
Co-starring: Sylva Koscina.

Darling Lili, Paramount, 1970 (Blake Edwards).
Co-starring: Julie Andrews.

Pretty Maids All in a Row, MGM, 1971 (Roger Vadim).
Co-starring: Angie Dickinson, Telly Savalas, Roddy McDowall, Keenan Wynn.

Showdown, Universal, 1973 (George Seaton).
Co-starring: Dean Martin, Susan Clark.

Embryo, Cine Artists, 1976 (Ralph Nelson).
Co-starring: Diane Ladd, Barbara Carrera, Roddy McDowall.

Avalanche, New World Pictures, 1978 (Corey Allen).
Co-starring: Mia Farrow, Robert Forster.

The Mirror Crack'd, EMI Films, 1980 (Guy Hamilton).
Co-starring: Elizabeth Taylor, Tony Curtis, Edward Fox, Geraldine Chaplin, Kim Novak, Angela Lansbury, Wendy Morgan, Margaret Courtenay.

The Ambassador, Cannon Films, 1984 (J. Lee Thompson).
Co-starring: Robert Mitchum, Ellen Burstyn, Donald Pleasance.

Television Features

Once Upon a Dead Man, NBC, 1971 (Leonard Stern).
Co-starring: Susan Saint James, John Schuck, Stacy Keach.

Wheels, NBC, 1978 (Jerry London).
Co-starring: Lee Remick, Ralph Bellamy, Tony Franciosa.

The Martian Chronicles, Charles Fries Productions, 1980 (Michael Anderson).
Co-starring: Roddy McDowall, Maria Schell.

The Starmarker, NBC, 1981 (Lou Antonio).
Co-starring: Suzanne Pleshette, Melanie Griffith, Ed McMahon.

World War III, Telepictures Corp, 1982 (David Greene).
Co-starring: David Soul, Brian Keith, Cathy Lee Crosby.

Las Vegas Strip Wars, ITC Entertainment, 1984 (George Englund).
Co-starring: James Earl Jones, Pat Morita, Sharon Stone.

The Films of James Dean

East of Eden, Warner Brothers, 1955 (Elia Kazan).
Co-starring: Raymond Massey, Richard Davalos, Julie Harris, Jo Van Fleet.

Rebel Without a Cause, Warner Brothers, 1955 (Nicholas Ray).
Co-starring: Natalie Wood, Jim Backus, Ann Doran, Rochelle Hudson, William Hopper, Sal Mineo, Corey Allen, Dennis Hopper, Virginia Brissac, Ian Wolfe, Nick Adams, Edward Platt.

Giant, Warner Brothers, 1956 (George Stevens).
Co-starring: Elizabeth Taylor, Rock Hudson, Carroll Baker, Jane Withers, Chill Wills, Mercedes McCambridge, Sal Mineo, Dennis Hopper.

Sources

The author and publishers are grateful to the following for permission to reprint brief extracts from previously published works: W. H. Allen, London, for *Past Imperfect* by Joan Collins; W. H. Allen, London, and Bantam Books, New York, for *Doris Day: Her Own Story*; Angus & Robertson (UK) and Doubleday, New York, for *My Husband, Rock Hudson* by Phyllis Gates (with Bob Thomas); Bantam Books, London and New York, for *His Way: the Unauthorised Biography of Frank Sinatra* by Kitty Kelley; André Deutsch, London, and Alfred A. Knopf, New York, for *Elia Kazan: a Life*; Doubleday, New York, for *The Whole Truth and Nothing But* by Hedda Hopper (with James Brough); Hamish Hamilton, London, for *Capote: a Biography* by Gerald Clarke; Harper & Row, New York, for *Judy* by Gerold Frank; William Morrow & Co., New York, for *Monty: the Biography of Montgomery Clift* by Robert LaGuardia; St Martin's Press, New York, for *James Dean: the Mutant King* by David Dalton; Sidgwick and Jackson, London, for *Burton: the Man Behind the Myth* by Penny Junor; Simon & Schuster, New York, for *Norman Mailer: His Life and Times* by Peter Manso.

Bibliography

Adkins, Dick, *Hollywood Explained: Method to the Madness*, Prince Publishers, Livingston, NJ, 1975.

Alleman, Richard, *The Movie Lover's Guide to Hollywood*, Harper & Row, New York, 1985.

Anger, Kenneth, *Hollywood Babylon*, Dell Publishing Co. edn, New York, 1981.

Astor, Mary, *My Story: an Autobiography*, Doubleday, New York, 1959.

——, *A Life on Film*, Delacorte Press, New York, 1967.

Bacon, James, *Made in Hollywood*, Warner Books, New York, 1977.

Bast, William, *James Dean: a Biography*, Ballantine Books, New York, 1956.

Baxter, John, *The Hollywood Exiles*, Taplinger, New York, 1976.

Beath, Warren Newton, *The Death of James Dean*, Grove Press, New York, 1986.

Bentley, Eric (ed.), *Thirty Years of Treason: Excerpts from Hearings Before the House Committee on Un-American Activities 1938–1968*, Viking, New York, 1971.

Boller, Paul F., Jr, and Davis, Ronald L., *Hollywood Anecdotes*, Macmillan, London, 1988.

Bosworth, Patricia, *Montgomery Clift: a Biography*, Harcourt Brace Jovanovich, New York, 1978.

Brode, Douglas, *The Films of the Fifties*, The Citadel Press, Secaucus, NJ, 1976.

Chaplin, Charles, *My Autobiography*, Simon & Schuster, New York, 1964.

Clarke, Gerald, *Capote: a Biography*, Hamish Hamilton, London, 1988.

Collins, Joan, *Past Imperfect*, Coronet edn, London, 1979.

Cohn, Art, *The Nine Lives of Mike Todd*, Random House, New York, 1958.

Dalton, David, *James Dean: the Mutant King*, St Martin's Press, New York, 1987.

Davidson, Bill, *Spencer Tracy: Tragic Idol*, Sidgwick & Jackson, London, 1987.

Day, Doris (with A. E. Hotchner), *Doris Day: Her Own Story*, W. H. Allen (Star edn), London, 1988.

de Dienes, André, *Marilyn, Mon Amour*, Sidgwick & Jackson, London, 1986.

Devillers, Marceau, *James Dean on Location*, Sidgwick & Jackson, London, 1987.

Downing, David, *Marlon Brando*, W. H. Allen, London, 1984.

Dmytryk, Edward, *It's a Hell of a Life But Not a Bad Living*, Times Books, New York, 1978.

Eames, John Douglas, *The MGM Story: the Complete History of Fifty Roaring Years*, Crown Publishers, New York, 1975.

Edwards, Anne, *Katharine Hepburn: a Biography*, Coronet edn, London, 1987.

Ferber, Edna, *Giant*, Doubleday, New York, 1952.

Ferris, Paul, *Richard Burton*, Weidenfeld & Nicolson, London, 1981.

Frank, Gerold, *Judy*, Harper & Row, New York, 1975.

Friedrich, Otto, *City of Nets; a Portrait of Hollywood in the 1940s*, Headline, London, 1987.

Fuchs, Wolfgang, *James Dean: Footsteps of a Giant*, TACO Publishers, Berlin, 1986.

Garfield, David, *The Actors Studio: a Player's Place*, Collier Macmillan, New York, 1984.

Gates, Phyllis (with Bob Thomas), *My Husband, Rock Hudson*, Angus & Robertson, London, 1987.

Geist, Kenneth L., *Pictures Will Talk: the Life and Films of Joseph L. Mankiewicz*, Frederick Muller, London, 1978.

Gitlin, Todd, *The Sixties: Years of Hope, Days of Rage*, Bantam Books, New York, 1987.

Goldman, Albert, *Elvis*, McGraw-Hill, New York, 1981.

Goodman, Ezra, *The Fifty-Year Decline and Fall of Hollywood*, Simon & Schuster, New York, 1981.

Graham, Sheilah, *The Rest of the Story*, Bantam Books, New York, 1965.

——, *Confessions of a Hollywood Columnist*, Morrow, New York, 1969.

——, *Hollywood Revisited: a Fiftieth Anniversary Celebration*, St Martins Press, New York, 1986.

Greene, Myrna, *The Eddie Fisher Story*, Paul S. Erikson, Middlebury, 1978.

Harris, Warren G., *Natalie and RJ: Hollywood's Star-Crossed Lovers*, Doubleday (Dolphin), New York, 1988.

Hellman, Lillian, *An Unfinished Woman: a Memoir*, Bantam Books, New York, 1970.

Herndon, Venable, *James Dean: a Short Life*, New American Library, New York, 1974.

Heston, Charlton, *The Actor's Life: Journals 1956–1976*, E. P. Dutton, New York, 1978.

Higham, Charles, *Warner Brothers*, Scribner, New York, 1975.

——, *Kate: the Life of Katharine Hepburn*, Norton, New York, 1975.

——, *Marlene: the Life of Marlene Dietrich*, Norton, New York, 1977.

——, *Bette: the Life of Bette Davis*, Macmillan, New York, 1981.

——, *Brando: the Unauthorised Biography*, New American Library (Signet edn), New York, 1987.

Hopper, Hedda (with James Brough), *The Whole Truth and Nothing But*, Doubleday, New York, 1962.

Hudson, Rock (with Sara Davidson), *Rock Hudson: His Story*, Bantam edn, London, 1987.

Huston, John, *An Open Book*, Ballantine, New York, 1981.

Hyams, Joe, *Mislaid In Hollywood*, Peter H. Wyden, New York, 1973.

Junor, Penny, *Burton: the Man Behind the Myth*, Sphere Books, London, 1986.

Kanin, Garson, *Hollywood: Stars and Starlets, Tycoons and Flesh Peddlars, Moviemakers and Moneymakers, Frauds and Geniuses, Hopefuls and Hasbeens, Great Lovers and Sex Symbols*, Viking, New York, 1974.

Kazan, Elia, *Elia Kazan: a Life*, André Deutsch, London, 1988.

Kelley, Kitty, *Elizabeth Taylor: the Last Star*, Simon & Schuster, New York, 1981.

——, *His Way: the Unauthorised Biography of Frank Sinatra*, Bantam edn, London, 1987.

Kidd, Charles, *Debrett Goes to Hollywood*, Weidenfeld & Nicolson, London, 1986.

LaGuardia, Robert, *Monty: the Biography of Montgomery Clift*, Arbor House, New York, 1977.

Law, Lisa, *Flashing on the Sixties*, Chronicle Books, San Francisco, 1987.

Lesley, Cole (with Graham Payn and Sheridan Morley), *Noël Coward and His Friends*, Weidenfeld & Nicolson, London, 1979.

Linet, Beverly, *Susan Hayward: Portrait of a Survivor*, Atheneum, New York, 1980.

Massey, Raymond, *A Hundred Different Lives: an Autobiography*, Little, Brown and Co., Boston, 1979.

Manso, Peter, *Norman Mailer: His Life and Times*, Simon & Schuster, New York, 1985.

Maychick, Diana (with L. Avon Borgo), *Heart to Heart with Robert Wagner*, St Martin's Press, New York, 1986.

Mosley, Leonard, *Zanuck: the Rise and Fall of Hollywood's Last Tycoon*, Little, Brown and Co., Boston, 1984.

Munshower, Suzanne, *Warren Beatty: His Life. His Loves. His Work*, St Martin's Press, New York, 1983.

Nickens, Christopher, *Natalie Wood: a Biography in Photographs*, Doubleday (Dolphin), New York, 1986.

Niven, David, *The Moon's a Balloon*, Dell edn, New York, 1976.

——, *Bring On the Empty Horses*, Coronet edn, London, 1976.

Norman, Barry, *Film Greats*, BBC/Hodder & Stoughton, London, 1985.

——, *Talking Pictures: the Story of Hollywood*, BBC/Hodder & Stoughton, London, 1987.

Oppenheimer, Jerry (with Jack Vitek), *Idol: the unauthorised Biography of Rock Hudson*, Bantam edn, London, 1987.

Parker, John, *King of Fools*, St Martin's Press edn, New York, 1989.

Peary, Danny, *Close-Ups: the Movie Star Book* (10th anniversary edn), Simon & Schuster, New York, 1988.

Poitier, Sidney, *This Life*, Ballantine, New York, 1981.

Powdermaker, Hortense, *Hollywood: the Dream Factory*, Little, Brown and Co., Boston, 1950.

Schary, Dore, *Heyday: an Autobiography*, Little, Brown & Co., Boston, 1979.

Sheppard, Dick, *Elizabeth: the Life and Career of Elizabeth Taylor*, Doubleday, New York, 1974.

Spada, James (with George Zeno), *Monroe: Her Life*, Sidgwick & Jackson, London, 1982.

Selznick, David O., *Memo from David O. Selznick* (ed. Rudy Behlmer), Viking, New York, 1972.

Schatt, Roy, *James Dean: a Portrait*, Delilah, New York, 1982.

Spiegel, Penina, *McQueen: the Untold Story of a Bad Boy in Hollywood*, Berkley edn, New York, 1987.

Stock, Dennis, *James Dean Revisited*, Penguin edn, Harmondsworth, 1978.

Steinbeck, John, *East of Eden*, Viking, New York, 1952.

Strasberg, Susan, *Bittersweet*, Putnam, New York, 1980.

Summers, Anthony, *Goddess: the Secret Lives of Marilyn Monroe*, Macmillan, New York, 1987.

Swanson, Gloria, *Swanson on Swanson: an Autobiography*, Random House, New York, 1980.

Taylor, Elizabeth, *Elizabeth Taylor by Elizabeth Taylor*, Harper & Row, New York, 1964.

——, *Elizabeth Takes Off*, Macmillan, London, 1988.

Taylor, John Russell, *King Cohn: the Life and Times of Harry Cohn*, Putnam, New York, 1967.

Thomas, Bob, *Marlon: Portrait of the Rebel as an Artist*, Random House, New York, 1973.

Waterbury, Ruth, *Elizabeth Taylor*, Appleton–Century, New York, 1964.

West, Nathaniel, *Miss Lonelyhearts*, New Directions, New York (no date).

Winters, Shelley, *Shelley: Also Known As Shirley*, William Morrow, New York, 1980.

Wood, Lana, *Natalie: a Memoir*, Putnam, New York, 1984.

Zec, Donald, *Elizabeth Taylor*, Mirror Books, London, 1972.

Index